Official Catholic Teachings

bible interpretation

bible interpretation

James J. Megivern

A Consortium Book

from McGrath Publishing Company
Wilmington, North Carolina 1978

Copyright © 1978 McGrath Publishing Company
All rights reserved. No portion of this book may be reproduced without
permission in writing from the publisher.
Manufactured in the United States of America

Library of Congress Card Catalog Number: 78-53846
ISBN: 0-8434-0715-8
ISBN: 0-8434-0721-2 paper

The publisher gratefully acknowledges permission to quote from the
following copyrighted publications.

ROLAND H. BAINTON
MURATORIAN FRAGMENT (CANON), "Early Christianity",
Van Nostrand Reinhold, ©1960.

BENZIGER BROTHERS
ST. THOMAS AQUINAS, SUMMA THEOLOGICA, ©1928.

CATHOLIC BIBLICAL QUARTERLY
*PONTIFICAL BIBLICAL COMMISSION RESPONSE ON THE USE
OF VERSIONS OF SACRED SCRIPTURE IN THE VERNACU-
LAR,* "Catholic Biblical Quarterly", Volume 10, ©1948.

CATHOLIC UNIVERSITY OF AMERICA PRESS, INC.
ST. AUGUSTINE ON CHRISTIAN INSTRUCTION, "The Fathers
of the Church", Volume 2, © 1947.
ST. CYRIL OF JERUSALEM CATECHESIS IV, "The Fathers of
the Church", Volume 61, © 1969.
*ST. EUSEBIUS PAMPHILI ECCLESIASTICAL HISTORY: BOOK
III,* "The Fathers of the Church", Volume 19, © 1953.
*ST. JOHN OF DAMASCUS EXPOSITIONS OF ORTHODOX
FAITH, BOOK IV,* "The Fathers of the Church", Volume 37,
©1958.

CHRISTIAN LITERATURE CO.
*TERTULLIAN, ON PRESCRIPTION OF HERETICS: ORIGEN,
LETTER TO GREGORY THAUMATURGIS; ORIGEN, BOOK
II OF COMMENTARY AND GOSPEL OF MATTHEW; BISHOP
OF ALEXANDRIA, LETTER XXXIX, ATHANASIUS,* "Ante-
Nicene Fathers", 1885-96.
*JEROME, LETTER TO POPE DAMASUS; JEROME, PREFACES
TO TRANSLATIONS OF NEW TESTAMENT BOOKS; AUGUS-
TINE, THE HARMONY OF THE GOSPELS; POPE LEO I,
LETTER XV TO TURRIBIUS; GREGORY' LETTER XXXI TO
THEODORUS,* "Select Library of Nicene and Post-Nicene
Father of the Christian Church", 1886-1900.

COLUMBIA UNIVERSITY
ISIDORE OF SEVILLE, ETYMOLOGIES, BOOK VI, "An Ency-
clopedist of the Dark Ages", by Ernest Brehaut, ©1912.

DECLARATION OF THE SACRED CONGREGATION FOR THE DOCTRINE OF FAITH (EXCERPT NO. 5), "The Pope Speaks", Volume 18, Number 2, ©1973.

ADDRESS OF POPE PAUL VI TO THE PBC ON THE ECCLESIAL ROLE OF BIBLICAL STUDIES, "The Pope Speaks", Volume 19, Number 1, ©1974.

DOCUMENT ISSUED BY THE SACRED CONGREGATION FOR CATHOLIC EDUCATION ON PRIESTLY FORMATION (EXCERPT), "The Pope Speaks", Volume 21, Number 4, ©1976.

JOHN HENRY PARKER
GREGORY I, MORALS ON THE BOOK OF JOB, Oxford, 1845.

ST. MEINRAD ARCHABBEY
PROVIDENTISSIMUS DEUS; VIGILANTIAE; FOURTEEN DECISIONS OF THE PONTIFICAL BIBLICAL COMMISSION; QUONIAM IN RE BIBICA; PRAESTANTIA SACRAE SCRIPTURAE; SPIRITUS PARACLITUS; PONTIFICAL BIBLICAL COMMISSION DECISION ON TWO TEXTS; PONTIFICAL BIBLICAL COMMISSION LETTER TO ITALIAN HIERARCHY; DIVINO AFFLANTE SPIRITU; PONTIFICAL BIBLICAL COMMISSION LETTER TO CARDINAL SUHARD; INSTRUCTION OF PONTIFICAL BIBLICAL COMMISSION OF THE PROPER WAY TO TEACH SACRED SCRIPTURE IN THE SEMINARIES; LETTER TO BISHOP O'HARA FROM PIUS XII; HUMANI GENERIS (EXCERPTS); PONTIFICAL BIBLICAL COMMISSION INSTRUCTION ON BIBLICAL ASSOCIATIONS, AND ON BIBLICAL CONVENTIONS AND MEETINGS, "Rome and The Study of Scripture", Abbey Press, ©1958.

J. STEVENSON
VINCENT OF LERINS, COMMONITORIUM II; IRENAEUS, AGAINST HERESIES (III 1-3), "Creeds, Councils and Controversies", SPCK, ©1966.

THEOLOGICAL PUB. IN INDIA
COUNCIL OF TRENT; SYLLABUS OF ERRORS; CONSTITUTION DEI FILIUS, "The Christian Faith in the Doctrinal Documents of the Catholic Church", ©1975.

THEOLOGICAL STUDIES, INC.
PBC INSTRUCTION CONCERNING THE HISTORICAL TRUTH OF THE GOSPELS, Joseph A. Fitzmyer in "Theological Studies", Volume 25, Number 3, Pages 386-408, ©1964.

JOSEPH F. WAGNER, INC.
LAMENTABILI; MONITUM OF THE HOLY OFFICE, "A Companion to Scripture Studies", ©1962.

THE WESTMINSTER PRESS
LETTER TO LEANDER, "Early Medieval Theology", Library of Christian Classics, Volume IX, translated and edited by George E. McCracken, published in the USA by The Westminster Press, 1957.

Table of Contents

Introduction

This collection of documents spans eighteen centuries of
Christian history. It contains necessarily a wide diversity of
examples, some reflecting the time when the decisions about
what works belonged in the Bible had not yet been firmly
made; some demonstrating how Christian pastors understood,
approached, and used the Bible in practice. In the later
period a different kind of concern is to be found: Church
leaders trying to define precise regulations on how the Bible
was to be used, attempting to prevent its being appealed to as
a source of division or novelty. The selection process inevitably involved a fair measure of subjectivity, so that one
can fault the inclusion of some and the exclusion of other
documents. The justification for what is here presented is
made in terms of the insight that can be gained by trying to
view these works in historical perspective, seeing them as
pieces in an intriguing story with dramatic ups and downs.
The collection is presented at this time in the conviction that
the contemporary scene is absolutely unparalleled. Never
before in history has Catholic Biblical scholarship been so
advanced in competence and at the same time so favorably
viewed by Church authorities. That unique combination of
circumstances augurs well for the future, so much so that
when it comes time to provide a supplement of later writings
to those contained here, it is safe to conjecture that those
newer documents will surpass most of what is to be found

here. That is as it should be, and if the volume in any way
fosters such growth, it will be more than worth the efforts
involved in producing it.

Documents in many ways speak for themselves. It is always
preferable to have the exact text related to historical events
than to be limited to second-hand summaries. Yet, as experience amply shows, some elements of context are required
to avoid misunderstanding documents by reading into them
anachronistic or otherwise extraneous concerns. The rest of
the remarks in this introduction are meant to provide something of an overview in which to situate these writings. The
history of the Catholic Church, especially in the last few centuries, has been characterized by some terribly difficult
complications in relation to the Bible. Appreciating them
may give one both sympathy for the struggles of the past and
hope in the promise of the future.

The Bible and the Christian Church are intimately related.
The history of one cannot be told without the history of the
other. This fact is easily overlooked in modern times, when
multiple translations by a wide variety of groups proliferate
and circulate as if the Bible had no historical matrix but was
somehow, somewhere, sometime dropped from heaven. This
seeming independence of the Bible is intelligible only if one
appreciates the numerous historical events that led to the
contemporary situation. However positively or negatively
one evaluates those events, the undeniable fact remains that
the various books of the Bible were produced by particular
historical religious communities.

Late in the first century, when the Christian movement
broke definitively with Judaism, the Greek translation of the
Hebrew Scriptures (Septuagint) had been so completely
appropriated by Christian preachers that it was repudiated
by the Rabbis. For the first few generations of Christianity,
when "the Scriptures" were spoken of, it was these writings
that were meant, later called "the Old Testament."

Thus interpretation of the Scriptures for the first century
and a half of Christianity meant the discovery of Jesus in the
Old Testament. The overriding concern of second-century
Christian writers was to show that the Law, the Prophets, and

the Writings of Judaism were fulfilled in Jesus as the Christ.
To do this effectively the most important tool utilized was
the allegorical method developed by the school of Alexandria.

Alongside of this process of interpreting the writings of
Israel, however, was the related phenomenon of a growing
body of Christian writings. Sayings of Jesus, stories about
Him, letters explaining His significance, and similar materials
circulated among the Christian communities. Written accounts
were exchanged, read in Church services, and discussed. These
works began to form collections and a complication arose
when a spate of inferior works emerged alongside them causing confusion and raising the question as to which among
these writings should be judged reliable. In the middle of the
second century the Gnostic Basilides and especially Marcion
gave a great impetus to the process of sifting when they made
their own decisions and started eliminating the best with the
worst. The only way to counteract such arbitrariness was for
the Christian Church at large to come to a consensus on what
were and what were not acceptable writings.

There is no detailed record of precisely how this process of
selection occurred, or how these "New Testament" writings
(as Tertullian first designated them) gradually came to be
placed on a par with the Old Testament writings, to form the
Christian Bible which is today so taken for granted. The first
document in this collecttion, the Muratorian fragment, is
usually considered to be the earliest list, but its precise dating
is still under dispute. Irenaeus (c. 180) seems to be the first
whom we can identify as having something like our New
Testament, although his collection only contained twenty-
two writings. With him these begin to be called "Scripture"
in the way that the Old Testament works were.

The formation of the New Testament canon involved the
acceptance of three different groups of writings. The first
group was the four accounts dealing with the sayings and
works of Jesus, which were called Gospels. There was early
second-century agreement on these. The second group also
caused little controversy and was agreed upon by the end of
the second century: Acts, I Peter, I John, and thirteen letters
of Paul. But besides these twenty works, another group was

competing for acceptance, and it was two more centuries before firm decisions were made, excluding several prestigious works and including the final seven to be admitted as part of the New Testament. This third group consisted of II and III John, II Peter, James, Jude, Hebrews and the Apocalypse.

These early developments are recalled for a couple of reasons. First, they make us much more aware of the complex relationship between Bible and Church. The biblicist who wants to contend that God gave the world a Book to answer all its problems can maintain such a stance only by denying or ignoring serious history. The Bible is a book by believers about believers for believers, and belief is always historically conditioned. It is not an isolated phenomenon but a communal response, a social reality. God calls, God saves, God loves individuals, but He does all these things corporately, i.e., within the context of a community. That community out of which these writings emerged to express and define its communal faith is indispensable for understanding their meaning, for interpreting their full significance.

Secondly, this very process goes far to explain why there is so little explicit concern for Bible interpretation in those formative centuries. Interpretation was something that was practiced, not discussed. It took place in the context of the communal celebrations when passages were proclaimed, explained, applied, and meditated upon. There was little occasion for or need to theorize or formulate principles of exegesis. This would come only after conditions arose which forced reflection on the whole earlier process.

One of the facts of history which the earlier works in the present collection make amply evident is the predominance of allegorical interpretation among the Fathers. Origen set the tone in the East and later Augustine did much the same in the West. Jerome says he tried to steer his course "between history and allegory," but the latter always had a special attraction because it provided so much leeway, so many possibilities for finding the hidden depths of the Spirit's meaning. It is a method that is too artificial and arbitrary for modern tastes, so that it has been almost entirely abandoned. Despite the very real criticisms that can be leveled against it, the role it played in early Christianity was too large simply to ignore and omit. The examples included here (especially from Augustine) serve to underline another reason why modern methods of interpretation met such strenuous opposition. The sober approach of recent scholarship could hardly be farther apart from the untrammeled fancy that ruled the allegorist.

It is well known that the school of Alexandria with its influential allegorical method did have a rival in early Christian centuries that might have tempered the abuses of allegorism, viz., the school of Antioch. This approach insisted on taking the literal sense much more seriously. The existence of a spiritual sense which transcended the literal was admitted, but was restricted to typology. If the Alexandrians thought that each word carried a hidden meaning that could be unveiled only through allegory, the Antiochenes insisted on substantial arguments to prove that any given passage was indeed prophetic. The only reason for mentioning this rival school, however, is to note the fact that it exercised next to no influence in Western Christianity. Origen's shadow stretches across the Mediterranean and the centuries to dominate medieval scholarship in the Western Church. If the Antiochene instead of the Alexandrian influence had prevailed, the story of Bible interpretation in the West would have been far different, with attention given to the literal sense long centuries before modern scholarship did so.

But the Antiochene method had been so completely lost and forgotten that when the thirteenth century followers of Aristotle began to rediscover the value of the literal sense, they were not even aware that any Christians had been down that road before. The sources at their disposal reflected the fact that the allegorical method had swept the Latin world, virtually eliminating any alternative. One reason was that, when compared with classical Latin literature, much of the Bible seemed so artless, so rustic, even shallow. When an allegorical exposition was applied, however, it took on all manner of new depths which challenged the most active of imaginations. Meanings were found that illustrated incredible ingenuity on the part of the expositor. Augustine admits how much this aspect of the preaching of Ambrose affected him.

From the fifth to the ninth century the only place in the West where any kind of study could be done was in a monastery. The "lectio divina" prescribed in the monastic rules assured that the Bible would continue to be the object of reflection and concentration, even though the general state of education allowed for little advance. The Bible that had been produced in the midst of the early Christian communities was now preserved, illuminated, and handed on in the midst of the communities gathered in the Christian monasteries. If our collection has little to offer from these centuries, it is because they were years when survival was much more the issue than progress. Had it not been for the industry of the Christian monks of these centuries, there would have been no Bible available for more critical study in later ages.

A truly representative collection of documents that would do justice to the way in which the Bible was interpreted in the Middle Ages is simply unavailable in English. The lament of Miss Beryl Smalley nearly forty years ago has not really been remedied: "Historians of medieval culture have neglected a vital factor in the object of their studies . . . since not even the vast quantity of works on the Bible has succeeded in catching their attention. The bulk of medieval commentaries remains in manuscript. Of the tiny proportion that have been printed the editions, with very rare exceptions, are old and uncritical. Many have been ascribed to the wrong authors . . ."[1] English translations are, of course, virtually non-existent. The overall result is the perpetuation of the time-honored Anglo-American prejudice against things medieval. The myth goes on that the Bible was a closed book in those centuries. The selections included here, because they are too few, will not go far to dismiss that myth, but that cannot be helped. The present volume is chiefly concerned to present the documentation of the modern era.

Nonetheless the passage from the *Summa Theologica* of Thomas Aquinas signals the advent of a new era when the literal sense has become much more central for interpretation. That is not to deny that problems remain which prevent further advance, e.g., the fact that it was not the original text but the Latin translation that was being worked with. But whether we look at the earlier work of Peter Comestor, Peter the Charger, Stephen Langton, Hugh of St. Cher and the Victorines, or at the later achievements of Bonaventure, Albert the Great, and Thomas Aquinas, it is evident today that medieval Christian theology was far more concerned with, based upon, and reflective of the Bible than has usually been acknowledged.

The 14th century was undoubtedly a period of decline which prepared the way for later troubles. One complicating factor that influenced the attitude of Catholic authorities for the next five centuries was the obvious connection between efforts to translate the Bible into vernacular languages and efforts to introduce novel theological positions, conflicting with what had become traditional. From John Wycliffe to Martin Luther this pattern resulted in Roman reactions that could only be viewed as opposed to Biblical progress. Without attempting to apportion blame, it is certainly understandable that suspicions were raised any time anyone began to deal with the Bible in a different way. The Decree for the Jacobites produced by the Council of Florence in 1441 proclaimed the traditional doctrine concerning the canon, naming both the protocanonical and the deuterocanonical books (those whose inspiration was questioned in the early church) was soon to become one of those side issues that developed its own symbolism in the clash between Catholic and Protestant. Their inclusion or exclusion would largely constitute the difference between "Catholic" and "Protestant" Bibles.

The Council of Trent set about the task of clarifying and standardizing orthodox Bible interpretation. In view of the chaos of the time, however, it is not at all surprising that the stance taken would have been one of restraint. Conflict and controversy are never conducive to balance, and the "odium theologicum" that existed on all sides hardly provided an atmosphere favorable to scholarly probing. Too much energy was absorbed in polemics to allow for anything more fruitful. In face of the Protestant downgrading of the deuterocanonical books, Trent reaffirmed the canon endorsed at Florence so that the battle lines were clearly drawn on this one biblical issue. A second decree goes on to declare that the Latin Vulgate translation was to be considered "the authentic edition for public reading, disputations, sermons, and explanations." Once again the circumstances of the time must be taken into account. Jerome's Vulgate had been the Bible of the Western world for over a millenium. The Renaissance revival of Greek and Hebrew studies was still in its relatively early stages. Besides reverence for the tradition the other chief motive behind the Decree was fear, fear that some would "distort Scripture to fit meanings of their own that are contrary to the meanings that Holy Mother Church has held and now holds."

If the conditions following the Reformation led to an implementation of Trent's decrees that made them overly restrictive, the advent of the Enlightenment brought even greater problems. Clement XI's Constitution condemning Quesnel (1713) gives some idea of the negative style that the authorities felt was required to meet the new threat of rationalism. It is poignant to recall that Richard Simon died the year before that Constitution, a man ahead of his times who had blazed a trail that his Church would not find acceptable for another two to three centuries. Simon was the first to realize and declare openly that the Catholic Church had nothing to fear from critical investigation of the Bible, but in his lifetime he was a voice crying in the wilderness.

When Pius VII and Leo XII condemned the mass distribution of vernacular translations which the flourishing Bible Societies were engaging in early in the 19th century, they were not condemning Bible reading. Yet, that is the way it must have seemed to many outside Catholic circles. The real objection was to the kind of translations and especially the doctrinal notes they contained, often explicitly anti-Catholic in nature. Later in the century, when Pius IX published his *Syllabus of Errors* (1864), there was no way to avoid the conclusion that Catholic leadership was as yet unable to cope with developments that had been accelerating for over a century. The Catholic world was stupefied at the time, and if it had not been for the modifying interpretation that Bishop

Dupanloup of Orleans popularized, it would have been even worse.

Today it is difficult to reconstruct the atmosphere that existed, making such statements possible. As the Papal States were dismantled and so much of the Risorgimento increased hostility between secular and religious forces, the Papacy had to seem impossibly out of date. "To the ordinary reader it (the Syllabus) appeared to condemn not only progress, liberalism, and modern civilization, but a whole lot of other things which Englishmen and Americans, in particular, had come to hold sacred, such as freedom of speech, freedom of the press, religious toleration, and the separation of Church and State . . . The Syllabus also checkmated a growing Catholic intellectual movement which was particularly strong in Germany."[2] Little positive could be expected as an old order grudgingly gave way in the face of the new. Hindsight provides a far better perspective but is only to be purchased with the coin of time.

But things were to get worse before they got better. On September 19, 1870, after the Vatican Council I had hastily disbanded as troops marched on Rome, Pius IX sadly retreated into the Vatican to live as a virtual prisoner. If often in the next sixty years Papal declarations were marked by what has been called the "siege mentality," it is only fair to recall that it did indeed involve a very real siege. In 1871 the Eternal City, which for so many centuries had been ruled by the Pope, was officially proclaimed to be the capital of the new Kingdom of Italy. The awkward position of the Papacy would continue until Pius XI negotiated the Lateran treaty with Mussolini, creating the Vatican State in 1929.

When this background is kept in view, the surprising thing is that there was any progress at all. Yet Leo XIII in 1893 opened a new era in Catholic biblical interpretation with his encyclical *Providentissimus*. That document reflects hostility and distrust of higher criticism, as one would expect. The historical relationship between the Bible and the Church combined with the ecclesiology that could see no validity to any but the Roman Church led to the inevitable conclusion: "The sense of Holy Scripture can nowhere be found incorrupt outside the Church." That was the predictable part of the encyclical. What was more important for the future was this scholarly Pontiff's recognition of the value of the new tools themselves.

To Catholics of the time the early 1890s must have looked like the dawning of a new day. Leo XIII opened the Vatican archives to historians, instituted a Biblical Commission, called for renewed study of Thomas Aquinas, provided unparalleled leadership in social questions with his famous *Rerum Novarum* of 1891, and in general showed a determined spirit to meet the needs of the modern world in a courageous, flexible and sensible way. Moderate progressives like Henry Edward Manning in England and James Gibbons in the United States were given recognition as cardinals. *Providentissimus* could be read in the light of *Rerum Novarum* as abandoning the negative defensive stance of the past and adopting a moderately progressive position that would try to incorporate the best of new techniques in Biblical studies.

That may well be the spirit in which Leo prepared the document, but complications were soon to prevail which offset it. As the new century opened, it was becoming more and more evident that a third crisis regarding the Bible was building, which was going to have a powerful impact for decades to come. The first crisis had been the Protestant Reformation, and Rome's reply was the Council of Trent; the second crisis was that of Enlightenment rationalism, and insofar as it was addressed at all, Rome's reply was Vatican I. Now the third crisis was to be known as Modernism and it differed from the other two in an important way. This time the "enemies" were not outsiders but insiders. Opinions still vary as to whether less drastic measures could have brought the Catholic community safely through the crisis, but such speculation is not our concern here. These observations are intended simply to throw light on why the early 20th century Roman statements are all so powerfully negative. Many of the propositions condemned in *Lamentabili* were taken directly from the writings of Alfred Loisy, who was finally excommunicated in 1908.

Leo XIII set up the Pontifical Biblical Commission in 1902, and this was viewed positively at the time, but by the time it started issuing the decrees found herein (1905–1915), it had become one more instrument of warfare in Pius X's all-out campaign against Modernism. "A coin struck on June 29, 1908, to commemorate the fifth anniversary of Pius X's pontificate bore a fitting emblem—it showed him in the act of slaying the Modernist dragon. And slay it he did. Under pressure of the measures he applied, the Modernist movement simply collapsed . . . Modernism was indeed successfully stamped out, but at a tremendous price; the Catholic intelligence was inoculated against error, but the dosage was almost fatal . . . Many of the Church's most brilliant thinkers were silenced or driven out of theology and into a kind of spiritual schizophrenia . . . Whoever deserves the most blame, the Modernist crisis was a catastrophe for the Church. It led to an intellectual sterility that still weighs heavily on its life . . ."[3]

The cautious beginnings of Leo XIII thus came to a screeching halt under Pius X in 1907. "By 1910, after only three years of papal exertion, it was all over. And as the bickering fell silent, so too did practically all creative biblical scholarship . . . Since then, great men had fallen. Lagrange, called in from Jerusalem, was forbidden to publish on touchy subjects . . . Loisy and Houtin had both had their publications put on the Index, and had been unfrocked and excommunicated. Even old Pierre Batiffol fell afoul of the authorities and was dismissed from the rectorship of the Institut Catholique de Toulouse. Franz von Hummelauer lost his teaching position. Giovanni Semeria was sent into exile by his Italian superiors, and Salvatore Minocchi was suspended. David Fleming had been eased out of Rome back to Britain, and Giovanni Genocchi had been dismissed from his chair at the Appolinare in that city. George Tyrrell died excommunicate without a Catholic funeral, and Friedrich von Hügel found that he was more welcome in non-Catholic circles than amidst his own folk. Henry Poels was expelled from the Catholic University of America and sent home to Holland. And a number of new periodicals that had recently displayed remarkable

erudition and promise now perished in the general fright . . .
All the replies (of the PBC) were rigorously negative, and
although their small print carried qualifications enough to
allow of further investigation into most issues, their tone was
so discouraging that Catholic scholars got the message that
new ideas, especially if imported from Protestant critics, were
unwanted by Rome. Finally in 1910 a loyalty oath against
Modernism was imposed on all clerics . . . Unfortunately too
little discrimination was made between petulant unbelievers
such as Loisy, and open-faced researchers like Lagrange. It
was generally understood that if men wished to continue
teaching and publishing, they must not hazard any hypotheses
that could not be comprehended by the consultors of the
Inquisition."[4]

If one is inclined to try to put the best possible interpretation on the strategy against Modernism, it can be viewed as a
kind of "holding action". The state of Catholic biblical
scholarship was so low in the 19th century that the sudden
mushrooming of new studies, outlooks, and opinions concerning the Bible found the Church unprepared and unqualified
to deal with them. The Ecole Biblique in Jerusalem was not
officially opened until 1890, and the Pontifical Biblical
Institute in Rome did not come into existence until 1909. In
view of what happened in the meantime, it is not surprising
to find that in some ways Benedict XV's Encyclical *Spiritus
Paraclitus* in 1920 is more negatively conservative than
Leo XIII's of 1893. It would still be several decades before a
cadre of competent Catholic scholars could be raised up to
enter into the field of Biblical studies in a fully professional
manner.

To understand some of the later resistance to Biblical
studies it is necessary to keep in mind this history. Many
present-day Catholics, including the clergy, were raised in the
anti-modernist atmosphere that identified the Bible with
trouble and preferred to stay away from it. "The professors
of that day transmitted their attitude to their students, and
the priests who were educated at that time popularized the
same attitude in their sermons and instructions. Books which
are still on our bookshelves and are still read today were

written in the same spirit. As is normal in the process of cultural development, the attitude began at the top and gradually descended to and penetrated the popular level."[5]

The years between the two World Wars were a time of quiet growth. When the Jesuit Rector of the Biblical Institute, Leopold Fonck, had drafted *Spiritus Paraclitus* for Benedict XV, he had reflected the ultra-conservatism of the post-Modernist period. When his counterpart 23 years later, Augustin Bea, did the same for Pius XII's *Divino Afflante Spiritu*, enough had happened to begin loosening the bonds. He helped "the reigning pontiff smile upon biblical scholars for the first time in four decades. It is the change of climate, the Roman thaw of 1943, that marks the end of incomparably sterile years and invites a second spring of biblical studies."[6]

It is easy both to overestimate and to underestimate the significance of *Divino Afflante Spiritu*. On the one hand, most of its positions were commonplace among the better scholars of a half-century earlier. On the other hand, in view of what had been standard fare in the interim, it was "an undeniable about-face in attitude toward biblical criticism. The encyclical . . . instructed Catholic scholars to use the methods of a scientific approach to the Bible that had hitherto been forbidden to them. Within about ten years teachers trained in biblical criticism began to move in large numbers into Catholic classrooms in seminaries and colleges, so that the mid-1950's really marked the watershed. By that time the pursuit of the scientific method had led Catholic exegetes to abandon almost all the positions on biblical authorship and composition taken by Rome at the beginning of the century . . . This dramatic change of position was tacitly acknowledged in 1955 by the secretary of the PBC who stated that now Catholic scholars had "complete freedom" with regard to those decrees of 1905–1915 except where they touched on faith or morals (and very few of them did)."[7]

That is not to say that *Divino Afflante Spiritu* changed the atmosphere overnight. It was in fact destined to meet stiff resistance even within Roman universities for two long decades. Some of those raised in the anti-Modernist age became more and more frightened that the specter of Modernism was rising again as Catholic representatives took their place in the international field of Biblical scholarship. When Pius XII died in 1958, conservatives in key positions made their move to reverse the trend. The Congregation of Seminaries voiced disapproval of a progressive French Catholic textbook; public attacks were orchestrated against leading Scripture scholars; two of them were ousted from their teaching positions at the Biblical Institute; the Holy Office issued its 1961 Monitum, which the press presented as even more negative than it was (since it overlooked the fact that it was aimed at popularizers, not scholars). Then word went forth that the schema on Revelation prepared for Vatican II, which was to open in the fall of 1962, represented a rejection of recent developments and a return to the sterile positions of the anti-Modernist era.

The potential fourth crisis threatening Catholic biblical studies did not materialize because of what happened when Vatican II actually convened. The spirit of John XXIII was contagious enough to prevent those whom he called "the prophets of doom" from imposing once more on Catholic scholars the kind of strait-jackets legislated for the earlier era, which would have been disastrous in the new situation. Due to his personal intervention, the retrogressive schema was rejected and the Council adopted the forward-looking approach that was to become its trademark. When Paul VI was elected in 1963, any lingering doubts about Rome's attitude toward modern Biblical studies were soon removed. The two professors at the Biblical Institute were restored to their chairs; some of the most qualified scholars were appointed consultors to the PBC; and in April 1964 the PBC issued its *Instruction on the Historical Truth of the Gospels.* This officially endorsed the awareness of the three "dimensions" of the Gospels as they have come down to us: 1) material from the Public Ministry of the historical Jesus; 2) modifications reflecting the concerns of the early Christian communities as the preached tradition was applied to these later circumstances; and 3) adaptations introduced by each Evangelist to suit his literary plan and purpose.

In some ways the 1964 Instruction is more important than the 1965 Constitution on Revelation of Vatican II. If 1893 and 1943 are singled out as earlier watersheds, marking the periods of modern Catholic concern with the Bible, 1964 finally stands as the year then the zigzag stopped. Even though some of the later documents found here contain what would have to be described as conservative statements, there is nothing comparable to those of the anti-Modernist period. Catholic Biblical scholarship has come of age and in doing so has been fully accepted by Church authorities. Ready evidence of this on the American scene is available in such developments as the *New American Bible*, the *Jerome Biblical Commentary* and the enhanced status of the *Catholic Biblical Quarterly*.

One might argue in light of the above that this collection might better have begun with the 1943 encyclical or the 1964 Instruction, since so much of the earlier material is rather useless for contemporary purposes. Much of it is extremely time conditioned. But such a contention would ironically repudiate the very source of so much of the progress—the scientific study of history. These documents are part of the record. They mark the road that the Roman Catholic tradition has had to travel. Even those from the darkest periods ought to serve as occasions of gratitude, because they demonstrate better than anything else how far things have since progressed. And those since 1964 reveal the commitment to contemporary scholarship that promises an ever more Biblical approach in the Catholic thought of the future. This was the explicit prayer and prediction of the Church in Vatican II: "So may it happen that, by the reading and study of the sacred books, 'the Word of God may speed on and triumph' (2 Thess. 3:1) and the treasure of Revelation entrusted to the Church may more and more fill the hearts of men. . . . a new impulse of spiritual life may be expected from increased veneration of the Word of God, which stands forever."[8]

1   *The Study of the Bible in the Middle Ages*, p. xii, Notre Dame Press, 1964.

2   E. E. Y. Hales, *The Catholic Church in the Modern World*, Doubleday 1958, p. 124, 129.

3   Thomas Bokenkotter, *A Concise History of the Catholic Church*, Doubleday, 1977, pp. 333-335.

4   James T. Burtchaell, *Catholic Theories of Biblical Inspiration Since 1810*, Cambridge University Press, 1969, pp. 230-232.

5   Luis Alonso Schökel, *Understanding Biblical Research*, Herder & Herder, 1963, p. 32f.

6   Burtchaell, *op. cit.*, p. 239.

7   Raymond E. Brown, *Biblical Reflection on Crises Facing the Church*, Paulist Press, 1975, p. 6f.

8   *Constitution on Revelation*, closing paragraph.

Subject Index

The Muratorian Fragment
c. 170 A.D.

. . . but at some he was present, and so he set them down [referring to Mark].

The third book of the Gospel, that according to Luke, was compiled in his own name on Paul's authority by Luke the physician, when after Christ's ascension Paul had taken him to be with him like a legal expert. Yet neither did he see the Lord in the flesh; and he too, as he was able to ascertain events, begins his story from the birth of John.

The fourth of the Gospels was written by John, one of the 2 disciples. When exhorted by his fellow-disciples and bishops, he said, 'Fast with me this day for three days; and what may be revealed to any of us, let us relate it to one another.' The same night it was revealed to Andrew, one of the apostles, that John was to write all things in his own name, and they were all to certify.

And therefore, though various ideas are taught in the 3 several books of the Gospels, yet it makes no difference to the faith of believers, since by one sovereign Spirit all things are declared in all of them concerning the Nativity, the Passion, the Resurrection, the conversation with his disciples and his two comings, the first in lowliness and contempt, which has come to pass, the second glorious with royal power, which is to come.

What marvel therefore if John so firmly sets forth each 4 statement in his Epistles too, saying of himself, "What we have seen with our eyes and heard with our ears and our hands have handled, these things we have written to you"? For so he declares himself not an eyewitness and a hearer only, but a writer of all the marvels of the Lord in order.

5   The Acts, however, of all the Apostles are written in one book. Luke, to the most excellent Theophilus, includes events because they were done in his own presence, as he also plainly shows by leaving out the passion of Peter, and also the departure of Paul from the City on his journey to Spain.

6   The Epistles, however, of Paul themselves make plain to those who wish to understand it, what epistles were sent by him, and from what place or for what cause. He wrote at some length first of all to the Corinthians, forbidding the schisms of heresy; next to the Galatians, forbidding circumcision; then he wrote to the Romans at greater length, impressing on them the rule of the Scriptures, and also that Christ is the first principle of them, concerning which severally it is not necessary for us to discuss. For the blessed Apostle Paul himself, following the rule of his predecessor John, writes only by name to seven churches in the following order—to the Corinthians a first, to the Ephesians a second, to the Philippians a third, to the Colossians a fourth, to the Galatians a fifth, to the Thessalonians a sixth, to the Romans a seventh; although for the sake of admonition there is a second to the Corinthians and to the Thessalonians, yet one Church is recognized as being spread over the entire world. For John too in the Apocalypse, though he writes to seven churches, yet speaks to all. Howbeit to Philemon one, to Titus one, and to Timothy two were put in writing from personal inclination and attachment, to be in honour however with the Catholic Church for the ordering of ecclesiastical discipline. There is in circulation also one to the Laodicenes, another to the Alexandrians, both forged in Paul's name to suit the heresy of Marcion, and several others, which cannot be received into the Catholic Church; for it is not fitting that gall be mixed with honey.

7   The Epistle of Jude no doubt, and the couple bearing the name of John, are accepted in the Catholic Church; and the Wisdom written by the friends of Solomon in his honour.

The Apocalypse also of John, and of Peter only we receive, which some of our friends will not have read in the Church. But the Shepherd was written quite lately in our times in the city of Rome by Hermas, while his brother Pius, the bishop, was sitting in the chair of the church of the city of Rome; and therefore it ought indeed to be read, but it cannot to the end of time be publicly read in the Church to the people, either among the prophets, who are complete in number, or among the Apostles.

But of Arsinous, called also Valentinus, or of Miltiades we receive nothing at all; those who have also composed a new book of Psalms for Marcion, together with Basileides and the Asian founder of the Cataphrygians are rejected.

ß

Irenaeus
Against Heresies
Book III, 1-3
c. 180 A.D.

The Lord of all gave to his apostles the power of the gospel, and by them we also have learned the truth, that is, the teaching of the Son of God—as the Lord said to them, 'He who hears you hears me, and he who despises you despises me, and him who sent me' [*Luke* 10: 16].

10   For we learned the plan of our salvation from no others than from those through whom the gospel came to us. They first preached it abroad, and then later by the will of God handed it down to us in Scriptures, to be the foundation and pillar of our faith. For it is not right to say that they preached before they had come to perfect knowledge, as some dare to say, boasting that they are the correctors of the apostles. For after our Lord had risen from the dead, and they were clothed with the power from on high when the Holy Spirit came upon them, they were filled with all things and had perfect knowledge. They went out to the ends of the earth, preaching the good things that come to us from God, and proclaiming peace from heaven to men, all and each of them equally being in possession of the gospel of God.

11   So Matthew among the Hebrews issued a written version of the gospel in their own tongue, while Peter and Paul were preaching the gospel at Rome and founding the Church. After their decease Mark, the disciple and interpreter of Peter, also handed down to us in writing what Peter had preached. Luke also, the follower of Paul recorded in a book

the gospel as it was preached by him. Finally John, the disciple of the Lord, who had also lain on his breast, himself published the gospel, while he was residing at Ephesus in Asia.

All of these handed down to us that there is one God,   12
maker of heaven and earth, proclaimed by the law and the prophets, and one Christ the Son of God. If anyone does not agree with them he despises the companions of the Lord, he despises the Lord himself, he even despises the Father, and he is self-condemned, resisting and refusing his own salvation, as all the heretics do.

But when they are refuted from the Scriptures they turn   13
around and attack the Scriptures themselves, saying that they are not correct, or authoritative, that they are mutually inconsistent and that the truth cannot be found from them by those who are not acquainted with the tradition. For this, they say, was not handed down in writing, but orally, which is why Paul said, 'We speak wisdom among the perfect, but not the wisdom of this world' [*1 Cor.* 2:6]. Each of them utters a wisdom which he has made up, or rather a fiction; so that according to them, the truth was at one time to be found quite properly in Valentinus, then at another time in Marcion, at another time in Cerinthus, then later in Basilides, or in anyone who opposes the Church and has no saving message to utter. Each one of them is wholly perverse, and is not ashamed to preach himself, corrupting the rule of faith.

But when we appeal again to that tradition which has   14
come down from the apostles and is guarded by the successions of elders in the churches, they oppose the tradition, saying that they are wiser not only than the elders, but even than the apostles, and have found the genuine truth. For the apostles, they say, mixed matters of the law with the words of the Saviour, and not only the apostles, but even the Lord himself, spoke sometimes from the Demiurge, sometimes from the middle power, sometimes from the highest, while they know the hidden mystery without doubt or corruption, and in its purity. This is nothing less than shameless blasphemy against their Maker. What it comes to is that they will not agree with either Scriptures or tradition.

15   It is such people, my dear friend, that we have to fight with, who like slippery snakes are always trying to escape us. Therefore we must resist them on all sides, hoping that we may so rebut and confound them that we may be able to bring some of them to turn to the truth. For although it is not easy for a soul which has been seized by error to turn back, still it is not absolutely impossible to put error to flight by putting the truth beside it.

16   The tradition of the apostles, made clear in all the world, can be seen in every church by those who wish to behold the truth. We can enumerate those who were established by the apostles as bishops in the churches, and their successors down to our time, none of whom taught or thought of anything like their mad ideas. Even if the apostles had known of hidden mysteries, which they taught to the perfect secretly and apart from others, they would have handed them down especially to those whom they were entrusting the churches themselves. For they certainly wished those whom they were leaving as their successors, handing over to them their own teaching position, to be perfect and irreproachable, since their sound conduct would be a great benefit, and failure on their part the greatest calamity.

17   To enumerate the successions of all the churches would take up too much space in a volume of this kind. But in order to put to shame all of those who in any way, either through self-conceit, or through vain-glory, or through blind and evil opinion, gather as they should not, I need only cite the case of that very great, most ancient and universally known church founded and established at Rome by those two most glorious apostles Peter and Paul and draw attention to the tradition which that church has received from the apostles and to the faith it preaches which has come down to our time through the succession of bishops. For in view of the outstanding pre-eminence of this church, there cannot be any disagreement between it and every other church (that is, the faithful in every place)—every church, that is, in which men in every place have at all times preserved the apostolic tradition.

When the blessed apostles had founded and built up the   **18**
church they handed over the ministry of the episcopate to
Linus. Paul mentions this Linus in his Epistles to Timothy.
Anencletus succeeded him. After him Clement received the
lot of the episcopate in the third place from the apostles. He
had seen the apostles and associated with them, and still had
their preaching sounding in his ears and their tradition before
his eyes—and not he alone, for there were many still left in
his time who had been taught by the apostles. In this Clement's time no small discord arose among the brethren in
Corinth, and the church in Rome sent a most appropriate
letter to the Corinthians, leading them to peace, renewing
their faith, and declaring the tradition which they had recently received from the apostles, which declared one almighty
God, maker of heaven and earth and fashioner of man, who
brought about the deluge, and called Abraham; who brought
out the people from the land of Egypt; who spoke with
Moses; who ordained the law and sent the prophets; and who
has prepared fire for the devil and his angels. Those who care
to can learn from this writing that he was proclaimed by the
churches as the Father of our Lord Jesus Christ, and so
understand the apostolic tradition of the Church, since this
epistle is older than those present false teachers who make up
lies about another God above the demiurge and maker of all
these things that are. Evarestus succeeded to this Clement,
and Alexander to Evarestus; then Xystus was installed as the
sixth from the apostles, and after him Telesphorus, who met
a glorious martyrdom; then Hyginus, then Pius, and after him
Anicetus. Soter followed Anicetus, and Eleutherus now in
the twelfth place from the apostles holds the lot of the
episcopate. In this very order and succession the apostolic
tradition in the church and the preaching of the truth has
come down even to us. This is a full demonstration that it is
one and the same life-giving faith which has been preserved in
the Church from the apostles to the present, and is handed
on in truth.

Similarly there was Polycarp, who not only was taught by   **19**
apostles and associated with many who had seen the Lord,

but also was installed by apostles in Asia as bishop in the church in Smyrna. I saw him myself in my early youth, for he survived for a long time and was of a ripe old age when he departed this life by a glorious and magnificent martyrdom. He too always taught what he learnt from the apostles. This is what the Church continues to hand on. This alone is true. The churches in Asia all bear witness to this, as do those who have succeeded Polycarp down to the present time; he is certainly a much more trustworthy and dependable witness to the truth than Valentinus and Marcion and the other false thinkers. When he visited Rome under Anicetus, he converted many followers of the above-mentioned heretics to the Church of God, proclaiming that he had received from the apostles the one and only truth, the same which is handed on by the Church. There are those who have heard him tell how when John the disciple of the Lord went to bathe at Ephesus, and saw Cerinthus inside, he rushed out of the baths without washing, but crying out, 'let us escape, lest the baths should fall while Cerinthus the enemy of the truth is in them.' Polycarp himself, when Marcion once met him and said, 'Acknowledge me!', answered, 'I acknowledge you—I acknowledge the first-born of Satan.' The apostles and their disciples took such great care not even to engage in conversations with the corrupters of the truth, as Paul also said, 'A heretical man after a first and second warning avoid, knowing that such a man has fallen away and is a sinner, being self-condemned' [*Titus* 3:10-11]. There is also a most appropriate letter of Polycarp addressed to the Philippians, from which those who care to, and are concerned for their own salvation, can learn the character of his faith and his preaching of the truth. The church in Ephesus also, which was founded by Paul, and where John survived until the time of Trajan, is a true witness of the traditions of the apostles,

Tertullian
On Prescription of Heretics
c. 207 A.D.

Chapter XV

We are therefore come to (the gist of) our position; for at this point we were aiming, and for this we were preparing in the preamble of our address (which we have just completed),—so that we may now join issue on the contention to which our adversaries challenge us. They put forward the Scriptures, and by this insolence of theirs they at once influence some. In the encounter itself, however, they weary the strong, they catch the weak, and dismiss waverers with a doubt. Accordingly, we oppose to them this step above all others, of not admitting them to any discussion of the Scriptures.

If in these lie their resources, before they can use them, it 21 ought to be clearly seen to whom belongs the possession of the Scriptures, that none may be admitted to the use thereof who has no title at all to the privilege.

Chapter XVI

I might be thought to have laid down this position to 22 remedy distrust in my case, or from a desire of entering on the contest in some other way, were there not reasons on my side, especially this, that our faith owes deference to the apostle, who forbids us to enter on "questions," or to consort with a heretic "after the first and second admonition," not, (be it observed,) after discussion. Discussion he has inhibited in this way, by designating *admonition* as the purpose of dealing with a heretic, and the *first* one too, because he is not a Christian; in order that he might not, after the manner of a Christian, seem to require correction again and again, and "before two or three witnesses," seeing that he ought to be corrected, for the very reason that he is not to be disputed with; and in the next place, because a controversy over the Scriptures can, clearly, produce no other effect than help to upset either the stomach or the brain.

Chapter XVII

23   Now this heresy of yours does not receive certain Scriptures; and whichever of them it does receive, it perverts by means of additions and diminutions, for the accomplishment of it own purpose; and such as it does receive, it receives not only in their entirety; but even when it does receive any up to a certain point as entire, it nevertheless perverts even these by the contrivance of diverse interpretations. Truth is just as much opposed by an adulteration of its meaning as it is by a corruption of its text. Their vain presumptions must needs refuse to acknowledge the (writings) whereby they are refuted. They rely on those which they have falsely put together, and which they have selected, because of their ambiguity. Though most skilled in the Scriptures, you will make no progress, when everything which you maintain is denied on the other side, and whatever you deny is (by them) maintained. As for yourself, indeed, you will lose nothing but your breath, and gain nothing but vexation from their blasphemy.

Chapter XVIII

24   But with respect to the man for whose sake you enter on the discussion of the Scriptures, with the view of strengthening him when afflicted with doubts, (let me ask) will it be to the truth, or rather to heretical opinions that he will lean? Influenced by the very fact that he sees you have made no

progress, whilst the other side is on an equal footing (with yourself) in denying and in defence, or at any rate on a like standing he will go away confirmed in his uncertainty by the discussion, not knowing which side to adjudge heretical. For, no doubt, they too are able to retort these things on us. It is indeed a necessary consequence that they should go so far as to say that adulterations of the Scriptures, and false expositions thereof, are rather introduced by ourselves, inasmuch as they, no less than we maintain that truth is on their side.

Chapter XIX

Our appeal, therefore, must not be made to the Scriptures;   25
nor must controversy be admitted on points in which victory will either be impossible, or uncertain, or not certain enough. But even if a discussion from the Scriptures should not turn out in such a way as to place both sides on a par, (yet) the natural order of things would require that this point should be first proposed, which is now the only one which we must discuss: "With whom lies that very faith to which the Scriptures belong? From what and through whom, and when, and to whom, has been handed down that rule, by which men become Christians?" For whatever it shall be manifest that the true Christian rule and faith shall be, *there* will likewise be the true Scriptures and expositions thereof, and all the Christian traditions.

Chapter XXXVII

Since this is the case, in order that the truth may be ad-   26
judged to belong to us, "as many as walk according to the rule," which the church has handed from the apostles, the apostles from Christ, *and* Christ from God, the reason of our position is clear, when it determines that heretics ought not to be allowed to challenge an appeal to the Scriptures, since we, without the Scriptures, prove that they have nothing to do with the Scriptures. For as they are heretics, they cannot be true Christians, because it is not from Christ that they get that which they pursue of their own mere choice, and from

the pursuit incur and admit the name of heretics. Thus, not being Christians, they have acquired no right to the Christian Scriptures; and it may be very fairly said to them, "Who are you? When and whence did you come? As you are none of mine, what have you to do with that which is mine? Indeed, Marcion, by what right do you hew my wood? By whose permission, Valentinus, are you diverting the streams of my fountain? By what power, Apelles, are you removing my land-marks? This is my property. Why are you, the rest, sowing and feeding here at your own pleasure? This (I say) is my property. I have long possessed it; I possessed it before you. I hold sure title-deeds from the original owners themselves, to whom the estate belonged. I am the heir of the apostles. Just as they carefully prepared their will and testament, and committed it to a trust, and adjured (the trustees to be faith-ful to their charge), even so do I hold it. As for you, they have, it is certain, always held you as disinherited, and re-jected you as strangers—as enemies. But on what ground are heretics strangers and enemies to the apostles, if it be not from the difference of their teaching, which each individual of his own mere will has either advanced or received in oppo-sition to the apostles?"

Chapter XXXVIII

27   Where diversity of doctrine is found, *there*, then, must be the corruption both of the Scriptures and the expositions thereof be regarded as existing. On those whose purpose it was to teach differently, lay the necessity of differently arranging the instruments of doctrine. They could not possibly have effected their diversity of teaching in any other way than by having a difference in the means whereby they taught. As in their case, corruption in doctrine could not possibly have succeeded without a corruption also if its instruments, so to ourselves also integrity of doctrine could not have accrued, without integrity in those means by which doctrine is managed. Now, what is there in our Scriptures which is contrary to us? What of our own have we introduced, that we should have to take it away again, or else add to it, or

alter it, in order to restore to its natural soundness anything
which is contrary to it, and contained in the Scriptures? What
we are ourselves, that also the Scriptures are (and have been)
from the beginning. Of them we have our being, before there
was in any other way, before they were interpolated by you.
Now, inasmuch as all interpolation must be believed to be a
later process, for the express reason that it proceeds from
rivalry which is never in any case previous to nor home-born
with that which it emulates, it is as incredible to every man
of sense that we should seem to have introduced any corrupt
text into the Scriptures, existing, as we have been, from the
very first, and being the first, as it is that they have not in
fact introduced it, who are both later in date and opposed (to
the Scriptures). One man perverts the Scriptures with his
hand, another their meaning by his exposition. For although
Valentinus seems to use the entire volume, he has none the
less laid violent hands on the truth only with a more cunning
mind and skill than Marcion. Marcion expressly and openly
used the knife, not the pen, since he made such an excision
of the Scriptures as suited his own subject-matter. Valentinus,
however, abstained from such excision, because he did not
invent Scriptures to square with his own subject-matter, but
adapted his matter to the Scriptures; and yet he took away
every particular word, and added fantastic arrangements of
things which have no real existence.

Chapter XXXIX

These were the ingenious arts of "spiritual wickednesses,"   28
wherewith we also, my brethren, may fairly expect to have "to
wrestle," as necessary for faith, that the elect may be made
manifest, (and) that the reprobate may be discovered. And
therefore they possess influence, and a facility in thinking
out and fabricating errors, which ought not to be wondered
at as if it were a difficult and inexplicable process, seeing that
in profane writings also an example comes ready to hand of a
similar facility. You see in our own day, composed out of
Virgil, a story of a wholly different character, the subject-
matter being arranged according to the verse, and the verse

according to the subject-matter. In short, Hosidius Geta has most completely pilfered his tragedy of *Meda* from Virgil. A near relative of my own, among some leisure productions of his pen, has composed out of the same poet *The Table of Cebes*. On the same principle, those *poetasters* are commonly called *Homerocentones*, "collectors of Homeric odds and ends," who stitch into one piece, patchwork fashion, works of their own from the lines of Homer, out of many scraps put together from this passage and from that (in miscellaneous confusion). Now, unquestionably, the Divine Scriptures are more fruitful in resources of all kinds for this sort of facility. Nor do I risk contradiction in saying that the very Scriptures were even arranged by the will of God in such a manner as to furnish materials for heretics, inasmuch as I read that "there must be heresies," which there cannot be without the Scriptures.

Chapter XL

29   The question will arise, By whom is to be interpreted the sense of the passages which make for heresies? By the devil, of course, to whom pertain those wiles which pervert the truth, and who, by the mystic rites of his idols, vies even with the essential portions of the sacraments of God. He, too, baptizes some—that is, his own believers and faithful followers; he promises the putting away of sins by a laver (of his own); and if my memory still serves me, Mithra there, (in the kingdom of Satan,) sets his marks on the foreheads of his soldiers; celebrates also the oblation of bread, and introduces an image of a resurrection, and before a sword wreathes a crown. What also must we say to (Satan's) limiting his chief priest to a single marriage? He, too, has his virgins; he, too, has his proficients in continence. Suppose now we revolve in our minds the superstitions of Numa Pompilius, and consider his priestly offices and badges and privileges, his sacrificial services, too, and the instruments and vessels of the sacrifices themselves, and the curious rites of his expiations and vows: is it not clear to us that the devil imitated the well-known moroseness of the Jewish law? Since, therefore, he has shown

such emulation in his great aim of expressing, in the concerns of his idolatry, those very things of which consists the administration of Christ's sacraments, it follows, of course, that the same being, possessing still the same genius, both set his heart upon, and succeeded in, adapting to his profane and rival creed the very documents of divine things and of the Christian saints—his interpretations from their interpretations, his words from their words, his parables from their parables. For this reason, then, no one ought to doubt, either that "spiritual wickednesses," from which also heresies come, have been introduced by the devil, or that there is any real difference between heresies and idolatry, seeing that they appertain both to the same author and the same work that idolatry does. They either pretend that there is another god in opposition to the Creator, or, even if they acknowledge that the Creator is the one only God, they treat Him as a different being from what He is in truth. The consequence is, that every lie which they speak of God is in a certain sense a sort of idolatry.

Origen
Letter to Gregory Thaumaturgus
c. 235 A.D.

All hail to thee in God, most excellent and reverend Sir, son Gregory, from Origen. A natural quickness of understanding is fitted, as you are well aware, if it be diligently exercised, to produce a work which may bring its owner so far as is possible, if I may so express myself, to the consummation of the art which he desires to practise, and your natural aptitude is sufficient to make you a consummate Roman lawyer and a Greek philosopher too of the most famous schools. But my desire for you has been that you should direct the whole force of your intelligence to Christianity as your end, and that in the way of production. And I would wish that you should take with you on the one hand those parts of the philosophy of the Greeks which are fit, as it were, to serve as general or preparatory studies for Christianity, and on the other hand so much of Geometry and Astronomy as may be helpful for the interpretation of the Holy Scriptures. The children of the philosophers speak of geometry and music and grammar and rhetoric and astronomy as being ancillary to philosophy; and in the same way we might speak of philosophy itself as being ancillary to Christianity.

31   It is something of this sort perhaps that is enigmatically indicated in the directions God is represented in the Book of Exodus as giving to the children of Israel. They are directed to beg from their neighbours and from those dwelling in their

tents vessels of silver and of gold, and raiment; thus they are
to spoil the Egyptians, and to obtain materials for making the
things they are told to provide in connection with the worship of God. For out of the things of which the children of
Isarel spoiled the Egyptians the furniture of the Holy of
Holies was made, the ark with its cover, and the cherubim
and the mercy-seat and the gold jar in which the manna, that
bread of angels, was stored. These probably were made from
the finest of the gold of the Egyptians, and from a second
quality, perhaps, the solid golden candlestick which stood
near the inner veil, and the lamps on it, and the golden table
on which stood the shewbread, and between these two the
golden altar of incense. And if there was gold of a third and
of a fourth quality, the sacred vessels were made of it. And of
the Egyptian silver, too, other things were made; for it was
from their sojourn in Egypt that the children of Israel derived
the great advantage of being supplied with such a quanitity of
precious materials for the use of the service of God. Out of
the Egyptian raiment probably were made all those requisites
named in Scripture in embroidered work; the embroiderers
working with the wisdom of God, such garments for such
purposes, to produce the hangings and the inner and outer
courts. This is not a suitable opportunity to enlarge on such a
theme or to show in how many ways the children of Israel
found those things useful which they got from the Egyptians.
The Egyptians had not made a proper use of them; but the
Hebrews used them, for the wisdom of God was with them,
for religious purposes. Holy Scripture knows, however, that it
was an evil thing to descend from the land of the children of
Israel into Egypt; and in this a great truth is wrapped up. For
some it is of evil that they should dwell with the Egyptians,
that is to say, with the learning of the world, after they have
been enrolled in the law of God and in the Israelite worship
of Him. Ader the Edomite, as long as he was in the land of
Israel and did not taste the bread of the Egyptians, made no
idols; but when he fled from the wise Solomon and went
down into Egypt, as one who had fled from the wisdom of
God he became connected with Pharaoh, marrying the sister
of his wife, and begetting a son who was brought up among

the sons of Pharaoh. Therefore, though he did go back to the land of Israel, he came back to it to bring division into the people of God, and to cause them to say to the golden calf, "These are thy gods, O Israel, which brought thee up out of the land of Egypt." I have learned by experience and can tell you that there are few who have taken of the useful things of Egypt and come out of it, and have then prepared what is required for the service of God; but Ader the Edomite on the other hand has many a brother. I mean those who, founding on some piece of Greek learning, have brought forth heretical ideas, and have as it were made golden calves in Bethel, which is, being interpreted, the house of God. This appears to me to be intended to convey that such persons set up their own images in the Scriptures in which the Word of God dwells, and which therefore are tropically called Bethel. The other image is said in the word to have been set up in Dan. Now the borders of Dan are at the extremities and are contiguous to the country of the heathens, as is plainly recorded in the Book of Jesus, son of Nave. Some of these images, then, are close to the borders of the heathen, which the brothers, as we showed, of Ader have devised.

32   Do you then, sir, my son, study first of all the divine Scriptures. Study them I say. For we require to study the divine writings deeply, lest we should speak of them faster than we think; and while you study these divine works with a believing and God-pleasing intention, knock at that which is closed in them, and it shall be opened to thee by the porter, of whom Jesus says,[1] "To him the porter openeth." While you attend to this divine reading seek aright and with unwavering faith in God the hidden sense which is present in most passages of the divine Scriptures. And do not be content with knocking and seeking, for what is most necessary for understanding divine things is prayer, and in urging us to this the Saviour says not only,[2] "Knock, and it shall be opened to you," and "Seek, and ye shall find," but also "Ask, and it shall be given you." So much I have ventured on account of my fatherly love to you. Whether I have ventured well or not, God knows, and His Christ, and he who has part of the Spirit of God and the Spirit of Christ. May you par-

take in these; may you have an always increasing share of
them, so that you may be able to say not only, "We are partakers of Christ,"[3] but also "We are partakers of God."

Origen
Commentary on the Gospel According to Matthew
c. 247 A.D.

Book II

"**B** *lessed are the peacemakers. . . .*"[1] To the man who is
a peacemaker in either sense there is in the Divine
oracles nothing crooked or perverse, for they are all
plain to those who understand.[2] And because to such an one
there is nothing crooked or perverse, he sees therefore abundance of peace[3] in all the Scriptures, even in those which
seem to be at conflict, and in contradiction with one another.
And likewise he becomes a third peacemaker as he demonstrates that that which appears to others to be a conflict in
the Scriptures is no conflict, and exhibits their concord and
peace, whether of the Old Scriptures with the New, or of the
Law with the Prophets, or of the Gospels with the Apostolic
Scriptures, or of the Apostolic Scriptures with each other.
For, also, according to the Preacher, all the Scriptures are
"words of the wise like goads, and as nails firmly fixed which
were given by agreement from one shepherd;"[4] and there is
nothing superfluous in them. But the Word is the one Shepherd of things rational which may have an appearance of
discord to those who have not ears to hear, but are truly at
perfect concord. For as the different chords of the psalter or
the lyre, each of which gives forth a certain sound of its own
which seems unlike the sound of another chord, are thought
by a man who is not musical and ignorant of the principle of

musical harmony, to be inharmonious, because of the dissimilarity of the sounds, so those who are not skilled in hearing the harmony of God in the sacred Scriptures think that
the Old is not in harmony with the New, or the Prophets
with the Law, or the Gospels with one another, or the Apostle
with the Gospel, or with himself, or with the other Apostles.
But he who comes instructed in the music of God, being a
man wise in word and deed, and, on this account, like another
David—which is, by interpretation, skilful with the hand—will
bring out the sound of the music of God, having learned from
this at the right time to strike the chords, now the chords of
the Law, now the Gospel chords in harmony with them, and
again the Prophetic chords, and, when reason demands it, the
Apostolic chords which are in harmony with the Prophetic,
and likewise the Apostolic with those of the Gospels. For he
knows that all the Scripture is the one perfect and harmonised
instrument of God, which from different sounds gives forth
one saving voice to those willing to learn, which stops and
restrains every working of an evil spirit, just as the music of
David laid to rest the evil spirit in Saul, which also was
choking him.[5] You see, then, that he is in the third place a
peacemaker, who sees in accordance with the Scripture the
peace of it all, and implants this peace in those who rightly
seek and make nice distinctions in a genuine spirit.

Eusebius
Ecclesiastical History: Book Three
312 A.D.

Chapter 3

Now, one letter of Peter, his so-called first Epistle, is admitted to be genuine, and the ancient presbyters made use of this Epistle as undisputed in their own writings. The reputed second Epistle we have ascertained to be not canonical; nevertheless, since it appeared useful to many, it has been studied together with the other Scriptures. However, the writing of the Acts imputed to him, and the Gospel that bears his name, and the Preaching spoken of as his, and the so-called Revelation we know have not been handed down at all among Catholics, because no orthodox writer among the ancients or in our own time has made use of their testimonies. As my history proceeds, I shall make it a point to indicate in succession which of the orthodox writers in each period made use of any of the disputed works and what they said about the canonical and accepted writings and what about those which are not so. But, such are the works which are called Peter's, among which I recognize only one Epistle as genuine and so acknowledged by the presbyters of old. And the fourteen Epistles of Paul are manifest and clear, yet it is not right to ignore that some have rejected the Epistle to the Hebrews as spurious, saying that it was disputed by the Church of Rome, on the ground that it was not by Paul. I shall set forth at the proper time what was said about this

Epistle by our predecessors. Indeed, not even have I received his so-called Acts among the undisputed writings. But since the same Apostle in the salutations at the end of the Epistle to the Romans has made mention among others of Hermas, whose, they say, is the Book of the Shepherd, we must realize that this also was rejected by some, and because of these it should not be placed among approved works, but by others it has been judged as most indispensable for those especially who need elementary instruction. We know that for this purpose it has been used publicly in the churches in recent times, and I have found that some of the most ancient authors have drawn on it. Let these words suffice to establish the divine writings that are undisputed and those which are not acknowledged by all.

Chapter 4

It should be clear from Paul's own words, and from what Luke has related in the Acts, that Paul, when preaching to the Gentiles, laid the foundation of the churches 'from Jerusalem round about as far as unto Illyricum.' And from the very words of Peter, from the Epistle which we have mentioned as indisputably his, in which he writes to the Hebrews who were in the dispersion of Pontus, Galatia, Cappadocia, Asia, and Bithynia, it should be clear in how many provinces he, too, handed down the word of the New Testament by preaching the Gospel of Christ to those of the circumcision. But it is not easy to say how many and who of these became genuinely zealous and were judged able to be pastors of the churches founded by them, except such as one might list from the words of Paul. His fellow workers and fellow soldiers, as he himself called them, numbered many thousands, the majority of whom he considered worthy of an everlasting memorial, for he has made his testimony to them unceasing in his own letters. Moreover, Luke also, as he lists those known to him, makes mention of them by name. So Timothy is recorded as the first to receive the bishopric of the diocese of Ephesus, as also was Titus of the churches in Crete. Luke, who was by race an Antiochian and by profession a physician,

35

had long been a companion of Paul, and had more than a casual acquaintance with the rest of the Apostles. He has left us in two inspired books examples of the art of healing for souls which he obtained from them: namely, the Gospel, which he testifies that he planned according to what those who were eye-witnesses from the beginning and ministers of the word had handed down to him, all of whom he says he had followed from the first, and the Acts of the Apostles, which he composed on the evidence not of hearsay but of his own eyes. And they say that Paul was actually accustomed to quote the Gospel according to St. Luke, since when writing about some Gospel as his own he used to say, 'According to my Gospel.' Of the rest of Paul's followers, there is evidence from Paul himself that Crescens was sent to Gaul, and Linus, whom he mentioned in the second Epistle to Timothy as being with him in Rome, has already been shown to have been the first after Peter to have been appointed to the episcopacy of the Church in Rome. And of Clement, also, who was himself appointed the third Bishop of the Church at Rome, there is evidence from Paul that he was his co-worker and fellow soldier. Besides these, that member of the Areopagus, Dionysius by name, whom Luke records in the Acts as having received the faith for the first time after Paul's public address to the Athenians in the Areopagus, is described by one of the ancients, another Dionysius, shepherd of the diocese of Corinth, as having been the first Bishop of the Church at Athens. As we proceed on our way, we will relate at the proper time the chronological details of the succession of the Apostles; meanwhile, let us go on with the succeeding events of our history.

Chapter 24

36   But, come, let us point out the irrefutable writings of this Apostle. Let the Gospel according to him, which is read in all the churches under heaven, be first recognized. That it has with good reason been listed by the ancients in the fourth place after the other three may be made evident as follows. Those inspired and truly divine men, I mean the Apostles of

Christ, had completely purified their life, and had adorned their souls with every virtue, but they were unskilled in speech. Although they indeed had confidence in the divine and wonder-working power granted them by the Saviour, they neither knew how nor desired to proclaim the doctrines of their teacher in persuasive and artistic language, but they used only the proof of the divine Spirit that worked with them, and the wonder-working power of Christ which was brought to fulfillment through them. Thus they proclaimed the knowledge of the kingdom of heaven to the whole world, and gave little consideration to care in composing written words. And they did this because they were serving a greater and superhuman ministry. At any rate, Paul, the most able of all in the handling of language and the most vigorous in thought, put in writing no more than the briefest Epistles, although he was able to express countless ineffable things, for he had touched the vision of the third heaven and had been caught up to the divine paradise itself and had been thought worthy of hearing ineffable words there. Now, the other pupils of our Saviour were not without experience in the same things—the twelve Apostles, the seventy disciples, and countless others in addition to these. Yet, of all these, only Matthew and John have left us recollections of the conversations of the Lord, and tradition has it that they took to writing by force. For Matthew, who had first preached to the Hebrews, when he was about to go among others, by committing the Gospel according to himself to writings in his native language, compensated by his writing for the lack of his presence those from whom he was being sent. And Mark and Luke had already given out the Gospels according to themselves, but it is said that John all the same made use of an unwritten message, and finally resorted to writing for the following reason. When the three Gospels which had been written before had been distributed among all including himself, it is said that he accepted them and bore witness to their truth, but said that there was only lacking in the writing the description of what was done by Christ in the first days and at the beginning of His preaching. And the statement is indeed true. It is at least possible to see that the three Evangelists described only what the Saviour had accomplished in the one year after John the Baptist was confined to prison and that they made this very point at the beginning of their narrative. Anyhow, after the fast of forty days and the temptation following upon this, Matthew shows the time of his own writing by saying: 'having heard John had been betrayed, he retired from Judaea into Galilee,' and Mark likewise says: 'After John was delivered up, Jesus came into Galilee.' And Luke also, before beginning the acts of Jesus, similarly observes, saying that Herod added to the evil deeds which he had done, and 'shut up John in prison.' Thus they say that the Apostle John was asked for this reason to hand down in his own Gospel an account of the period passed over in silence by the former Evangelists and of the things done at this time by the Saviour (and those were what He did before the imprisonment of the Baptist), and that he pointed this out when he said on one occasion, 'this beginning of miracles did Jesus,' and on another occasion, by mentioning the Baptist in the midst of the acts of Jesus as then still baptizing in Enon near Salim, and that he makes this clear by saying, 'for John was not yet cast into prison.' Thus John hands down by the writing of his own Gospel the things which were done by Christ when the Baptist had not yet been thrown under guard, and the other three Evangelists relate the events after the casting of the Baptist into prison. To one who has grasped this, the Gospels no longer appear to be at variance with one another, because that according to John includes the first of the acts of Christ, and the others the story of what He did at the end of the period, and because John then probably passed over the genealogy of our Saviour inasmuch as it had already been described by Matthew and Luke, and he began with His divinity since it had been reserved for him by the Divine Spirit as for one greater than they.

37   Let so much suffice for us regarding the writing of the Gospel according to John, and the reason for that according to Mark has been made clear above. Luke himself has also set forth, as he began his account, the reason why he made his composition, pointing out that, since many others had attempted rather rashly to form a narrative of the matters of

which he himself had full knowledge, to relieve us of the
doubtful opinions of others he of necessity through his own
Gospel handed down the accurate account of those events of
which he himself had well grasped the truth, aided by his
association and life with Paul and by his intercourse with the
other Apostles. So much do we present on these matters at
this time, but on a more fitting occasion we will try to show
by quotations from the ancients what has been said by others
concerning them.

Of the writings of John besides the Gospel, the first of the   38
Epistles is acknowledged without controversy by men of today as well as by the ancients, but the other two are disputed,
and opinion on the Apocalypse with most persons even today
tends in either direction. However, at the proper time, this
also will receive consideration from the testimony of the
ancients.

Chapter 25

It seems reasonable, having arrived at this point, to summa-   39
rize the writings of the New Testament which have been mentioned. First, we must put the holy quaternion of the Gospels,
and the writing of the Acts of the Apostles follows these.
After this we must reckon the Epistles of Paul. Next to these
in order we must recognize the Epistle of John called the first
and similarly the Epistle of Peter. After these, if it seem well,
we must place the Apocalypse of John, the arguments concerning which we will set forth at the proper time. These are
among the recognized books. Among the disputed works, but
yet known to most, are extant the so-called Epistle of James,
that of Jude, the second Epistle of Peter, and the so-called
second and third Epistle of John, whether they really belong
to the Evangelist or even to another of the same name.
Among the spurious works must be placed the work of the
Acts of Paul and the so-called Shepherd, and the Apocalypse
of Peter, and in addition to these the extant letter of Barna-
bas and the so-called Teachings of the Apostles, and again, as
I have said, the Apocalypse of John, if it should so appear.
Some, as I have said, reject it, but others classify it among

the accepted books. Now, among these some have also placed the Gospel according to the Hebrews, in which the Hebrews who have accepted Christ especially delight. All these might be among the disputed books, but we have nevertheless, of necessity, made a list of them, distinguishing those writings which according to the tradition of the Church are true, genuine, and recognized from those which are different from these in that they are not canonical but disputed, although known by most of the writers of the Church, in order that we might be able to know these works themselves and the writings which are published by the heretics under the name of the Apostles, including Gospels such as those of Peter and Thomas and Matthias, and some others besides these, or Acts such as those of Andrew and John and the other Apostles. To none of these has anyone belonging to the succession of the writers of the Church considered it right to refer in his writings. Furthermore, the character of the phraseology is at variance with apostolic style, and both the thought and the purpose of what is related in them is especially in discord with true orthodoxy and clearly proves that they really are forgeries by heretics. They ought, therefore, to be placed not even among spurious works, but should be shunned as altogether absurd and impious.

Chapter 39

40   Now, the acknowledged writing of Clement is well known and the works of Ignatius and Polycarp have been mentioned; and of Papias five treatises are in circulation which bear the title, 'Interpretation of the Oracles of the Lord.' And Irenaeus makes mention of these as the only ones written by him, speaking as follows: 'These things, too, Papias, an ancient man, who was a hearer of John and a companion of Polycarp, attests in writing in the fourth of his books, for five books were composed by him. Such are the words of Irenaeus. Papias himself, however, according to the preface of his treatises, makes it clear that he was never a hearer or eyewitness of the holy Apostles, but he shows that he received the doctrines of the faith from those who knew them, and he

does so in these words: 'I shall not hesitate to set down for you together with my interpretations all that I have ever learned well from the presbyters and recall well, being confident of their truth. For, unlike most, I did not take pleasure in those who say much, but in those who teach the truth, and not in those who relate the commandments of others, but in those who relate the commandments given to the faith by the Lord and derived from the truth itself; but if ever anyone came who had carefully followed the presbyters, I inquired as to the words of the presbyters, what Andrew or what Peter said, or what Philip or what Thomas or James or what John or Matthew or any other of the disciples of the Lord, and what Aristion and the presbyter John, the Lord's disciples, were saying. For I did not suppose that information from books helped me so much as that from a living and abiding voice.'

His mentioning the name of John twice is worth noting here. The first of these he reckons along with Peter and James and Matthew and the other Apostles, meaning clearly the Evangelist, but the other John, after expanding his statement, he places outside the number of the Apostles, placing Aristion before him, and he distinctly calls him a presbyter. Thus, by these words is proved the truth of the story of those who have said that two persons in Asia bore the same name, and that there were two tombs in Ephesus and each of these even today is said to be John's. We must give attention to this, for it is probable that the second (unless you would prefer the first) saw the Revelation which passes under the name of John. And Papias, who is now being explained by us, confesses that he had received the words of the Apostles from their followers, but says that he himself was a hearer of Aristion and the presbyter John. At any rate, he mentions them many times and presents their traditions in his writings. Let us at least say this much to good purpose. But it is worth while to add to the words of Papias already quoted other expressions of his by which he describes certain marvels and other matters which probably reached him through tradition. Now, it has already been pointed out above that Philip the Apostle lived at Hierapolis with his daughters, but it must

41

now be noted that Papias, who was a contemporary of theirs, reveals that he received a marvelous story from the daughters of Philip, for he relates that a resurrection of a corpse took place in his time, and again that another miracle took place in connection with Justus surnamed Barsabas, who drank a deadly poison and through the grace of the Lord suffered no harm. The book of Acts relates in these words that the holy Apostles, after the ascension of the Saviour, appointed this Justus together with Matthias and prayed over them for the choice of one in the place of Judas to fill up their number. 'And they appointed two, Joseph, called Barsabas, who was surnamed Justus, and Matthias; and praying, they said,' And the same author presents other accounts as having come to him from unwritten tradition, and some strange parables of the Saviour and teachings of His and other more mythical accounts. Among these he says that there will be a period of about a thousand years after the resurrection of the dead, when the kingdom of Christ will be established on this earth in material form. I suppose that he got these ideas through a perverse reading of the accounts of the Apostles, not realizing that these were expressed by them mystically in figures. For he appears to be a man of very little intelligence, to speak judging from his books, but he was responsible for the great number of Church writers after him holding the same opinion as himself, who proposed in their support the antiquity of the man, as, for instance, Irenaeus and whoever else appeared to hold similar views.

42   In his own writing he also passes on interpretations of the Lord's words from Aristion, who has been mentioned before, and traditions from John the presbyter. After referring the studious to these, we shall now of necessity add to his words already quoted a tradition about Mark who wrote the Gospel, which he gives in these words: 'This also the Presbyter used to say, "When Mark became Peter's interpreter, he wrote down accurately, although not in order, all that he remembered of what was said or done by the Lord. For he had not heard the Lord nor followed Him, but later, as I have said, he did Peter, who made his teaching fit his needs without, as it were, making any arrangement of the Lord's oracles, so that

Mark made no mistake in thus writing some things down as he remembered them. For to one thing he gave careful attention, to omit nothing of what he heard and to falsify nothing in this." ' Now, this has been related by Papias regarding Mark, and regarding Matthew he has spoken as follows: 'Now Matthew collected the oracles in the Hebrew language, and each one interpreted them as he was able.'

The same writer has used testimonies from the first Epistle 43 of John and likewise from that of Peter, and he has set forth another story about a woman who was accused before the Lord of many sins, which is contained in the Gospel according to the Hebrews. Let us observe this much, out of a feeling of necessity, in addition to what has already been quoted.

Cyril, Bishop of Jerusalem
Catechesis IV (Excerpts)
c. 348 A.D.

Believe also in the Holy Spirit and cherish the right knowledge concerning Him; since there are many strangers to the Holy Spirit and they teach blasphemous things about Him. Learn then that this Holy Spirit is one and indivisible, His powers manifold; various as are the effects He produces, He is not Himself divided. He knows the mysteries, and "searches all things, even the deep things of God."[1] It is He who descended upon the Lord Jesus Christ in the form of a dove, who wrought in the Law and the Prophets, yes, who even now, at the time of baptism, puts a seal upon your soul; of His holiness every intellectual nature stands in need. If any man dare to blaspheme against Him, "It will not be forgiven him, either in this world or in the world to come";[2] who is ranked in honor of dignity with Father and Son; of whom also Thrones, Dominations, Principalities, and Powers have need. For there is one God, the Father of Christ, and One Lord Jesus Christ, the Only-begotten Son of the One God, and One Holy Spirit who sanctifies and deifies all, who spoke in the Law and the Prophets, both in the Old and the New Testaments.

45   17. Keep this seal in mind at all times. I have spoken of it summarily, touching the main points, but if the Lord grant, I shall discuss it more fully later, to the best of my power, with proof from the Scriptures. For in regard to the divine and holy mysteries of the faith, not even a casual statement

should be delivered without the Scriptures, and we must not be drawn aside merely by probabilities and artificial arguments. Do not believe even me merely because I tell you these things, unless you receive from the inspired Scriptures the proof of the assertions. For this saving faith of ours depends not on ingenious reasonings but on proof from the inspired Scriptures.

33. The teaching you have heard is that of the divinely-inspired Scriptures, both of the Old and the New Testament. For there is One God of the two Testaments, who foretold in the Old Testament the Christ who appeared in the New, and who, through the preparatory school of the Law and the Prophets, led us to Christ. For "before the faith came, we were guarded under the Law";[3] and, "the Law trained us for Christ's school."[4] And so, if ever you hear any heretic blaspheming the Law or the Prophets, quote that saving word against him: Jesus came not to destroy the Law, but to fulfill it.[5] Be eager to learn, and from the Church, what are the books of the Old Testament, what of the New; and I pray you read none of the apocryphal books. For why should you, when you do not know the books acknowledged by all, trouble yourself needlessly with those whose authenticity is disputed? Read the divine Scriptures, these twenty-two books of the Old Testament translated by the seventy-two interpreters.[6]

34. When Alexander, king of Macedon, died, his empire was divided into four kingdoms, Babylon and Macedon, Asia and Egypt. One of the Egyptian dynasty, Ptolemy Philadelphus, a great lover of learning, when he became king and was collecting books from every quarter, heard from Demetrius of Phalerum, the curator of his library, of the divine Scriptures of the Law and the Prophets. He judged it far better not to get the books by force from unwilling persons, but rather to win over the possessors with gifts and friendship, since he knew that what is forced from men, because it is given against their will, is often adulterated, while that which is freely offered is given with all sincerity. When he had sent to Eleazar, the High Priest at that time, very many gifts for the temple here at Jerusalem, he had six men out of each of the

46

47

twelve tribes of Israel dispatched to him for the work of translation. Then, to prove whether the books were divine or not, and to prevent collusion by the members of the mission, he assigned to each of the interpreters a separate dwelling in the place called Pharus, lying near Alexandria, and committed to each all the Scriptures to translate. When they had completed their task in seventy-two days, the king compared all their translations, which they had made in separate cells without communicating with one another, and found that they exactly agreed, not only in sense, but even in words. For the process did not admit of a naturalistic explanation, nor was it any contrivance of human ingenuity; no, but the translation of the divine Scriptures, spoken by the Holy Spirit, was completed by the Holy Spirit.

48   35. Of these, read the twenty-two books, and have nothing to do with the apocryphal writings. Study earnestly only those books which we read openly in Church. For far wiser and more devout than yourself were the Apostles and the ancient bishops, the rulers of the Church, who handed down these books. Therefore, since you are a child of the Church, do not transgress her ordinances. Of the Old Testament, then, as it has been said, study these twenty-two books and, if you are eager to learn, strive to fix them by name in your memory as I enumerate them. For of the Law the books of Moses are the first five, Genesis, Exodus, Leviticus, Numbers, Deuteronomy; then Josue, the son of Nun, and the book of Judges, which, along with Ruth, is numbered the seventh. Of the remaining historical books, the first and second books of Kings are among the Hebrews one book, and the third and fourth one book. Likewise, the first and second books of Paralipomenon make one book, and the first and second books of Esdras are reckoned as one. The book of Esther is the twelfth; and these are the historical books. The books written in verse are five, Job, the book of Psalms, Proverbs, Ecclesiastes, and the Canticle of Canticles, which is the seventeenth book. There follow the five prophetic books: the one book of the twelve prophets, of Isaia one, of Jeremia with Baruch, the Lamentations and the Epistle one; the Ezechiel, and the book of Daniel, the twenty-second of the Old Testament.

36. Of the New Testament, there are only four gospels; for   49
the rest are not genuine and are harmful. The Manichaeans
also wrote a "Gospel according to Thomas," which, through
the spurious odor of sanctity conferred by its title, corrupts
simple folk. Receive also the Acts of the Twelve Apostles;
and in addition to these, the seven Catholic Epistles of James,
Peter, John, and Jude; then, as a seal upon all of them, and
the last work of the disciples, the fourteen Epistles of St.
Paul.[7] But let all the rest be put in the second rank; and whatever books are not read in the churches read not by yourself,
in accordance with what you have been told. Thus far concerning these matters.

37. Flee every diabolical influence[8] and hearken not to the   50
apostate Serpent, who of his own deliberate choice was transformed from a good nature; who can persuade the willing,
but can force no one. Attend not to the fabulous divinations
of the Greeks. As for sorcery, incantation, and the wicked
practices of necromancy, do not admit them within your
hearing. Stand aloof from every form of intemperance, being
neither a glutton nor a lover of pleasure, and, above all, from
covetousness and usury. Venture not among the assemblies
of the heathen spectacles; never use amulets in times of sick-
ness; put aside also the defilement of frequenting taverns.
Fall not into the sect of the Samaritans or into Judaism; for
henceforth Jesus Christ has redeemed you. Stand aloof from
all observation of Sabbaths and speak not of any of the in-
different meats as common or unclean. But abhor especially
all the assemblies of the wicked heretics; and in every way
make your own soul safe, by fasting, prayers, alms, and the
reading of the divine oracles, that living in temperance and in
the observance of pious doctrines for the rest of your time in
the flesh, you may enjoy the one salvation of the laver of
baptism, and so, enrolled in the heavenly hosts by God the
Father, you may be deemed worthy of the heavenly crowns,
in Christ Jesus our Lord, to whom be glory forever and ever.
Amen.

Athanasius, Bishop of Alexandria
Letter XXXIX
367 A.D.

They have fabricated books which they call books of tables, in which they shew stars, to which they give the names of Saints. And therein of a truth they have inflicted on themselves a double reproach: those who have written such books, because they have perfected themselves in a lying and contemptible science; and as to the ignorant and simple, they have led them astray by evil thoughts concerning the right faith established in all truth and upright in the presence of God.

52   But since we have made mention of heretics as dead, but of ourselves as possessing the Divine Scriptures for salvation; and since I fear lest, as Paul wrote to the Corinthians, some few of the simple should be beguiled from their simplicity and purity, by the subtilty of certain men, and should henceforth read other books—those called apocryphal—led astray by the similarity of their names with the true books; I beseech you to bear patiently, if I also write, by way of remembrance, of matters with which you are acquainted, influenced by the need and advantage of the Church.

53   In proceeding to make mention of these things, I shall adopt, to commend my undertaking, the pattern of Luke the Evangelist, saying on my own account: 'Forasmuch as some have taken in hand, to reduce into order for themselves the books termed apocryphal, and to mix them up with the divinely inspired Scripture, concerning which we have been

fully persuaded, as they who from the beginning were eyewitnesses and ministers of the Word, delivered to the fathers;
it seemed good to me also, having been urged thereto by true
brethren, and having learned from the beginning, to set before you the books included in the Canon, and handed down,
and accredited as Divine; to the end that any one who has
fallen into error may condemn those who have led him astray;
and that he who has continued stedfast in purity may again
rejoice, having these things brought to his remembrance.

There are, then, of the Old Testament, twenty-two books   54
in number; for, as I have heard, it is handed down that this is
the number of the letters among the Hebrews; their respective order and names being as follows. The first is Genesis,
then Exodus, next Leviticus, after that Numbers, and then
Deuteronomy. Following these there is Joshua, the son of
Nun, then Judges, then Ruth. And again, after these four
books of Kings, the first and second being reckoned as one
book, and so likewise the third and fourth as one book. And
again, the first and second of the Chronicles are reckoned as
one book. Again Ezra, the first and second are similarly one
book. After these there is the book of Psalms, then the Proverbs, next Ecclesiastes, and the Song of Songs. Job follows,
then the Prophets, the twelve being reckoned as one book.
Then Isaiah, one book, then Jeremiah with Baruch, Lamentations, and the epistle, one book; afterwards, Ezekiel and
Daniel, each one book. Thus far constitutes the Old Testament.

Again it is not tedious to speak of the [books] of the New   55
Testament. These are, the four Gospels, according to Matthew, Mark, Luke, and John. Afterwards, the Acts of the
Apostles and Epistles (called Catholic), seven, viz. of James,
one; of Peter, two; of John, three; after these, one of Jude. In
addition, there are fourteen Epistles of Paul, written in this
order. The first, to the Romans; then two to the Corinthians;
after these, to the Galatians; next, to the Ephesians; then to
the Philippians; then to the Colossians; after these, two to the
Thessalonians, and that to the Hebrews; and again, two to
Timothy; one to Titus; and lastly, that to Philemon. And
besides, the Revelation of John.

56   These are fountains of salvation, that they who thirst may be satisfied with the living words they contain. In these alone is proclaimed the doctrine of godliness. Let no man add to these, neither let him take ought from these. For concerning these the Lord put to shame the Sadducees, and said, 'Ye do err, not knowing the Scriptures.' And He reproved the Jews, saying, 'Search the Scriptures, for these are they that testify of Me.'

57   But for greater exactness I add this also, writing of necessity; that there are other books besides these not indeed included in the Canon, but appointed by the Fathers to be read by those who newly join us, and who wish for instruction in the word of godliness. The Wisdom of Solomon, and the Wisdom of Sirach, and Esther, and Judith, and Tobit, and that which is called the Teaching of the Apostles, and the Shepherd. But the former, my brethren, are included in the Canon, the latter being [merely] read; nor is there in any place a mention of apocryphal writings. But they are an invention of heretics, who write them when they choose, bestowing upon them their approbation, and assigning to them a date, that so, using them as ancient writings, they may find occasion to lead astray the simple.

Jerome
Letter to Pope Damasus
383 A.D.

You urged me to revise the old Latin version, and, as it were, to sit in judgment on the copies of the Scriptures which are now scattered throughout the whole world; and, inasmuch as they differ from one another, you would have me decide which of them agree with the Greek original. The labour is one of love, but at the same time both perilous and presumptuous; for in judging others I must be content to be judged by all; and how can I dare to change the language of the world in its hoary old age, and carry it back to the early days of its infancy? Is there a man, learned or unlearned, who will not, when he takes the volume into his hands, and perceives that what he reads does not suit his settled tastes, break out immediately into violent language, and call me a forger and a profane person for having the audacity to add anything to the ancient books, or to make any changes or corrections therein? Now there are two consoling reflections which enable me to bear the odium—in the first place, the command is given by you who are the supreme bishop; and secondly, even on the showing of those who revile us, readings at variance with the early copies cannot be right. For if we are to glean the truth from a comparison of *many*, why not go back to the original Greek and correct the mistakes introduced by inaccurate translators, and the blundering alterations of confident but ignorant critics, and, further, all that has been inserted or changed by copyists more asleep than awake? I am not discussing the Old Testament, which was turned into Greek by the Seventy elders, and has reached us by a descent of three steps. I do not ask what Aquila and Symmachus think, or why Theodotion takes a middle course between the ancients and the moderns. I am willing to let that be the true translation which had apostolic approval. I am now speaking of the New Testament. This was undoubtedly composed in Greek, with the exception of the work of Matthew the Apostle, who was the first to commit to writing the Gospel of Christ, and who published his work in Judæa in Hebrew characters. We must confess that as we have it in our language it is marked by discrepancies, and now that the stream is distributed into different channels we must go back to the fountainhead. I pass over those manuscripts which are associated with the names of Lucian and Hesychius, and the authority of which is perversely maintained by a handful of disputatious persons. It is obvious that these writers could not amend anything in the Old Testament after the labours of the Seventy; and it was useless to correct the New, for versions of Scripture which already exist in the languages of many nations show that their additions are false. I therefore promise in this short Preface the four Gospels only, which are to be taken in the following order, Matthew, Mark, Luke, John, as they have been revised by a comparison of the Greek manuscripts. Only early ones have been used. But to avoid any great divergences from the Latin which we are accustomed to read, I have used my pen with some restraint, and while I have corrected only such passages as seemed to convey a different meaning, I have allowed the rest to remain as they are.

Jerome
Prefaces to Translation of New Testament Books
388-398 A.D.

MATTHEW

The first evangelist is Matthew, the publican, who was surnamed Levi. He published his Godpel in Judæa in the Hebrew language, chiefly for the sake of Jewish believers in Christ, who adhered in vain to the shadow of the law, although the substance of the Gospel had come. The second is Mark, the amanuensis of the Apostle Peter, and first bishop of the Church of Alexandria. He did not himself see our Lord and Saviour, but he related the matter of his Master's preaching with more regard to minute detail than to historical sequence. The third is Luke, the physician, by birth a native of Antioch, in Syria, whose praise is in the Gospel. He was himself a disciple of the Apostle Paul, and composed his book in Achaia and Bœotia. He thoroughly investigates certain particulars and, as he himself confesses in the preface, describes what he had heard rather than what he had seen. The last is John, the Apostle and Evangelist, whom Jesus loved most, who reclining on the Lord's bosom, drank the purest streams of doctrine, and was the only one thought worthy of the words from the cross, "Behold! thy mother." When he was in Asia, at the time when the seeds of heresy were springing up (I refer to Cerinthus, Ebion, and the rest who say that Christ has not come in the flesh, whom he in his own epistle calls Antichrists, and whom the Apostle Paul frequently assails), he was urged by almost all the bishops of Asia then living, and by deputations from many Churches, to write more profoundly concerning the divinity of the Saviour, and to break through all obstacles so as to attain to the very Word of God (if I may so speak) with a boldness as successful as it appears audacious. Ecclesiastical history relates that, when he was urged by the brethren to write, he replied that he would do so if a general fast were proclaimed and all would offer up prayer to God; and when the fast was over, the narrative goes on to say, being filled with revelation, he burst into the heaven-sent Preface: "In the beginning was the Word, and the Word was with God, and the Word was God: this was in the beginning with God."

60   . . . Jerome then applies the four symbolical figures of Ezekiel to the Gospels: the Man is Matthew, the Lion, Mark, the Calf, Luke, "because he began with Zacharias the priest," and the Eagle, John. He then describes the works of his predecessors: Origen with his twenty-five volumes, Theophilus of Antioch, Hippolytus the martyr, Theodorus of Heraclea, Apollinaris of Laodicæa, Didymus of Alexandria, and of the Latins, Hilary, Victorinus, and Fortunatianus; from these last, he says, he had gained but little. He continues as follows:

But you urge me to finish the composition in a fortnight, when Easter is now rapidly approaching, and the spring breezes are blowing; you do not consider when the shorthand writers are to take notes, when the sheets are to be written, when corrected, how long it takes to make a really accurate copy; and this is the more surprising, since you know that for the last three months I have been so ill that I am now hardly beginning to walk; and I could not adequately perform so great a task in so short a time. Therefore, neglecting the authority of ancient writers, since I have no opportunity of reading or following them, I have confined myself to the brief exposition and translation of the narrative which you particularly requested; and I have sometimes thrown in a few of the flowers of the spiritual interpretation, while I reserve the perfect work for a future day.

ST. LUKE

A few days ago you told me that you had read some commentaries on Matthew and Luke, of which one was equally dull in perception and expression, the other frivolous in expression, sleepy in sense. Accordingly you requested me to translate, without regarding such rubbish, our Adamantius' thirty-nine "homilies" on Luke, just as they are found in the original Greek; I replied that it was an irksome task and a mental torment to write, as Cicero phrases it, with another man's heart not one's own; but yet I will undertake it, as your requests reach no higher than this. The demand which the sainted Blesilla once made, at Rome, that I should translate into our language his twenty-five volumes on Matthew, five on Luke, and thirty-two on John is beyond my powers, my leisure, and my energy. You see what weight your influence and wishes have with me. I have laid aside for a time my books on Hebrew Questions because you think my labour will not be in vain, and turn to the translation of these commentaries, which, good or bad, are his work and not mine. I do this all the more readily because I hear on the left of me the raven—that ominous bird—croaking and mocking in an extraordinary way at the colours of all the other birds, though he himself is nothing if not a bird of gloom. And so, before he change his note, I confess that in these treatises Origen is like a boy amusing himself with the dice-box; there is a wide difference between his mature efforts and the serious studies of his old age. If my proposal meet with your approbation, if I am still able to undertake the task, and if the Lord grant me opportunity to translate them into Latin after completing the work I have now deferred, you will then be able to see—aye, and all who speak Latin will learn through you—how much good they knew not, and how much they have now begun to know. Besides this, I have arranged to send you shortly the Commentaries of Hilary, that master

61

of eloquence, and of the blessed martyr Victorinus, on the Gospel of Matthew. Their style is different, but the grace of the Spirit which wrought in them is one. These will give you some idea of the study which our Latins also have, in former days, bestowed upon the Holy Scriptures.

GALATIANS

62   Only a few days have elapsed since, having finished my exposition of the Epistle of Paul to Philemon, I had passed to Galatians, turning my course backwards and passing over many intervening subjects. But all at once letters unexpectedly arrived from Rome with the news that the venerable Albina has been recalled to the presence of the Lord, and that the saintly Marcella, bereft of the company of her mother, demands more than ever such solace as you can give, my dear Paula and Eustochium. This for the present is impossible on account of the great distance to be traversed by sea and land, and I could, therefore, wish to apply to the wound so suddenly inflicted at least the healing virtue of Scripture. I know full well her zeal and faith; I know how brightly the fire burns in her bosom, how she rises superior to her sex, and soars so far above human nature itself, that she crosses the Red Sea of this world, sounding the loud timbrel of the inspired volumes. Certainly, when I was at Rome, she never saw me for ever so short a time without putting some questions to me respecting the Scriptures, and she did not, like the Pythagoreans, accept the "Ipse dixit" of her teacher, nor did authority, unsupported by the verdict of reason, influence her; but she tested all things, and weighed the whole matter so sagaciously that I perceived I had not a disciple so much as a judge. And so, believing that my labours would be most acceptable to her who is at a distance, and profitable for you who are with me here, I will approach a work unattempted by any writers in our language before me, and which scarcely any of the Greeks themselves have handled in a manner worthy of the dignity of the subject.

. . . Jerome then speaks of Victorinus, who had published   63
a commentary on St. Paul, but "was busily engaged with
secular literature and knew nothing of the Scriptures,"
and of the great Greek writers, Origen, Didymus, and
Appolinaris, Eusebius of Emesa, and Theodorus of Heraclea, and says he has plucked flowers out of their gardens,
so that the Commentary is more theirs than his. The expository part of the Preface is chiefly remarkable as giving
the view of St. Paul's rebuke of St. Peter in Galatians ii.,
which occasioned the controversy between Jerome and
Augustin. Jerome says:

Paul does not go straight to the point, but is like a man
walking in secret passages: his object is to exhibit Peter as
doing what was expedient for the people of the circumcision committed to him, since, if a too sudden revolt took
place from their ancient mode of life, they might be offended
and not believe in the Cross; he wished, moreover, to show,
inasmuch as the evangelisation of the Gentiles had been entrusted to himself, that he had justice on his side in defending
as true that which another only pretended was a dispensation. That wretch Porphyry Bataneotes by no means understood this, and, therefore, in the first book of the work
which he wrote against us, he raised the objection that Peter
was rebuked by Paul for not walking uprightly as an evangelical teacher. His desire was to brand the former with error and
the latter with impudence, and to bring against us as a body
the charge of erroneous notions and false doctrine, on the
ground that the leaders of the Churches are at variance
among themselves.

     . . . In the Preface to Book II. Jerome describes the origin   64
of the Galatians as a Gaulish tribe settled in Asia; but he
takes them as slow of understanding, and says that the
Gauls still preserve this character, just as the Roman
Church preserves the character for which it was praised by
St. Paul, for it still has crowds frequenting its churches and
the tombs of its martyrs, and "nowhere else does the
Amen resound so loudly, like spiritual thunder, and shake

the temples of the idols"; and similarly the traits of the churches of Corinth and Thessalonica are still preserved; in the first, the looseness of behaviour and of doctrine, and the conceit of worldly knowledge; in the second, the love of the brethren side by side with the disorderly conduct of busybodies. And he speaks of the condition of Galatia in his own day as follows:

Any one who has seen by how many schisms Ancyra, the metropolis of Galatia, is rent and torn, and by how many differences and false doctrines the place is debauched, knows this as well as I do. I say nothing of Cataphrygians, Ophites, Borborites, and Manichæans; for these are familiar names of human woe. Who ever heard of Passaloryncitæ, and Ascodrobi, and Artotyritæ, and other portents—I can hardly call them names—in any part of the Roman Empire? The traces of the ancient foolishness remain to this day. One remark I must make, and so fulfil the promise with which I started. While the Galatians, in common with the whole East, speak Greek, their own language is almost identical with that of the Treviri; and if through contact with the Greek they have acquired a few corruptions, it is a matter of no moment. The Africans have to some extent changed the Phenician language, and Latin itself is daily undergoing changes through differences of place and time.

65   . . . The Preface to Book III. opens with the following passage, describing, in contrast with his own simple exposition, the arts of the preachers of his day.

We are now busily occupied with our third book on Galatians, and, my friends, Paula and Eustochium, we are well aware of our weakness, and are conscious that our slender ability flows in but a small stream and makes little roar and rattle. For these are the qualities (to such a pass have we come) which are now expected even in the Churches; the simplicity and purity of apostolic language is neglected; we meet as if we were in the Athenæum, or the lecture rooms, to kindle the applause of the bystanders; what is now required is a discourse painted and tricked out with spurious rhetorical skill, and which, like a strumpet in the streets, does not aim at instructing the public, but at winning their favour; like a psaltery or a sweet-sounding lute, it must soothe the ears of the audience; and the passage of the prophet Ezekiel is suitable for our times, where the Lord says to him, "Thou art become unto them as the sound of a pleasant lute which is well made, for they hear thy words but do them not."

How far I have profited by my unflagging study of Hebrew 66
I leave to others to decide; what I have lost in my own language, I can tell. In addition to this, on account of the weakness of my eyes and bodily infirmity generally, I do not write with my own hand; and I cannot make up for my slowness of utterance by greater pains and diligence, as is said to have been the case with Virgil, of whom it is related that he treated his books as a bear treats her cubs, and licked them into shape. I must summon a secretary, and either say whatever comes uppermost; or, if I wish to think a little and hope to produce something superior, my helper silently reproves me, clenches his fist, wrinkles his brow, and plainly declares by his whole bearing that he has come for nothing.

How few there are who now read Aristotle. How many are 67
there who know the books, or even the name of Plato? You may find here and there a few old men, who have nothing else to do, who study them in a corner. But the whole world speaks the language of our Christian peasants and fishermen, the whole world re-echoes their words. And so their simple words must be set forth with simplicity of style; for the word *simple* applies to their *words*, not their meaning. But if, in response to your prayers, I could, in expounding their epistles, have the same spirit which they had when they dictated them, you would then see in the Apostles as much majesty and breadth of true wisdom as there is arrogance and vanity in the learned men of the world. To make a brief confession of the secrets of my heart, I should not like any one who wished to understand the Apostle to find a difficulty in understanding my writings, and so be compelled to find some one to interpret the interpreter.

Council of Hippo
Canon 36
393 A.D.

(The same canon was endorsed by the 3rd Council of Carthage in 397 as Canon 47, and repeated by the 4th Council of Carthage in 419 as Canon 29.)

It has been decided that nothing except the Canonical Scriptures should be read in the church under the name of the Divine Scriptures. But the Canonical Scriptures are: Genesis, Exodus, Leviticus, Numbers, Deuteronomy, Josue, Judges, Ruth, four books of Kings, Paralipomenon two books, Job, the Psalter of David, five books of Solomon, twelve books of the Prophets, Isaias, Jeremias, Daniel, Ezechiel, Tobias, Judith, Esther, two books of Esdras, two books of the Machabees. Moreover of the New Testament: Four books of the Gospels, the Acts of the Apostles one book, thirteen epistles of Paul the Apostle, one of the same to the Hebrews, two of Peter, three of John, one of James, one of Jude, the Apocalypse of John. Thus [it has been decided] that the Church beyond the sea may be consulted regarding the confirmation of that canon; also that it be permitted to read the sufferings of the martyrs, when their anniversary days are celebrated.

Augustine, Bishop of Hippo
On Christian Instruction
397 A.D.

Prologue

There are several norms for expounding Scripture. These
I am convinced can be profitably presented to those
devoted to the study of this subject, so that they may
benefit, not only by acquiring knowledge from others who
have unveiled the mysteries of sacred writings, but by disclos-
ing these mysteries to others themselves. I am undertaking to
transmit these principles to those who are able and willing to
grasp them, if only God our Lord will not refuse to supply
me as I write with the same help which He usually grants me
when I reflect upon this matter. Before I begin this, I think
that I should reply to those who will censure these principles,
or who would do so if I did not pacify them first. But if some,
even after this, find fault, at least they will not influence
others, whom they could influence unless they were previously fortified and equipped. nor will they entice them from
beneficial study to the indolence of ignorance.

Some will censure my work because they have failed to
comprehend those principles of which I shall treat. Others,
when they have desired to employ the principles which they
have learned and have endeavored to explain the Sacred
Scriptures according to these principles, but have failed to
disclose and elucidate what they want, will think that I have
labored uselessly; and, because they themselves have not been

70

aided by this work, will think that no one could profit from it. The third category of critics comprises those who either actually interpret Scripture well, or seem to in their own estimation. These observe, or think they observe, that they have gained the ability to explain sacred writings, although they have studied none of the regulations of the sort that I have now determined to recommend. Accordingly, they will protest that those principles are essential to no one, but that whatever is convincingly revealed about the obscurities of those writings could be achieved more effectively by divine assistance alone.

71   Briefly answering all those who do not comprehend the matters about which I am writing, I make this statement: I should not be criticized because they do not understand, just as they should not become enraged at me if, wishing to see the waning moon, the new moon, or some barely distinguishable star which I was indicating with my finger, they did not have sufficiently keen vision to see even my finger. In fact, those who cannot discern the obscure points of Sacred Scripture, even after studying and learning these rules, would believe that they could indeed see my finger, but could not see the stars which it was extended to indicate. Consequently, these two groups ought to refrain from criticizing me and beg that vision be granted them from heaven. For, if I can lift my finger to indicate something, I cannot on the other hand illumine the eyes of individuals to see either my act of indicating or that subject to which I am anxious to direct attention.

72   However, there are some who boast about the grace of God, and pride themselves upon the fact that they appreciate and are able to interpret Sacred Scripture without rules such as I have undertaken to propose, and for that reason they consider unnecessary what I have planned to write. These persons should moderate their anxiety, so that, although they may well be glad for the wonderful grace of God, they may still keep in mind that they have learned these matters through men or books. They should not be despised by Anthony, the saintly Egyptian hermit, simply because he, without any knowledge of reading, is said to have memorized the Sacred

Scripture by merely hearing it and to have penetrated its meaning by profound reflection. Nor should they be scorned by that foreign Christian slave, about whom we learned not long ago from very eminent and reliable persons. Although no one taught him how to read, he acquired proficiency by praying that the secrets might be disclosed to him. After three days' prayer he received the answer to his petition, with the result that he astounded the spectators by reading at sight the book they handed him.

If anyone believe that these accounts are false, I am not   73 going to argue violently about it. Certainly, since my case deals with Christians who rejoice that they understand Sacred Scripture without human instruction (and if this is so, they rejoice in a true and by no means insignificant blessing), they must concede that any one of us has learned his own language simply from hearing it habitually from childhood, and that we have acquired a knowledge of any other language—Greek, Hebrew, or any one of the others similarly—either by hearing them or by some person's instruction. Now then, are we to admonish all our brethren not to train their children in these subjects, since in a single instant the Apostles,[1] filled with grace by the coming of the Holy Ghost, spoke in the tongues of all peoples; or are we to admonish anyone who has not enjoyed such privileges to think that he is not a Christian or to doubt that he has received the Holy Ghost? On the contrary, let whatever should be acquired through human means be acquired humbly, and let anyone who is instructing another pass on to him whatever he has received[2] without haughtiness or grudging. Let us not tempt Him whom we have believed,[3] lest, deceived by such cunning of the Devil and by our own stubbornness, we may even decline to go to church to listen to the Gospel itself or to learn about it, or to refuse to read a book, or to pay attention to a reader or a preacher, but expect, as the Apostle says, to be caught 'up to the third heaven . . . whether in the body or out of the body,'[4] and there hear 'secret words that man may not repeat,' or there see the Lord Jesus Christ[5] and learn the Gospel from Him rather than from men.

74   We should guard against such presumptuous and perilous snares. Instead, we should reflect that the Apostle Paul himself,[6] even though he was thrown to the ground and instructed by the divine Voice from heaven, was nevertheless sent to a human being to receive the sacraments and be united to the Church. We should also consider that the centurion Cornelius,[7] though an angel informed him that his prayers had been heard and his alms regarded with approval, was still sent to Peter to be guided and not only to receive from him the sacraments, but also to learn what he was to believe in, hope for, and love. All these things might well have been accomplished by an angel, but human nature would have been lowered in dignity if God had seemed unwilling to transmit His word to men through human means. Indeed, how would there be truth in the statement, 'for holy is the temple of God, and this temple you are,'[8] if God did not grant replies from a human temple, but announced from heaven through angels all the learning which He desired to have imparted to men? Then charity itself, which unites men to one another with the bond of unity, would have no way of joining and almost fusing souls with each other, if men learned nothing from other men.

75   Again, the Apostle did not send to an angel the eunuch[9] who failed to comprehend what he read in the prophet Isaias. What he did not understand was not taught him by an angel, nor was it revealed to him by divine inspiration. He sat with him and explained in human terms and language what had been veiled in that passage of Scripture. God spoke to Moses,[10] did he not? Yet Moses very prudently and humbly yielded to the advice of his father-in-law, foreigner though he was, with regard to governing and directing such a mighty nation. For he realized that, from whatever intellect right counsel proceeded, it should be attributed not to him who conceived it but to Him who is the Truth, the immutable God.

76   Finally, whoever glories in understanding by the grace of God whatever things are obscure in the Scriptures, although he has not been guided by any principles, believes correctly indeed (and it is true) that that ability is not his own as if it

came into existence from him, but it was committed to him from heaven (for thus he seeks the glory of God and not his own). But, when he reads and understands without anyone's explanation, why does he try to explain to others? Instead, why does he not send them to God so that they also may understand, not through human agency, but by His teaching within their souls? Of course, he is afraid that he may hear from the Lord:[11] 'Wicked servant, thou shouldst have entrusted my money to the bankers.' Therefore, just as these individuals instruct others either orally or by their writings in matters they understand, I certainly should not be criticized by them if I, too, teach not only the points which they understand, but also the principles they observe in order to come to an understanding. Nevertheless no one should consider anything his own except, perhaps, falsehood,[12] since all truth comes from Him who has said:[13] 'I am the Truth,' For what have we that we have not received? But, if we have received it, why do we boast as if we had not received it?[14]

He who reads written matter to listeners pronounces what he understands. But, he who teaches reading does so that others will also learn how to read; yet, both transmit what they have been taught. So also, he who explains to his hearers the thoughts which he understands in Sacred Scripture acts like one who in the office of reader pronounces the words which he understands. On the other hand, he who teaches how to understand is like a person teaching reading. It is his task to teach reading in such a way that the man who knows how to read has no need of another reader, when he comes upon a book, to tell him what is written in it. Similarly, the person who has accepted the principles which we are trying to propose, when he comes upon any obscurity in books, observes certain rules, as he did in reading, and does not require another person as interpreter to lay open for him whatever is obscure. Rather, by following certain indications, he may arrive at the hidden meaning himself, without any false step, or, at least, will not fall into the foolishness of misguided thought. Therefore, although it may be clear enough in this work itself that no one can in justice criticize this undertaking of mine which is intended to be useful, nevertheless, it seemed fitting to answer any objectors in a preface such as this. This, then, presented itself to me as the starting point of the course I propose to follow in this book.

BOOK ONE

Chapter 1

78   The entire treatment of the Scriptures is based upon two factors: the method of discovering what we are to understand and the method of teaching what has been understood. I shall discuss first the method of discovery and then the method of teaching. This is a worthy and laborious task, and, though it should prove hard to accomplish, I fear that I am rash enough to undertake it. Indeed, I should be, if I were relying solely upon myself. However, since all my confidence of finishing this work depends upon Him from whom I have already received much inspiration through meditation, I need not fear that He will cease to grant me further inspiration when I shall have begun to employ that which He has already granted. Everything which is not exhausted by being given away is not yet owned as it ought to be, so long as we hold on to it and do not give it away. 'For,' He has said:[15] 'He that hath to him shall be given.' Therefore, He will give to those who already have; this is, He will increase and heap up[16] what He has given, when they dispense with generosity what they have received. There were five loaves of bread and, on another occasion, seven loaves, before they were distributed to the hungry multitude.[17] Afterwards, although the hunger of so many thousands was satisfied, they filled baskets and baskets. And so, just as that bread increased after it was broken, the Lord has now granted me the thoughts which are necessary for beginning this work, and they will be increased by His inspiration when I have begun to dispense them.[18] As a result, I shall not only suffer no poverty of thought in this ministry of mine, but shall even exult in a remarkable abundance of ideas.

Chapter 36

Whoever, then, appears in his own opinion to have compre-   79
hended the Sacred Scriptures, or even some part of them, yet
does not build up with that knowledge the two-fold love of
God and his neighbor, 'has not yet known as he ought to
know.'[19] Yet, if anyone has derived from them an idea that
may be useful to him in building up this love, but has not
expressed by it what the author whom he is reading demon-
strably intended in that passage, he is not erring dangerously
nor lying at all. For, inherent in lying is the will to speak
falsehoods. We find many persons who wish to lie, but no
one who wishes to be deceived. Therefore, since a man de-
ceives with knowledge, but is deceived through ignorance, it
is sufficiently evident, in any one instance, that he who is
deceived is better than he who lies, since it is better to suffer
injustice than to commit it.[20] Everyone who lies acts unjust-
ly, and, if lying ever seems useful to anyone, it is possible
that injustice sometimes seems useful to him. No liar preserves faith in that about which he lies. He wishes that he to
whom he lies may have faith in him, but he does not preserve
this faith by lying to him. Every breaker of faith is unjust.
Therefore, either injustice is sometimes useful (a thing which
is impossible) or lying is always hurtful.

Whoever understands in the Sacred Scriptures something   80
other than the writer had in mind is deceived, although they
do not lie. Yet, as I began to say, if he is deceived in an interpretation by which, however, he builds up charity (which is
the end of the precept[21]), he is deceived in the same way as
is someone who leaves the road through error, but makes his
way through the field to the place where the road also leads.
Nevertheless, he must be corrected and must be shown how it
is more advantageous not to leave the road, lest by a habit of
deviating he may be drawn into a crossroad or even go the
wrong way.

Chapter 37

81   By rashly asserting something which the author did not intend, he frequently runs into other passages which he cannot reconcile to that interpretation. If he agrees that these latter are true and definite, then the opinion which he had formed concerning the former cannot be true, and it happens, in some way or other, that by loving his own opinion he begins to be more vexed at Scripture than at himself. If he allows this error to creep in, he will be utterly destroyed by it. 'For we walk by faith and not by sight.'[22] Faith will totter, if the authority of Sacred Scriptures wavers. Indeed, even charity itself grows weak, if faith totters. If anyone falls from faith, it is inevitable that he also falls from charity. For, he cannot love what he does not believe exists. But, if he both believes and loves, by leading a good life and by obeying the commandments of good morals, he gives himself reason to hope that he may arrive at that which he loves. And so 'there abide faith, hope, and charity, these three'[23] which all knowledge and all prophecy serve.

Chapter 38

82   But the vision which we shall see takes the place of faith and that blessedness to which we shall attain takes the place of hope, but charity will be all the more increased as those former die away. If by faith we love what we do not yet see, how much more shall we love when we have begun to see? If through hope we love what we have not yet attained, how much more shall we love when we have attained it? There is this difference between temporal goods and eternal goods, that something temporal is loved more before we have it, but becomes worthless when it has come into our possession. It does not content the soul, whose true and appointed abode is eternity. But, an eternal good is loved more ardently when we have obtained it than it was when we were seeking it. No one who desires it can value it higher than inherently it is

worth, with the result that it would become worthless to him when he discovers that it was less than his valuation of it. But, however highly anyone may value it while he was coming to it, he will find it more valuable when he has obtained it.

Chapter 39

And so, a man who relies upon faith, hope, and charity   83
and resolutely holds fast to them does not need the Scriptures, except to teach others. And many by means of these three virtues live in solitude without the Sacred Scriptures. It seems to me that in them is already exemplified the saying:[24] 'Whereas prophecies will disappear, and tongues will cease, and knowledge will be destroyed,' Yet, by these devices, so to speak, such a great building of faith, hope, and charity has risen in them that, holding on to something perfect—perfect, of course, insofar as it is possible in this life—they do not seek after those things which are only partially so.[25] For, in comparison with the life to come, no just or holy man has a perfect life here. Hence, the Apostle says:[26] 'There abide faith, hope, and charity, these three; but the greatest of these is charity'; since, even when we have attained to the eternal goods, although the other two die away, charity will remain forever, increased and more firmly established.

Chapter 40

Therefore, when anyone recognizes that 'the end of the   84
precept is charity from a pure heart and a good conscience and faith unfeigned,[27] and proposes to refer his whole comprehension of Sacred Scriptures to these three virtues, he may approach the interpretation of those books fearlessly. for, when he spoke of 'charity,' the Apostle added 'from a pure heart,' so that nothing would be loved except that which ought to be. He joined to it 'a good conscience' for the sake of our hope, because a person upon whom the anxiety of a bad conscience is weighing despairs of attaining that which he has faith in and loves. Third, he said 'and faith

unfeigned.' For, if our faith is untainted by falsehood, then we do not feel affection for what we ought not to love; by living rightly, we hope that our hope may not be deceived in any way.

85   I have wished to speak of matters concerning faith only insofar as I considered them of benefit for the time being, because much has been said already in other works, either by other writers or by me. And so, let this be the limit of this book. As for the rest, I shall treat of signs, as far as God gives me inspiration.

BOOK TWO

Chapter 1

86   When I was writing about things, I began with a forcible reminder that one should only consider in them what they are in themselves, even when they are signs of something else. But now, when I come to the treatment of signs, one should not consider in them what they are, but rather direct his attention to the fact that they are signs, namely, that they signify something. A sign is a thing which, apart from the impression that it presents to the senses, causes of itself some other thing to enter our thoughts. For example, at the sight of a footprint, we think that the animal whose track it is has passed this way; at the sight of smoke, we learn there is a fire nearby; at the sound of a living voice, we direct our attention to the idea in that person's mind; at the sound of a trumpet, soldiers know whether to advance or retreat, or whether the action requires them to do something else.

87   Some signs are natural; others are conventional. Natural signs are those that, independently of any purpose or desire of being a sign of anything except themselves, cause something else to be recognized. Such is the case when smoke indicates fire. It is not a will to signify that causes this. Rather, through observation and attention to our experiences we learn that fire is near at hand, even when only the smoke is visible. The footprint of a passing animal also belongs to this category. The face of an angry or sad person indicates his

state of mind, although this may not be the intention of the person who is angry or sad. Every other operation of the mind is revealed by the testimony of our facial expression, even when we are not endeavoring to betray it. But it is not my aim to treat here of this type of signs. However, since it has a place in my division of the subject, I could not disregard it entirely; it is sufficient to have alluded to it to this extent.

Chapter 2

Conventional signs are those which living creatures give to   88
one another. They thus indicate, as far as possible, either the operations of their minds or anything perceived by sense or intellect. The only reason we have for indicating by signs is that we may call forth and transfer to another's mind what is in our mind as we give the sign. I intend, therefore, to examine and treat of this type of signs, insofar as it pertains to men. This I do because even the signs communicated by inspiration which are included in Holy Scripture were disclosed to us by the men who wrote them. Even beasts have certain signs among themselves by which they reveal the desires they feel. After the cock finds food, he gives a sign with his voice to the hen to hurry to him; and the dove calls his mate or is called to her by cooing. We are accustomed to observe many such signs. Whether these, such as the expression or outcry of a man in pain, conform to the operation of the mind with no intention of giving a sign, or whether they are given for the specific purpose of signifying, is another issue. It has no reference to the matter under discussion and I am omitting it from this work as irrelevant.

Chapter 3

Of the symbols by which men express their ideas to one   89
another, some involve the sense of sight; many, the sense of hearing; and a very few, the other senses. When we nod, we are giving a sign only to the eyes of the person whom we desire through this sign to make a sharer of our will. Some express ever so much by the movements of their hands. Actors

by the motions of all their limbs give certain signs to those who understand and, in a certain sense, speak to their eyes. Banners and military standards make known through the eyes of the intention of the leaders. All these signs are like visible words. But, as we have said, there are more which have to do with hearing and these are principally expressed in words. The trumpet, the flute, and the harp often produce not only a pleasing sound, but also one full of meaning. All these signs are very infrequent, in contrast to words. Words have gained, by far, a pre-eminence among men for expressing whatever operations of the mind a person might desire to reveal. The Lord, it is true, gave a sign by means of the perfume of the ointment with which His feet were anointed.[1] He made known through taste what He intended in the Sacrament of His Body and Blood.[2] And when the woman was healed by touching 'the tassel of His cloak,'[3] the act signified something. But, an incalculable number of signs by which men convey their ideas are based upon words. I could express in words all those signs of the kinds I have mentioned briefly, but I would not at all be able to make words clear by those signs.

Chapter 4

90 Since, after words have reverberated upon the air, they pass away and last no longer than the sound they make, signs of words have been provided by means of letters. In this manner voice-sounds are presented to the eye, not through themselves, but through certain characteristic signs. Those signs could not be the same for all nations, because of the sin of human dissension, in which each one seizes the first place for himself. An evidence of this pride is that tower raised up to heaven where impious men merited the just penalty of having not only their minds, but also their tongues, confounded.[4]

Chapter 5

91 The result was this. Although Sacred Scripture, which heals such grave maladies of human hearts, began from one

language,[5] by which it could be spread abroad through the whole world at the proper time, it was scattered far and wide by the various languages of translators, and only thus became known to the nations for their salvation. In reading it, men are desirous only of discovering the thoughts and intentions of those by whom it was written. Through these in turn they discover the will of God, according to which we believe such men spoke.

Chapter 6

Those who read indiscreetly are deceived by numerous and varied instances of obscurity and vagueness, supposing one meaning instead of another. In some passages they do not find anything to surmise even erroneously, so thoroughly do certain texts draw around them the most impenetrable obscurity. I am convinced that this whole situation was ordained by God in order to overcome pride by work and restrains from haughtiness our minds which usually disdain anything they have learned easily. There are holy and perfect men by whose lives and example the Church of Christ rids those who come to her of superstition and incorporates them with herself through the imitation of these good men. These good and truly faithful servants of God, ridding themselves of worldly cares, have come to the holy laver of baptism, and arising from it, produce by the infusion of the Holy Ghost the fruit of a two-fold charity: a love of God and of their neighbor. Why is it, then, I ask, that, when anyone asserts these facts, he affords less charm to his listener than when he explains with the same interpretation that text from the Canticle of Canticles where the Church is alluded to as a beautiful woman who is being praised: 'Thy teeth are as flocks of sheep that are shorn, which come up from the washing, all with twins, and there is none barren among them'?[6] Does one learn anything more than when he hears that same thought phrased in the simplest words, without the aid of this simile? But, somehow or other, I find more delight in considering the saints when I regard them as the teeth of the Church. They bite off men from their heresies and carry them over to the

92

body of the Church, when their hardness of heart has been softened as if by being bitten off and chewed. With very great delight I look upon them also as shorn sheep that have put aside worldly cares, as if they were fleece. Coming up from the washing, that is, the baptismal font, all bear twins, that is, the two precepts of love, and I see no one destitute of that holy fruit.

93   But it is hard to explain why I experience more pleasure in this reflection than if no such comparison were derived from the Sacred Books, even though the matter and the knowledge are the same. This is another question. However, no one is uncertain now that everything is learned more willingly through the use of figures, and that we discover it with much more delight when we have exprelenced some trouble in searching for it. Those who do not find what they are seeking are afflicted with hunger, but those who do not seek, because they have it in their possession, often waste away in their pride. Yet, in both cases, we must guard against discouragement. The Holy Ghost, therefore, has generously and advantageously planned Holy Scripture in such a way that in the easier passages He relieves our hunger; in the ones that are harder to understand He drives away our pride. Practically nothing is dug out from those unintelligible texts which is not discovered to be said very plainly in another place.

Chapter 7

94   Primarily, we must be led by the fear of God that we may recognize His will, what He orders us to seek after and what we must flee from. It is inevitable that this fear should awaken reflection upon our mortal nature and the death that will be ours. By it all our emotions of pride are fastened to the wood of the cross, as it were, by nailing our flesh. Then we must become gentle through piety. We ought not to protest against Holy Scripture, either when we understand it and it is attacking some of our faults, or when we do not understand it and think that we ourselves could be wiser and give better advice. In this latter case we must rather reflect and believe that

what is written there is more beneficial and more reasonable, even if hidden, than what we could know of ourselves.

After those two steps of fear and piety we come to the third step, that of knowledge, which I have now begun to discuss. Everyone devoted to the study of the Holy Scriptures trains himself in this. In them he will find nothing else except that God must be loved for His own sake, and our neighbor for the sake of God; and to love God with his whole heart, and with his whole soul, and with his whole mind, and his neighbor as himself;[7] that is, that our entire love of our neighbor as also of ourselves is to be referred to God. I treated of these two precepts in the previous book when I was discussing things. It is inevitable, then, that at first, each one should discover in the Scriptures that he has been enmeshed by the love of this world, that is, of temporal things, and has been far separated from such a great love of God and of his neighbor as Scripture itself prescribes. Then, truly, that fear with which he meditates upon the judgment of God and that piety through which he must needs believe in and yield to the authority of the Holy Books should force him to mourn over himself. That knowledge of a good hope causes a man to be not boastful, but sorrowful. In this disposition he begs, through unceasing prayers, the consolation of divine assistance, that he may not be crushed by despair. He thus begins upon the fourth step, that of fortitude, where he hungers and thirsts for justice. In this state he withdraws himself from every deadly pleasure of passing things. In turning aside from these, he turns toward the love of eternal things, namely, the unchangeable Trinity in Unity.

When, as well as he can, he has observed this gleaming from a distance, and has plainly perceived that he cannot bear that light because of the weakness of his vision, he is at the fifth step, that is, in the counsel of mercy. Here he cleanses sordid thoughts from his soul, which is somehow confused and annoying to him because of its craving for inferior things. It is here that he zealously practices the love of his neighbor and perfects himself in it. Now, full of hope and spiritually vigorous, when he has attained even to the love of his enemy, he

95

96

rises to the sixth step. There he cleanses the sight itself which can see God, so far as He can be seen by those who die to this world as far as they can. They see in proportion to the extent that they die to this world, but, insofar as they live to it, they do not see. And so, although the splendor of that light begins to appear more definite now, and is not only more endurable, but even more pleasant, it is still said to be seen 'through a mirror in an obscure manner.'[8] This is because we walk more 'by faith' than 'by sight' while 'we are exiled'[9] in this life, although 'our citizenship is in heaven.'[10] At this level, however, he so cleanses the eye of his heart that he does not prefer or compare even his neighbor to the Truth, and therefore, not himself either, since he does not so exalt the one he loves as himself. Therefore, that holy man will be so sincere and clean of heart that he will not be turned away from truth, either through a desire of gratifying men or through an intention of evading whatever inconveniences disturb this life. Such a child of God mounts to Wisdom, which is the last and seventh step, and this he fully enjoys with perfect calm and serenity. For, 'the fear of the Lord is the beginning of wisdom.[11] From that fear until we arrive even at Wisdom, it is through these steps that we make our way.

Chapter 8

97   Let us now turn our attention to that third step which I have determined to discuss and reflect upon as the Lord may prompt me. The most intelligent investigator of Sacred Scriptures will be the man who has in the first place read them all and obtained a knowledge of them. Perhaps he has not yet acquired the knowledge of understanding; yet, he may have some grasp of them through reading, at least with respect to those which are called canonical Scriptures. For, fortified by the belief of truth, he will read the others more securely, that they may not preoccupy a weak mind, nor, deluding it with dangerous lies and imaginations, prejudice it against a wholesome understanding. In the canonical Scriptures he should follow the authority of the majority of Catholic Churches,

among which are surely those that have deserved to have apostolic sees and receive epistles. He will keep to this method in canonical Scriptures, therefore preferring those which are accepted by all Catholic Churches to those which some do not accept. Among those which are not accepted by all, let him favor those which the greater number of more eminent churches accept, rather than those upheld by a minority of churches of less authority.[12] If he discovers that some are accepted by the greater number of churches and others by the more important ones, although he cannot discover this easily, I believe the authority in the two cases should be considered as equal.

The whole canon of the Scriptures on which I maintain   98
that this consideration should depend is contained in these books: the five of Moses, that is, Genesis, Exodus, Leviticus, Numbers, and Deuteronomy; one book of Josue; one of Judges; a little book which is called Ruth, which seems rather to pertain to the beginning of Kings; then four books of Kings and two of Paralipomenon, which do not follow them in thought, but, as it were, are collaterally joined and proceed together with them. These are the books of history which contain a connected narrative of the times and have an orderly arrangement. There are others, histories of a different order which are not united to the aforementioned order or to one another, such as the books of Job, Tobias, Esther, Judith, the two books of the Machabees, and the two of Esdras. These last two follow the orderly history up to its termination in the books of Kings and Paralipomenon. Then the Prophets, in which there are one book of the Psalms of David and three of Solomon: Proverbs, the Canticles of Canticles, and Ecclesiastes. As to the two books, one of which is entitled Wisdom and the other Ecclesiasticus, these are said to have been Solomon's, because of a certain likeness of style. Yet Jesus the son of Sirach is asserted most consistently to have written them.[13] However, they must be counted among the prophetical books, because they have deserved recognition for their authority. The rest are the books which are properly termed Prophets, twelve separate books of the Prophets, which are connected with one another and are considered as

one, since they have never been separated. These are the names of the prophets: Osee, Joel, Amos, Abdias, Jonas, Micheas, Nahum, Habacuc, Sophonias, Aggeus, Zacharias, and Malachias. Then the four major prophets: Isaias, Jeremias, Daniel, and Exechiel. The authority of the Old Testament is contained in these forty-four books.[14] The authority of the New Testament rests in the following: the four books of the Gospel, according to Matthew, Mark, Luke, and John; the fourteen Epistles of Paul the Apostle; to the Romans, two to the Corinthians, to the Galatians, to the Ephesians, to the Philippians, two to the Thessalonians, to the Colossians, two to Timothy, to Titus, to Philemon, and to the Hebrews; two Epistles of Peter; three of John; one of Jude; and one of James; the Acts of the Apostles in one book; and one book of the Apocalypse of John.

Chapter 9

99   In all these books those who fear God and are meek in their devotion seek the will of God. The first care of this task and endeavor, as I have said, is to know these books. Although we may not yet understand them, nevertheless, by reading them we can either memorize them or become somewhat acquainted with them. Then, those things which are clearly asserted in them as rules, governing either life or belief, should be studied more intelligently and more attentively. The more anyone learns about these, the more capable of discernment he is. For, among those things which have been clearly expressed in the Scriptures, we discover all those which involve faith and the rules of living, namely, hope and charity, of which I treated in the previous book. Then, after a certain intimacy with the language of the Holy Scriptures has been achieved, we should begin to uncover and examine thoroughly those passages which are obscure, selecting examples from clearer texts to explain such as are more obscure, and allowing some proofs of incontestable texts to remove the uncertainty from doubtful passages. In this endeavor the memory is of very great value. If this is wanting, it cannot be imparted by these precepts.

Chapter 10

Things which have been written fail to be understood for   **100**
two reasons; they are hidden by either unknown or ambiguous signs. These signs are either literal or figurative. They are
literal when they are employed to signify those things for
which they were instituted. When we say *bos* we mean an ox,
because all men call it by this name in the Latin language just
as we do. Signs are figurative when the very things which we
signify by the literal term are applied to some other meaning;
for example, we say *bos* and recognize by that word an ox to
which we usually give that name; but again, under the figure
of the ox, we recognize a teacher of the gospel. This is inti-
mated by Holy Scripture, according to the interpretation of
the Apostle, in the text:[15] 'Thou shalt not muzzle the ox
that treads out the grain.'

Chapter 11

A knowledge of languages is an efficacious cure for an ig-   **101**
norance of literal signs. Men who know the Latin language,
whom I have now begun to teach, have need of two others in
order to understand the Sacred Scriptures. These are Hebrew
and Greek, by which they may turn back to the originals if
the infinite variances of Latin translators cause any uncertainty. And yet, in these books we may often come upon
Hebrew words that have not been translated, such as *Amen,
Alleluia, Raca, Hosanna,* and some others. Some of these,
although they could have been translated, have been kept
unchanged, like *Amen* and *Alleluia,* because of their holier
authority. Some, on the other hand, are not considered
capable of being translated into another language, such as the
other two which I specified. There are some expressions in
certain languages which cannot pass over into the usage of
another language through translation. This occurs especially
with interjections; these words indicate an impulse of the
mind, rather than any part of reasoned thought. The two

last are cited as such, for they maintain that *Raca* is the expression of an indignant person, and *Hosanna* of a person who is rejoicing. However, an understanding of the languages named is indispensable, not because of these few examples, which are very easy to observe and investigate, but because of the variances of translators, as I mentioned. For we can enumerate those who have translated the Scriptures from Hebrew to Greek, but the Latin translators are innumerable. In the first ages of the faith, when a Greek text came into the possession of anyone who considered himself slightly capable in both languages, he attempted to translate it.

Chapter 12

102   In fact, this diversity has helped rather than impeded understanding, if readers would only be discerning. A close study of a number of texts frequently has clarified some of the more obscure phrases, for instance that of the Prophet Isaias which one translator expresses:[16] 'And do not despise the domestics of thy seed'; while another interprets it thus:[17] 'And despise not thy own flesh.' Each one confirms the other, for the one is interpreted from the other. 'Flesh' can be understood in its literal sense, and this one could believe that he has been warned not to despise his own body, and figuratively, 'the domestics of thy seed' could be taken to mean Christians who, together with us, have been given spiritual birth from the same seed, the Word. However, after we have compared the opinions of the translators, a more probable meaning occurs to us. The precept, literally, is not to despise one's relations, because, when we associate 'domestics, of the seed' with 'flesh,' relations come particularly to mind. That, I think, is the source of the Apostle's statement:[18] 'In the hope that I may provoke to jealousy those who are my flesh, and may save some of them.' By this he means, through zealously imitating those who had believed, they themselves might also believe. For, he designates the Jews his own flesh because of his blood-relationship to them. Likewise, that text of the Prophet Isaias:[19] 'If ye will not believe, ye shall not understand,' has also been translated:[20] 'If you will not be-

lieve, you shall not continue.' It is open to question which one of these conforms to the literal meaning, unless we read the texts in the original language. However, something valuable in both is impressed upon those who read with understanding. It is difficult for translators to become so different from one another that they do not converge by some resemblance. Now, the essence of knowledge is the eternal Vision, while faith nourishes us as babes, upon milk, in the cradles of earthly things (for now 'we walk by faith and not by sight.'[21]) If, however, we do walk by faith, we shall not be able to arrive at sight, which does not vanish, but continues through our intellect once cleansed by our union with the Truth. Therefore it is that one translator says: 'If ye will not believe, ye shall not understand,' and the other declares: 'If you will not believe, you shall not continue.'

Frequently, a translator who does not understand the sense very well is led astray by an obscure expression in the original language. He therefore translates it with a meaning which is utterly foreign to that of the writer. For example, some texts have: 'Their feet are sharp to shed blood.' *Oxus* in Greek means both 'sharp' and 'swift.' So, he who translated as 'Their feet are swift to shed blood,'[22] recognized the true meaning; the other, drawn in the opposite direction by an equivocal term, made a mistake. Such translations are not ambiguous; they are erroneous, and there is a great difference between the two things. For we must be taught not how to understand such texts, but rather how to rectify them. On this account, because in Greek *móschos* means 'calf,' some did not know that *moscheúmata* are 'transplantings,' and they have translated it as 'calves.' This mistake has crept into so many texts that it can hardly be found written otherwise. Yet, the sense if very apparent, since it is clarified by the words which follow. It is more consistent to say 'Bastard slips shall not take deep root'[23] than to speak of calves. Calves walk upon the earth with their feet and do not hold fast to it by roots. Other expressions in this passage defend this interpretation.

103

Chapter 13

104   The meaning which the various translators attempt to give, each in accordance with his own skill and opinion, is not obvious unless it is studied in the language which is being translated. Very often, also, a translator, unless he is a very learned man, deviates from the sense of the author. Accordingly, we must either strive after a mastery of those languages from which Holy Scripture is translated into Latin or we must use the translations of those who have adhered unduly to the actual words. It is not that such translations are adequate, but through them we may detect the looseness or error of others who have preferred to conform to the meaning rather than to the actual words in translating. Often times they translate, not only individual words, but even whole phrases which cannot be translated at all into a customary Latin expression, if we are desirous of preserving the idiom of the ancients who spoke Latin. These expressions sometimes take nothing from our comprehension. However, they do irritate those who find more charm in things when in their signs a certain appropriate correctness is preserved. What is called a solecism is nothing but a combination of words contrary to the rule used by the ancients who spoke with any authority. It does not concern a seeker after truth whether we say *inter homines* or *inter hominibus* [among men]. Likewise, what else is a barbarism but a word either spelled or pronounced other than was the custom of those who spoke Latin before our time? Whether *ignoscere* [forgive] is pronounced with a long or a short third syllable is not much of a worry to a man begging God to forgive his sins in whatever way he can utter that word. What is purity of language, therefore, but the preservation of the idiom, supported by the authority of the earlier speakers?

105   The weaker men are, the more they are annoyed by this. And they are weak in proportion as they wish to appear learned, not in the knowledge of the things by which we may be instructed, but rather in a knowledge of signs. Through

this knowledge it is very easy to become proud, since even the knowledge of things often raises up our pride,[24] unless it can be curbed by the yoke of the Master. To one who understands, what harm comes because a passage is written this way: *Quae est terra in qua isti insidunt super eam, si bona est an nequam, et quae sunt civitates in quibus ipsi inhabitant in pisis?*[25] ['Of what sort is the land in which those people dwell, whether it is good or bad, and what manner of cities there are in which they live.'] I consider that this is rather the expression of a foreign language than that it has any more profound significance. There is also that text which we are now unable to take away from the chant of the faithful: *Super ipsum autem floriet sanctificatio mea*[26] ['But upon him shall my sanctification flourish']. Assuredly, this detracts nothing from the sense, but a more instructed reader would rather have this corrected so that we would say not *floriet*, but *florebit*. Moreover, nothing prevents this revision except the custom of the changers. These defects, then, can be easily overlooked by anyone who is unwilling completely to avoid them, for they do not at all detract from a sound meaning. Then, there is that text of the Apostle:[27] '*Quod stultum est Dei, sapientius est hominibus; et quod infirmum est Dei, fortius est hominibus*' [For the foolishness of God is wiser than men, and the weakness of God is stronger than men']. Suppose someone had wished to preserve the Greek idiom in this text and had said *Quod stultum est Dei, sapientius est hominum, et quod infirmum est Dei, fortius est hominum*. The attention of a watchful reader would certainly go on to the truth of the passage, but someone rather slow of comprehension would either not understand it at all or else would interpret it the wrong way. For, such a phrase is not only incorrect in the Latin language, but it even tends to obscurity, so that it might seem that the foolishness or the weakness of men is wiser or stronger than God's. And yet, even that phrase *sapientius est hominibus* [is wiser than men] is not untainted by ambiguity, although it is exempt from solecism. It is not clear whether *hominibus* is a dative plural or ablative plural, except through a recognition of its meaning. Accordingly, it would be better expressed: *sapientius est quam homines* and *fortius est quam homines*.

Chapter 14

106   I shall speak about ambiguous signs later on. Now I am discussing unknown signs, of which there are two forms insofar as they apply to words. Obviously, an unknown word or an unknown expression causes the reader to be perplexed. If these come from foreign languages, we must ask about them from men who use those languages, or learn the languages, if we have the time and the ability, or study a comparison of the various translators. If we are unfamiliar with some words or expressions of our own language, they become known to us through repeated usage in reading or hearing them. Indeed, the best things for us to memorize are those classes of words or expressions which we do not know. Thus, we may be able easily, by the assistance of our memory, to study and acquire a knowledge of them, either when a more educated man whom we may question happens along, or when we come upon a text such that, either by the preceding or the following context or both, it indicates the import or meaning of that which we did not understand. Yet, so powerful is the effect of habit even in learning, that those who have in a certain sense been nourished and reared in the Holy Scriptures wonder more at other expressions, and consider them less perfect Latin than the ones they have learned in the Scriptures, but which are not found in Latin authors. Here also the multitude of translators is a very important aid, when they have been considered and debated upon by a comparison of texts. However, avoid all that is positively false. For, in correcting texts, the ingenuity of those who desire to know the Sacred Scriptures should be exercised principally in such a way that uncorrected passages, at least those coming from a single source of translation, yield to those that have been rectified.

Chapter 15

In the case of translations themselves, however, the Itala[28] is to be preferred to the others, since it combines greater precision of wording with clearness of thought. In emending any Latin translations, we must consult the Greek texts; of these, the reputation of the seventy translators[29] is most distinguished in regard to the Old Testament. These translators are now considered by the more learned Churches to have translated under such sublime inspiration of the Holy Ghost that from so many men there was only one version. According to tradition and to many deserving of our trust, these men, while translating, were isolated from one another in separate cells. Nevertheless, nothing was discovered in the work of any one of them which was not discovered in the others expressed in the same words and the same arrangement of words. Who, then, would venture to put anything on a level with this authority; still less, esteem anything better? But, if they consulted one another so that one version was produced by the united treatment and opinion of all of them, even then it is certainly not reasonable or proper for any one man, regardless of his knowledge, to presume to reform the common opinion of so many older and more learned men. Therefore, even if we discover something in the Hebrew original other than they have interpreted it, it is my opinion that we should yield to the divine direction. This guidance was accomplished through them so that the books which the Jewish nation refused to transmit to other nations, either because of reverence or jealousy, were revealed so far ahead of time, with the aid of the authority of King Ptolemy, to those nations who would believe through our Lord. It may be that they translated according to the manner in which the Holy Ghost, who directed them and caused them all to speak the same words, decided was adapted to those persons. Yet, as I said before, a comparison of those translators, also, who have adhered more persistently to the actual words is often effica-

107

cious in interpreting a thought. As I began to say then, the Latin texts of the Old Testament should be corrected, if they need correction. They ought to follow the model of the Greek texts, and especially the version of those who, although seventy in number, are declared to have translated with complete agreement. Moreover, there is no doubt that the books of the New Testament, if there is any confusion resulting from the differences in Latin translations, ought to defer to the Greek texts, especially the ones that are found in the Churches of greater and more diligent learning.

Chapter 16

108   However, in reference to figurative expressions, if, by chance, the reader is caused perplexity by any unknown signs, he must decipher them partly through a knowledge of languages, partly through a knowledge of things. The pool of Siloe,[30] where the Lord ordered the man whose eyes He had smeared with clay made of spittle to wash his face, is applicable in some degree as an analogy and unquestionably alludes to some mystery. Nevertheless, if the Evangelist had not explained that name from an unknown language, such an essential implication would be hidden from us. So also, many Hebrew names which have not been interpreted by the authors of those books unquestionably have no small power to help toward explaining the obscurities of the Scriptures, if someone is able to translate them. Some men, expert in that language, have rendered a truly valuable service to succeeding ages by having interpreted all these words apart from the Scriptures and by having given the meanings for *Adam, Eve, Abraham,* and *Moses,* and also for the interpretation of the name of places like *Jerusalem, Sion, Jericho, Sinai, Lebanon, Jordan,* or whatever other names in that language are unknown to us. Because these have been revealed and translated, many figurative passages in the Scriptures are interpreted.

109   In addition, an imperfect knowledge of things causes figurative passages to be obscure; for example, when we do not recognize the nature of the animals, minerals, plants, or other things which are very often represented in the Scrip-

tures for the sake of an analogy. It is well known that a serpent exposes its whole body, rather than its head, to those
attacking it, and how clearly that explains the Lord's meaning when He directed us to be 'wise as serpents.'[31] We should,
therefore, expose our body to persecutors, rather than our
head, which is Christ.[32] Thus, the Christian faith, the head so
to speak, may not be killed in us, as it would be if, preserving
our body, we were to reject God! There is also the belief
that, having forced itself through a small opening in disposing
of its old skin, the serpent gains renewed vigor. How well this
agrees with imitating the wisdom of the serpent and stripping
off the 'old man'[33] that we may put on the new, as the
Apostle expresses it; and we must strip it off passing through
narrow places, since the Lord says: 'Enter by the narrow
gate.'[34] A knowledge of the nature of the serpent, therefore,
explains many analogies which Holy Scripture habitually
makes from that animal; so a lack of knowledge about other
animals to which Scripture no less frequently alludes for
comparisons hinders a reader very much. The same is true of
an ignorance of minerals and plants, or whatever is held fast
by roots. Knowledge of the carbuncle, which glitters in darkness, also illumines many obscure passages of these books
wherever it is proposed for the sake of comparison, and an
ignorance of the beryl or the diamond frequently closes the
doors to understanding. It is easy to comprehend that everlasting peace is signified by the olive branch which the dove,
returning, brought back to the ark,[35] in no other way than
through our knowledge that the smooth surface of oil is not
readily marred by a different liquid and that the olive tree
itself is always in leaf. Indeed, many, through an ignorance of
hyssop—not knowing its potency, either for purifying the
lungs or, as it is said, for penetrating rocks with its roots, although it is a little, unpretentious plant—cannot discover at
all why it has been said:[36] 'Thou shalt sprinkle me with
hyssop, and I shall be cleansed.'

An ignorance of numbers is the reason why many things   110
expressed figuratively and mystically in the Scriptures are not
understood. Certainly a sincere nature cannot help being concerned about the significance of the fact that Moses, Elias,

and the Lord Himself fasted forty days.[37] The figurative perplexity of this act is solved only by a knowledge and study of this number. It is composed of four times ten; as it were, the knowledge of all things joined together by time. The course of the day and year are accomplished through the number four; the days are carried through in intervals of hours: morning, noon, evening, and night; the years, by the spring, summer, autumn, and winter months. But, while we are living in time, we must abstain and fast from all pleasure in time because of the eternity in which we hope to live; although, by the passage of time, that very doctrine of despising temporal things and striving for eternal goods is recommended to us. Further, the number ten symbolizes the knowledge of the Creator and the creature. For a trinity is present in the Creator, while the number seven signifies the creature, by reason of his life and body. In the case of his life, there are three Commandments to love God with our whole heart, our whole soul, and our whole mind;[38] with regard to the body, there are four very discernible elements of which it is composed. So, while the number ten is being impressed upon us in the sense of time, that is, multiplied by four, we are being instructed to live virtuously and temperately, free from the delights of time—in other words, to fast for forty days. This instruction comes from the Law, exemplified by Moses, from the prophecies, exemplified by Elias, and from the Lord Himself. He, as if claiming the testimony of the Law and the prophets, revealed Himself on the mount between those two to His three watching and wondering disciples.[39] The next question is: How the number fifty, which is especially sacred in our religion because of Pentecost, proceeds from forty; also, how this number multiplied by three[40]—because of the three periods of time (before the Law, under the Law, and under grace) or, because of the Name of the Father, the Son, and the Holy Ghost, eminently increased by the Holy Trinity Itself—is applied to the mystery of the most Holy Church and equals the hundred and fifty-three fishes which were caught in the net cast 'on the right side' after the Resurrection of the Lord. And so, certain mysteries of comparison are expressed in the Sacred Books in many other numbers and arrangements of numbers, which are hidden from readers because of their ignorance of numbers.

An ignorance of certain elements of music also encloses and conceals many other things. A certain author[41] has beautifully interpreted some figurative passages from the dissimilarity between the psaltery and the harp.[42] It is also reasonable that learned men strive to discover whether the psaltery with its ten chords is dependent upon any musical law requiring only that number of strings, or, if it is not, whether that number itself should be regarded as all the more sacred because of the Ten Commandments. Just so, if there would be any question about this number, it should be ascribed to the Creator and the creature, because of the number ten itself as explained above. That number of forty-six years required for the building of the Temple, which is related in the Gospel,[43] has a certain musical sound. Applied to the formation of the Lord's body (because of which He mentioned the Temple), it constrains some heretics to acknowledge that the Son of God has clothed Himself not with a counterfeit, but with a truly human, body. Indeed, in many places in the Sacred Scriptures we discover both number and music alluded to with respect.

111

Chapter 17

We must not approve of the superstitions of the pagans who taught that the nine Muses were the daughters of Jupiter and Memory. Varro disproves these errors and I know of no one among the ancients more learned or diligent in such matters. He says that a certain state (I do not remember the name) made an agreement with three artists each for three statues of the Muses to present as an offering in the temple of Apollo. There was one condition, however, that it would choose and buy, in preference to all others, the statues of whichever of the artists had fashioned the most beautiful ones. It turned out that the artists all produced works equally beautiful and that all nine satisfied the state. Therefore, all were purchased to be enshrined in the temple of Apollo. He declares that the poet Hesiod later ascribed names to them.

112

Consequently, Jupiter did not produce the nine Muses, but three workmen chiseled three statues each. Besides, that state had not arranged for three because it had witnessed them in dreams or because such a number of Muses had shown themselves to any of the inhabitants. It did so because it was easy to observe that all sound which is the material of songs is by nature three-fold. It is caused either by the voice, as in the case of those who sing from their throats without an instrument, or by the breath, as in playing trumpets or flutes, or by striking, as is true of harps, drums, or any other instruments which produce tone through percussion.

Chapter 41

113   When the student of the Holy Scriptures, after being instructed in this manner, begins his examination of them, he should not fail to reflect upon that observation of the Apostle:[44] 'Knowledge puffs up, but charity edifies.' In that way he will realize that, although he leaves Egypt a rich man, still, unless he has observed the passover, he cannot be saved. Besides, 'Christ our passover has been sacrificed.[45] The most important lesson this sacrifice teaches Christians is the one that He Himself proclaimed to those whom He saw laboring as in Egypt under Pharoah.[46] Come to me, you who labor and are burdened, and I will give you rest. Take my yoke upon you, and learn from me, for I am meek and humble of heart; and you will find rest for your souls. For my yoke is easy, and my burden light.' To whom was He speaking, except to the meek and humble of heart, whom knowledge does not puff up, but whom charity edifies? Therefore, they are to bear in mind that those who celebrated the passover at the time through figures and shadows, when they were commanded to mark their door-post with the blood of the lamb, marked them with hyssop.[47] This is a mild and humble plant, but has very strong and penetrating roots. So, 'being rooted and grounded in love,' we may be able 'to comprehend with all the saints what is the breadth and length and height and depth,'[48] that is, the Cross of the Lord. Its breadth is signified by the transverse beam on which the hands are extended;

the length from the ground to that cross-bar is where the whole body from the hands down is fastened; the height, from the cross-bar up to the top which is near the head; the depth is that part which is concealed, driven into the earth. In this Sign of the Cross the whole Christian life is defined: to perform good works in Christ and cling to Him perseveringly, to aspire to heavenly goods, and not to profane the Sacraments. Cleansed by means of this action, we shall be able 'to know Christ's love which surpasses knowledge,' by which He is equal to the Father, through whom all things were made in order that we 'may be filled unto all the fullness of God.'[49] There is also a cleansing power in hyssop, lest the breast, arrogant because of the knowledge which puffs up, should boast haughtily about the riches carried away from Egypt. So the Psalmist says,[50] 'Thou shalt sprinkle me with hyssop, and I shall be cleansed. Thou shalt wash me, and I shall be made whiter than snow. To my hearing Thou shalt give joy and gladness.' Then he continues in the following words to show that a cleansing from pride is signified by the hyssop: 'and the bones that have been humbled shall rejoice.'

Chapter 42

Yet, all the knowledge gathered from the works of the pagans, however useful it is, when it is compared to the knowledge of Sacred Scriptures, is as inferior as the abundance of gold, silver, and clothing, which the Israelites carried out of Egypt with them is in comparison with the wealth which they afterwards acquired at Jerusalem, especially during the rule of King Solomon.[51] Whatever a man has learned apart from Scripture is censured there, if it is harmful; if it is useful, he finds it there. And, although everyone may have found there everything which he learned profitably somewhere else, he will discover there, in much greater profusion, things which he can learn nowhere else at all, except in the admirable profundity and surprising simplicity of the Scriptures alone. Therefore, when unfamiliar signs do not ensnare the reader provided with this instruction—meek and humble of heart, easily brought under the yoke of Christ and weighed down

114

by His light burden, grounded, rooted, and built up in love, beyond the power of knowledge to puff him up—let him advance to the study and thorough investigation of the ambiguous signs in the Scriptures. In the third book, I shall begin to say about these signs whatever our Lord will deign to grant me to say.

BOOK THREE

Chapter 1

115   A man who fears God carefully searches for His Will in the Holy Scriptures. Gentle in his piety, so that he has no affection for wrangling; fortified by a knowledge of languages, that he may not be perplexed over unknown words and modes of expression; protected also by an appreciation of certain indispensable things, that he may not be unaware of the power and nature of those which are employed for the sake of analogy; aided, too, by the integrity of the texts which an intelligent accuracy in correction has assured;—let him approach, thus trained, to the investigation and explanation of the obscurities of the Scriptures. As a consequence, he will not be deceived by ambiguous signs, so far as I can teach him. It is possible, however, that, because of the stature of his genius or the clarity of his greater inspiration, he may laugh at, as being childish, those ways which I intend to show him. However, as I began to say, one who has such a disposition of soul that he is able to learn from me, as far as I can teach him, will understand that the ambiguity of Scripture consists in either literal or figurative use of words. I defined these classes in the second book.

Chapter 2

116   When literal words cause Scripture to be ambiguous, our first concern must be to see that we have not punctuated them incorrectly or mispronounced them. Then, when a careful scrutiny reveals that it is doubtful how it should be punctuated or pronounced, we must consult the rule of faith

which we have learned from the clearer passages of the Scriptures and from the authority of the Church. I said enough about this matter when I discussed things in the first book. If both meanings or even all of them, if there should be several, sound obscure after recourse has been had to faith, we must consult the context of both the preceding and the following passage to ascertain which of the several meanings indicated it would consent to and permit to be incorporated with itself.

Now, consider some examples. Some heretics punctuate a 117 certain passage thus: *In principio erat verbum et verbum erat apud Deum et Deus erat,* so that the next sentence would be, *Verbum hoc erat in principio apud Deum* ['In the beginning was the Word and the Word was with God and God was.' 'This Word was in the beginning with God']. They were unwilling to acknowledge that the Word is God. This, however, must be shown to be false according to the rule of faith, which teaches us to say of the equality of the Holy Trinity:[1] *Et Deus erat verbum;* then to add: *Hoc erat in principio apud Deum.* ['and the Word was God.' 'he was in the beginning with God'].

There is an obscurity of punctuation that is not opposed 118 to faith through either interpretation and must therefore be determined from the context itself in this statement of the Apostle:[2] 'And I do not know which to choose. Indeed I am hard pressed from both sides—desiring to depart and to be with Christ, [for this is] a lot by far the better; yet to stay on in the flesh is necessary for your sake.' It is doubtful whether we are to understand *ex duobus concupiscentiam habens* ['desiring two things'] or *Compellor autem ex duobus* ['Indeed I am hard pressed from both sides'], that we may add *concupiscentiam habens dissolvi et esse cum Christo* ['desiring to depart and to be with Christ']. But, since the following words are *multo enim magis optimum* ['a lot by far the better'], it is clear that he is saying that he desires what is better, so that, although he is hard pressed from both sides, he recognizes a desire for one, but a need for the other: that is to say, a desire to be with Christ, and a necessity to stay on in the flesh. This ambiguity is decided by one word which follows and which is translated *enim* ['for']. The translators who have taken away that particle have been more influenced by the opinion that he appeared to be not only hard pressed from both sides, but that he also desired both. Consequently, we must punctuate this way: *Et quid eligam ignoro. Compellor autem ex duobus* ['And I do not know which to choose. Indeed I am hard pressed from both sides']. There follows this mark of punctuation: *concupiscentiam habens dissolvi et esse cum Christo* ['desiring to depart and to be with Christ']. And, as if he were asked why he had more of a desire of this, he says: *multo enim magis optimum* ['for this is by far the better lot']. Then, why is he hard pressed from two sides? Because there is a necessity for his staying on; so he adds this: *manere in carne necessarium propter vos* ['to stay on in the flesh is necessary for your sake'].

119   But, when the ambiguity can be explained neither through a principle of faith nor through the context itself, there is nothing to prevent our punctuating the sentence according to any interpretation that is made known to us. This is a case in the letter to the Corinthians:[3] 'Having therefore these promises, beloved, let us cleanse ourselves from all defilement of the flesh and of the spirit, perfecting holiness in the fear of God. Make room for us. We have wronged no one.' As a matter of fact, it is uncertain whether we should read: *Mundemus nos ab omni coinquinatione carnis et spiritus* ['Let us cleanse ourselves from all defilement of the flesh and of the spirit'], as in the passage:[4] 'that she may be holy in body and in spirit,' or whether we should read: *Mundemus nos ob omni coinquinatione carnis* ['let us cleanse ourselves from all defilement of the flesh']. In this case, the next sentence would be: *Et spiritus perficientes sanctificationem in timore Dei, capite nos* ['And perfecting holiness of spirit in the fear of God, make room for us']. Such ambiguities of punctuation, then, are subject to the reader's judgment.

Chapter 27

120   Not only one but perhaps two or more interpretations are understood from the same words of Scripture. And so, even

if the meaning of the writer is unknown, there is no danger, provided that it is possible to show from other passages of the Scriptures that any one of them is in accord with truth. A man who thoroughly examines the Holy Scriptures in an endeavor to find the purpose of the author (through whom the Holy Ghost brought Holy Scripture into being), whether he attains this goal or whether he elicits from the words another meaning which is not opposed to the true faith, is free from blame, if he has proof from some other passage of the Holy Scriptures. In fact, the author perhaps saw that very meaning, too, in the same words which we are anxious to interpret. And, certainly, the Spirit of God who produced these words through him also foresaw that this very meaning would occur to the reader or listener; further, He took care that it should occur to him because it also is based upon truth. For, what could God have provided more generously and more abundantly in the Holy Scriptures than that the same words might be understood in several ways, which other supporting testimonies no less divine endorse?

Chapter 28

When such a meaning is elicited that its uncertainty cannot be explained by the unerring testimonies of the Holy Scriptures, however, it remains for us to explain it by the proof of reason, even if the man whose words we are seeking to understand were perhaps unaware of that meaning. This, however, is a dangerous practice. It is much safer to walk by means of the Holy Scriptures. When we are trying to search out those passages that are obscured by figurative words, we may either start out from a passage which is not subject to dispute, or, if it is disputed, we may settle the question by employing the testimonies that have been discovered everywhere in the same Scripture.

Chapter 29

Furthermore, learned men should know that our authors have used all the modes of expression which grammarians call

by their Greek name, 'tropes,' and they have employed them
in greater numbers and more eloquently than those who do
not know these writers, and have learned the figures in other
works, can suppose or believe. Yet, those who know these
tropes recognize them in the Holy Scriptures, and the knowledge of them is a considerable aid in understanding the Scriptures. But, it is not proper for me at this point to teach them
to the inexperienced, lest I should appear to be teaching
grammar. To be sure, I suggest that they be learned apart
from this work, although I have already given this advice
above in the second book, when I discussed the necessary
knowledge of languages. The letters from which grammar
derives its name—the Greeks call letters *grammata*—are
certainly the signs of sounds that relate to the articulate voice
with which we speak. In the Holy Books there are seen not
only examples of these tropes, just as of all figures, but even
the names of some of them; for example, 'allegory,' 'enigma,'
and 'parable.' And yet, almost all of these tropes which are
said to be learned in the liberal arts are also discovered in the
speech of those who have not studied under any grammarians,
but are satisfied with the manner of speech which ordinary
people use. For, who does not say: 'So may you flourish'?
This trope is called a 'metaphor.' Who does not speak of a
fishpond, even when it contains no fish and was not made for
fish, but still it derives its name from fish? This trope is
called 'catachresis.'

123   It would be tedious to describe the others in this fashion.
The speech of the common people employs even those which
are more unusual because they mean the opposite of what
they say; examples are those called 'irony' and 'antiphrasis.'
Irony shows by the inflection of the voice what it intends us
to understand, as when we say to a man who is behaving
badly, 'You are doing well.' Antiphrasis, on the other hand, is
not made to signify contrary meanings by an inflection of
voice, but uses its own words, whose origin is from the contrary, as when a grove is called *lucus* because it has very little
light; or when we say 'Yes,' even though, on the contrary,
it would be 'No,' as when we are seeking what is not in a
place and we receive the answer: 'There is plenty'; or, by add-

ing words, we cause what we say to be understood in the
contrary sense, as 'Beware of him, because he is a good man.'
What unlearned man does not use such expressions, and still
is utterly unaware of the nature or the names of these tropes?
A knowledge of them is necessary in explaining the obscurities of the Scriptures, because, when the meaning is unreason-
able if understood in the literal signification of the words, we
must, of course, try to find out whether it has been expressed
in some figure or other which we do not know. And so, many
passages which were obscure have been interpreted.

Augustine
The Harmony of the Gospels
Book I
400 A.D.

Chapter I

In the entire number of those divine records which are contained in the sacred writings, the gospel deservedly stands pre-eminent. For what the law and the prophets aforetime announced as destined to come to pass, is exhibited in the gospel in its realization and fulfilment. The first preachers of this gospel were the apostles, who beheld our Lord and Saviour Jesus Christ in person when He was yet present in the flesh. And not only did these men keep in remembrance the words heard from His lips, and the deeds wrought by Him beneath their eyes; but they were also careful, when the duty of preaching the gospel was laid upon them, to make mankind acquainted with those divine and memorable occurrences which took place at a period antecedent to the formation of their own connection with Him in the way of discipleship, which belonged also to the time of His nativity, His infancy, or His youth, and with regard to which they were able to institute exact inquiry and to obtain information, either at His own hand or at the hands of His parents or other parties, on the ground of the most reliable intimations and the most trustworthy testimonies. Certain of them also—namely, Matthew and John—gave to the world, in their respective books, a written account of all those matters which it seemed needful to commit to writing concerning Him.

And to preclude the supposition that, in what concerns the   125
apprehension and proclamation of the gospel, it is a matter of
any consequence whether the enunciation comes by men
who were actual followers of this same Lord here when He
manifested Himself in the flesh and had the company of His
disciples attendant on Him, or by persons who with due
credit received facts with which they became acquainted in a
trustworthy manner through the instrumentality of these
former, divine providence, through the agency of the Holy
Spirit, has taken care that certain of those also who were
nothing more than followers of the first apostles should have
authority given them not only to preach the gospel, but also
to compose an account of it in writing. I refer to Mark and
Luke. All those other individuals, however, who have attempted to dare to offer a written record of the acts of the
Lord or of the apostles, failed to commend themselves in their
own times as men of the character which would induce the
Church to yield them its confidence, and to admit their
compositions to the canonical authority of the Holy Books.
And this was the case not merely because they were persons
who could make no rightful claim to have credit given them
in their narrations, but also because in a deceitful manner
they introduced into their writings certain matters which are
condemned at once by the catholic and apostolic rule of
faith, and by sound doctrine.

Chapter II

Now, those four evangelists whose names have gained the   126
most remarkable circulation over the whole world, and whose
number has been fixed as four,—it may be for the simple reason that there are four divisions of that world through the
universal length of which they, by their number as by a kind
of mystical sign, indicated the advancing extension of the
Church of Christ,—are believed to have written in the order
which follows: first Matthew, then Mark, thirdly Luke, lastly
John. Hence, too, [it would appear that] these had one order
determined among them with regard to the matters of their
personal knowledge and their preaching [of the gospel], but

a different order in reference to the task of giving the written narrative. As far, indeed, as concerns the acquisition of their own knowledge and the charge of preaching, those unquestionably came first in order who were actually followers of the Lord when He was present in the flesh, and who heard Him speak and saw Him act; and [with a commission received] from His lips they were despatched to preach the gospel. But as respects the task of composing that record of the gospel which is to be accepted as ordained by divine authority, there were (only) two, belonging to the number of those whom the Lord chose before the passover, that obtained places,—namely, the first place and the last. For the first place in order was held by Matthew, and the last by John. And thus the remaining two, who did not belong to the number referred to, but who at the same time had become followers of the Christ who spoke in these others, were supported on either side by the same, like sons who were to be embraced, and who in this way were set in the midst between these twain.

127   Of these four, it is true, only Matthew is reckoned to have written in the Hebrew language; the others in Greek. And however they may appear to have kept each of them a certain order of narration proper to himself, this certainly is not to be taken as if each individual writer chose to write in ignorance of what his predecessor had done, or left out as matters about which there was no information things which another nevertheless is discovered to have recorded. But the fact is, that just as they received each of them the gift of inspiration, they abstained from adding to their several labours any superfluous conjoint compositions. For Matthew is understood to have taken it in hand to construct the record of the incarnation of the Lord according to the royal lineage, and to give an account of most part of His deeds and words as they stood in relation to this present life of men. Mark follows him closely, and looks like his attendant and epitomizer. For in his narrative he gives nothing in concert with John apart from the others: by himself separately, he has little to record; in conjunction with Luke, as distinguished from the rest, he has still less; but in concord with Matthew, he has a very large number of passages. Much, too, he narrates in words almost numeri-

cally and identically the same as those used by Matthew, where the agreement is either with that evangelist alone, or with him in connection with the rest. On the other hand, Luke appears to have occupied himself rather with the priestly lineage and character of the Lord. For although in his own way he carries the descent back to David, what he has followed is not the royal pedigree, but the line of those who were not kings. That genealogy, too, he has brought to a point in Nathan the son of David,[1] which person likewise was no king. It is not thus, however, with Matthew. For in tracing the lineage along through Solomon the king,[2] he has pursued with strict regularity the succession of the other kings; and in enumerating these, he has also conserved that mystical number of which we shall speak hereafter.

Chapter III

For the Lord Jesus Christ, who is the one true King and the one true Priest, the former to rule us, and the latter to make expiation for us, has shown us how His own figure bore these two parts together, which were only separately commended [to notice] among the Fathers. This becomes apparent if (for example) we look to that inscription which was affixed to His cross—"King of the Jews:" in connection also with which, and by a secred instinct, Pilate replied, "What I have written, I have written."[3] For it had been said aforetime in the Psalms, "Destroy not the writing of the title."[4] The same becomes evident, so far as the part of priest is concerned, if we have regard to what He has taught us concerning offering and receiving. For thus it is that He sent us before hand a prophecy respecting Himself, which runs thus, "Thou art a priest for ever, after the order of Melchisedek."[5] And in many other testimonies of the divine Scriptures, Christ appears both as King and as Priest. Hence, also, even David himself, whose son He is, not without good reason, more frequently declared to be than he is said to be Abraham's son, and whom Matthew and Luke have both alike held by,—the one viewing him as the person from whom, through Solomon, His lineage can be traced down, and the other taking him for

128

the person to whom, through Nathan, His genealogy can be carried up,—did represent the part of a priest, although he was patently a king, when he ate the shew-bread. For it was not lawful for any one to eat that, save the priests only. To this it must be added that Luke is the only one who mentions how Mary was discovered by the angel, and how she was related to Elisabeth, who was the wife of Zacharias the priest. And of this Zacharias the same evangelist has recorded the fact, that the woman whom he had for wife was one of the daughters of Aaron, which is to say she belonged to the tribe of the priests.[7]

129   Whereas, then, Matthew had in view the kingly character, and Luke the priestly, they have at the same time both set forth pre-eminently the humanity of Christ: for it was according to His humanity that Christ was made both King and Priest. To Him, too, God gave the throne of His father David, in order that of His kingdom there should be no end.[8] And this was done with the purpose that there might be a mediator between God and men, the man Christ Jesus,[9] to make intercession for us. Luke, on the other hand, had no one connected with him to act as his summarist in the way that Mark was attached to Matthew. And it may be that this is not without a certain solemn significance. For it is the right of kings not to miss the obedient following of attendants; and hence the evangelist, who had taken it in hand to give an account of the kingly character of Christ, had a person attached to him as his associate who was in some fashion to follow in his steps. But inasmuch as it was the priest's wont to enter all alone into the holy of holies, in accordance with that principle, Luke, whose object contemplated the priestly office of Christ, did not have any one to come after him as a confederate, who was meant in some way to serve as an epitomizer of his narrative.

Chapter IV

130   These three evangelists, however, were for the most part engaged with those things which Christ did through the vehicle of the flesh of man, and after the temporal fashion.

But John, on the other hand, had in view that true divinity
of the Lord in which He is the Father's equal, and directed
his efforts above all to the setting forth of the divine nature
in his Gospel in such a way as he believed to be adequate to
men's needs and notions. Therefore he is borne to loftier
heights, in which he leaves the other three far behind him; so
that, while in them you see men who have their conversation
in a certain manner with the man Christ on earth, in him
you perceive one who has passed beyond the cloud in which
the whole earth is wrapped, and who has reached the liquid.
heaven from which, with clearest and steadiest mental eye,
he is able to look upon God the Word, who was in the
beginning with God, and by whom all things were made.[10]
And there, too, he can recognise Him who was made flesh in
order that He might dwell amongst us;[11] [that Word of whom
we say,] that He assumed the flesh, not that He was changed
into the flesh. For had not this assumption of the flesh been
effected in such a manner as at the same time to conserve the
unchangeable Divinity, such a word as this could never have
been spoken,—namely, "I and the Father are one."[12] For
surely the Father and the flesh are not one. And the same
John is also the only one who has recorded that witness
which the Lord gave concerning Himself, when He said: "He
that hath seen me, hath seen the Father also;" and "I am in
the Father, and the Father is in me;"[13] "that they may be
one, even as we are one;"[14] and, "Whatsoever the Father
doeth, these same things doeth the Son likewise."[15] And
whatever other statements there may be to the same effect,
calculate; to betoken, to those who are possessed of right
understanding, that divinity of Christ in which He is the
Father's equal, of all these we might almost say that we are
indebted for their introduction into the Gospel narrative to
John alone. For he is like one who has drunk in the secret of
His divinity more richly and somehow more familiarly than
others, as if he drew it from the very bosom of his Lord on
which it was his wont to recline when He sat at meat.[16]

Chapter V

131   Moreover, there are two several virtues (or talents) which
have been proposed to the mind of man. Of these, the one is
the active, and the other the contemplative: the one being
that whereby the way is taken, and the other that whereby
the goal is reached; the one that by which men labour in order
that the heart may be purified to see God, and the other that
by which men are disengaged and God is seen. Thus the
former of these two virtues is occupied with the precepts for
the right exercise of the temporal life, whereas the latter
deals with the doctrine of that life which is everlasting. In
this way, also the one operates, the other rests; for the
former finds its sphere in the purging of sins, the latter moves
in the light of the purged. And thus, again, in this mortal
life the one is engaged with the work of a good conversation;
while the other subsists rather on faith, and is seen only in
the person of the very few, and through the glass darkly,
and only in part in a kind of vision of the unchangeable
truth.[17] Now these two virtues are understood to be presented emblematically in the instance of the two wives of
Jacob. Of these I have discoursed already up to the measure
of my ability, and as fully as seemed to be appropriate to my
task, (in what I have written) in opposition to Faustus the
Manichaean. For Lia, indeed, by interpretation means "la-
bouring," whereas Rachel signifies "the first principle seen."
And by this it is given to us to understand, if one will only
attend carefully to the matter, that those three evangelist who,
with pre-eminent fulness, have handled the account of the
Lord's temporal doings and those of His sayings which were
meant to bear chiefly upon the moulding of the manners of
the present life, were conversant with that active virtue; and
that John, on the other hand, who narrates fewer by far of
the Lord's doings, but records with greater carefulness and
with larger wealth of detail the words which He spoke, and
most especially those discourses which were intended to
introduce us to the knoweldge of the unity of the Trinity

and the blessedness of the life eternal, formed his plan and framed his statement with a view to commend the contemplative virtue to our regard.

Chapter VI

For these reasons, it also appears to me, that of the various 132 parties who have interpreted the living creatures in the Apocalypse as significant of the four evangelists, those who have taken the lion to point to Matthew, the man to Mark, the calf to Luke, and the eagle to John, have made a more reasonable application of the figures than those who have assigned the man to Matthew, the eagle to Mark, and the lion to John. For, in forming their particular idea of the matter, these latter have chosen to keep in view simply the beginnings of the books, and not the full design of the several evangelists in its completeness, which was the matter that should, above all, have been thoroughly examined. For surely it is with much greater propriety that the one who has brought under our notice most largely the kingly character of Christ, should be taken to be represented by the lion. Thus is it also that we find the lion mentioned in conjunction with the royal tribe itself, in that passage of the Apocalypse where it is said, "The lion of the tribe of Judah hath prevailed."[18] For in Matthew's narrative the magi are recorded to have come from the east to inquire after the King, and to worship Him whose birth was notified to them by the star. Thus, too, Herod, who himself also was a king, is [said there to be] afraid of the royal child, and to put so many little children to death in order to make sure that the one might be slain.[19] Again, that Luke is intended under the figure of the calf, in reference to the preeminent sacrifice made by the priest, has been doubted by neither of the two [sets of interpreters]. For in that Gospel the narrator's account commences with Zacharias the priest. In it mention is also made of the relationship between Mary and Elisabeth.[20] In it, too, it is recorded that the ceremonies proper to the earliest priestly service were attended to in the case of the infant Christ;[21] and a careful examination brings a variety of other matters under our notice in this Gospel, by

which it is made apparent that Luke's object was to deal with
the part of the priest. In this way it follows further, that
Mark, who has set himself neither to give an account of the
kingly lineage, nor to expound anything distinctive of the
priesthood, whether on the subject of the relationship or on
that of the consecration, and who at the same time comes
before us as one who handles the things which the man Christ
did, appears to be indicated simply under the figure of the
man among those four living creatures. But again, those three
living creatures, whether lion, man, or calf, have their course
upon the earth; and in like manner, those three evangelists
occupy themselves chiefly with the things which Christ did
in the flesh, and with the precepts which He delivered to men,
who also bear the burden of the flesh, for their instruction in
the rightful exercise of this mortal life. Whereas John, on the
other hand, soars like an eagle above the clouds of human
infirmity, and gazes upon the light of the unchangeable truth
with those keenest and steadiest eyes of the heart.

Chapter VII

133   Those sacred chariots of the Lord, however, in which He is
borne throughout the earth and brings the peoples under His
easy yoke and His light burden, are assailed with calumnious
charges by certain persons who, in impious vanity or in ignorant temerity, think to rob of their credit as veracious historians those teachers by whose instrumentality the Christian
religion has been disseminated all the world over, and through
whose efforts it has yielded fruits so plentiful that unbelievers
now scarcely dare so much as to mutter their slanders in
private among themselves, kept in check by the faith of the
Gentiles and by the devotion of all the peoples. Nevertheless,
inasmuch as they still strive by their calumnious disputations
to keep some from making themselves acquainted with the
faith, and thus prevent them from becoming believers, while
they also endeavour to the utmost of their power to excite
agitations among others who have already attained to belief,
and thereby give them trouble; and further, as there are some
brethren who, without detriment to their own faith, have a

desire to ascertain what answer can be given to such questions, either for the advantage of their own knowledge or for
the purpose of refuting the vain utterances of their enemies,
with the inspiration and help of the Lord our God (and
would that it might prove profitable for the salvation of such
men), we have undertaken in this work to demonstrate the
errors or the rashness of those who deem themselves able to
prefer charges, the subtilty of which is at least sufficiently
observable, against those four different books of the gospel
which have been written by these four several evangelists.
And in order to carry out this design to a successful conclusion, we must prove that the writers in question do not
stand in any antagonism to each other. For those adversaries
are in the habit of adducing this as the palmary allegation in
all their vain objections, namely, that the evangelists are not
in harmony with each other.

But we must first discuss a matter which is apt to present a   134
difficulty to the minds of some. I refer to the question why
the Lord has written nothing Himself, and why He has thus
left us to the necessity of accepting the testimony of other
persons who have prepared records of His history. For this is
what those parties—the pagans more than any—allege when
they lack boldness enough to impeach or blaspheme the Lord
Jesus Christ Himself, and when they allow Him—only as a
man, however—to have been possessed of the most distinguished wisdom. In making that admission, they at the same
time assert that the disciples claimed more for their Master
than He really was; so much more indeed that they even called
Him the Son of God, and the Word of God, by whom all
things were made, and affirmed that He and God are one.
And in the same way they dispose of all other kindred passages in the epistles of the apostles, in the light of which we
have been taught that He is to be worshipped as one God with
the Father. For they are of opinion that He is certainly to be
honoured as the wisest of men, but they deny that He is to
be worshipped as God.

Wherefore, when they put the question why He has not   135
written in His own person, it would seem as if they were
prepared to believe regarding Him whatever He might have

written concerning Himself, but not what others may have given the world to know with respect to His life, according to the measure of their own judgment. Well, I ask them in turn why, in the case of certain of the noblest of their own philosophers, they have accepted the statements which their disciples left in the records they have composed, while these sages themselves have given us no written accounts of their own lives? For Pythagoras, than whom Greece in those days did not possess any more illustrious personage in the sphere of that contemplative virtue, is believed to have written absolutely nothing, whether on the subject of his own personal history or on any other theme whatsoever. And as to Socrates, to whom, on the other hand, they have adjudged a position of supremacy above all others in that active virtue by which the moral life is trained, so that they do not hesitate also to aver that he was even pronounced to be the wisest of men by the testimony of their deity Apollo,—it is indeed true that he handled the fables of Aesop in some short verses, and thus made use of words and numbers of his own in the task of rendering the themes of another. But this was all. And so far was he from having the desire to write anything himself, that he declared that he had done even so much only because he was constrained by the imperial will of his demon, as Plato, the noblest of all his disciples, tells us. That was a work, also, in which he sought to set forth in fair form not so much his own thoughts, as rather the ideas of another. What reasonable ground, therefore, have they for believing, with regard to those sages, all that their disciples have committed to record in respect of their history, while at the same time they refuse to credit in the case of Christ what His disciples have written on the subject of His life? And all the more may we thus argue, when we see how they admit that all other men have been excelled by Him in the matter of wisdom, although they decline to acknowledge Him to be God. Is it, indeed, the case that those persons whom they do not hesitate to allow to have been by far His inferiors, have had the faculty of making disciples who can be trusted in all that concerns the narrative of their careers, and that He failed in that capacity? But if that is a most absurd statement to

venture upon, then in all that belongs to the history of that
Person to whom they grant the honour of wisdom, they
ought to believe not merely what suits their own notions, but
that they read in the narratives of those who learned from
this sage Himself those various facts which they have left on
record on the subject of His life.

Chapter VIII

Besides this, they ought to tell us by what means they have   136
succeeded in acquiring their knowledge of this fact that He
was the wisest of men, or how it has had the opportunity of
reaching their ears. If they have been made acquainted with it
simply by current report, then is it the case that common report forms a more trustworthy informant on the subject of
His history than those disciples of His who, as they have gone
and preached of Him, have disseminated the same report like
a penetrating savour throughout the whole world? In fine,
they ought to prefer the one kind of report to the other, and
believe that account of His life which is the superior of the
two. For this report, indeed, which is spread abroad with a
wonderful clearness from that Church catholic at whose
extension through the whole world those persons are so
astonished, prevails in an incomparable fashion over the
unsubstantial rumours with which men like them occupy
themselves. This report, furthermore, which carries with it
such weight and such currency, that in dread of it they can
only mutter their anxious and feeble snatches of paltry objections within their own breasts, as if they were more afraid
not of being heard than wishful to receive credit, proclaims
Christ to be the only-begotten Son of God, and himself God,
by whom all things were made. If, therefore, they choose
report as their witness, why does not their choice fix on this
special report, which is so pre-eminently lustrous in its remarkable definiteness? And if they desire the evidence of
writings, why do they not take those evangelical writings
which excel all others in their commanding authority? On
our side, indeed, we accept those statements about their
deities which are offered at once in their most ancient

writings and by most current report. But if these deities are to be considered proper objects for reverence, why then do they make them the subject of laughter in the theatres? And if, on the other hand, they are proper objects for laughter, the occasion for such laughter must be all the greater when they are made the objects of worship in the theatres. It remains for us to look upon those persons as themselves minded to be witnesses concerning Christ, who, by speaking what they know not, divest themselves of the merit of knowing what they speak about. Or if, again, they assert that they are possessed of any books which they can maintain to have been written by Him, they ought to produce them for our inspection. For assuredly those books (if there are such) must be most profitable and most wholesome, seeing they are the productions of one whom they acknowledge to have been the wisest of men. If, however, they are afraid to produce them, it must be because they are of evil tendency; but if they are evil, then the wisest of men cannot have written them. They acknowledge Christ, however, to be the wisest of men, and consequently Christ cannot have written any such thing.

Chapter IX

137   But, indeed, these persons rise to such a pitch of folly as to allege that the books which they consider to have been written by Him contain the arts by which they think He wrought those miracles, the fame of which has become prevalent in all quarters. And this fancy of theirs betrays what they really love, and what their aims really are. For thus, indeed, they show us how they entertain this opinion that Christ was the wisest of men only for the reason that He possessed the knowledge of I know not what illicit arts, which are justly condemned, not merely by Christian discipline, but even by the administration of earthly government itself. And, in good sooth, if there are people who affirm that they have read books of this nature composed by Christ, then why do they not perform with their own hand some such works as those which so greatly excite their wonder when

wrought by Him, by taking advantage of the information
which they have derived from these books?

Chapter X

Nay more, as by divine judgment, some of those who either   138
believe, or wish to have it believed, that Christ wrote matter
of that description, have even wandered so far into error as to
allege that these same books bore on their front, in the form
of epistolary superscription, a designation addressed to Peter
and Paul. And it is quite possible that either the enemies of
the name of Christ, or certain parties who though that they
might impart to this kind of execrable arts the weight of
authority drawn from so glorious a name, may have written
things of that nature under the name of Christ and the apostles. But in such most deceitful audacity they have been so
utterly blinded as simply to have made themselves fitting
objects for laughter, even with young people who as yet
know Christian literature only in boyish fashion, and rank
merely in the grade of readers.

For when they made up their minds to represent Christ   139
to have written in such strain as that to His disciples, they
bethought themselves of those of His followers who might
best be taken for the persons to whom Christ might most
readily be believed to have written, as the individuals who
had kept by Him on the most familiar terms of friendship.
And so Peter and Paul occurred to them, I believe, just
because in many places they chanced to see these two apostles represented in pictures as both in company with Him.
For Rome, in a specially honourable and solemn manner,
commends the merits of Peter and of Paul, for this reason
among others, namely, that they suffered [martyrdom] on
the same day. Thus to fall most completely into error was the
due desert of men who sought for Christ and His apostles not
in the holy writings, but on painted walls. Neither is it to be
wondered at, that these fiction-limners were misled by the
painters. For throughout the whole period during which
Christ lived in our mortal flesh in fellowship with His disciples,
Paul had never become His disciple. Only after His passion,

after His resurrection, after His ascension, after the mission of the Holy Spirit from heaven, after many Jews had been converted and had shown marvellous faith, after the stoning of Stephen the deacon and martyr, and when Paul still bore the name Saul, and was grievously persecuting those who had become believers in Christ, did Christ call that man [by a voice] from heaven, and made him His disciple and apostle.[22] How, then, is it possible that Christ could have written those books which they wish to have it believed that He did write before His death, and which were addressed to Peter and Paul, as those among His disciples who had been most intimate with Him, seeing that up to that date Paul had not yet become a disciple of His at all?

Chapter XI

140   Moreover, let those who madly fancy that it was by the use of magical arts that He was able to do the great things which He did, and that it was by the practice of such rites that He made His name a sacred thing to the peoples who were to be converted to Him, give their attention to this question,—namely, whether by the exercise of magical arts, and before He was born on this earth, He could also have filled with the Holy Spirit those mighty prophets who afore-time declared those very things concerning Him as things destined to come to pass, which we can now read in their accomplishment in the gospel, and which we can see in their present realization in the world. For surely, even if it was by magical arts that He secured worship for Himself, and that, too, after His death, it is not the case that He was a magician before He was born. Nay, for the office of prophesying on the subject of His coming, one nation had been most specially deputed; and the entire administration of that common-wealth was ordained to be a prophecy of this King who was to come, and who was to be found a heavenly state drawn out of all nations.

Chapter XII

Furthermore, that Hebrew nation, which, as I have said, 141
was commissioned to prophesy of Christ, had no other God
but one God, the true God, who made heaven and earth, and
all that herein is. Under His displeasure they were oft-
times given into the power of their enemies. And now, indeed,
on account of their most heinous sin in putting Christ to
death, they have been thoroughly rooted out of Jerusalem
itself, which was the capital of their kingdom, and have been
made subject to the Roman empire. Now the Romans were in
the habit of propitiating the deities of those nations whom
they conquered by worshipping these themselves, and they
were accustomed to undertake the charge of their sacred
rites. But they declined to act on that principle with regard
to the God of the Hebrew nation, either when they made
their attack or when they reduced the people. I believe that
they perceived that, if they admitted the worship of this
Deity, whose commandment was that He only should be worshipped, and that images should be destroyed, they would
have to put away from them all those objects to which formerly they had undertaken to do religious service, and by the
worship of which they believed their empire had grown. But
in this the falseness of their demons mightily deceived them.
For surely they ought to have apprehended the fact that it is
only by the hidden will of the true God, in whose hand
resides the supreme power in all things, that the kingdom was
given them and has been made to increase, and that their
position was not due to the favour of those deities who, if
they could have wielded any influence whatever in that
matter, would rather have protected their own people from
being over-mastered by the Romans, or would have brought
the Romans themselves into complete subjection to them.

Certainly they cannot possibly affirm that the kind of piety 142
and manners exemplified by them became objects of love and
choice on the part of the gods of the nations which they conquered. They will never make such an assertion, if they only

recall their own early beginnings, the asylum for abandoned criminals and the fratricide of Romulus. For when Remus and Romulus established their asylum, with the intention that whoever took refuge there, be the crime what it might be with which he stood charged, should enjoy impunity in his deed, they did not promulgate any precepts of penitence for bringing the minds of such wretched men back to a right condition. By this bribe of impunity did they not rather arm the gathered band of fearful fugitives against the states to which they properly belonged, and the laws of which they dreaded? Or when Romulus slew his brother, who had perpetrated no evil against him, is it the case that his mind was bent on the vindication of justice, and not on the acquisition of absolute power? And is it true that the deities did not take their delight in manners like these, as if they were themselves enemies to their own states, in so far as they favoured those who were the enemies of these communities? Nay rather, neither did they by deserting them harm the one class, nor did they by passing over to their side in any sense help the other. For they have it not in their power to give kingship or to remove it. But that is done by the one true God, according to His hidden counsel. And it is not His mind to make those necessarily blessed to whom He may have given an earthly kingdom, or to make those necessarily unhappy whom He has deprived of that position. But He makes men blessed or wretched for other reasons and by other means, and either by permission or by actual gift distributes temporal and earthly kingdoms to whomsoever He pleases, and for whatsoever period He chooses, according to the fore-ordained order of the ages.

Chapter XIII

143   Hence also they cannot meet us fairly with this question: Why, then, did the God of the Hebrews, whom you declare to be the supreme and true God, not only not subdue the Romans under their power, but even fail to secure those Hebrews themselves against subjugation by the Romans? For there were open sins of theirs that went before them, and on

account of which the prophets so long time ago predicted
that this very thing would overtake them; and above all, the
reason lay in the fact, that in their impious fury they put
Christ to death, in the commission of which sin they were
made blind [to the guilt of their crime] through the deserts
of other hidden transgressions. That His sufferings also would
be for the benefit of the Gentiles, was foretold by the same
prophetic testimony. Nor, in another point of view, did the
fact appear clearer, that the kingdom of that nation, and its
temple, and its priesthood, and its sacrificial system, and that
mystical unction which is called χρῖσμα in Greek, from which
the name of *Christ* takes its evident application, and on account of which that nation was accustomed to speak of its
kings as *anointed ones*, were ordained with the express object
of prefiguring Christ, than has the kindred fact become
apparent, that after the resurrection of the Christ who was
put to death began to be preached unto the believing Gentiles,
all those things came to their end, all unrecognised as the
circumstance was, whether by the Romans, through whose
victory, or by the Jews, through whose subjugation, it was
brought about that they did thus reach their conclusion.

Chapter XIV

Here indeed we have a wonderful fact, which is not re-   **144**
marked by those few pagans who have remained such,—
namely, that this God of the Hebrews who was offended by
the conquered, and who was also denied acceptance by the
conquerors, is now preached and worshipped among all
nations. This is that God of Israel of whom the prophet
spake so long time since when he thus addressed the people
of God: "And He who brought thee out, the God of Israel,
shall be called (the God) of the whole earth." What was thus
prophesied has been brought to pass through the name of the
Christ, who comes to men in the form of a descendant of
that very Israel who was the grandson of Abraham, with
whom the race of the Hebrews began. For it was to this Israel
also that it was said, "In thy seed shall all the tribes of the
earth be blessed."[2 3] Thus it is shown that the God of Israel,

the true God who made heaven and earth, and who administers human affairs justly and mercifully in such wise that neither does justice exclude mercy with Him, nor does mercy hinder justice, was not overcome Himself when His Hebrew people suffered their overthrow, in virtue of His permitting the kingdom and priesthood of that nation to be seized and subverted by the Romans. For now, indeed, by the might of this gospel of Christ, the true King and Priest, the advent of which was prefigured by that kindom and priesthood, the God of Israel Himself is everywhere destroying the idols of the nations. And, in truth, it was to prevent that destruction that the Romans refused to admit the sacred rites of this God in the way that they admitted those of the gods of the other nations whom they conquered. Thus did He remove both kingdom and priesthood from the prophetic nation, because He who was promised to men through the agency of that people had already come. And by Christ the King He has brought into subjection to His own name that Roman empire by which the said nation was overcome; and by the strength and devotion of Christian faith, He has converted it so as to effect a subversion of those idols, the honour ascribed to which precluded His worship from obtaining entrance.

145   I am of opinion that it was not by means of magical arts that Christ, previous to His birth among men, brought it about that those things which were destined to come to pass in the course of His history, were pre-announced by so many prophets, and prefigured also by the kingdom and priesthood established in a certain nation. For the people who are connected with that now abolished kingdom, and who in the wonderful providence of God are scattered throughout all lands, have indeed remained without any unction from the true King and Priest; in which anointing the import of the name of Christ is plainly discovered. But notwithstanding this, they still retain remnants of some of their observances; while, on the other hand, not even in their state of overthrow and subjugation have they accepted those Roman rites which are connected with the worship of idols. Thus they still keep the prophetic books as the witness of Christ; and in this way in the documents of His enemies we find proof presented

of the truth of this Christ who is the subject of prophecy.
What, then, do these unhappy men disclose themselves to be,
by the unworthy method in which they laud the name of
Christ? If anything relating to the practice of magic has been
written under His name, while the doctrine of Christ is so
vehemently antagonistic to such arts, these men ought rather
in the light of this fact to gather some idea of the greatness
of that name, by the addition of which even persons who live
in opposition to His precepts endeavour to dignify their
nefarious practices. For just as, in the course of the diverse
errors of men, many persons have set up their varied heresies
against the truth under the cover of His name, so the very
enemies of Christ think that, for the purposes of gaining
acceptance for opinions which they propound in opposition
to the doctrine of Christ, they have no weight of authority
at their service unless they have the name of Christ.

Chapter XV

But what shall be said to this, if those vain eulogizers of
Christ, and those crooked slanderers of the Christian religion,
lack the daring to blaspheme Christ, for this particular reason
that some of their philosophers, as Porphyry of Sicily has
given us to understand in his books, consulted their gods as
to their response on the subject of [the claims of] Christ, and
were constrained by their own oracles to laud Christ? Nor
should that seem incredible. For we also read in the Gospel
that the demons confessed Him;[24] and in our prophets it is
written in this wise: "For the gods of the nations are demons."[25] Thus it happens, then, that in order to avoid attempting aught in opposition to the responses of their own
deities, they turn their blasphemies aside from Christ, and
pour them forth against His disciples. It seems to me, however,
that these gods of the Gentiles, whom the philosophers of
the pagans may have consulted, if they were asked to give
their judgment on the disciples of Christ, as well as on Christ
Himself, would be constrained to praise them in like manner.

146

Chapter XVI

147   Nevertheless these persons argue still to the effect that this demolition of temples, and this condemnation of sacrifices, and this shattering of all images, are brought about, not in virtue of the doctrine of Christ Himself, but only by the hand of His apostles, who, as they contend, taught something different from what He taught. They think by this device, while honouring and lauding Christ, to tear the Christian faith in pieces. For it is at least true, that it is by the disciples of Christ that at once the works and the words of Christ have been make known, on which this Christian religion is established, with which a very few people of this character are still in antagonism, who do not now indeed openly assail it, but yet continue even in these days to utter their mutterings against it. But if they refuse to believe that Christ taught in the way indicated, let them read the prophets, who not only enjoined the complete destruction of the superstitions of idols, but also predicted that this subversion would come to pass in Christian times. And if these spoke falsely, why is their word fulfilled with so mighty a demonstration? But if they spoke truly, why is resistance offered to such divine power?

Chapter XVII

148   However, here is a matter which should meet with more careful consideration at their hands,—namely, what they take the God of Israel to be, and why they have not admitted Him to the honours of worship among them, in the way that they have done with the gods of other nations that have been made subject to the imperial power of Rome? This question demands an answer all the more, when we see that they are of the mind that all the gods ought to be worshipped by the man of wisdom. Why, then, has He been excluded from the number of these others? If He is very mighty, why is He the only deity that is not worshipped by them? If He has little

or no might, why are the images of other gods broken in pieces by all the nations, while He is now almost the only God that is worshipped among these peoples? From the grasp of this question these men shall never be able to extricate themselves, who worship both the greater and the lesser deities, whom they hold to be gods, and at the same time refuse to worship this God, who has proved Himself stronger than all those to whom they do service. If He is [a God] of great virtue, why has He been deemed worthy only of rejection? And if He is [a God] of little or no power, why has He been able to accomplish so much, although rejected? If He is good, why is He the only one separated from the other good deities? And if He is evil, why is He, who stands thus alone, not subjugated by so many good deities? If He is truthful, why are His precepts scorned? And if He is a liar, why are His predictions fulfilled?

Chapter XVIII

In fine, they may think of Him as they please. Still, we may ask whether it is the case that the Romans refuse to consider evil deities as also proper objects of worship,—those Romans who have erected fanes to Pallor and Fever, and who enjoin both that the good demons are to be entreated and that the evil demons are to be propitiated. Whatever their opinion, then, of Him may be, the question still is, Why is He the only Deity whom they have judged worthy neither of being called upon for help, nor of being propitiated? What God is this, who is either one so unknown, that He is the only one not discovered as yet among so many gods, or who is one so well known that He is now the only one worshipped by so many men? There remains, then, nothing which they can possibly allege in explanation of their refusal to admit the worship of this God, except that His will was that He alone should be worshipped; and His command was, that those gods of the Gentiles that they were worshipping at the time should cease to be worshipped. But an answer to this other question is rather to be required of them, namely, what or what manner of deity they consider this God to be,

149

who has forbidden the worship of those other gods for whom they erected temples and images,—this God, who has also been possessed of might so vast that His will has prevailed more in effecting the destruction of their images than theirs has availed to secure the non-admittance of His worship. And, indeed, the opinion of that philosopher of theirs is given in plain terms, whom, even on the authority of their own oracle, they have maintained to have been the wisest of all men. For the opinion of Socrates is, that every deity whatsoever ought to be worshipped just in the manner in which he may have ordained that he should be worshipped. Consequently it became a matter of the supremest necessity with them to refuse to worship the God of the Hebrews. For if they were minded to worship Him in a method different from the way in which He had declared that He ought to be worshipped, then assuredly they would have been worshipping not this God as He is, but some figment of their own. And, on the other hand, if they were willing to worship Him in the manner which He had indicated, then they could not but perceive that they were not at liberty to worship those other deities whom He interdicted them from worshipping. Thus was it, therefore, that they rejected the service of the one true God, because they were afraid that they might offend the many false gods. For they thought that the anger of those deities would be more to their injury, than the goodwill of this God would be to their profit.

Chapter XIX

150   But that must have been a vain necessity and a ridiculous timidity. We ask now what opinion regarding this God is formed by those men whose pleasure it is that all gods ought to be worshipped. For if He ought not to be worshipped, how are all worshipped when He is not worshipped? And if He ought to be worshipped, it cannot be that all others are to be worshipped along with Him. For unless He is worshipped alone, He is really not worshipped at all. Or may it perhaps be the case, that they will allege Him to be no God at all, while they call those gods who, as we believe, have no power

to do anything except so far as permission is given them by His judgment,—have not merely no power to do good to any one, but no power even to do harm to any, except to those who are judged by Him, who possesses all power, to merit so to be harmed? But, as they themselves are compelled to admit, those deities have shown less power than He has done. For if those are held to be gods whose prophets, when consulted by men, have returned responses which, that I may not call them false, were at least most convenient for their private interests, how is not He to be regarded as God whose prophets have not only given the congruous answer on subjects regarding which they were consulted at the special time, but who also, in the case of subjects respecting which they were not consulted, and which related to the universal race of man and all nations, have announced prophetically so long time before the event those very things of which we now read, and which indeed we now behold? If they gave the name of god to that being under whose inspiration the Sibyl sung of the fates of the Romans, how is not He (to be called) God, who, in accordance with the announcement aforetime given, has shown us how the Romans and all nations are coming to believe in Himself through the gospel of Christ, as the one God, and to demolish all the images of their fathers? Finally, if they designate those as gods who have never dared through their prophets to say anything against this God, how is not He (to be designated) God, who not only commanded by the mouth of His prophets the destruction of their images, but who also predicted that among all the Gentiles they would be destroyed by those who should be enjoined to abandon their idols and to worship Him alone, and who, on receiving these injunctions, should be His servants?

Chapter XX

Or let them aver, if they are able, that some Sibyl of theirs,   151
or any one whatever among their other prophets, announced long ago that it would come to pass that the God of the Hebrews, the God of Israel, would be worshipped by all nations, declaring, at the same time, that the worshippers of other gods

before that time had rightly rejected Him; and again, that the compositions of His prophets would be in such exalted authority, that in obedience to them the Roman government itself would command the destruction of images, the said seers at the same time giving warning against acting upon such ordinances;—let them, I say, read out any utterances like these, if they can, from any of the books of their prophets. For I stop not to state that those things which we can read in their books repeat a testimony on behalf of our religion, that is, the Christian religion, which they might have heard from the holy angels and from our prophets themselves; just as the very devils were compelled to confess Christ when He was present in the flesh. But I pass by these matters, regarding which, when we bring them forward, their contention is that they were invented by our party. Most certainly, however, they may themselves be pressed to adduce anything which has been prophesied by the seers of their own gods against the God of the Hebrews; as, on our side, we can point to declarations so remarkable at once for number and for weight recorded in the books of our prophets against their gods, in which also we can both note the command and recite the prediction and demonstrate the event. And over the realization of these things, that comparatively small number of heathens who have remained such are more inclined to grieve than they are ready to acknowledge that God has had the power to foretell these things as events destined to be made good; whereas in their dealings with their own false gods, who are genuine demons, they prize nothing else so highly as to be informed by their responses of something which is to take place with them.

Chapter XXI

152   Seeing, then, that these things are so, why do not these unhappy men rather apprehend the fact that this God is the true God, whom they perceive to be placed in a position so thoroughly separated from the company of their own deities, that, although they are compelled to acknowledge Him to be God, those very persons who profess that all gods ought to be

worshipped are nevertheless not permitted to worship Him along with the rest? Now, since these deities and this God cannot be worshipped together, why is not He selected who forbids those others to be worshipped; and why are not those deities abandoned, who do not interdict Him from being worshipped? Or if they do indeed forbid His worship, let the interdict be read. For what has greater claims to be recited to their people in their temples, in which the sound of no such thing has ever been heard? And, in good sooth, the prohibition directed by so many against one ought to be more notable and more potent than the prohibition launched by one against so many. For if the worship of this God is impious, then those gods are profitless, who do not interdict men from that impiety; but if the worship of this God is pious, then, as in that worship the commandment is given that these others are not to be worshipped, their worship is impious. If, again, those deities forbid His worship, but only so diffidently that they rather fear to be heard than dare to prohibit, who is so unwise as not to draw his own inference from the fact, who fails to perceive that this God ought to be chosen, who in so public a manner prohibits their worship, who commanded that their images should be destroyed, who foretold that demolition, who Himself effected it, in preference to these deities of whom we know not that they ordained abstinence from His worship, of whom we do not read that they foretold such an event, and in whom we do not see power sufficient to have it brought about? I put the question, let them give the answer: Who is this God, who thus harasses all the gods of the Gentiles, who thus betrays all their sacred rites, who thus renders them extinct?

Chapter XXII

But why do I interrogate men whose native wit has deserted them in answering the question as to who this God is? Some say that He is Saturn. I fancy the reason of that is found in the sanctification of the Sabbath; for those men assign that day to Saturn. But their own Varro, than whom they can point to no man of greater learning among them, thought

153

that the God of the Jews was Jupiter, and he judged that it
mattered not what name was employed, provided the same
subject was understood under it; in which, I believe, we see
how he was subdued by His supremacy. For, inasmuch as the
Romans are not accustomed to worship any more exalted
object than Jupiter, of which fact their Capitol is the open
and sufficient attestation, and deem him to be the king of all
gods; when he observed that the Jews worshipped the supreme
God, he could not think of any object under that title other
than Jupiter himself. But whether men call the God of the
Hebrews Saturn, or declare Him to be Jupiter, let them tell us
when Saturn dared to prohibit the worship of a second deity.
He did not venture to interdict the worship even of this very
Jupiter, who is said to have expelled him from his kingdom,—
the son thus expelling the father. And if Jupiter, as the more
powerful deity and the conqueror, has been accepted by his
worshippers, then they ought not to worship Saturn, the
conquered and expelled. But neither, on the other hand, did
Jove put his worship under the ban. Nay, that deity whom he
had power to overcome, he nevertheless suffered to continue
a god.

Chapter XXIII

154   These narratives of yours, say they, are but fables which
have to be interpreted by the wise, or else they are fit only to
be laughed at; but we revere that Jupiter of whom Maro says
that

> "All things are full of Jove,"
> —Virgil's *Eclogues*, iii. v. 60;

that is to say, the spirit of life that vivifies all things. It is not
without some reason, therefore, that Varro thought that Jove
was worshipped by the Jews; for the God of the Jews says by
His prophet, "I fill heaven and earth."[26] But what is meant
by that which the same poet names Ether? How do they take
the term? For he speaks thus:

"Then the omnipotent father Ether, with fertilizing showers,
Came down into the bosom of his fruitful spouse."
                                    —Virgil's *Georgics*, ii. 325.

They say, indeed that his Ether is not spirit, but a lofty body
in which the heaven is stretched above the air. Is liberty conceded to the poet to speak at one time in the language of the
followers of Plato, as if God was not body, but spirit, and at
another time in the language of the Stoics, as if God was a
body? What is it, then, that they worship in their Capitol? If
it is a spirit, or if again it is, in short, the corporeal heaven
itself, then what does that shield of Jupiter there which they
style the Aegis? The origin of that name, indeed, is explained
by the circumstance that a goat nourished Jupiter when he
was concealed by his mother. Or is this a fiction of the poets?
But are the capitols of the Romans, then, also the mere
creations of the poets? And what is the meaning of that, certainly not poetical, but unmistakeably farcical, variability of
yours, in seeking your gods according to the ideas of philosophers in books, and revering them according to the notions
of poets in your temples?

But was that Euhemerus also a poet, who declares both   155
Jupiter himself, and his father Saturn, and Pluto and Neptune
his brothers, to have been men, in terms so exceedingly plain
that their worshippers ought all the more to render thanks to
the poets, because their inventions have not been intended so
much to disparage them as rather to dress them up? Albeit
Cicero mentions that this same Euhemerus was translated
into Latin by the poet Ennius. Or was Cicero himself a poet,
who, in counselling the person with whom he debates in his
Tusculan Disputations, addresses him as one possessing knowledge of things secret, in the following terms: "If, indeed, I
were to attempt to search into antiquity, and produce from
thence the subjects which the writers of Greece have given to
the world, it would be found that even those deities who are
reckoned gods of the higher orders have gone from us into
heaven. Ask whose sepulchres are pointed out in Greece: call
to mind, since you have been initiated, the things which are
delivered in the mysteries: then, doubtless, you will com-

prehend how widely extended this belief is." This author certainly makes ample acknowledgment of the doctrine that those gods of theirs were originally men. He does, indeed, benevolently surmise that they made their way into heaven. But he did not hesitate to say in public, that even the honour thus given them in general repute was conferred upon them by men, when he spoke of Romulus in these words: "By good will and repute we have raised to the immortal gods that Romulus who founded this city." How should it be such a wonderful thing, therefore, to suppose that the more ancient men did with respect to Jupiter and Saturn and the others what the Romans have done with respect to Romulus, and what, in good truth, they have thought of doing even in these more recent times also in the case of Caesar? And to these same Virgil has addressed the additional flattery of song, saying:

"Lo, the star of Caesar, descendant of Dione, arose."
—Eclogue, ix. ver. 47.

Let them see to it, then, that the truth of history do not turn out to exhibit to our view sepulchers erected for their false gods here upon the earth! and let them take heed lest the vanity of poetry, instead of fixing, may be but feigning stars for their deities there in heaven. For, in reality, that one is not the star of Jupiter, neither is this one the star of Saturn; but the simple fact is, that upon these stars, which were set from the foundation of the world, the names of those persons were imposed after their death by men who were minded to honour them as gods on their departure from this life. And with respect to these we may, indeed, ask how there should be such ill desert in chastity, or such good desert in voluptuousness, that Venus should have a star, and Minerva be denied one among those luminaries which revolve along with the sun and moon?

156   But it may be said that Cicero, the Academic sage, who has been bold enough to make mention of the sepulchres of their gods, and to commit the statement to writing, is a more doubtful authority than the poets; although he did not pre-

sume to offer that assertion simply as his own personal opinion, but put it on record as a statement contained among the
traditions of their own sacred rites. Well, then, can it also be
maintained that Varro either gives expression merely to an
invention of his own, as a poet might do, or puts the matter
only dubiously, as might be the case with an Academician,
because he declares that, in the instance of all such gods, the
matters of their worship had their origin either in the life
which they lived, or in the death which they died, among
men? Or was that Egyptian priest, Leon, either a poet or an
Academician, who expounded the origin of those gods of
theirs to Alexander of Macedon, in a way somewhat different
indeed from the opinion advanced by the Greeks, but nevertheless so far accordant therewith as to make out their
deities to have been originally men?

But what is all this to us? Let them assert that they worship   157
Jupiter, and not a dead man, let them maintain that they
have dedicated their Capitol not to a dead man, but to.the
Spirit that vivifies all things and fills the world. And as to
that shield of his, which was made of the skin of a she-goat
in honour of his nurse, let them put upon it whatever interpretation they please. What do they say, however, about
Saturn? What is it that they worship under the name of
Saturn? Is not this the deity that was the first to come down
to us from Olympus (of whom the poet sings):

> "Then from Olympus' height came down
> Good Saturn, exiled from his crown
>   By Jove, his mightier heir:
> He brought the race to union first
> Erewhile on mountain-tops dispersed,
> And gave them statues to obey,
> And willed the land wherein he lay
>   Should Latium's title bear."
> —Virgil's *Aeneid*, viii. 320-324, Conington's trans.

Does not his very image, made as it is with the head covered,
present him as one under concealment? Was it not he that
made the practice of agriculture known to the people of

Italy,—a fact which is expressed by the reaping-hook? No, say they, for you may see whether the being of whom such things are recorded was a man, and indeed one particular king: we, however, interpret Saturn to be *universal Time*, as is signified also by his name in Greek: for he is called *Chronus*, which word, with the aspiration thus given it, is also the vocable for *time*: whence too, in Latin he gets the name of *Saturn*, as if it meant that he is *sated* with years. But now, what we are to make of people like these I know not, who, in their very effort to put a more favourable meaning upon the names and the images of their gods, make the confession that the very god who is their major deity, and the father of the rest, is Time. For what else do they thus betray but, in fact, that all those gods of theirs are only temporal, seeing that the very parent of them all is made out to be Time?

158   Accordingly, their more recent philosophers of the Platonic school, who have flourished in Christian times, have been ashamed of such fancies, and have endeavoured to interpret Saturn in another way, affirming that he received the name Χρόνος in order to signify, as it were, the fulness of intellect; their explanation being, that in Greek *fulness* is expressed by the term χόρος, and *intellect* or *mind* by the term νοῦς which etymology seems to be favoured also by the Latin name, on the supposition that the first part of the word (Saturnus) came from the Latin, and the second part from the Greek: so that he got the title saturnus as an equivalent to *satur, νοῦς*. For they saw how absurd it was to have that Jupiter regarded as a son of Time, whom they either considered, or wished to have considered, eternal deity. Furthermore, however, according to this novel interpretation, which it is marvellous that Cicero and Varro should have suffered to escape their notice, if their ancient authorities really had it, they call Jupiter the son of Saturn, thus denoting him, it may be, as the spirit that proceedeth forth from that supreme mind—the spirit which they choose to look upon as the soul of this world, so to speak, filling alike all heavenly and all earthly bodies. Whence comes also that saying of Maro, which I have cited a little ago, namely, "All things are full of Jove"? Should they not, then, if they are possessed of the ability, alter the

superstitions indulged in by men, just as they alter their interpretation; and either erect no images at all, or at least build capiols to Saturn rather than to Jupiter? For they also maintain that no rational soul can be produced gifted with wisdom, except by participation in that supreme and unchangeable wisdom of his; and this affirmation they advance not only with respect to the soul of a man, but even with respect to that same soul of the world which they also designate Jove. Now we not only concede, but even very particularly proclaim, that there is a certain supreme wisdom of God, by participation in which every soul whatsoever that is constituted truly wise acquires its wisdom. But whether that universal corporeal mass, which is called the world, has a kind of soul, or, so to speak, its own soul, that is to say, a rational life by which it can govern its own movements, as is the case with every sort of animal, is a question both vast and obscure. That is an opinion which ought not to be affirmed, unless its truth is clearly ascertained. And what will it matter to man, even should this question remain for ever unsolved, since, in any case, no soul becomes wise or blessed by drawing from any other soul but from that one supreme and immutable wisdom of God?

The Romans, however, who have founded a Capitol in honour of Jupiter, but none in honour of Saturn, as also these 159 other nations whose opinion it has been that Jupiter ought to be worshipped pre-eminently and above the rest of the gods, have certainly not agreed in sentiment with the persons referred to; who, in accordance with that mad view of theirs, would dedicate their loftiest citadels rather to Saturn, if they had any power in these things, and who most particularly would annihilate those mathematicians and nativity-spinners by whom this Saturn, whom their opponents would designate the maker of the wise, has been placed with the character of a deity of evil among the other stars. But this opinion, nevertheless, has prevailed so mightily against them in the mind of humanity, that men decline even to name that god, and call him *Ancient* rather than Saturn; and that in so fearful a spirit of superstition, that the Carthaginians have now gone very near to change the designation of their town, and call it the town of the Ancient more frequently than the town of Saturn.

Chapter XXIV

160   It is well understood, therefore, what these worshippers of images are convicted in reality of revering, and what they attempt to colour over. But even these new interpreters of Saturn must be required to tell us what they think of the God of the Hebrews. For to them also it seemed right to worship all the gods, as is done by the heathen nations, because their pride made them ashamed to humble themselves under Christ for the remission of their sins. What opinion, therefore, do they entertain regarding the God of Israel? For if they do not worship Him, then they do not worship all gods; and if they do worship Him, they do not worship Him in the way that He has ordained for His own worship, because they worship others also whose worship He has interdicted. Against such practices He issued His prohibition by the mouth of those same prophets by whom He also announced before-hand the destined occurrence of those very things which their images are now sustaining at the hands of the Christians. For whatever the explanation may be, whether it be that the angels were sent to those prophets to show them figuratively, and by the congruous forms of visible objects, the one true God, the Creator of all things, to whom the whole universe is made subject, and to indicate the method in which He enjoined His own worship to proceed; or whether it was that the minds of some among them were so mightily elevated by the Holy Spirit, as to enable them to see those things in that kind of vision in which the angels themselves behold objects; in either case it is the incontestable fact, that they did serve that God who has prohibited the worship of other gods; and, moreover, it is equally certain, that with the faithfulness of piety in the kingly and in the priestly office, they ministered at once for the good of their country, and in the interest of those sacred ordinances which were significant of the coming of Christ as the true King and Priest.

Chapter XXV

But further, in the case of the gods of the Gentiles (in their   161
willingness to worship whom they exhibit their unwillingness
to worship that God who cannot be worshipped together
with them), let them tell us the reason why no one is found
in the number of their deities who thinks of interdicting the
worship of another; while they institute them in different
offices and functions, and hold them to preside each one over
objects which pertain properly to his own special province.
For if Jupiter does not prohibit the worship of Saturn, because he is not to be taken merely for a man, who drove
another man, namely his father, out of his kingdom, but
either for the body of the heavens, or for the spirit that fills
both heaven and earth, and because thus he cannot prevent
that supernal mind from being worshipped, from which he is
said to have emanated: if, on the same principle also, Saturn
cannot interdict the worship of Jupiter, because he is not [to
be supposed to be merely] one who was conquered by that
other in rebellion,—as was the case with a person of the same
name, by the hand of some one or other called Jupiter, from
whose arms he was fleeing when he came into Italy,—and
because the primal mind favours the mind that springs from
it: yet Vulcan at least might [be expected to] put under the
ban the worship of Mars, the paramour of his wife, and
Hercules [might be thought likely to interdict] the worship
of Juno, his persecutor. What kind of foul consent must
subsist among them, if even Diana, the chaste virgin, fails to
interdict the worship, I do not say merely of Venus, but even
of Priapus? For if the same individual decides to be at once a
hunter and a farmer, he must be the servant of both of these
deities; and yet he will be ashamed to do even so much as
erect temples for them side by side. But they may aver, that
by interpretation Diana means a certain virtue, be it what they
please; and they may tell us that Priapus really denotes the
deity of fecundity,—to such an effect, at any rate, that Juno
may well be ashamed to have such a coadjutor in the task of

making females fruitful. They may say what they please; they may put any explanation upon these things which in their wisdom they think fit: only, in spite of all that, the God of Israel will confound all their argumentations. For in prohibiting all those deities from being worshipped, while His own worship is hindered by none of them, and in at once commanding, foretelling, and effecting destruction for their images and sacred rites, He has shown with sufficient clearness that they are false and lying deities, and that He Himself is the one true and truthful God.

162   Moreover, to whom should it not seem strange that those worshippers, now become few in number, of deities both numerous and false, should refuse to do homage to Him of whom, when the question is put to them as to what deity He is, they dare not at least assert, whatever answer they may think to give, that He is no God at all? For if they deny His deity, they are very easily refuted by His works, both in prophecy and in fulfilment. I do not speak of those works which they deem themselves at liberty not to credit, such as His work in the beginning, when He made heaven and earth, and all that is in them.[27] Neither do I specify here those events which carry us back into the remotest antiquity, such as the translation of Enoch, the destruction of the impious by the flood,[28] and the saving of righteous Noah and his house from the deluge, by means of the [ark of] wood.[29] I begin the statement of His doings among men with Abraham. To this man, indeed, was given by an angelic oracle an intelligible promise, which we now see in its realization. For to him it was said, "In thy seed shall all nations be blessed."[30] Of his seed, then, sprang the people of Israel, whence came the Virgin Mary, who was the mother of Christ; and that in Him all the nations are blessed, let them now be bold enough to deny if they can. This same promise was made also to Isaac the son of Abraham.[31] It was given again to Jacob the grandson of Abraham. This Jacob was also called Israel, from whom that whole people derived both its descent and its name so that indeed the God of this people was called the God of Israel: not that He is not also the God of the Gentiles, whether they are ignorant of Him or now know Him; but

that in this people He willed that the power of His promises should be made more conspicuously apparent. For that people, which at first was multiplied in Egypt, and after a time was delivered from a state of slavery there by the hand of Moses, with many signs and portents, saw most of the Gentile nations subdued under it, and obtained possession also of the land of promise, in which it reigned in the person of kings of its own, who sprang from the tribe of Judah. This Judah, also, was one of the twelve sons of Israel, the grandson of Abraham. And from him were descended the people called the Jews, who, with the help of God Himself did great achievements, and who also, when He chastised them, endured many sufferings on account of their sins, until the coming of that Seed to whom the promise was given, in whom all the nations were to be blessed, and [for whose sake] they were willingly to break in pieces the idols of their fathers.

Chapter XXVI

For truly what is thus effected by Christians is not a thing which belongs only to Christian times, but one which was predicted very long ago. Those very Jews who have remained enemies to the name of Christ, and regarding whose destined perfidy these prophetic writings have not been silent, do themselves possess and peruse the prophet who says: "O Lord my God, and my refuge in the day of evil, the Gentiles shall come unto Thee from the ends of the earth, and shall say, Surely our fathers have worshipped mendacious idols, and there is no profit in them."[32] Behold, that is now being done; behold, now the Gentiles are coming from the ends of the earth to Christ, uttering things like these, and breaking their idols! Of signal consequence, too, is this which God has done for His Church in its world-wide extension, in that the Jewish nation, which has been deservedly overthrown and scattered abroad throughout the lands, has been made to carry about with it everywhere the records of our prophecies, so that it might not be possible to look upon these predictions as concocted by ourselves; and thus the enemy of our faith has been made a witness to our truth. How, then, can it be

163

possible that the disciples of Christ have taught what they have not learned from Christ, as those foolish men in their silly fancies object, with the view of getting the superstitious worship of heathen gods and idols subverted? Can it be said also that those prophecies which are still read in these days, in the books of the enemies of Christ, were the inventions of the disciples of Christ?

164   Who, then, has effected the demolition of these systems but the God of Israel? For to this people was the announce-made by those divine voices which were addressed to Moses: "Hear, O Israel; the Lord thy God is one God."[33] "Thou shalt not make unto thee any graven image, or any likeness of anything that is in heaven above or that is in the earth beneath."[34] And again, in order that this people might put an end to these things wherever it received power to do so, this commandment was also laid down upon the nation: "Thou shalt not bow down to their gods, nor serve them; thou shalt not do after their works, but thou shalt utterly overthrow them, and quite break down their images."[35] But who shall say that Christ and Christians have no connection with Israel, seeing that Israel was the grandson of Abraham, to whom first, as afterwards to his son Isaac, and then to his grandson Israel himself, that promise was given, which I have already mentioned, namely: "In thy seed shall all nations be blessed"? That prediction we see now in its fulfilment in Christ. For it was of this line that the Virgin was born, concerning whom a prophet of the people of Israel and of the God of Israel sang in these tems: "Behold, a virgin shall conceive, and bear a son; and they shall call His name Emmanuel." For by interpretation, Emmanuel means, "God with us."[36] This God of Israel, therefore, who has interdicted the worship of other gods, who has interdicted the making of idols, who has commanded their destruction, who by His prophet has predicted that the Gentiles from the ends of the earth would say, "Surely our fathers have worshipped mendacious idols, in which there is no profit;" this same God is He who, by the name of Christ and by the faith of Christians, has ordered, promised, and exhibited the overthrow of all these superstitions. In vain, therefore, do these unhappy men, knowing

that they have been prohibited from blaspheming the name
of Christ, seek to make it out, that this kind of doctrine is
something strange to Him, in the power of which the Christians dispute against idols, and root out all those false religions,
wherever they have the opportunity.

Chapter XXVII

Let them now give their answer with respect to the God of   165
Israel, to whom, as teaching and enjoining such things, witness
is borne not only by the books of the Christians, but also by
those of the Jews. Regarding Him, let them ask the counsel
of their own deities, who have prevented the blaspheming of
Christ. Concerning the God of Israel, let them give a con-
tumelious response if they dare. But whom are they to consult?
or where are they to ask counsel now? Let them peruse the
books of their own authorities. If they consider the God of
Israel to be Jupiter, as Varro has written (that I may speak
for the time being in accordance with their own way of thinking), why then do they not believe that the idols are to be
destroyed by Jupiter? if they deem Him to be Saturn, why
do they not worship Him? Or why do they not worship
Him in that manner in which, by the voice of those prophets
through whom He has made good the things which He has
foretold, He has ordained His worship to be conducted? Why
do they not believe that images are to be destroyed by Him,
and the worship of other gods forbidden? If He is neither
Jove nor Saturn (and surely, if He were one of these, He would
not speak out so mightily against the sacred rites of their
Jove and Saturn), who then is this God, who, with all their
consideration for other gods, is the only Deity not worshipped
by them, and who, nevertheless, so manifestly brings it about
that He shall Himself be the sole object of worship, to the
overthrow of all other gods, and to the humiliation of everything proud and highly exalted, which has lifted itself up
against Christ in behalf of idols, persecuting and slaying Christians? But, in good truth, men are now asking into what
secret recesses these worshippers withdraw, when they are
minded to offer sacrifice; or into what regions of obscurity

they thrust back these same gods of theirs, to prevent their being discovered and broken in pieces by the Christians. Whence comes this mode of dealing, if not from the fear of those laws and those rulers by whose instrumentality the God of Israel discovers His power, and who are now made subject to the name of Christ. And that it should be so He promised long ago, when He said by the prophet: "Yea, all kings of the earth shall worship Him: all nations shall serve Him."[3][7]

Chapter XXVIII

166   It cannot be questioned that what was predicted at sundry times by His prophets is now being realized,—namely, the announcement that He would disclaim His impious people (not indeed, the people as a whole, because even of the Israelites many have believed in Christ; for His apostles themselves belonged to that nation), and would humble every proud and injurious person, so that He should Himself alone be exalted, that is to say, alone be manifested to men as lofty and mighty; until idols should be cast away by those who believe, and be concealed by those who believe not; when the earth is broken by His fear, that is to say, when the men of earth are subdued by fear, to wit, by fearing His law, or the law of those who, being at once believers in His name and rulers among the nations, shall interdict such sacrilegious practices.

167   For these things, which I have thus briefly stated in the way of introduction, and with a view to their readier apprehension, are thus expressed by the prophet: And now, O house of Jacob, come ye, and let us walk in the light of the Lord. For He has disclaimed His people the house of Israel, because the country was replenished, as from the beginning, with their soothsayings as with those of strangers, and many strange children were born to them. For their country was replenished with silver and gold, neither was there any numbering of their treasure; their land also is full of horses, neither was there any numbering of their chariots: their land also is full of the abominations of the works of their own hands, and they have worshipped that which their own

fingers have made. And the mean man has bowed himself, and the great man has humbled himself, and I will not forgive it them. And now enter ye into the rocks, and hide yourself in the earth from before the fear of the Lord, and from the majesty of His power, when He arises to crush the earth: for the eyes of the Lord are lofty, and man is low; and the haughtiness of men shall be humbled, and the Lord alone shall be exalted in that day. For the day of the Lord of Hosts shall be upon every one that is injurious and proud, and upon every one that is lifted up and humbled, and they shall be brought low; and upon every cedar of Lebanon of the high ones and the lifted up, and upon every tree of the Lebanon of Bashan, and upon every mountain, and upon every high hill, and upon every ship of the sea, and upon every spectacle of the beauty of ships. And the contumely of men shall be humbled and shall fall, and the Lord alone shall be exalted in that day; and all things made by hands they shall hide in dens, and in holes of the rocks, and in caves of the earth, from before the fear of the Lord, and from the majesty of His power, when He arises to crush the earth: for in that day a man shall cast away the abominations of gold and silver, the vain and evil things which they made for worship, in order to go into the clefts of the solid rock, and into the holes of the rocks, from before the fear of the Lord, and from the majesty of His power, when He arises to break the earth in pieces.[38]

Chapter XXIX

What do they say of this God of Sabaoth, which term, by   168
interpretation, means the God of powers or of armies, inasmuch as the powers and the armies of the angels serve Him?
What do they say of this God of Israel; for He is the God of
that people from whom came the seed wherein all the nations
were to be blessed? Why is He the only deity excluded from
worship by those very persons who contend that all the gods
ought to be worshipped? Why do they refuse their belief to
Him who both proves other gods to be false gods, and also
overthrows them? I have heard one of them declare that he
had read, in some philosopher or other, the statement that,

from what the Jews did in their sacred observances, he had come to know what God they worshipped. "He is the deity," said he, "that presides over those elements of which this visible and material universe is constructed;" when in the Holy Scriptures of His prophets it is plainly shown that the people of Israel were commanded to worship that God who made heaven and earth, and from whom comes all true wisdom. But what need is there for further disputation on this subject, seeing that it is quite sufficient for my present purpose to point out how they entertain any kind of presumptuous opinions regarding that God whom yet they cannot deny to be a God? If, indeed, He is the deity that presides over the elements of which this world consists, why is He not worshipped in preference to Neptune, who presides over the sea only? Why not, again, in preference to Silvanus, who presides over the fields and woods only? Why not in preference to the Sun, who presides over the day only, or who also rules over the entire heat of heaven? Why not in preference to the Moon, who presides over the night only, or who also shines pre-eminent for power over moisture? Why not in preference to Juno, who is supposed to hold possession of the air only? For certainly those deities, whoever they may be, who preside over the parts, must cenessarily be under that Deity who wields the presidency over all the elements, and over the entire universe. But this Deity prohibits the worship of all those deities. Why, then, is it that these men, in opposition to the injunction of One greater than those deities, not only choose to worship them, but also decline, for their sakes, to worship Him? Not yet have they discovered any constant and intelligible judgment to pronounce on this God of Israel; neither will they ever discover any such judgment, until they find out that He alone is the true God, by whom all things were created.

Chapter XXX

169   Thus it was with a certain person named Lucan, one of their great declaimers in verse. For a long time, as I believe, he endeavored to find out, by his own cogitations, or by the

perusal of the books of his own fellow-countrymen, who the God of the Jews was; and failing to prosecute his inquiry in the way of piety, he did not succeed. Yet he chose rather to speak of Him as the uncertain God whom he did not find out, than absolutely to deny the title of God to that Deity of whose existence he perceived proofs so great. For he says:

> "And Judaea, devoted to the worship
> Of an uncertain God."
> —Lucan, Book ii. towards the end.

And as yet this God, the holy and true God of Israel, had not done by the name of Christ among all nations works so great as those which have been wrought after Lucan's times up to our own day But now who is so obdurate as not to be moved, who so dull as not to be inflamed, seeing that the saying of Scripture is fulfilled, "For there is not one that is hid from the heat thereof;"[39] and seeing also that those other things which were predicted so long time ago in this same Psalm from which I have cited one little verse, are now set forth in their accomplishment in the clearest light? For under this term of the "heavens" the apostles of Jesus Christ were denoted, because God was to preside in them with a view to the publishing of the gospel. Now, therefore, the heavens have declared the glory of God, and the firmament has proclaimed the works of His hands. Day unto day has given forth speech, and night unto night has shown knowledge. Now there is no speech or language where their voices are not heard. Their sound has gone out into all the earth, and their words to the end of the world. Now hath He set His tabernacle in the sun, that is, in manifestation, which tabernacle is His Church. For in order to do so (as the words proceed in the passage) He came forth from His chamber like a bridegroom; that is to say, the Word, wedded with the flesh of man, came forth from the Virgin's womb. Now has He rejoiced as a strong man, and has run His race. Now has His going forth been made from the height of heaven, and His return even to the height of heaven.[40] And accordingly, with the completest propriety, there follows upon this the verse which I have already mentioned: "And there is not one that is hid from the heat thereof [or, His heat]." And still these men make choice of their little, weak, prating objections, which are like stubble to be reduced to ashes in that fire, rather than like gold to be purged of its dross by it; while at once the fallacious monuments of their false gods have been brought to nought, and the veracious promises of that uncertain God have been proved to be sure.

Chapter XXXI

170   Wherefore let those evil applauders of Christ, who refuse to become Christians, desist from making the allegation that Christ did not teach that their gods were to be abandoned, and their images broken in pieces. For the God of Israel, regarding whom it was declared aforetime that He should be called the God of the whole earth, is now indeed actually called the God of the whole earth. By the mouth of His prophets He predicted that this would come to pass, and by Christ He did bring it eventually to pass at the fit time. Assuredly, if the God of Israel is now named the God of the whole earth, what He has commanded must needs be made good; for He who has given the commandment is now well known. But, further, that He is made known by Christ and in Christ, in order that His Church may be extended throughout the world, and that by its instrumentality the God of Isarel may be named the God of the whole earth, those who please may read in a little earlier in the same prophet. That paragraph may also be cited by me. It is not so long as to make it requisite for us to pass it by. Here there is much said about the presence, the humility, and the passion of Christ, and about the body of which He is the Head, that is, His Church, where if is called barren, like one that did not bear. For during many years the Church, which was destined to subsist among all the nations with its children, that is, with its saints, was not apparent, as Christ remained yet unannounced by the evangelists to those to whom He had not been declared by the prophets. Again, it is said that there shall be more children

for her who is forsaken than for her who has a husband, under which name of a husband the Law was signified, or the King whom the people of Israel first received. For neither had the Gentiles received the Law at the period at which the prophet spake; nor had the King of Christians yet appeared to the nations, although from these Gentile nations a much more fruitful and numerous multitude of saints has now proceeded. It is in this manner, therefore, that Isaiah speaks, commencing with the humility of Christ, and turning afterwards to an address to the Church, on to that verse which we have already instanced, where he says: And He who brought thee out, the same God of Israel, shall be called the God of the whole earth.[41] Behold, says he, my Servant shall deal prudently, and shall be exalted and honoured exceedingly. As many shall be astonied at Thee; so shall Thy marred visage, nevertheless, be seen by all, and Thine honour by men. For so shall many nations be astonied at Him, and the kings shall shut their mouths. For they shall see to whom it has not been told of Him; and those who have not heard shall understand. O Lord, who hath believed our report, and to whom is the arm of the Lord revealed? We have proclaimed before Him as a servant, as a root in a thirsty soil; He hath no form nor comeliness. And we have seen Him, and He had neither beauty nor seemliness; but His countenance is despised, and His state rejected by all men: a man stricken, and acquainted with the bearing of infirmities; on account of which His face is turned aside, injured, and little esteemed. He bears our infirmities, and is in sorrows for us. And we did esteem Him to be in sorrows, and to be stricken and in punishment. But He was wounded for our transgressions, and He was enfeebled for our iniquities; the chastisement of our peace was upon Him, and with His stripes we are healed. All we, like sheep, have gone astray, and the Lord hath given Him up for our sins. And whereas He was evil entreated, He opened not His mouth; He was brought as a sheep to the slaughter; and as a lamb before him who shears it is dumb, so He opened not His mouth. In humility was His judgment taken. Who shall declare His generation? For His life shall be cut off out of the land; by the iniquities of my people is He led to death. Therefore shall I give the wicked for His sepulture, and the rich on account of His death; because He did no iniquity, neither was any deceit in His mouth. The Lord is pleased to clear Him in regard to His stroke. If ye shall give your soul for your offences, ye shall see the seed of the longest life. And the Lord is pleased to take away His soul from sorrows, to show Him the light, and to set Him forth in sight, and to justify the righteous One who serves many well; and He shall bear their sins. Therefore shall He have many for His inheritance, and shall divide the spoils of the strong; for which reason His soul was delivered over to death, and He was numbered with the transgressors, and He bare the sins of many, and was delivered for their iniquities. Rejoice, O barren, thou that doest not bear: exult, and cry aloud, thou that dost not travail with child; for more are the children of the desolate than those of her who has a husband. For the Lord hath said, Enlarge the place of thy tent, and fix thy courts; there is no reason why thou shouldst spare: lengthen thy cords, and strengthen thy stakes firmly. Yea, again and again break thou forth on the right hand and on the left. For thy seed shall inherit the Gentiles, and thou shalt inhabit the cities which were desolate. There is nothing for thee to fear. For thou shalt prevail, and be not thou confounded as if thou shalt be put to shame. For thou shalt forget thy confusion for ever: thou shalt not remember the shame of thy widowhood, since I who made thee am the Lord; the Lord is His name: and He who brought thee out, the very God of Israel, shall be called the God of the whole earth.[42]

171   What can be said in opposition to this evidence, and this expression of things both foretold and fulfilled? If they suppose that His disciples have given a false testimony on the subject of the divinity of Christ, will they also doubt the passion of Christ? No: they are not accustomed to believe that He rose from the dead; but, at the same time, they are quite ready to believe that He suffered all that men are wont to suffer, because they wish Him to be held to be a man and nothing more. According to this, then, He was led like a sheep to the slaughter; He was numbered with the transgressors; He was wounded for our sins; by His stripes were we

healed; His face was marred, and little esteemed, and smitten with the palms and defiled with the spittle; His position was disfigured on the cross; He was led to death by the iniquities of the people Israel; He is the man who had no form nor comeliness when He was buffeted with the fists, when He was crowned with the thorns, He was derided as He hung (upon the tree); He is the man who, as the lamb is dumb before its shearer, opened not His mouth, when it was said to Him by those who mocked Him, "Prophesy to us, thou Christ."[43] Now, however, He is exalted verily, now He is honoured exceedingly; truly many nations are now astonied at Him.[44] Now the kings have shut their mouth, by which they were wont to promulgate the most ruthless laws against the Christians. Truly those now see to whom it was not told of Him, and those who have not heard understand.[45] For those Gentile nations to whom the prophets made no announcement, do now rather see for themselves how true these things are which were of old reported by the prophets; and those who have not heard Isaiah speak in his own proper person, now understand from his writings the things which he spoke concerning Him. For even in the said nation of the Jews, who believed that report of the prophets, or to whom was that arm of the Lord revealed, which is this very Christ who was announced by them,[46] seeing that by their own hands they perpetrated those crimes against Christ, the commission of which had been predicted by the prophets whom they possessed? But now, indeed He possesses many by inheritance; and He divides the spoils of the strong, since the devil and the demons have now been cast out and given up, and the possessions once held by them have been distributed by Him among the fabrics of His churches and for other necessary services.

Chapter XXXII

What, then, do these men, who are at once the perverse applauders of Christ and the slanderers of Christians, say to these facts? Can it be that Christ, by the use of magical arts, caused those predictions to be uttered so long ago by the

172

prophets? or have His disciples invented them? Is it thus that the Chuch, in her extension among the Gentile nations, though once barren, has been made to rejoice now in the possession of more children than that synagogue had which, in its Law or its King, had received, as it were, a husband? or is it thus that this Church has been led to enlarge the place of her tent, and to occupy all nations and tongues, so that now she lengthens her cords beyond the limits to which the rights of the empire of Rome extend, yea, even on to the territories of the Persians and the Indians and other barbarous nations? or that, on the right hand by means of true Christians, and on the left hand by means of pretended Christians, His name is being made known among such a multitude of peoples? or that His seed is made to inherit the Gentiles, so as now to inhabit cities which had been left desolate of the true worship of God and the true religion? or that His Church has been so little daunted by the threats and furies of men, even at times when she has been covered with the blood of martyrs, like one clad in purple array, that she has prevailed over persecutors at once so numerous, so violent, and so powerful? or that she has not been confounded, like one put to shame, when it was a great crime to be or to become a Christian? or that she is made to forget her confusion for ever, because, where sin had abounded, grace did much more abound? or that she is taught not to remember the shame of her widowhood, because only for a little was she forsaken and subjected to opprobrium, while now she shines forth once more with such eminent glory? or, in fine, is it only a fiction concocted by Christ's disciples, that the Lord who made her, and brought her forth from the denomination of the devil and the demons, the very God of Israel is now called the God of the whole earth; all which, nevertheless, the prophets, whose books are now in the hands of the enemies of Christ, foretold so long before Christ became the Son of man?

173   From this, therefore, let them understand that the matter is not left obscure or doubtful even to the slowest and dullest minds: from this, I say, let these perverse applauders of Christ and execrators of the Christian religion understand that the disciples of Christ have learned and taught, in opposition to

their gods, precisely what the doctrine of Christ contains. For the God of Israel is found to have enjoined in the books of the prophets that all these objects which those men are minded to worship should be held in abomination and be destroyed, while He Himself is now named the God of the whole earth, through the instrumentality of Christ and the Church of Christ, exactly as He promised so long time ago. For if, indeed, in their marvellous folly, they fancy that Christ worshipped their gods, and that it was only through them that He had power to do things so great as these, we may well ask whether the God of Israel also worshipped their gods, who has now fulfilled by Christ what He promised with respect to the extension of His own worship through all the nations, and with respect to the detestation and subversion of those other deities?[48] Where are their gods? Where are the vaticinations of their fanatics, and the divination of their prophets? Where are the auguries, or the auspices, or the soothsayings, or the oracles of demons? Why is it that, out of the ancient books which constitute the records of this type of religion, nothing in the form either admonition or of prediction is advanced to oppose the Christian faith, or to controvert the truth of those prophets of ours, who have now come to be so well understood among all nations? "We have offended our gods," they say in reply, "and they have deserted us for that reason: that explains it also why the Christians have prevailed against us, and why the bliss of human life, exhausted and impaired, goes to wreck among us." We challenge them, however, to take the books of their own seers, and read out to us any statement purporting that the kind of issue which has come upon them would be brought on them by the Christians: nay, we challenge them to recite any passages in which, if not Christ (for they wish to make Him out to have been a worshipper of their own gods), at least this God of Israel, who is allowed to be the subverter of other deities is held up as a deity destined to be rejected and worthy of detestation. But never will they produce any such passage, unless, perchance, it be some fabrication of their own. And if ever they do cite any such statement, the fact that it is but a fiction of their own will betray itself in the unnoticeable manner in which a matter of so grave importance is found adduced; whereas, in good truth, before what has been predicted should have come to pass, it behoved to have been proclaimed in the temples of the gods of all nations, with a view to the timeous preparation and warning of all who are now minded to be Christians.

Chapter XXXIII

174   Finally, as to the complaint which they make with respect to the impairing of the bliss of human life by the entrance of Christian times, if they only peruse the books of their own philosophers, who reprehend those very things which are now being taken out of their way in spite of all their unwillingness and murmuring, they will indeed find that great praise is due to the times of Christ. For what diminution is made in their happiness, unless it be in what they most basely and luxuriously abused, to the great injury of their Creator? or unless, perchance, it be the case that evil times originate in such circumstances as these, in which throughout almost all states the theatres are falling, and with them, too, the dens of vice and the public profession of iniquity: yea, altogether the forums and cities in which the demons used to be worshipped are falling. How comes it, then, that they are falling, unless it be in consequence of the failure of those very things, in the lustful and sacrilegious use of which they were constructed? Did not their own Cicero, when commending a certain actor of the name of Roscius, call him a man so clever as to be the only one worthy enough to make it due for him to come upon the stage; and yet, again, so good a man as to be the only one so worthy as to make it due for him not to approach it? What else did he disclose with such remarkable clearness by this saying, but the fact that the stage was so base there, that a person was under the greater obligation not to connect himself with it, in proportion as he was a better man than most? And yet their gods were pleased with such things of shame as he deemed fit only to be removed to a distance from good men. But we have also an open confession of the same Cicero, where he says that he had to appease Flora, the

mother of sports, by frequent celebration; in which sports such an excess of vice is wont to be exhibited, that, in comparison with them, others are respectable, from engaging in which, nevertheless, good men are prohibited. Who is this mother Flora, and what manner of goddess is she, who is thus conciliated and propitiated by a practice of vice indulged in with more than usual frequency and with looser reins? How much more honourable now was it for a Roscius to step upon the stage, than for a Cicero to worship a goddess of this kind! If the gods of the Gentile nations are offended because the supplies are lessened which are instituted for the purpose of such celebrations, it is apparent of what character those must be who are delighted with such things. But if, on the other hand, the gods themselves in their wrath diminish these supplies, their anger yields us better services than their placability. Wherefore let these men either confute their own philosophers, who have reprehended the same practices on the side of wanton men; or else let them break in pieces those gods of theirs who have made such demands upon their worshippers, if indeed they still find any such deities either to break in pieces or to conceal. But let them cease from their blasphemous habit of charging Christian times with the failure of their true prosperity,—a prosperity, indeed, so used by them that they were sinking into all that is base and hurtful,—lest thereby they be only putting us all the more emphatically in mind of reasons for the ampler praise of the power of Christ.

Chapter XXXIV

Much more might I say on this subject, were it not that the requirements of the task which I have undertaken compel me to conclude this book, and revert to the object originally proposed. When, indeed, I took it in hand to solve those problems of the Gospels which meet us where the four evangelists, as it seems to certain critics, fail to harmonize with each other, by setting forth to the best of my ability the particular designs which they severally have in view, I was met first by the necessity of discussing a question which some are accus-

175

tomed to bring before us,—the question, namely, as to the reason why we cannot produce any writings composed by Christ Himself. For their aim is to get Him credited with the writing of some other composition, I know not of what sort, which may be suitable to their inclinations, and with having indulged in no sentiments of antagonism to their gods, but rather with having paid respect to them in a kind of magical worship; and their wish is also to get it believed that His disciples not only gave a false account of Him when they declared Him to be the God by whom all things were made, while He was really nothing more than a man, although certainly a man of the most exalted wisdom, but also that they taught with regard to these gods of theirs something different from what they had themselves learned from Him. This is how it happens that we have been engaged preferentially in pressing them with arguments concerning the God of Israel, who is now worshipped by all nations through the medium of the Church of the Christians, who is also subverting their sacrilegious vanities the whole world over, exactly as He announced by the mouth of the prophets so long ago, and who has now fulfilled those predictions by the name of Christ, in whom He had promised that all nations should be blessed. And from all this they ought to understand that Christ could neither have known nor taught anything else with regard to their gods than what was enjoined and foretold by the God of Israel through the agency of these prophets of His by whom He promised, and ultimately sent, this very Christ, in whose name, according to the promise given to the fathers, when all nations were pronounced blessed, it has come to pass that this same God of Israel should be called the God of the whole earth. By this, too, they ought to see that His disciples did not depart from the doctrine of their Master when they forbade the worship of the gods of the Gentiles, with the view of preventing us from addressing our supplications to insensate images, or from having fellowship with demons, or from serving the creature rather than the Creator with the homage of religious worship.

Chapter XXXV

Wherefore, seeing that Christ Himself is that Wisdom of   176
God by whom all things were created, and considering that
no rational intelligence, whether of angels or of men, receive
wisdom except by participation in this Wisdom wherewith we
are united by that Holy Spirit through whom charity is shed
abroad in our hearts[49] (which Trinity at the same time constitutes one God), Divine Providence, having respect to the
interests of mortal men whose time-bound life was held
engaged in things which rise into being and die, decreed that
this same Wisdom of God, assuming into the unity of His
person the (nature of) man, in which He might be born according to the conditions of time, and live and die and rise again,
should utter and perform and bear and sustain things congruous to our salvation; and thus, in exemplary fashion, show at
once to men on earth the way for a return to heaven, and to
those angels who are above us, the way to retain their position
in heaven. For unless, also, in the nature of the reasonable
soul, and under the conditions of an existence in time,
something came newly into being,—that is to say, unless that
began to be which previously was not,—there could never be
any passing from a life of utter corruption and folly into one
of wisdom and true goodness. And thus, as truth in the
contemplative lives in the enjoyment of things eternal, while
faith in the believing is what is due to things which are made,
man is purified through that faith which is conversant with
temporal things, in order to his being made capable of
receiving the truth of things eternal. For one of their noblest
intellects, the philosopher Plato, in the treatise which is
named the *Timaeus*, speaks also to this effect: "As eternity
is to that which is made, so truth to faith." Those two belong
to the things above,—namely, eternity and truth; these two
belong to the things below,—namely, that which is made and
faith. In order, therefore, that we may be called off from the
lowest objects, and led up again to the highest, and in order
also that what is made may attain to the eternal, we must

come through faith to truth. And because all contraries are reduced to unity by some middle factor, and because also the iniquity of time alienated us from the righteousness of eternity, there was need of some mediatorial righteousness of a temporal nature; which mediatizing factor might be temporal on the side of those lowest objects, but also righteous on the side of these highest, and thus, by adapting itself to the former without cutting itself off from the latter, might bring back those lowest objects to the highest. Accordingly, Christ was named the Mediator between God and men, who stood between the immortal God and mortal man, as being Himself both God and man,[50] who reconciled man to God, who continued to be what He (formerly) was, but was made also what He (formerly) was not. And the same Person is for us at once the (centre of the) said faith in things that are made, and the truth in things eternal.

177   This great and unutterable mystery, this kingdom and priesthood, was revealed by prophecy to the men of ancient time, and is now preached by the gospel to their descendants. For it behoved that, at some period or other, that should be made good among all nations which for a long time had been promised through the medium of a single nation. Accordingly, He who sent the prophets before His own descent also despatched the apostles after His ascension. Moreover, in virtue of the man assumed by Him, He stands to all His disciples in the relation of the head to the members of His body. Therefore, when those disciples have written matters which He declared and spake to them, it ought not by any means to be said that He has written nothing Himself; since the truth is, that His members have accomplished only what they became acquainted with by the repeated statements of the Head. For all that He was minded to give for our perusal on the subject of His own doings and sayings, He commanded to be written by those disciples, whom He thus used as if they were His own hands. Whoever apprehends this correspondence of unity and this concordant service of the members, all in harmony in the discharge of diverse offices under the Head, will receive the account which he gets in the Gospel through the narratives constructed by the disciples, in the

same kind of spirit in which he might look upon the actual hand of the Lord Himself, which He bore in that body which was made His own, were he to see it engaged in the act of writing. For this reason let us now rather proceed to examine into the real character of those passages in which these critics suppose the evangelists to have given contradictory accounts (a thing which only those who fail to understand the matter aright can fancy to be the case); so that, when these problems are solved, it may also be made apparent that the members in that body have preserved a befitting harmony in the unity of the body itself, not only by identity in sentiment, but also by constructing records consonant with that identity.

Vincent of Lerins
Commonitorium, II 4—III 8
434 A.D.

I have often inquired most earnestly and attentively from very many experts in sanctity and learning, how, and by what definite and, as it were, universal rule I might distinguish the truth of the Catholic Faith from the falsity of heretical perversion; and I have always received an answer of this kind from almost all of them, namely, that whether I, or any one else, wished to detect the frauds of newly rising heretics and to avoid their snares, and to remain sound and whole in the sound faith, one ought, with the Lord's help, to fortify one's faith in a twofold manner: first, by the authority of the Divine Law, and secondly, by the tradition of the Catholic Church.

179   Here perhaps some one will ask, Since the canon of Scripture is complete and is in itself sufficient, and more than sufficient on all points, what need is there to join to it the authority of ecclesiastical interpretation? The answer of course is that, owing to the very depth of holy Scripture itself, all do not receive it in one and the same sense; but one in one way and another in another interprets the declarations of the same writer, so that it seems possible to elicit from it as many opinions as there are men. For Novatian expounds it one way, Photinus another, Sabellius another, Donatus another, Arius, Eunomius, and Macedonius another, Apollinarius and Priscillian another, Jovinian, Pelagius, and Celestius another, and quite lately Nestorius another. Whence it is most necessary, on account of the great intricacies of such

various errors, that the rule for the interpretation of the
Prophets and Apostles should be laid down in accordance
with the standard of the ecclesiastical and Catholic understanding of them.

Also in the Catholic Church itself we take great care that   180
we hold that which has been believed everywhere, always, by
all. For that is truly and properly "Catholic", as the very

how, which comprehends
we shall observe this rule
, consent. We shall follow
Faith to be true which the
rld confesses; antiquity if
interpretations which it is
thers proclaimed; consent
ollow the definitions and
priests and doctors alike.

hristian do if any part of   181
n the communion of the
refer the soundness of the
pt member?

seek to infect the whole   182
ortion of it? Then he will
which cannot now be led

be detected on the part of   183
ity, or even of a province?
r the decrees of an ancient
he rashness and ignorance

concerning which nothing   184
he must take pains to find
the ancients, provided, of
communion and faith of
gh they lived in different
times and places, conspicuous and approved teachers; and
whatever he shall find to have been held, written, and taught,
not by one or two only, but by all equally and with one consent, openly, frequently and persistently, that he must understand is to be believed by himself also without the slightest
hesitation.

XIV

In the thirteenth place comes their assertion that the whole body of the canonical Scriptures is to be accepted, under the names of the patriarchs: because those twelve virtues which work the reformation of the inner man are pointed out in their names, and without this knowledge no soul can effect its reformation, and return to that substance from which it came forth. But this wicked delusion the Christian wisdom holds in disdain, for it knows that the nature of the true Godhead is inviolable and immutable: but the soul, whether living in the body or separated from the body, is subject to many passions: whereas, of course, if it were part of the divine essence, no adversity could happen to it. And therefore there is no comparison between them: One is the Creator, the other is the creature. For He is always the same, and suffers no change: but the soul is changeable, even if not changed, because its power of not changing is a gift, and not a property.

XV

186   14. Under the fourteenth heading their sentiments upon the state of the body are stated, viz., that it is, on account of its earthly properties, held under the power of stars and con-

various errors, that the rule for the interpretation of the Prophets and Apostles should be laid down in accordance with the standard of the ecclesiastical and Catholic understanding of them.

Also in the Catholic Church itself we take great care that   180
we hold that which has been believed everywhere, always, by all. For that is truly and properly "Catholic", as the very force and meaning of the word show, which comprehends everything almost universally. And we shall observe this rule if we follow universality, antiquity, consent. We shall follow universality if we confess that one Faith to be true which the whole Church throughout the world confesses; antiquity if we in no wise depart from those interpretations which it is plain that our holy ancestors and fathers proclaimed; consent if in antiquity itself we eagerly follow the definitions and beliefs of all, or certainly nearly all, priests and doctors alike.

What, then, will the Catholic Christian do if any part of   181
the Church has cut itself off from the communion of the universal Faith? What surely but prefer the soundness of the whole body to a pestilent and corrupt member?

What if some novel contagion seek to infect the whole   182
Church, and not merely a small portion of it? Then he will take care to cling to antiquity, which cannot now be led astray by any novel deceit.

What if in antiquity itself error be detected on the part of   183
two or three men, or perhaps of a city, or even of a province? Then he will look to it that he prefer the decrees of an ancient general council, if such there be to the rashness and ignorance of a few.

But what if some error spring up concerning which nothing   184
of this kind is to be found? Then he must take pains to find out and compare the opinions of the ancients, provided, of course, that such remained in the communion and faith of the One Catholic Church, although they lived in different times and places, conspicuous and approved teachers; and whatever he shall find to have been held, written, and taught, not by one or two only, but by all equally and with one consent, openly, frequently and persistently, that he must understand is to be believed by himself also without the slightest hesitation.

Pope Leo I
Letter XV to Turribius
447 A.D.

XIV

In the thirteenth place comes their assertion that the whole body of the canonical Scriptures is to be accepted, under the names of the patriarchs: because those twelve virtues which work the reformation of the inner man are pointed out in their names, and without this knowledge no soul can effect its reformation, and return to that substance from which it came forth. But this wicked delusion the Christian wisdom holds in disdain, for it knows that the nature of the true Godhead is inviolable and immutable: but the soul, whether living in the body or separated from the body, is subject to many passions: whereas, of course, if it were part of the divine essence, no adversity could happen to it. And therefore there is no comparison between them: One is the Creator, the other is the creature. For He is always the same, and suffers no change: but the soul is changeable, even if not changed, because its power of not changing is a gift, and not a property.

XV

186   14. Under the fourteenth heading their sentiments upon the state of the body are stated, viz., that it is, on account of its earthly properties, held under the power of stars and con-

stellations, and that many things are found in the holy books which have reference to the outer man with this object, that in the Scriptures themselves a certain opposition may be seen at work between the divine and the earthly nature: and that that which the powers that rule the soul claim for themselves may be distinguished from that which the fashioners of the body claim. These stories are invented that the soul may be maintained to be part of the divine substance, and the flesh believed to belong to the bad nature: since the world itself, with its elements, they hold to be not the work of the good God, but the outcome of an evil author: and that they might disguise these sacrilegious lies under a fair cloak, they have polluted almost all the divine utterances with the colouring of their unholy notions.

XVI

15. And on this subject your remarks under the fifteenth head make a complaint, and express a well-deserved abhorrence of their devilish presumption, for we too have ascertained this from the accounts of trustworthy witnesses, and have found many of their copies most corrupt, though they are entitled canonical. For how could they deceive the simple-minded unless they sweetened their poisoned cups with a little honey, lest what was meant to be deadly should be detected by its over-nastiness? Therefore care must be taken, and the priestly diligence exercised to the uttermost, to prevent falsified copies that are out of harmony with the pure Truth being used in reading. And the apocryphal scriptures, which, under the names of Apostles, form a nursery-ground for many falsehoods, are not only to be proscribed, but also taken away altogether and burnt to ashes in the fire. For although there are certain things in them which seem to have a show of piety, yet they are never free from poison, and through the allurements of their stories they have the secret effect of first beguiling men with miraculous narratives, and then catching them in the noose of some error. Wherefore if any bishop has either not forbidden the possession of apocryphal writings in men's houses, or under the name of being

187

canonical has suffered those copies to be read in church which are vitiated with the spurious alterations of Priscillian, let him know that he is to be accounted heretic, since he who does not reclaim others from error shows that he himself has gone astray.

Pope Gregory I
Morals on the Book of Job (Excerpt)
c. 585 A.D.

Book XX

Although all knowledge and all lore Sacred Scripture without all comparison far excels, to say nothing that it tells forth what is true; that it bids to the heavenly country; that it changes the heart of him that reads it from earthly desires to the embracing of things Above; that by its obscurer statements it exercises the strong, and by its humble strain speaks gently to the little ones; that it is neither so shut up, that it should come to be dreaded, nor so open to view as to become contemptible; that by use it removes weariness, and is the more delighted in the more it is meditated on; that the mind of him, who reads it, by words of a low pitch it assists, and by meanings of a lofty flight uplifts; that in some sort it grows with the persons reading, that by uninstructed readers it is in a manner reviewed, and yet by the well instructed is always found new; so then to say nothing of the weightiness of the subjects, it goes beyond all forms of knowledge and teaching even by the mere manner of its style of speaking, because in one and the same thread of discourse, while it relates the text, it declares a mystery, and has the art so to tell the past, that merely by that alone it knows how to announce the future, and the order of telling remaining unaltered, is instructed by the very self-same forms of speech at once to describe things done before, and to tell things destined to be done, just as it is with these same words of blessed Job, who while he tells his own circumstances foretels ours, and while he points out his own sorrows in respect of the phrase, sounds of the cases and occasions of Holy Church in respect of the meaning.

Pope Gregory I
Letter to Leander (Excerpt)
594 A.D.

The expounder of Holy Scripture ought to be like a river, for if the stream flowing along in its bed should on its flanks come into contact with curving valleys, it at once turns into them its powerful current, and when it has filled them full, it suddenly pours back again into its channel. That is how, certainly, the expounder of the divine Word should be, so that when he discusses any topic, if perchance he finds an opportunity presented to him suitable for edification, he may turn the streams of his eloquence into it as if it were a nearby valley, and when he has poured over this adjacent field of instruction, he may fall back into the channel of speech he had originally set before him.

3. You must know, however, that we run over some topics in historical exposition, and in some we search for allegorical meaning in our examination of types; in still others we discuss morality but through the allegorical method; and in several instances we carefully make an attempt to apply all three methods. In the first instance we lay the historical foundation; in the second, through the typological sense we erect a structure of the mind to be a citadel of faith; finally, through the grace of moral instruction, we clothe the edifice, as it were, with a coat of color. What must one really believe the words of truth to be but food taken for the refreshment[23] of the mind? When we discuss these topics in various methods, changing them often, we set a feast before the mouth, in such

190

a way as to eliminate distaste from our reader who, dining like a banqueter, scrutinizes what is offered him and takes what he sees is more palatable.

191   But at times we neglect to expound the obvious words of the narrative so as not to reach too late the obscure meanings. At times they cannot be understood literally because, when the obvious meaning is taken, they engender in the readers, not instruction, but error. For see what is said: "Under whom those who carry the world are bowed down."[24] Who would not know that so great a man as Job is not following the empty tales of the poets so as to view the great bulk of the world as borne aloft on the sweat of a giant?[25] Again, struck by calamities, he says: "My soul has chosen hanging and my bones death."[26] Who in his right mind would believe that a man of such great fame, who, of course, as all agree, received from the eternal Judge rewards in proportion to the virtue of his patience, had determined in the midst of his afflictions to end his life by hanging? In some instances, also, the words themselves militate against the possibility of their literal interpretation. For he says, "Let the day perish on which I was born and the night on which it was said, 'A man has been conceived.' "[27] And a little later he adds, "Let the darkness seize it and let it be covered over with bitterness."[28] And as a curse for the same night he adds, "Let that night be unique."[29] Surely this day of his birth, rolling round in the onrush of time itself, could not stand still. How, then, could it have become veiled in darkness? Having passed away, of course, it no longer existed, nor yet if, in the nature of creation, it still were to exist, could it feel bitterness. It is clear, then, that he is not speaking at all of an insensate day when he wishes it to be struck by a sense of bitterness. And if the night of his conception had passed away like other nights, how could he wish that it be unique? As from the lapse of time, it could not now be fixed, so also it could not be separated from contact with the other nights. Again he says, "How long wilt thou not spare me nor let me go until I swallow my spittle?"[30] And yet a little while before he had said, "My soul was hitherto unwilling to touch them, and now from necessity they are my food."[31] Who does not know

that spittle is more easily swallowed than food? Since he says
he is taking food, it is absolutely unbelievable that he cannot swallow spittle. Another time he says, "I have sinned;
what shall I do to thee, thou guardian of men?"[32] And
surely, "Thou wantest me to consume the iniquities of my
youth,"[33] And in another reply he adds, "My heart shall
not reproach me throughout my whole life."[34] How, then, is
he not reproached by his heart throughout his whole life
when he openly testifies that he has sinned? For never do
guilt of deed and irreproachability of heart coincide in the
same man. But surely the literal sense of the words, when
they are compared, cannot be made to agree, and it shows
that something different should be sought in them, as if the
words were explicitly to say, "Though you see that we, in so
far as our obvious meaning is concerned, are destroyed,
nevertheless seek in us something logical and consistent that
may be found to reside in us."

4. At time, however, he who fails to take the words of   192
the story in a literal sense hides the light of truth that has
been offered to him, and when he labors to find in them
some other inner meaning, he loses what he could easily have
arrived at on the surface. For the holy man says, "If I have
denied to the poor what they desired, or have made the eyes
of the widow to wait; if I have eaten my morsel alone, and
the orphan has not eaten of it; . . . if I have seen anyone per-
ishing because he had no clothing, or a poor man without
covering; if his loins have not blessed me, and if he was not
warmed with the fleece of my sheep . . ."[35] If we forcibly
twist such a passage into an allegorical sense, we make all
these deeds of mercy to be as naught. For as the divine Word
stimulates the wise with mysteries, so it often kindles the
simple with an obvious statement. It holds in the open the
means of feeding children, but keeps in secret the means of
causing souls to hang upon the adoration of the sublime. Indeed, it is, as I said, like a river, shallow and deep, in which a
lamb may walk and an elephant may swim. As therefore the
opportunity of each and every passage demands, so the
course of exposition is studiously changed. In order that it

may the more truly discover the sense of the divine Word, as each topic demands, it varies according to the case.

193   5. This exposition, then, I have transmitted to your beatitude for revision, not because I owed it to you as something worthy of you, but because I remember that when you asked for it, I promised it. Whatever in it your holiness may find mediocre or unpolished, may you as quickly grant me your pardon as you do not overlook the fact that I speak poorly. For when the body is worn with trouble, so when the mind is afflicted, eagerness for speaking grows dull. Now many years have rolled round in their courses since I began to be tortured by frequent pains of the flesh, and each hour and each moment I grow faint with lack of good digestion,[36] and I breathe with difficulty under mild yet constant fevers.

194   Meanwhile, I give serious attention to the saying in the Scripture, "Everyone who is received by God is beaten,"[37] and the harder I am pressed by these present evils, so the more certainly do I breathe with anticipation of the eternal. And perhaps it was the design of divine providence that, afflicted thus, I should expound Job who was also thus afflicted, and that I should, under the lash, the better understand the mind of the one who was also lashed. Nevertheless, it is clear to those who rightly think about it that weariness of the flesh is no small obstacle to my enthusiasm for my work, in that when the power of the flesh scarcely is sufficient for the function of speaking, the mind cannot express its feelings in proper fashion. For what is the duty of the body except to serve as the instrument of the heart? And no matter how skilled a man may be in the art of singing, he cannot realize the fulfillment of this art unless for this purpose his external functions are in harmony, because the instruments, when shaken, do not give forth the song in proper tones, nor does the breath produce an artistic sound if the reed rattles when it is split. How much more seriously impaired is the quality of my exposition in which the broken instrument diminishes the grace of rhetoric so that it contains no artistic skill? When you run through the pages of this work, please do not look for literary nosegays, because in expounders of Holy Writ the lightness of fruitless verbosity is

carefully repressed, and since the planting of a grove in God's temple is forbidden.[38] And we are all clearly aware that as often as the tops of the grain stalks luxuriate into undesirable leafage, the heads of the grain do not fill out so well. This is why I have foreborne to employ the very art of rhetoric which the examples of superficial learning teach. For as the sense of this letter proclaims, I do not flee from the collision of metacism,[39] I do not avoid the confusion of a barbarism, and I disdain to preserve the rules of position and order[40] and the cases of prepositions, because I consider it very unbecoming that I should tie down the words of the heavenly oracles to the rules of Donatus.[41] No precedent of the translators of sacred Scripture requires these rules to be observed by any exegetes. Because our exposition takes its origin surely from this authority, it is surely proper for that which issues forth like a shoot to model itself on the appearance of its mother. I am using here, however, the new translation,[42] but as the necessity of proof demands, I take now the new, now the old, so that, because the Apostolic See, over which, with God's design, I preside, uses both, the labor of my study may be supported by both.

Pope Gregory I
Letter to Theodorus, Physician to the Emperor
595 A.D.

Letter XXXI (Excerpt)

For what is sacred Scripture but a kind of epistle of Almighty God to His creature? And surely, if your Glory were resident in any other place, and were to receive letters from an earthly emperor, you would not loiter, you would not rest, you would not give sleep to your eyes, till you had learnt what the earthly emperor had written.

196   The Emperor of Heaven, the Lord of men and angels, has sent thee his epistles for thy life's behoof; and yet, glorious son, thou neglectest to read these epistles ardently. Study then, I beseech thee, and daily meditate on the words of thy Creator. Learn the heart of God in the words of God, that thou mayest sigh more ardently for the things that are eternal, that your soul may be kindled with greater longings for heavenly joys. For a man will have the greater rest here in proportion as he has now no rest in the love of his Maker. But, that you may act thus, may Almighty God pour into you the Spirit the Comfortor: may He fill your soul with His presence, and in filling it, compose it.

Isidore
Etymologies, Book VI (Excerpts)
630 A.D.

Chapter 1

The Old Testament is so-called because when the New came it was at an end, of which the Apostle speaks: Vetera transierunt, et ecce facta sunt omnia nova.

2. The New Testament is so-called because it brings in the new. For men do not learn it, except those renewed from their former state through grace and now belonging to the New Testament, which is the kingdom of heaven.

3. The Hebrews accept on Esdras' authority twenty-two books of the Old Testament, according to the number of their letters, dividing them into three series, namely, the Law, the Prophets, and the Hagiographi.

4. The first series of the Law is accepted in five books, of which the first is Beresith, which is Genesis; the second, Veele Samoth, which is Exodus; the third, Vaicra, which is Leviticus; the fourth, Vajedabber, which is Numbers; the fifth, Elleaddebarium, which is Deuteronomy.

6. The second series is that of the Prophets, in which eight books are contained, of which the first is Josue Ben-Nun, which in Latin is called Jesu Nave; the second, Sophtin, which is Judges; the third, Samuel, which is the first of Kings; the fourth, Malachim, which is the second of Kings; the fifth, Isaias; the sixth, Jeremias; the seventh, Ezechiel; the eighth, Thereazer, which is called 'Of the Twelve Prophets,' which

198

199

200

201

books are taken as one since they are placed together on account of their brevity.

202   7. The third is the series of the Hagiographi, that is, those who write what is holy, in which are nine books, of which the first is Job; the second, the Psalms; the third, Misse, which is the Proberbs of Solomon; the fourth, Coheleth, which is Ecclesiastes; the fifth, Sir Hassirim, which is the Song of Songs; the sixth, Daniel; the seventh, Dibrehajamin, which is Verba dierum, *i. e.*, Paralipomenon (Chronicles); the eighth, Esdras; the ninth, Esther. And all of these together, five, eight, and nine, make twenty-two just as they were inclusively given above.

203   8. Certain add Ruth and Cinoth, which in the Latin is Lamentatio Jeremiae, to the hagiographa and make twenty-four volumes of the Old Testament, like the twenty-four elders who stand in the sight of the Lord.

204   9. There is with us a fourth series consisting of those books of the Old Testament which are not in the Hebrew canon. Of which the first is the book of Wisdom (Sapientiae); the second, Ecclesiasticus; the third, Thobias; the fourth, Judith; the fifth and sixth, of the Machabees. Although the Jews set these aside as apocryphal, still the church of Christ honors and preaches them among the divine books.

205   10. In the New Testament are two series: first the Ēvangelic, in which are Matthew, Mark, Luke and John; second, the apostolic, in which are Paul in fourteen epistles, Peter in two, John in three, James and Jude in one each, the Acts of the Apostles and the Apocalypse of John.

206   11. Moreover the whole of each Testament is triply divided, that is, into history, morals, and allegory. Again those three have many divisions, for example, what was done and said by God, what by the angels, or by men, what was foretold by the prophets of Christ and his body; what of the devil and his members; what of the old and the new people; what of the present age, and the coming kingdom, and the judgment.

Chapter 2

1. These are said to be the authors of the Old Testament   **207**
according to the Hebrew tradition. First Moses wrote a cos-
mography of divine history in five volumes, which is named
Pentateuch.

8. The book of Josue received its name from Jesus, son of   **208**
Nave, whose history it contains, and the Hebrews assert that
the name Josue was its writer, in the text of which, after the
crossing of the Jordan, the kingdoms of the enemy are overthrown and the land divided among the people, and by the
separate cities, villages, mountains and boundaries the spiritual realms of the church and the heavenly Jerusalem are prefigured.

18. Solomon, son of David, king of Israel, wrote three vol-   **209**
umes according to the number of his names, of which the
first is in Hebrew, Misle, which the Greeks name Parabolae,
the Latins, Proverbia, because in it he sets forth figurative
expressions and likenesses of the truth under the form of a
parallel.

19. The truth itself he has reserved to its readers to under-   **210**
stand. The second book is called Coheleth, which in the
Greek is Ecclesiastes, in Latin, Concionator, because its discourse is not especially addressed to one, as in Proverbs, but
generally to all, teaching that all things which we see in the
universe are perishable and short-lived, and for this reason
little to be desired.

20. The third book he called Sir Hassirim, which is trans-   **211**
lated Cantica Canticorum in the Latin, where in a marriage
song he sings in mystic fashion the union of Christ and the
church. . . .

21. The songs in these three books are said to be written   **212**
in hexameter and pentameter verse as Josephus and Hiero-
nymus say.

40. These are the four Evangelists whom the holy spirit   **213**
indicated in Ezechiel in the four animals. And there are four

animals, because the faith of the Christian religion is spread by their preaching through the four quarters of the world.

214   41. And they were called animals (*animalia*) because the Gospel of Christ is preached by them on account of the soul (*anima*) of man. And they were full of eyes within and without, since they perceive that what was said by the prophets and what had been promised was being fulfilled.

215   42. And their legs were straight because there is nothing crooked in the Gospels. And as for the six wings apiece that cover their legs and faces, those things which were hid are revealed at the coming of Christ.

216   50. These are the writers of the sacred books who, speaking by the holy spirit for our edification, wrote both the precepts of living and the rule for believing.

217   51. In addition to these there are other volumes called apocrypha, and they are called apocrypha, that is, set aside, because they are doubted. For their origin is hidden and was not clear to the Fathers from whom the authority of the genuine scriptures has come down to us by a most certain and well-known tradition. In these apocrypha, although some truth is found, there is no canonic authority, on account of the many things that are false, and it is rightly judged by the wise that they ought not to be believed [to be the work] of those to whom they are ascribed.

218   52. For many [works] were brought forward by the heretics under the name of the prophets, and many of later origin under the name of the apostles, and of all those after careful examination were separated from the authority of the canon, under the name of apocrypha.

Chapter 4

219   1. This man [Ptolemy Philadelphus] asked Eleazer the high-priest for the Scriptures of the Old Testament, and had them translated from Hebrew into Greek by seventy translators, and kept them in the library of Alexandria.

220   2. Being placed separately in separate cells they so translated all, by the influence of the holy spirit, that nothing was

found in the text of any one of them, that was different in the rest, even in the order of the words.

5. The priest, Jerome, being expert in the three languages, translated the Scriptures also from Hebrew into Latin and expressed them with eloquence, and his translation is rightly preferred to the rest. For it is nearer to the literal, and plainer because of the clearness of its expression, and truer, as being done by a Christian translator.

221

John Damascene
On the Orthodox Faith: Book Four
745 A.D.

Chapter 17

The God proclaimed by the Old Testament and the New is one, He who is celebrated and glorified in Trinity, for the Lord said: 'I am not come to destroy the law, but to fulfil.'[1] For He worked our salvation, for the sake of which all Scripture and every mystery has been revealed. And again: 'Search the scriptures: for these give testimony of me.'[2] And the Apostle too, says: 'God, who, at sundry times and in diverse manners, spoke in times past to the fathers by prophets, last of all, in these days, hath spoken to us by his Son.'[3] Through the Holy Ghost, then, both the Law and the Prophets, the evangelists, apostles, pastors, and teachers spoke.

223   Therefore, 'all scripture, inspired of God, is quite profitable.'[4] so that to search the sacred Scripture is very good and most profitable for the soul. For, 'like a tree which is planted near the running waters,'[5] so does the soul watered by sacred Scripture also grow fat and bear fruit in due season, which is the orthodox faith, and so is it adorned with its evergreen leaves, with actions pleasing to God, I mean. And thus we are disposed to virtuous action and untroubled contemplation by the sacred Scriptures. In them we find exhortation to every virtue and dissuasion from every vice. Therefore, if we are eager for knowledge, we shall also be rich in knowledge, for by diligence, toil, and the grace of God who grants it all things

succeed. 'For he that asketh receiveth: and he that seeketh findeth: and to him that knocketh it shall be opened.'[6] So let us knock at the very beautiful paradise of the Scriptures, the fragrant, most sweet and lovely paradise which fills our ears with the varied songs of inspired spiritual birds, which touches our heart, comforting it when grieving, calming it when angry, and filling it with everlasting joy, and which lifts our mind onto the back of the sacred dove, gleaming with gold and most brilliant,[7] who bears us with his most bright wings to the only-begotten Son and heir of the Husbandman of the spiritual vineyard and through Him on to the Father of lights. Let us not knock casually, but with eagerness and persistence, and let us not lose heart while knocking, for so it will be opened to us. Should we read once and then a second time and still not understand what we are reading, let us not be discouraged. Rather, let us persist, let us meditate and inquire, for it is written: 'Ask thy father, and he will declare to thee: thy elders and they will tell thee.'[8] For not all have knowledge.[9] From the fountain of paradise let us draw everflowing and most pure waters springing up into life everlasting.[10] Let us revel in them, let us revel greedily in them to satiety, for they contain the grace which cannot be exhausted. Should we, however, be able to get some profit from other sources, this is not forbidden. Let us be proved bankers and amass the genuine and pure gold, while we reject the spurious. Let us accept the best sayings, but let us throw to the dogs the ridiculous gods and unhealthy fables, for from the former we should be able to draw very great strength against the latter.

One must know that there are twenty-two books of the   **224** Old Testament, corresponding to the letters of the Hebrew alphabet,[11] for the Hebrews have twenty-two letters, of which five are doubled so as to make twenty-seven. Thus, *kaph, mem, nun, pe,* and *sade* are double. For this reason the books, too, are numbered this way and are found to be twenty-seven, because five of them are doubled. Ruth is combined with Judges and counted as one book by the Hebrews. Kings 1 and 2 make one book; 3 and 4 Kings, one book; 1 and 2 Paralipomenon, one book; and 1 and 2 Esdras, one book. Thus, the books fall into four groups of five, as follows.

There are five books of the Law: Genesis, Exodus, Leviticus, Numbers, and Deuteronomy. This first group of five is also called the Law. Then, another group of five books called the Writings, or, by some, the Sacred Books, which are as follows: Josue, son of Nave; Judges, together with Ruth; 1 and 2 Kings making one book; 3 and 4 Kings making one book; and the two Paralipomenons making one book. This is the second group of five books. A third group of five is made up of the poetical books, namely: Job, the Psalter, the Proverbs of Solomon, Ecclesiastes of the same, and the Canticle of Canticles of the same. A fourth group of five books is the prophetic, which is made up of the twelve minor Prophets, making one book, Isaias, Jeremias, Ezechiel, Daniel, and then the two books of Esdras combined into one, and Esther. The All-Virtuous Wisdom, however, that is to say, the Wisdom of Solomon—and the Wisdom of Jesus, which the father of Sirach composed in Hebrew but which was translated into Greek by his grandson, Jesus son of Sirach—these are indeed admirable and full of virtue, but they are not counted, nor were they placed in the Ark.

225   In the New Testament there are: four Gospels, those according to Matthew, Mark, Luke and John; the Acts of the holy Apostles by Luke the Evangelist; seven Catholic Epistles—one of James, two of Peter, three of John, and one of Jude; fourteen Epistles of the Apostle Paul; the Apocalypse of John the Evangelist; and the Canons of the Holy Apostles by Clement.[1 2]

Hugh of St. Victor
On the Sacraments of the Christian Faith
1140 A.D.

Prologue

Since, therefore, I previously composed a compendium on the initial instruction in Holy Scripture, which consists in their historical reading, I have prepared the present work for those who are to be introduced to the second stage of instruction, which is in allegory. By this work they may firmly establish their minds on that foundation, so to speak, of the knowledge of faith, so that such other things as may be added to the structure by reading or hearing may remain unshaken. For I have compressed this brief *summa*, as it were, of all doctrine into one continuous work, that the mind may have something definite to which it may affix and conform its attention, lest it be carried away by various volumes of writings and diversity of readings without order or direction.

I

Whoever approaches the reading of the Divine Scriptures   227
for instruction ought to consider first what the nature of the subject matter is with which their discourse is concerned; because if he has knowledge of those things about which Scripture is composed, he will more easily thereafter perceive the truth or profundity of its words.

II

228   The subject matter of all the Divine Scriptures is the works of man's restoration. For there are two works in which all that has been done is contained. The first is the work of foundation; the second is the work of restoration. The work of foundation is that whereby those things which were not came into being. The work of restoration is that whereby those things which had been impaired were made better. Therefore, the work of foundation is the creation of the world with all its elements. The work of restoration is the Incarnation of the Word with all its sacraments, both those which have gone before from the beginning of time, and those which come after, even to the end of the world. For the Incarnate Word is our King, who came into this world to war with the devil; and all the saints who were before His coming are soldiers as it were, going before their King, and those who have come after and will come, even to the end of the world, are soldiers following their King. And the King himself is in the midst of His army and proceeds protected and surrounded on all sides by His columns. And although in a multitude as vast as this the kind of arms differ in the sacraments and observance of the peoples preceding and following, yet all are really serving the one king and following the one banner; all are pursuing the one enemy and are being crowned by the one victory. In all these writings the works of restoration are considered, with which the whole intent of the Divine Scriptures is concerned. Worldly or secular writings have as subject matter the works of foundation. Divine Scripture has as subject matter the works of restoration. Therefore, it is rightly believed to be superior to all other writings insofar as the subject matter is the more dignified and the more sublime with which its consideration and discourse are concerned. For the works of restoration are of much greater dignity than the works of foundation, because the latter were made for servitude, that they might be subject to man standing; the former, for salvation, that they

might raise man fallen. Therefore, the works of foundation, as if of little importance, were accomplished in six days, but the works of restoration can not be completed except in six ages. Yet six are placed over against six that the Restorer may be proven to be the same as the Creator.

III

Now although the principal subject matter of Divine Scrip-   **229** ture is the works of restoration, yet, in order to approach the treatment of these more competently, it first, at the very commencement of its narrative, recounts briefly and truthfully the beginning and constitution of the works of foundation. For it could not fittingly have shown how man was restored, unless it first explained how he had fallen; nor, indeed, could it fittingly have shown his fall unless it first explained in what condition he was constituted by God. But to show the first condition of man, it was necessary to describe the foundation and creation of the whole world, because the world was made for the sake of man; the soul indeed, for the sake of God; the body, for the sake of the soul; the world, for the sake of the body of man, that the soul might be subject to God, the body to the soul, and the world to the body.

In this order, accordingly, Sacred Scripture describes first   **230** the creation of the world, which was made for the sake of man; then it relates how man when made was disposed in the way of justice and discipline; next how man fell; lastly how he was restored. First, therefore, it deals with the subject matter of man's creation and original disposition; next with his misery in sin and punishment; then with his restoration and piety in the knowledge of truth and love of virtue; finally with his true home land and the joy of heavenly happiness.

IV

Now of this subject matter Divine Scripture treats accord-   **231** ing to a threefold sense: that is, according to history, allegory, and tropology. History is the narration of events, which is contained in the first meaning of the letter; we have allegory when, through what is said to have been done, something else is signified as done either in the past or in the present or in the future; we have tropology when through what is said to have been done, it is signified that something ought to be done.

V

232   Wherefore, it is apparent how much Divine Scripture excels all other writings in subtlety and profundity, not only in its subject matter but also in its method of treatment, since indeed in other writings words alone are found to have meaning, but in it not only words but also things are significant. Hence, just as wherever the sense between words and things is uncertain, the knowledge of words is necessary, so in the case of that which exists between things and mystical acts done or to be done, the knowledge of things is necessary. But the knowledge of words is considered under two heads, namely: pronunciation and meaning. To pronunciation alone grammar applies, to meaning alone dialectic applies; to pronunciation and meaning together rhetoric applies. The knowledge of things is concerned with two points, form and nature. Form is in the exterior disposition; nature, in the interior quality. The form of things is considered either under number, to which arithmetic applies, or under proportion, to which music applies, or under dimension, to which geometry applies, or under motion to which astronomy applies. But the consideration of the interior nature of things belongs to physics.

VI

233   Therefore, it is clear that all the natural arts serve divine science, and that the lower wisdom, rightly ordered, leads to the higher. Accordingly, under the sense of the significance of words in relation to things history is contained, which, as has been said, is served by three sciences: grammar, dialectic, and rhetoric. Under that sense, however, consisting in the significance of things in relation to mystical facts, allegory is

contained. And under that sense, consisting in the meaning of things in relation to mystical things to be done, tropology is contained, and these two are served by arithmetic, music, geometry, astronomy, and physics. Besides these, there is above all that divine science to which the Divine Scripture leads, whether in allegory or in tropology; one division of this which is in allegory, teaches right faith, the other, which is in tropology, teaches good work. In these consist knowledge of truth and love of virtue; and this is the true restoration of man.

VII

Now that we have shown what the subject matter of the Divine Scriptures is, and how these treat of their subject matter in the three-fold sense of history, allegory, and tropology, it is now fitting to indicate of what books the work justly distinguished by the term "divine" consists. The whole body of Divine Scriptures is comprised of two Testaments: namely, the Old and the New. Both are divided into three parts. The Old Testament contains the Law, the Prophets, and the Hagiographers, which translated means holy writers or writers of holy things. In the Law are contained five works: namely, Genesis, Exodus, Leviticus, Numbers, Deuteronomy. Genesis, moreover, is so called from "generation;" Exodus, from "going out;" Leviticus, from the Levites. The book of numbers is so called, because in it are numbered the sons of Israel, Deuteronomy is the second law. In Hebrew these books are called bresith, hellesmoth, vagetra, vegedaber, adabarim.

In the division comprising the prophets there are eight works: the first, the book of Josue, who is also called Jesu Nave and Josue Bennun, that is, son of Nun; the second book, that of Judges, which is called Sopthim; the third book, that of Samuel, which is the first and second of Kings; the fourth, that of Malachim, which is translated of Kings, which is the third and fourth of Kings; the fifth is Isaias; the sixth, Jeremias; the seventh, Ezechiel; the eighth, the book of the twelve prophets which is called thareasra. These books are

234

235

called prophetical because they are of prophets, although they are not all prophecies. Now a prophet is defined in three ways: by his office, by his grace, by his mission. But in the common use of the word they rather are called prophets who are prophets either by their office or by their manifest mission, just as in this place. And according to this acceptance of the word David and Daniel and many others are not called prophets but hagiographers.

236   In the division comprising the hagiographers nine works are contained. The first is Job; the second, the book of Psalms; the third, the Proverbs of Solomon, which in Greek are called parabolae, in Hebrew masloth; the fourth, Ecclesiastes, which in Hebrew is translated coeleth, in Latin concionator; the fifth, syra syrim, that is the Canticle of Canticles; the sixth, Daniel; the seventh, Paralipomenon, which in Latin is translated verba dierum, in Hebrew, dabreniamin; the eighth, Esdras; the ninth, Esther. All these, that is the five and the eight and the nine together, make twenty-two, the number of letters also contained in the Hebrew alphabet, so that the life of the just may be instructed to salvation by the same number of books as is that of the letters by which the tongue of learners is instructed in speech. There are besides in the Old Testament certain other books which indeed are read, but are not written in the body of the text or in the canon of authority. Such are the books of Tobias, Judith, Machabees, the book which is entitled The Wisdom of Solomon, and Ecclesiasticus.

237   The New Testament contains the Gospels, the Apostles, and the Fathers. There are four Gospels: those of Matthew, Mark, Luke, and John. There are likewise four books of the Apostles: the Acts of the Apostles, the Epistles of Paul, the Canonical Epistles, and the Apocalypse These books combined with the twenty-two of the Old Testament mentioned above make thirty, and of this number the body of Divine Scripture is comprised. The writings of the Fathers are not reckoned in the body of the text, since they add nothing, but by explanation and a broader and clearer treatment they amplify the same matter contained in the books mentioned above.

Thomas Aquinas
Summa Theologica
Part I, Question I
1265 A.D.

Ninth Article

Whether Holy Scripture Should Use Metaphors?

We proceed thus to the Ninth Article:—

Objection 1. It seems that Holy Scripture should not use 238 metaphors. For that which is proper to the lowest science seems not to befit this science, which holds the highest place of all. But to proceed by the aid of various similitudes and figures is proper to poetry, the least of all the sciences. Therefore it is not fitting that this science should make use of such similitudes.

Objection 2. Further, this doctrine seems to be intended to 239 make truth clear. Hence a reward is held out to those who manifest it: *They that explain me shall have life everlasting* (Ecclus. xxiv. 31). But by such similitudes truth is obscured. Therefore to put forward divine truths by likening them to corporeal things does not befit this science.

Objection 3. Further, the higher creatures are, the nearer 240 they approach to the divine likeness. If therefore any creature be taken to represent God, this representation ought chiefly to be taken from the higher creatures, and not from the lower; yet this is often found in the Scriptures.

On the contrary, It is written (Osee xii. 10): *I have multi-* 241 *plied visions, and I have used similitudes by the ministry of the prophets.* But to put forward anything by means of similitudes is to use metaphors. Therefore this sacred science may use metaphors.

242   *I answer that,* It is befitting Holy Writ to put forward divine and spiritual truths by means of comparisons with material things. For God provides for everything according to the capacity of its nature. Now it is natural to man to attain to intellectual truths through sensible objects, because all our knowledge originates from sense. Hence in Holy Writ spiritual truths are fittingly taught under the likeness of material things. This is what Dionysius says (*Cælest. Hierarch.* i.): *We cannot be enlightened by the divine rays except they be hidden within the covering of many sacred veils.* It is also befitting Holy Writ, which is proposed to all without distinction of persons—*To the wise and to the unwise I am a debtor* (Rom. i. 14)—that spiritual truths be expounded by means of figures taken from corporeal things, in order that thereby even the simple who are unable by themselves to grasp intellectual things may be able to understand it.

243   *Reply Obj.* 1. Poetry makes use of metaphors to produce a representation, for it is natural to man to be pleased with representations. But sacred doctrine makes use of metaphors as both necessary and useful.

244   *Reply Obj.* 2. The ray of divine revelation is not extinguished by the sensible imagery wherewith it is veiled, as Dionysius says (*Cælest. Hierarch.* i.); and its truth so far remains that it does not allow the minds of those to whom the revelation has been made, to rest in the metaphors, but raises them to the knowledge of truths; and through those to whom the revelation has been made others also may receive instruction in these matters. Hence those things that are taught metaphorically in one part of Scripture, in other parts are taught more openly. The very hiding of truth in figures is useful for the exercise of thoughtful minds, and as a defence against the ridicule of· the impious, according to the words *Give not that which is holy to dogs* (Matth. vii, 6).

245   *Reply Obj.* 3. As Dionysius says, (*loc cit.*) it is more fitting that divine truths should be expounded under the figure of less noble than of nobler bodies, and this for three reasons.

Firstly, because thereby men's minds are the better preserved from error. For then it is clear that these things are not literal descriptions of divine truths, which might have been open to doubt had they been expressed under the figure of nobler bodies, especially for those who could think of nothing nobler than bodies. Secondly, because this is more befitting the knowledge of God that we have in this life. For what He is not is clearer to us than what He is. Therefore similitudes drawn from things farthest away from God form within us a truer estimate that God is above whatsoever we may say or think of Him. Thirdly, because thereby divine truths are the better hidden from the unworthy.

Tenth Article

Whether in Holy Scripture A Word May Have Several Senses?

We proceed thus to the Tenth Article:—

Objection 1. It seems that in Holy Writ a word cannot have 246
several senses, historical or literal, allegorical, tropological or moral, and anagogical. For many different senses in one text produce confusion and deception and destroy all force of argument. Hence no argument, but only fallacies, can be deduced from a multiplicity of propositions. But Holy Writ ought to be able to state the truth without any fallacy. Therefore in it there cannot be several senses to a word.

Objection 2. Further, Augustine says (*De util. cred.* iii.) 247
that *the Old Testament has a fourfold division as to history, etiology, analogy, and allegory.* Now these four seem altogether different from the four divisions mentioned in the first objection. Therefore it does not seem fitting to explain the same word of Holy Writ according to the four different senses mentioned above.

Objection 3. Further, besides these senses, there is the 248
parabolical, which is not one of these four.

On the contrary, Gregory says (*Moral.* xx., 1): *Holy Writ* 249
by the manner of its speech transcends every science, because in one and the same sentence, while it describes a fact, it reveals a mystery.

250   *I answer that,* The author of Holy Writ is God, in whose power it is to signify His meaning, not by words only (as man also can do), but also by things themselves. So, whereas in every other science things are signified by words, this science has the property, that the things signified by the words have themselves also a signification. Therefore that first signification whereby words signify things belongs to the first sense, the historical or literal. That signification whereby things signified by words have themselves also a signification is called the spiritual sense, which is based on the literal, and presupposes it. Now this spiritual sense has a threefold division. For as the Apostle says (Heb. x. 1) the Old Law is a figure of the New Law, and Dionysius says (*Cæl. Hier.* i.) *the New Law itself is a figure of future glory.* Again, in the New Law, whatever our Head has done is a type of what we ought to do. Therefore, so far as the things of the Old Law signify the things of the New Law, there is the allegorical sense; so far as the things done in Christ, or so far as the things which signify Christ, are types of what we ought to do, there is the moral sense. But so far as they signify what relates to eternal glory, there is the anagogical sense. Since the literal sense is that which the author intends, and since the author of Holy Writ is God, Who by one act comprehends all things by His intellect, it is not unfitting, as Augustine says (*Confess.* xii.), if, even according to the literal sense, one word in Holy Writ should have several senses.

251   *Reply Obj.* 1. The multiplicity of these senses does not produce equivocation or any other kind of multiplicity, seeing that these senses are not multiplied because one word signifies several things; but because the things signified by the words can be themselves types of other things. Thus in Holy Writ no confusion results, for all the senses are founded on one—the literal—from which alone can any argument be drawn, and not from those intended in allegory, as Augustine says (*Epist.* xlviii.). Nevertheless, nothing of Holy Scripture perishes on account of this, since nothing necessary to faith is contained under the spiritual sense which is not elsewhere put forward by the Scripture in its literal sense.

Reply Obj. 2. These three—history, etiology, analogy—are   252 grouped under the literal sense. For it is called history, as Augustine expounds (*loc. cit.*), whenever anything is simply related; it is called etiology when its cause is assigned, as when Our Lord gave the reason why Moses allowed the putting away of wives—namely, on account of the hardness of men's hearts; it is called analogy whenever the truth of one text of Scripture is shown not to contradict the truth of another. Of these four, allegory alone stands for the three spiritual senses. Thus Hugh of S. Victor (*Sacram.* iv. 4 *Prolog.*) includes the anagogical under the allegorical sense, laying down three senses only—the historical, the allegorical, and the tropological.

Reply Obj. 3. The parabolical sense is contained in the   253 literal, for by words things are signified properly and figuratively. Nor is the figure itself, but that which is figured, the literal sense. When Scripture speaks of God's arm, the literal sense is not that God has such a member, but only what is signified by this member, namely, operative power. Hence it is plain that nothing false can ever underlie the literal sense of Holy Writ.

Pope Clement V
Council of Vienne
Canon 11
1311 A.D.

Among the cares that weigh heavily upon us, not the least is our solicitude to lead the erring into the way of truth and with the help of God to win them for Him. This is what we ardently desire, to it we zealously direct the energies of our mind, and about it we are concerned *diligenti studio et studiosa diligentia*. We repeat, however, that for the attainment of our purpose an exposition of the Holy Scriptures is particularly appropriate and a faithful preaching thereof very opportune. Nor are we ignorant that even this will prove of no avail if directed to the ears of one speaking an unknown tongue. Therefore, following the example of Him whose representative we are on earth, who wished that the Apostles, about to go forth to evangelize the world, should have a knowledge of every language, we earnestly desire that the Church abound with Catholic men possessing a knowledge of the languages used by the infidels, who will be able to instruct them in Catholic doctrine and by holy baptism form them into a body of Christians. Therefore, that a knowledge of these languages may be easily obtained we, with the approval of the holy council, direct that for the teaching of the language named below, schools be established wherever the Roman curia may happen to reside and also in the Universities of Paris, Oxford, Bologna, and Salamanca, decreeing that in each of these Catholic men possessing a sufficient knowledge of the Hebrew, Greek, Arabic, and

Chaldaic languages be engaged, two for each language, who shall direct the schools, translate books from these languages into Latin, and teach these languages to others who, on being sufficiently instructed in them, may propagate the faith among the infidels. As regards the support of these instructors, we direct that those in the Roman curia be maintained by the Apostolic See, those at Paris by the King of France, those at Oxford by the King of England, Scotland, Ireland, and Wales, those at Bologna and Salamanca, by the prelates, monasteries, chapters, exempt and non-exempt religious communities, and rectors of churches of Italy and Spain respectively, a tax in proportion to the needs to be imposed on each, privileges and exemptions to the contrary notwithstanding, by which, however, we do not wish to create a disadvantage *quoad alia*.

Pope Eugene IV
Council of Florence
A Decree in Behalf of the Jacobites
from the Bull "Cantate Domino"
1442 A.D.

The sacrosanct Roman Church, founded by the voice of our Lord and Savior, firmly believes, professes, and preaches one true God omnipotent, unchangeable, and eternal, Father, Son, and Holy Ghost; one in essence, three in persons; Father unborn, Son born of the Father, Holy Spirit proceeding from Father and Son; that the Father is not Son or Holy Spirit, that Son is not Father or Holy Spirit; that Holy Spirit is not Father or Son; but Father alone is Father, Son alone is Son, Holy Spirit alone is Holy Spirit. The Father alone begot the Son of His own substance; the Son alone was begotten of the Father alone; the Holy Spirit alone proceeds at the same time from the Father and Son. These three persons are one God, and not three gods, because the three have one substance, one essence, one nature, one divinity, one immensity, one eternity, where no opposition of relationship interferes.

256   "Because of this unity the Father is entire in the Son, entire in the Holy Spirit; the Son is entire in the Father; entire in the Holy Spirit, the Holy Spirit is entire in the Father, entire in the Son. No one either excels another in eternity, or exceeds in magnitude, or is superior in power. For the fact that the Son is of the Father is eternal and without beginning and that the Holy Spirit proceeds from the Father and the Son is eternal and without beginning."[1] Whatever the Father is or has, He does not have from another, but from Himself;

and He is the principle without principle. Whatever the Son is
or has, He has from the Father, and is the principle from a
principle. Whatever the Holy Spirit is or has, He has simultaneously from the Father and the Son. But the Father and
the Son are not two principles of the Holy Spirit, but one
principle, just as the Father and the Son and the Holy Spirit
are not three principles of the creature, but one principle.

Whoever, therefore, have adverse and contrary opinions   257
the Church disapproves and anathematizes and declares to be
foreign to the Christian body which is the Church. Hence it
condemns Sabellius who confuses the persons and completely
takes away their real distinction. It condemns the Arians, the
Eunomians, the Macedonians who say that only the Father is
the true God, but put the Son and the Holy Spirit in the
order of creatures. It condemns also any others whatsoever
who place grades or inequality in the Trinity.

Most strongly it believes, professes, and declares that the   258
one true God, Father and Son and Holy Spirit, is the creator
of all things visible and invisible, who, when He wished, out
of His goodness created all creatures spiritual as well as cor-
poral; good indeed, since they were made by the highest
good, but changeable, since they were made from nothing,
and it asserts that nature is not evil, since all nature, in so far
as it is nature, is good. It professes one and the same God as
the author of the Old and New Testament, that is, of the Law
and the Prophets and the Gospel, since the saints of both
Testaments have spoken with the inspiration of the same
Holy Spirit, whose books, which are contained under the
following titles it accepts and venerates. [The books of the
canon follow].

Besides it anathematizes the madness of the Manichaeans,   259
who have established two first principles, one of the visible,
and another of the invisible; and they have said that there is
one God of the New Testament, another God of the Old
Testament.

Pope Leo X
Fifth Lateran Council
Fourth and Fifth Decrees
1515-1516

From the bull "Inter Sollicitudines", Session X
May 4, 1515

While a knowledge of the sciences can be easily obtained through the reading of books, and the art of printing, which through the divine goodness has been invented and in our own time greatly perfected, has brought untold blessings to mankind, because at a small cost a large number of books can be procured, by means of which those so disposed may easily devote themselves to a study of the sciences, and men versed in the languages, especially Catholics of whom we desire an ever increasing number for the Church, may conveniently improve themselves, and which are useful, moreover, for the instruction of infidels and for strengthening the faith of those who already possess it, nevertheless, many complaints have come to us and to the Apostolic See that some masters in the art of printing books in different countries presume to print and publicly sell books translated from the Greek, Hebrew, Arabic, and Chaldaic into the Latin language and different vernaculars, which contain errors in matters of faith and teachings contrary to the Christian religion; also attacks on persons holding positions of dignity and trust, the reading of which is not only not conducive to the intellectual well-being of the reader but also leads to grave errors in matters of faith and morals, whence have arisen numerous scandals and daily greater ones are to be feared.

Wherefore, that that invention, so advantageous to extend-   261
ing the glory of God, to the increase of the faith, and the diffusion of the arts and sciences, may not have the contrary result and become an obstacle to the salvation of souls, we have deemed it advisable to direct our attention to the print-ing of books, lest in the future thorns grow up with the good seed or poisons be mixed with the medicine. Wishing, there-fore, to provide an opportune remedy in regard to this matter, we, with the approval of the holy council, decree and ordain that in the future no one shall presume to print or cause to be printed, in Rome or in any other city or diocese, any book or any other writing whatsoever unless it has first been care-fully examined and its publication approved by our vicar and the master of the Sacred Palace, in other cities and dioceses by the bishops or by competent persons appointed by them and by the inquisitor of the city or diocese in which the books are to be printed. This approval must be given over the personal signatures of the censors, free of charge and without delay, under penalty of excommunication. Those who act contrary to this constitution shall, besides the loss and de-struction of such books by fire, the payment of 100 ducats toward the construction of the Basilica of St. Peter, and sus-pension from the printing of books for a period of one year, incur the sentence of excommunication, and, should they continue in their obstinacy, they shall be punished by the bishops or by our vicar with all the penalties of the law, so that from their example others may be deterred from com-mitting similar offenses.

From the bull "Supernae Majestatis Praesidio", Session XI
December 19, 1516

1. With the approval of the holy council we decree and   262
ordain that no clerics, whether seculars or members of any of the mendicant orders or any other order to which the office of preaching pertains by right, custom, privilege, or other-

wise, be admitted to exercise that office unless they have first been carefully examined by their respective superiors and found competent and fit as regards moral integrity, age, knowledge, uprightness, prudence, and exemplariness of life. Of this approved competency they must, wherever they may preach, acquaint the local ordinary by means of authentic letters or other instruments from those who examined and approved them for this work.

263   2. We command all who are engaged in this work and who will be so engaged in the future that they preach and explain the truth of the Gospel and the Holy Scriptures in accordance with the teaching, interpretation, and exposition of the doctors of the Church, whom the Church or long usage has approved and the reading of whom she has thus far accepted and in the future will accept, without adding thereto anything that is contrary to or in any way at variance with their teaching. Nor shall they presume to announce or predict in their sermons any fixed time of future evils, the coming of Antichrist or the day of the last judgment, since the truth says: "It is not for you to know the times and moments which the Father hath put in his own power" (*Acts* 1:7). Those who till now have made such and similar predictions have lied, and their conduct has been in no small measure a detriment to the esteem and work of those who preach well. Wherefore, no cleric, whether regular or secular, who engages in this work in the future is permitted in his sermons to foretell future events *ex litteris sacris* or to affirm that he has received his knowledge of them from the Holy Ghost or through divine revelation or to resort for proof of his statements to foolish divinations, but by divine command it is his duty to preach and explain the Gospel to every creature, to instil a hatred of sin and the cultivation of virtue, and to promote the peace and mutual charity so insistently counseled by our Redeemer. To realize this peace and charity, let him preserve undivided the seamless garment of Christ by abstaining from that scandalous practice of defaming the character of bishops, prelates, and other superiors before the people.

Council of Trent
Fourth Session
1546 A.D.

First Decree

The holy ecumenical and general Council of Trent . . . has always this purpose in mind that in the Church errors be removed and the purity of the Gospel be preserved. This Gospel was promised of old through the prophets in the Sacred Scriptures; Our Lord Jesus Christ, Son of God, first promulgated it from His own lips; He in turn ordered that it be preached through the apostles to all creatures as the source of all saving truth and rule of conduct. The Council clearly perceives that this truth and rule are contained in the written books and unwritten traditions which have come down to us, having been received by the apostles from the mouth of Christ Himself, or from the apostles by the dictation of the Holy Spirit, and have been transmitted as it were from hand to hand. Following, then, the example of the orthodox Fathers, it receives and venerates with the same sense of loyalty and reverence all the books of the Old and New Testaments, for God alone is the author of both—together with all the traditions concerning faith and morals, as coming from the mouth of Christ or being inspired by the Holy Spirit and preserved in continuous succession in the Catholic Church.

265   The Council has thought it proper to insert in this decree a list of the sacred books, so that no doubt may remain as to which books are recognised by this Council.

266   They are the following:

Old Testament: The five books of Moses, i.e., Genesis, Exodus, Leviticus, Numbers, Deuteronomy; Joshua, Judges, Ruth, four books of Kings, two of Chronicles, the first book of Ezra, the second book of Ezra called the book of Nehemiah, Tobit, Judith, Esther, Job, the book of Psalms of David containing 150 psalms, Proverbs, Ecclesiastes, the Song of Songs, Wisdom, Ecclesiasticus, Isaiah, Jeremiah with Baruch, Ezechiel, Daniel, the twelve minor prophets, i.e., Hosea, Joel, Amos, Obadiah, Jonah, Micah, Nahum, Habakkuk, Zephaniah, Haggai, Zachariah and Malachi; two books of Maccabees, i.e., the first and the second.

New Testament: The four Gospels according to Matthew, Mark, Luke and John; the Acts of the apostles written by Luke the Evangelist; fourteen epistles of the apostle Paul, i.e., to the Romans, two to the Corinthians, to the Galatians, Ephesians, Philippians, Colossians, two to the Thessalonians, two to Timothy, to Titus, Philemon, and the Hebrews; two epistles of the apostle Peter, three of the apostle John, one of the apostle James, one of the apostle Jude, and the Revelation

267   of the apostle John.

If anyone does not accept all these books in their entirety, with all their parts, as they are being read in the Catholic Church and are contained in the ancient Latin Vulgate edition, as sacred and canonical and knowingly and deliberately rejects the aforesaid traditions, *anathema sit.*

Second Decree

268

Moreover, because the same holy Council thought it very useful to the Church if it were known which of all the Latin editions of the sacred books now in circulation is to be regarded as the authentic version, it declares and decrees: This same ancient Vulgate version which has been preserved by the Church for so many centuries is to be regarded as the authentic translation in public readings, disputations, ser-

mons and expositions, and let no one dare or presume to
reject it on any grounds.

Furthermore, to restrain irresponsible minds, it decrees   269
that no one, relying on his own prudence, twist Holy Scripture in matters of faith and morals that pertain to the edifice
of Christian doctrine, according to his own mind, contrary to
the meaning that holy mother the Church has held and
—since it belongs to her to judge the true meaning and interpretation of Holy Scripture—and that no one dare to interpret
the Scripture in a way contrary to the unanimous consensus
of the Fathers, even though such interpretations be not intended for publication.

Council of Trent, Fifth Session
Second Decree
1547 A.D.

Chapter I

The same holy council, adhering to the pious decisions of   270
the sovereign pontiffs and of approved councils, and accepting and adding to them, that the heavenly treasure of the
sacred books which the Holy Ghost has with the greatest
liberality delivered to men may not lie neglected, has ordained
and decreed that in those churches in which there exists a
prebend or a benefice with an obligation attached, or other
income by whatever name it may be known, set aside for instructors in sacred theology, the bishops, archbishops, primates, and other ecclesiastical superiors of those localities
compel, even by a reduction of their revenues, those who
hold such prebend, benefice or income, to expound and
interpret the Holy Scriptures, either personally if they are
competent, otherwise by a competent substitute to be chosen
by the bishops, archbishops, primates, or other superiors of
those places. In the future such prebend, benefice and income shall be conferred only on competent persons and
those who can themselves discharge that office; a provision
made otherwise shall be null and void. In metropolitan and

cathedral churches, however, if the city be an outstanding and populous one, and also in collegiate churches that are situated in a prominent town, even though they do not belong to any diocese, provided the clergy there are numerous, where there is no prebend, benefice or income provided for this purpose, let the prebend that shall first become vacant in any manner whatever, except by resignation, and to which some other incompatible duty is not attached, be understood to be *ipso facto* and forever set aside and devoted to that purpose. And should it happen that in those churches there is not any or no sufficient income, let the metropolitan or the bishop himself, by assigning thereto the revenues of some simple benefice, the duties connected with it being nevertheless discharged, or by contributions of the *beneficiati* of his city and diocese, or otherwise, as may be most convenient, provide in such a way with the advice of the chapter that the instructions in Holy Scripture may be procured; so, however, that all other instructions, whether established by custom or any other agency, be by no means on that account omitted. Churches whose annual revenues are scanty and where the number of clergy and people is so small that instruction in theology cannot be conveniently had therein, may have at least a master, to be chosen by the bishop with the advice of the chapter, to teach grammar gratuitously to clerics and other poor students, so that afterwards they may with the help of God pass on to the study of Holy Scripture. For this purpose let the revenues of some simple benefice be assigned to that master of grammar, which he shall receive so long as he is engaged in teaching (provided, however, that that benefice be not deprived of the services due to it), or let some suitable remuneration be paid him out of the capitular or episcopal income, or finally, let the bishop himself devise some other arrangement suitable to his church and diocese, that this pious, useful and profitable provision may not under any feigned excuse be neglected. In the monasteries of monks also, where this can be conveniently done, let there be instructions in the Holy Scriptures. If abbots prove negligent in this matter, let the bishops of the localities, as the delegates herein of the Apostolic See, compel them thereto by suitable measures. In the convents of other regulars in which studies can conveniently flourish, let there be likewise instructions in the Holy Scriptures, which shall be assigned by the general and provincial chapters to the more worthy masters. In the public gymnasia also where instructions so profitable and of all the most necessary have not thus far been instituted, let them be introduced by the piety and charity of the most religious princes and governments for the defense and increase of the Catholic faith and the preservation and propagation of wholesome doctrine, and where once instituted and neglected, let them be restored. And that under the semblance of piety impiety may not be disseminated, the same holy council has decreed that no one be admitted to this office of instructor, whether such instruction be public or private, who has not been previously examined and approved by the bishop of the locality as to his life, morals and knowledge; which, however, is not to be understood of instructions in the monasteries of monks. Moreover, those who teach Holy Scripture, as long as they teach publicly in the schools, and also the students who study in those schools, shall fully enjoy and possess in case of absence all the privileges accorded by the common law with regard to the collection of the incomes of their prebends and benefices.

Chapter II

But since the preaching of the Gospel is no less necessary to the Christian commonwealth than the reading thereof, and since this is the chief duty of the bishops, the same holy council has ordained and decreed that all bishops, archbishops, primates and all other prelates of the churches are bound personally, if not lawfully hindered, to preach the holy Gospel of Jesus Christ. But if it should happen that bishops and the others mentioned above are hindered by a legitimate impediment, they shall be bound, in accordance with the provision of the general council, to appoint competent persons to discharge beneficially this office of preaching. If however anyone through contempt fails to observe this, let him be subject to severe punishment. Archpriests, priests and all

271

who in any manner have charge of parochial and other churches to which is attached the *cura animarum*, shall at least on Sundays and solemn festivals, either personally or, if they are lawfully impeded, through others who are competent, feed the people committed to them with wholesome words in proportion to their own and their people's mental capacity, by teaching them those things that are necessary for all to know in order to be saved, and by impressing upon them with briefness and plainness of speech the vices that they must avoid and the virtues that they must cultivate, in order that they may escape eternal punishment and obtain the glory of heaven. But if anyone of the above should neglect to discharge this duty, even on the plea that for some reason he is exempt from the jurisdiction of the bishop, even if the churches are said in some way to be exempt, or perhaps annexed or united to some monastery that is outside the diocese, if the churches are really within their dioceses, let not the watchful and pastoral solicitude of the bishops be wanting, lest that be fulfilled: *The little ones have asked for bread, and there was none to break it unto them.* Wherefore, if after having been admonished by the bishop they neglect their duty for a period of three months, let them be compelled by ecclesiastical censures or by other measures at the discretion of the bishop; and should he deem it expedient, let a fair remuneration be paid from the revenues of the benefices to another person to discharge that office, till the incumbent, having come to his senses, shall fulfil his own duty.

272   But if there should be found parochial churches subject to monasteries that are not in any diocese, and the abbots and regular prelates are negligent in the aforesaid matters, let them be compelled thereto by the metropolitans in whose provinces the dioceses are located, who in this matter shall act as delegates of the Apostolic See, and no custom or exemption, appeal, protest or counteraction shall impede the execution of this decree, till a competent judge, who shall proceed summarily and examine only into the truth of the fact, shall have taken the matter into consideration and given a decision. Regulars of whatever order, unless they have been examined by their superiors regarding life, morals and knowl-

edge and approved by them, may not without their permission preach even in the churches of their order, and they must present themselves personally with this permission before the bishops and ask from these the blessing before they begin to preach. In churches, however, that are not of their orders they must, in addition to the permission of their superiors, have also that of the bishop, without which they may not under any circumstances preach in churches that do not belong to their orders. This permission the bishops shall grant *gratis*. But if, which heaven avert, a preacher should spread errors or scandals among the people, let the bishop forbid him to preach, even though he preach in his own or in the monastery of another order. Should he preach heresies, let him proceed against him in accordance with the requirement of the law or the custom of the locality, even though that preacher should plead exemption by a general or special privilege; in which case the bishop shall proceed by Apostolic authority and as the delegate of the Apostolic See. But let bishops be careful that a preacher be not annoyed by false accusations or calumnies, or have just cause of complaint concerning such. Moreover, let bishops be on their guard not to permit anyone, whether of those who, being regulars in name, live outside their monasteries and the obedience of their religious institute, or secular priests, unless they are known to them and are of approved morals and doctrine, to preach in their city or diocese, even under pretext of any privilege whatsoever, till they have consulted the holy Apostolic See on the matter; from which See it is not likely that privileges of this kind are extorted by unworthy persons except by suppressing the truth or stating what is false.

Those soliciting alms, who are also commonly known as 273 questors, whatever their state, shall not in any manner presume to preach either *per se* or *per alium*, and shall, notwithstanding any privilege whatsoever, be absolutely restrained by suitable measures by the bishops and ordinaries of the localities.

Clement XI
Constitution UNIGENITUS
(Condemned Statements of P. Quesnel)
1713 A.D.

274   79. It is useful and necessary at all times, in all places, and for any kind of person, to study and to know the spirit, the piety, and the mysteries of Sacred Scripture.

275   80. The reading of Sacred Scripture is for all.

276   81. The sacred obscurity of the Word of God is no reason for the laity to dispense themselves from reading it.

277   82. The Lord's Day ought to be sanctified by Christians with reading of pious works and above all of the Holy Scriptures. It is harmful for a Christian to wish to withdraw from this reading.

278   83. It is an illusion to persuade oneself that knowledge of the mysteries of religion should not be communicated to women by the reading of Sacred Scriptures. Not from the simplicity of women, but from the proud knowledge of men has arisen the abuse of the Scriptures, and have heresies been born.

279   84. To snatch away from the hands of Christians the New Testament or to hold it closed against them by taking away from them the means of understanding it, is to close for them the mouth of Christ.

280   85. To forbid Christians to read Sacred Scriptures, especially the Gospels, is to forbid the use of light to the sons of light, and to cause them to suffer a kind of excommunication.

Pius VII
Letter to Archbishop of Mohileff (Excerpt)
September 3, 1816

We were overcome with great and bitter sorrow when We learned that a pernicious plan, by no means the first, had been undertaken whereby the most sacred books of the Bible are being spread everywhere in every vernacular tongue, with new interpretations which are contrary to the wholesome rules of the Church, and are skillfully turned into a distorted sense. For, from one of the versions of this sort already presented to Us we notice that such a danger exists against the sanctity of purer doctrine, so that the faithful might easily drink a deadly poison from those fountains from which they should drain "waters of saving wisdom" [*Ecclus.* 15:3]. . . .

282 For you should have kept before your eyes the warnings which Our predecessors have constantly given, namely, that, if the sacred books are permitted everywhere without discrimination in the vulgar tongue, more damage will arise from this than advantage. Furthermore, the Roman Church, accepting only the Vulgate edition according to the well-known prescription (see n. 268 f. of the Council of Trent, disapproves the sessions in other tongues and permits only those which are edited with the explanations carefully chosen from writings of the Fathers and Catholic Doctors, so that so great a treasure may not be exposed to the corruptions of novelties, and so that the Church, spread throughout the world, may be "of one tongue and of the same speech" [*Gen.* 2:1].

283   Since in vernacular speech we notice very frequent inter-changes, varieties, and changes, surely by an unrestrained license of Biblical versions that changelessness which is proper to the divine testimony would be utterly destroyed, and faith itself would waver, when, especially, from the meaning of one syllable sometimes an understanding about the truth of a dogma is formed. For this purpose, then, the heretics have been accustomed to make their low and base machinations, in order that in the publication of their vernacular Bibles, (of whose strange variety and discrepancy they, nevertheless, accuse one another and wrangle) they may, each one, treacherously insert their own errors wrapped in the more holy apparatus of divine speech. "For heresies are not born," St. Augustine used to say, "except when the true Scriptures are not well understood and when what is not well understood in them is rashly and boldly asserted."[1] But, if we grieve that men renowned for piety and wisdom have, by no means rarely, failed in interpreting the Scriptures, what should we not fear if the Scriptures, translated into every vulgar tongue whatsoever, are freely handed on to be read by an inexperienced people who, for the most part, judge not with any skill but with a kind of rashness? . . .

UBI PRIMUM
Encyclical Letter of Pope Leo XII (Excerpts)
May 5, 1824

... The wickedness of our enemies is progressing to such a 284
degree that, besides the flood of pernicious books hostile in
themselves to religion they are endeavoring to turn to the harm
of religion even the sacred Literature given to us by divine
Providence for the progress of religion itself. It is not unknown
to you, Venerable Brethren, that a certain "Society," commonly called "Biblical," is boldly spreading through the
whole world, which, spurning the traditions of the Holy
Fathers and against the well-known decree of the Council of
Trent, is turning with all its strength and means toward this:
to translate—or either mistranslate—the Sacred Books into
the vulgar tongue of every nation. . . .

And to avert this plague, Our predecessors have published 285
many Constitutions. . . . . We, also, in accord with our
Apostolic duty, encourage you, Venerable Brothers, to be
zealous in every way to remove your flock away from these
posionous pastures. "Reprove, entreat, be instant in season,
out of season, in all patience and doctrine" [II *Tim.* 4:2],
so that your faithful people, clinging exactly to the regulations of our Congregation of the Index, may be persuaded
that, "if the Sacred Books are permitted everywhere without
discrimination in the vulgar tongue, more harm will arise
therefrom than advantage, because of the boldness of men."
Experience demonstrates the truth of this.

Pope Pius IX
Syllabus of Condemned Errors, Number 7 (Excerpt)
1864 A.D.

Divine revelation is imperfect and hence subject to continual and indefinite progress, which ought to correspond to the progress of human reason.

287 The faith in Christ is detrimental to human reason; and divine revelation not only is of no use but is even harmful to man's perfection.

288 The prophecies and miracles set forth in the narration of the Sacred Scriptures are poetical fictions; the mysteries of the Christian faith are the outcome of philosophical reflections; in the books of both Testaments mythical tales are contained; Jesus Christ Himself is a mythical fiction.

Vatican I
Constitution DEI FILIUS
1870 A.D.

Chapter II: On Revelation

Further, this supernatural revelation, according to the universal belief of the Church, declared by the sacred Synod of Trent, "is contained in the written books and unwritten traditions which have come down to us, having been received by the apostles from the mouth of Christ Himself, or from the apostles themselves by the dictation of the Holy Spirit, and have been transmitted as it were from hand to hand" (*cf. n.* 210). These books of the Old and New Testaments are to be received as sacred and canonical in their integrity, with all their parts, as they are enumerated in the decree of the said Council and are contained in the ancient Latin edition of the Vulgate. These the Church holds to be sacred and canonical, not because, having been carefully composed by mere human industry, they were afterwards approved by her authority, nor merely because they contain revelation with no admixture of error, but because, having been written by the inspiration of the Holy Spirit, they have God for their author and have been delivered as such to the Church herself.

However, what the holy Council of Trent has laid down concerning the interpretation of the divine Scripture for the good purpose of restraining indisciplined minds, has been explained by certain men in a distorted manner. Hence we renew the same decree and declare this to be its sense: In

290

matters of faith and morals, affecting the building up of Christian doctrine, that is to be held as the true sense of holy Scripture which Holy Mother the Church has held and holds, to whom it belongs to judge of the true sense and interpretation of Holy Scriptures. Therefore no one is allowed to interpret the same sacred Scripture contrary to this sense, or contrary to the unanimous consent of the Fathers.

PROVIDENTISSIMUS DEUS
Encyclical Letter of Pope Leo XIII
on the Study of Holy Scripture
November 18, 1893

The God of all Providence, who in the adorable designs of His love at first elevated the human race to the participation of the divine nature, and afterwards delivered it to its primitive dignity, has, in consequence, bestowed upon man a splendid gift and safeguard—making known to him, by supernatural means, the hidden mysteries of His divinity, His wisdom and His mercy. For although in divine revelation there are contained some things which are not beyond the reach of unassisted reason, and which are made the objects of such revelation in order "that all may come to know them with facility, certainty, and safety from error, yet not on this account can supernatural revelation be said to be absolutely necessary; it is only necessary because God has ordained man to a supernatural end."[1] This supernatural revelation, according to the belief of the universal Church, is contained both in unwritten tradition and in written books, which are, therefore, called sacred and canonical because, "being written under the inspiration of the Holy Ghost, they have God for their author, and as such have been delivered to the Church."[2] This belief has been perpetually held and professed by the Church in regard to the books of both Testaments; and there are well-known documents of the gravest kind, coming down to us from the earliest times, which proclaim that God, who spoke first by the Prophets, then by His own mouth, and lastly by the Apostles, composed also the canonical Scripture,[3] and that these are His own oracles and words[4] —a Letter written by our Heavenly Father and transmitted by the sacred writers to the human race in its pilgrimage so far from its heavenly country.[5] If, then, such and so great is the excellence and the dignity of the Scriptures, that God Himself has composed them, and that they treat of God's marvelous mysteries, counsels, and works, it follows that the branch of sacred theology which is concerned with the defense and elucidation of these divine books must be excellent and useful in the highest degree.

292   Now We, who by the help of God, and not without fruit, have by frequent Letters and exhortation endeavored to promote other branches of study which seemed capable of advancing the glory of God and contributing to the salvation of souls, have for a long time cherished the desire to give an impulse to the noble science of Holy Scripture, and to impart to Scripture study a direction suitable to the needs of the present day. The solicitude of the apostolic office naturally urges and even compels Us, not only to desire that this grand source of Catholic revelation should be made safely and abundantly accessible to the flock of Jesus Christ, but also not to suffer any attempt to defile or corrupt it, either on the part of those who impiously and openly assail the Scriptures, or of those who are led astray into fallacious and imprudent novelties.

293   We are not ignorant, indeed, Venerable Brethren, that there are not a few Catholics, men of talent and learning, who do devote themselves with ardor to the defence of the sacred writings and to making them better known and understood. But whilst giving to these the commendation they deserve, We cannot but earnestly exhort others also, from whose skill and piety and learning We have a right to expect good results, to give themselves to the same most praiseworthy work. It is Our wish and fervent desire to see an increase in the number of the approved and persevering laborers in the cause of Holy Scripture; and more especially that those whom divine grace has called to Holy Orders, should, day by day, as their state demands, display greater diligence and industry in reading, meditating, and explaining it.

Among the reasons for which the Holy Scripture is so   294
worthy of commendation—in addition to its own excellence
and to the homage which we owe to God's Word—the chief
of all is, the innumerable benefits of which it is the source;
according to the infallible testimony of the Holy Spirit Himself, who says: "All Scripture is inspired by God and useful
for teaching, for reproving, for correcting, for instructing in
justice; that the man of God may be perfect, equipped for
every good work" (*II Tim.* 3:16-17).

That such was the purpose of God in giving the Scripture   295
to men is shown by the example of Christ our Lord and of
His apostles. For He Himself who "obtained authority by
miracles, merited belief by authority, and by belief drew to
Himself the multitude"[6] was accustomed in the exercise of
His divine mission, to appeal to the Scriptures. He uses them
at times to prove that He is sent by God, and is God Himself.
From them He cites instructions for His disciples and confirmation of His doctrine. He vindicates them from the calumnies of objectors; He quotes them against Sadducees and
Pharisees and retorts from them upon Satan himself when he
dares to tempt Him. At the close of His life His utterances are
from the Holy Scripture, and it is the Scripture that He expounds to His disciples after His resurrection, until He ascends
to the glory of His Father.

Faithful to His precepts, the Apostles, although He Him-   296
self granted "signs and wonders to be done by their hands"
(*Acts* 14:3), nevertheless used with the greatest effect the
sacred writings, in order to persuade the nations everywhere
of the wisdom of Christianity, to conquer the obstinacy of
the Jews, and to suppress the outbreak of heresy. This is
plainly seen in their discourses, especially in those of St.
Peter; these were often little less than a series of citations
from the Old Testament making in the strongest manner for
the new dispensation. We find the same thing in the Gospels
of St. Matthew and St. John and in the Catholic Epistles; and
most remarkably of all in the words of him who "boasts that
he learned the law at the feet of Gamaliel, in order that, being armed with spiritual weapons, he might afterwards say

with confidence, 'the arms of our warfare are not carnal but mighty unto God.' "[7]

297   Let all, therefore, especially the novices of the ecclesiastical army, understand how deeply the sacred books should be esteemed, and with what eagerness and reverence they should approach this great arsenal of heavenly arms. For those whose duty it is to handle Catholic doctrine before the learned or the unlearned will nowhere find more ample matter or more abundant exhortation, whether on the subject of God, the supreme Good and the All-perfect Being, or of the works which display His glory and His love. Nowhere is there anything more full or more express on the subject of the Savior of the world than is to be found in the whole range of the Bible.

298   As St. Jerome says, "to be ignorant of the Scripture is not to know Christ."[8] In its pages His Image stands out, living and breathing; diffusing everywhere around consolation in trouble, encouragement to virtue, and attraction to the love of God. And as to the Church, her institutions, her nature, her office, and her gifts, we find in Holy Scripture so many references and so many ready and convincing arguments, that as St. Jerome again most truly says: "A man who is well grounded in the testimonies of the Scripture is the bulwark of the Church."[9] And if we come to morality and discipline, an apostolic man finds in the sacred writings abundant and excellent assistance: most holy precepts, gentle and strong exhortation, splendid examples of every virtue, and finally the promise of eternal reward and the threat of eternal punishment, uttered in terms of solemn import, in God's name and in God's own words.

299   And it is this peculiar and singular power of Holy Scripture, arising from the inspiration of the Holy Spirit, which gives authority to the sacred orator, fills him with apostolic liberty of speech, and communicates force and power to his eloquence.

300   For those who infuse into their efforts the spirit and strength of the Word of God speak "not in word only but in power also, and in the Holy Spirit, and in much fulness" (*I Thess.* 1:5). Hence, those preachers are foolish and im-

provident who, in speaking of religion and proclaiming the things of God, use no words but those of human science and human prudence, trusting to their own reasonings rather than to those of God. Their discourses may be brilliant and fine, but they must be feeble and they must be cold, for they are without the fire of the utterance of God[10] and they must fall far short of that mighty power which the speech of God possesses: "for the Word of God is living and effectual, and keener than any two-edged sword; and extending unto the division of the soul and the spirit" (*Heb.* 4:12). But, indeed, all those who have a right to speak are agreed that there is in the Holy Scripture an eloquence that is wonderfully varied and rich, and worthy of great themes. This St. Augustine thoroughly understood and has abundantly set forth.[11] This, also, is confirmed by the best preachers of all ages, who have gratefully acknowledged that they owed their repute chiefly to the assiduous use of the Bible, and to devout meditation on its pages.

The holy Fathers well knew all this by practical experience, and they never cease to extol the sacred Scripture and its fruits. In innumerable passages of their writings we find them applying to it such phrases as "an inexhaustible treasury of heavenly doctrine,"[12] or "overflowing fountain of salvation,"[13] or putting it before us as fertile pastures and beautiful gardens in which the flock of the Lord is marvelously refreshed and delighted.[14] Let us listen to the words of St. Jerome, in his Epistle to Nepotian: "Often read the divine Scriptures; yea, let holy reading be always in thy hand; study that which thou thyself must preach. . . . Let the speech of the priest be ever seasoned with scriptural reading."[15] St. Gregory the Great, than whom no one has more admirably described the pastoral office, writes in the same sense. "Those," he says, "who are zealous in the work of preaching must never cease the study of the written Word of God."[16] St. Augustine, however, warns us that "vainly does the preacher utter the Word of God exteriorly unless he listens to it interiorly";[17] and St. Gregory instructs sacred orators "first to find in Holy Scripture the knowledge of themselves,

                                                301

and then to carry it to others, lest in reproving others they forget themselves."[18]

302   Admonitions such as these had, indeed, been uttered long before by the apostolic voice which had learned its lesson from Christ Himself, who "began to do and teach." It was not to Timothy alone, but to the whole order of the clergy, that the command was addressed: "Take heed to thyself and to thy teaching, be earnest in them. For in so doing thou wilt save both thyself and those who hear thee" (*I Tim.* 4:16). For the saving and for the perfection of ourselves and of others there is at hand the very best of help in the Holy Scriptures, as the Book of Psalms, among others, so constantly insists; but those only will find it who bring to this divine reading not only docility and attention but also piety and an innocent life. For the sacred Scripture is not like other books. Dictated by the Holy Spirit, it contains things of the deepest importance, which, in many instances, are most difficult and obscure. To understand and explain such things there is always required the "coming"[19] of the same Holy Spirit; that is to say, His light and His grace; and these, as the Royal Psalmist so frequently insists, are to be sought by humble prayer and guarded by holiness of life.

303   It is in this that the watchful care of the Church shines forth conspicuously. By admirable laws and regulations, she has always shown herself solicitous that "the celestial treasure of the sacred books, so bountifully bestowed upon man by the Holy Spirit, should not lie neglected."[20] She has prescribed that a considerable portion of them shall be read and piously reflected upon by all her ministers in the daily office of the sacred psalmody. She has ordered that in cathedral churches, in monasteries, and in other convents in which study can conveniently be pursued, they shall be expounded and interpreted by capable men; and she has strictly commanded that her children shall be fed with the saving words of the Gospel at least on Sundays and solemn feasts.[21] Moreover, it is owing to the wisdom and exertions of the Church that there has always been continued, from century to century, that cultivation of Holy Scripture which has been so remarkable and has borne such ample fruit.

And here, in order to strengthen Our teaching and Our exhortations, it is well to recall how, and from the beginning of Christianity, all who have been renowned for holiness of life and sacred learning, have given their deep and constant attention to Holy Scripture.   304

If we consider the immediate disciples of the Apostles, St. Clement of Rome, St. Ignatius of Antioch, St. Polycarp—or the apologists, such as St. Justin and St. Irenaeus, we find that in their letters and their books, whether in defense of the Catholic Faith or in its commendation, they drew faith, strength, and unction from the Word of God. When there arose, in various sees, catechetical and theological schools, of which the most celebrated were those of Alexandria and of Antioch, there was little taught in those schools, but what was contained in the reading, the interpretation, and the defense of the divine written word. From them came forth numbers of Fathers and writers whose laborious studies and admirable writings have justly merited for the three following centuries the appellation of the golden age of biblical exegesis. In the Eastern Church, the greatest name of all is Origen—a man remarkable alike for penetration of genius and for persevering labor; from whose numerous works and his great *Hexapla* almost all have drawn that came after him. Others who have widened the field of this science may also be named, as especially eminent; thus, Alexandria could boast of St. Clement and St. Cyril; Palestine, of Eusebius and the other St. Cyril; Cappadocia, of St. Basil the Great and the two St. Gregories, of Nazianzus and Nyssa; Antioch, of St. John Chrysostom, in whom the science of Scripture was rivalled by the splendor of his eloquence. In the Western Church there were many names as great: Tertullian, St. Cyprian, St. Hilary, St. Ambrose, St. Leo the Great, St. Gregory the Great; most famous of all, St. Augustine and St. Jerome, of whom the former was so marvelously acute in penetrating the sense of God's Word and so fertile in the use that he made of it for the promotion of the Catholic truth, and the latter has received from the Church, by reason of his preeminent knowledge of Scripture and his labors in promoting its use, the name, "great Doctor."   305

306   From this period down to the eleventh century, although biblical studies did not flourish with the same vigor and the same fruitfulness as before, yet they did flourish, and principally by the instrumentality of the clergy. It was their care and solicitude that selected the best and most useful things that the ancients had left, arranged them in order, and published them with additions of their own—as did St. Isidore of Seville, Venerable Bede, and Alcuin, among the most prominent; it was they who illustrated the sacred pages with "glosses" or short commentaries, as we see in Walafrid Strabo and St. Anselm of Laon, or expended fresh labor in securing their integrity, as did St. Peter Damian and Blessed Lanfranc. In the twelfth century many took up, with great success, the allegorical exposition of Scripture. In this kind, St. Bernard is preeminent; and his writings, it may be said, are Scripture all through. With the age of the scholastics came fresh and welcome progress in the study of the Bible. That the scholastics were solicitous about the genuineness of the Latin version is evident from the *Correctoria Biblica*, or lists of emendations, which they have left. But they expended their labors and industry chiefly on interpretation and explanation. To them we owe the accurate and clear distinction, such as had not been given before, of the various senses of the sacred words; the assignment of the value of each "sense" in theology; the division of books into parts, and the summaries of the various parts; the investigation of the objects of the writers; the demonstration of the connection of sentence with sentence, and clause with clause; all of which is calculated to throw much light on the more obscure passages of the sacred volume. The valuable work of the scholastics in Holy Scripture is seen in their theological treatises and in their Scripture commentaries; and in this respect the greatest name among them all is St. Thomas Aquinas.

307   When Our predecessor, Clement V, established chairs of Oriental literature in the Roman College and in the principal universities of Europe, Catholics began to make more accurate investigation of the original text of the Bible as well as of the Latin version. The revival amongst us of Greek learning, and, much more, the happy invention of the art of printing,

gave a strong impetus to biblical studies. In a brief space of time, innumerable editions, especially of the Vulgate, poured from the press and were diffused throughout the Catholic world; so honored and loved was Holy Scripture during that very period against which the enemies of the Church direct their calumnies. Nor must we forget how many learned men there were, chiefly among the religious orders, who did excellent work for the Bible between the Council of Vienne and that of Trent; men who, by the employment of modern means and appliances, and by the tribute of their own genius and learning, not only added to the rich stores of ancient times but prepared the way for the succeeding century, the century which followed the Council of Trent, when it almost seemed that the great age of the Fathers had returned. For it is well known, and We recall it with pleasure, that Our predecessors, from Pius IV to Clement VIII caused to be prepared the celebrated editions of the Vulgate and Septuagint, which, having been published by the command and authority of Sixtus V and of the same Clement, are now in common use. At this time, moreover, were carefully brought out various other ancient versions of the Bible, and the Polyglots of Antwerp and of Paris, most important for the investigation of the true meaning of the text; nor is there any one book of either Testament which did not find more than one expositor, nor any grave question which did not profitably exercise the ability of many inquirers, among whom there are not a few—more especially of those who made most use of the Fathers—who have acquired great reputation. From that time downwards the labor and solicitude of Catholics has never been wanting; for as time went on, eminent scholars have carried on biblical study with success, and have defended Holy Scripture against *rationalism* with the same weapons of philology and kindred sciences with which it had been attacked. The calm and fair consideration of what has been said will clearly show that the Church has never failed in taking due measures to bring the Scriptures within reach of her children, and that she has ever held fast and exercised profitably that guardianship conferred upon her by Almighty God for the protection and glory of His holy Word; so that she has never required, nor does she now require, any stimulation from without.

308   We must now, Venerable Brethren, as Our purpose demands impart to you such counsels as seem best suited for carrying on successfully the study of biblical science.

309   But first it must be clearly understood whom we have to oppose and contend against, and what are their tactics and their arms. In earlier times the contest was chiefly with those who, relying on private judgment and repudiating the divine traditions and teaching office of the Church, held the Scriptures to be the one source of revelation and the final appeal in matters of faith. Now, we have to meet the Rationalists, true children and inheritors of the older heretics, who, trusting in their turn to their own way of thinking, have rejected even the scraps and remnants of Christian belief which have been handed down to them. They deny that there is any such thing as revelation or inspiration or Holy Scriptures at all; they see, instead, only the forgeries and the falsehoods of men; they set down the Scripture narratives as stupid fables and lying stories: the prophecies and the oracles of God are to them either predictions made up after the event or forecasts formed by the light of nature; the miracles and the wonders of God's power are not what they are said to be, but the startling effects of natural law, or else mere tricks and myths; and the apostolic Gospels and writings are not the work of the Apostles at all.

310   These detestable errors, whereby they think they destroy the truth of the divine books, are obtruded on the world as the peremptory pronouncements of a certain newly-invented "free science," a science, however, which is so far from final that they are perpetually modifying and supplementing it. And there are some of them who, notwithstanding their impious opinions and utterances about God, and Christ, the Gospels and the rest of Holy Scripture, would fain be considered both theologians and Christians, and men of the gospel, and who attempt to disguise by such honorable names their rashness and their pride. To them we must add not a few professors of other sciences who approve their views and give them assistance and are urged to attack the Bible by a

similar intolerance of revelation. And it is deplorable to see these attacks growing every day more numerous and more severe.

It is sometimes men of learning and judgment who are as-   311
sailed; but these have little difficulty in defending themselves from evil consequences. The efforts and the arts of the enemy are chiefly directed against the more ignorant masses of the people. They diffuse their deadly poison by means of books, pamphlets, and newspapers; they spread it by addresses and by conversation; they are found everywhere; and they are in possession of numerous schools, taken by violence from the Church, in which, by ridicule and scurrilous jesting, they pervert the credulous and unformed minds of the young to the contempt of Holy Scripture. Should not these things, Venerable Brethren, stir up and set on fire the heart of every pastor, so that to this "so-called knowledge" (*I Tim.* 6:20), may be opposed the ancient and true wisdom which the Church, through the Apostles, has received from Christ, and that Holy Scripture may find the champions that are needed in so momentous a battle?

Let our first care, then, be to see that in seminaries and   312
academical institutions the study of Holy Scripture be placed on such a footing as its own importance and the circumstances of the time demand. With this view, the first thing which requires attention is the wise choice of professors. Teachers of sacred Scripture are not to be appointed haphazard out of the crowd; but they must be men whose character and fitness are proved by their love of, and their long familiarity with the Bible, and by suitable learning and study.

It is a matter of equal importance to provide in time for a   313
continuous succession of such teachers; and it will be well, wherever this can be done, to select young men of good promise who have successfully accomplished their theological course, and to set them apart exclusively for Holy Scripture, affording them facilities for full and complete studies. Professors thus chosen and thus prepared may enter with confidence on the task that is appointed for them; and that they may carry out their work well and profitably, let them take heed to the instructions We now proceed to give.

314   At the commencement of the course of Holy Scripture let the professor strive earnestly to form the judgment of the young beginners so as to train them equally to defend the sacred writings and to penetrate their meaning. This is the object of the treatise which is called "Introduction." Here the student is taught how to prove the integrity and authority of the Bible, how to investigate and ascertain its true sense, and how to meet and refute objections. It is needless to insist upon the importance of making these preliminary studies in an orderly and thorough fashion, with the accompaniment and assistance of theology; for the whole subsequent course must rest on the foundation thus laid and make use of the light thus acquired. Next, the teacher will turn his earnest attention to that more fruitful division of Scripture science which has to do with interpretation, wherein is imparted the method of using the Word of God for the advantage of religion and piety. We recognize, without hesitation, that neither the extent of the matter nor the time at disposal allows each single book of the Bible to be separately gone through. But the teaching should result in a definite and ascertained method of interpretation—and, therefore, the professor should equally avoid the mistake of giving a mere taste of every book, and of dwelling at too great length on a part of one book. If most schools cannot do what is done in the large institutions—that is, take the students through the whole of one or two books continuously and with a certain development—yet at least those parts which are selected should be treated with suitable fullness; in such a way that the students may learn from the sample that is thus put before them to love and use the remainder of the sacred book during the whole of their lives.

315   The professor, following the tradition of antiquity, will make use of the Vulgate as his text; for the Council of Trent decreed that "in public lectures, disputations, preaching, and exposition,"[22] the Vulgate is the "authentic" version; and this is the existing custom of the Church. At the same time, the other versions, which Christian antiquity has approved, should not be neglected, more especially the more ancient MSS. For, although the meaning of the Hebrew and Greek is substantially rendered by the Vulgate, nevertheless, wherever

there may be ambiguity or want of clearness, the "examination of older tongues,"[23] to quote St. Augustine, will be
useful and advantageous. But in this matter we need hardly
say that the greatest prudence is required, for the "office of
a commentator," as St. Jerome says, "is to set forth not what
he himself would prefer, but what his author says."[24] The
question of "reading" having been, when necessary, carefully
discussed, the next thing is to investigate and expound the
meaning. And the first counsel to be given is this: that the
more our adversaries contend to the contrary, so much the
more solicitously should we adhere to the received and approved canons of interpretation. Hence, whilst weighing the
meanings of words, the connection of ideas, the parallelism
of passages, and the like, we should by all means make use of
such illustrations as can be drawn from apposite erudition of
an external sort; but this should be done with caution, so as
not to bestow on questions of this kind more labor and time
than are spent on the sacred books themselves, and not to
overload the minds of the students with a mass of information that will be rather a hindrance than a help.

The professor may now safely pass on to the use of Scrip-   316
ture in matters of theology. On this head it must be observed
that in addition to the usual reasons which make ancient
writings more or less difficult to understand, there are some
which are peculiar to the Bible. For the language of the Bible
is employed to express, under the inspiration of the Holy
Spirit, many things which are beyond the power and scope of
the reason of man—that is to say, divine mysteries and all
that is related to them. There is sometimes in such passages a
fullness and a hidden depth of meaning which the letter
hardly expresses and which the laws of interpretation hardly
warrant. Moreover, the literal sense itself frequently admits
other senses, adapted to illustrate dogma or to confirm
morality.

Wherefore, it must be recognized that the sacred writings   317
are wrapt in a certain religious obscurity; and that no one can
enter into their interior without a guide; God so disposing,
as the holy Fathers commonly teach, in order that men may
investigate them with greater ardor and earnestness, and

that what is attained with difficulty may sink more deeply into the mind and heart, and, most of all, that they may understand that God has delivered the Holy Scripture to the Church, and that in reading and making use of His Work, they must follow the Church as their guide and their teacher. St. Irenaeus long since laid down, that where the charismata of God were, there the truth was to be learned, and the Holy Scripture was safely interpreted by those who had the apostolic succession.[26]

318   His teaching, and that of other holy Fathers, is taken up by the Council of the Vatican, which in renewing the decree of Trent declares its "mind" to be this—that "in things of faith and morals, belonging to the building up of Christian doctrine, that is to be considered the true sense of Holy Scripture, which has been held and is held by our Holy Mother the Church, whose place it is to judge of the true sense and interpretation of the Scriptures; and, therefore, that it is permitted to no one to interpret Holy Scripture against such sense or also against the unanimous agreement of the Fathers."[27] By this most wise decree the Church by no means prevents or restrains the pursuit of biblical science, but rather protects it from error, and largely assists its real progress.

319   A wide field is still left open to the private student, in which his hermeneutical skill may display itself with signal effect and to the advantage of the Church. On the one hand, in those passages of Holy Scripture which have not as yet received a certain and definite interpretation such labors may, in the benignant providence of God, prepare for and bring to maturity the judgment of the Church; on the other, in passages already defined the private student may do work equally valuable, either by setting them forth more clearly to the flock and more skillfully to scholars, or by defending them more powerfully from hostile attack. Wherefore the first and dearest object of the Catholic commentator should be to interpret these passages which have received an authentic interpretation either from the sacred writers themselves, under the inspiration of the Holy Spirit (as in many places of the New Testament), or from the Church, under the assistance of the same Holy Spirit, whether by her solemn judg-

ment or her ordinary and universal *magisterium*[28] —to interpret these passages in that identical sense, and to prove by all
the resources of science, that sound hermeneutical laws admit
of no other interpretation.

In the other passages the analogy of faith should be fol-　320
lowed, and Catholic doctrine, as authoritatively proposed by
the Church, should be held as the supreme law; for seeing
that the same God is the author both of the sacred books and
of the doctrine committed to the Church, it is clearly impossible that any teaching can, by legitimate means, be extracted
from the former, which shall, in any respect, be at variance
with the latter. Hence it follows that all interpretation is
foolish and false which either makes the sacred writers
disagree one with another, or is opposed to the doctrine of
the Church.

The professor of Holy Scripture, therefore, amongst other　321
recommendations, must be well acquainted with the whole
circle of theology and deeply read in the commentaries of the
holy Fathers and Doctors, and other interpreters of mark.
This is inculcated by St. Jerome,[29] and still more frequently
by St. Augustine, who thus justly complains: "If there is no
branch of teaching, however humble and easy to learn, which
does not require a master, what can be a greater sign of rashness and pride than to refuse to study the books of the divine
mysteries by the help of those who have interpreted them?"[30]
The other Fathers have said the same, and have confirmed it
by their example, for they "endeavored to acquire the understanding of the Holy Scriptures not by their own lights and
ideas, but from the writings and authority of the ancients,
who, in their turn, as we know, received the rule of interpretation in direct line from the Apostles."[31] The holy Fathers
"to whom, after the Apostles, the Church owes its growth—
who have planted, watered, built, governed and cherished
it,"[32] the holy Fathers, We say, are of supreme authority,
whenever they all interpret in one and the same manner any
text of the Bible, as pertaining to the doctrine of faith or
morals; for their unanimity clearly evinces that such interpretation has come down from the Apostles as a matter of
Catholic faith. The opinion of the Fathers is also of very

great weight when they treat of these matters in their capacity of Doctors unofficially; not only because they excel in their knowledge of revealed doctrine and in their acquaintance with many things which are useful in understanding the apostolic books, but because they are men of eminent sanctity and of ardent zeal for the truth, on whom God has bestowed a more ample measure of His light. Wherefore the expositor should make it his duty to follow their footsteps with all reverence, and to use their labors with intelligent appreciation.

322   But he must not on that account consider that it is forbidden when just cause exists, to push inquiry and exposition beyond what the Fathers have done; provided he carefully observes the rule so wisely laid down by St. Augustine—not to depart from the literal and obvious sense, except only where reason makes it untenable or necessity requires;[33] a rule to which it is the more necessary to adhere strictly in these times, when the thirst for novelty and unrestrained freedom of thought make the danger of error most real and proximate. Neither should those passages be neglected which the Fathers have understood in an allegorical or figurative sense, more especially when such interpretation is justified by the literal, and when it rests on the authority of many. For this method of interpretation has been received by the Church from the Apostles and has been approved by her own practice, as the holy Liturgy attests; although it is true that the holy Fathers did not thereby pretend directly to demonstrate dogmas of faith, but used it as a means of promoting virtue and piety, such as, by their own experience, they knew to be most valuable.

323   The authority of other Catholic interpreters is not so great; but the study of the Scriptures has always continued to advance in the Church and therefore these commentaries also have their own honorable place, and are serviceable in many ways for the refutation of assailants and the explanation of difficulties. But it is most unbecoming to pass by, in ignorance or contempt, the excellent work which Catholics have left in abundance, and to have recourse to the works of non-Catholics—and to seek in them, to the detriment of sound doctrine

and often to the peril of faith, the explanation of passages on
which Catholics long since have successfully employed their
talent and their labor. For although the studies of non-
Catholics, used with prudence, may sometimes be of use to
the Catholic student, he should, nevertheless, bear well in
mind—as the Fathers also teach in numerous passages[34]—that
the sense of Holy Scripture can nowhere be found incorrupt
outside the Church, and cannot be expected to be found in
writers who, being without the true faith, only gnaw the bark
of the sacred Scripture and never attain its pith.

Most desirable is it, and most essential, that the whole   324
teaching of theology should be pervaded and animated by the
use of the divine Word of God. This is what the Fathers and
the greatest theologians of all ages have desired and reduced
to practice. It was chiefly out of the sacred writings that they
endeavored to proclaim and establish the Articles of Faith
and the truth connected with it, and it was in them, together
with divine tradition, that they found the refutation of
heretical error, and the reasonableness, the true meaning, and
the mutual relation of the truths of Catholicism. Nor will any
one wonder at this who considers that the sacred books hold
such an eminent position among the sources of revelation that
without their assiduous study and use, theology cannot be
placed on its true footing, or treated as its dignity demands.

For although it is right and proper that students in acade-   325
mies and schools should be chiefly exercised in acquiring a
scientific knowledge of dogma, by means of reasoning from
the Articles of Faith to their consequences, according to the
rules of approved and sound philosophy—nevertheless the
judicious and instructed theologian will by no means pass by
that method of doctrinal demonstration which draws its
proof from the authority of the Bible; "for theology does not
receive her first principles from any other science, but immediately from God by revelation. And, therefore, she does
not receive of other sciences as from a superior, but uses
them as her inferiors or handmaids."[35] It is this view of
doctrinal teaching which is laid down and recommended by
the prince of theologians, St. Thomas Aquinas;[36] who,
moreover, shows—such being the essential character of Chris-

tian theology—how she can defend her own principles against attack: "If the adversary," he says, "do but grant any portion of the divine revelation, we have an argument against him; thus, against a heretic we can employ Scripture authority, and against those who deny one article, we can use another. But if our opponent reject divine revelation entirely, there is then no way left to prove the Articles of Faith by reasoning; we can only solve the difficulties which are raised against them"[38] Care must be taken, then, that beginners approach the study of the Bible well prepared and furnished; otherwise, just hopes will be frustrated, or, perchance, what is worse, they will unthinkingly risk the danger of error, falling an easy prey to the sophisms and labored erudition of the Rationalists. The best preparation will be a conscientious application to philosophy and theology under the guidance of St. Thomas Aquinas, and a thorough training therein—as We Ourselves have elsewhere pointed out and directed. By this means, both in biblical studies and in that part of theology which is called *positive*, they will pursue the right path and make satisfactory progress.

326   To prove, to expound, to illustrate Catholic doctrine by legitimate and skillful interpretation of the Bible is much; but there is a second part of the subject of equal importance and equal difficulty—the maintenance in the strongest possible way of its full authority. This cannot be done completely or satisfactorily except by means of the living and proper *magisterium* of the Church. The Church, "by reason of her wonderful propagation, her distinguished sanctity and inexhaustible fecundity in good, her Catholic unity, and her unshaken stability, is herself a great and perpetual motive of credibility, and an unassailable testimony to her own divine mission."[38] But since the divine and infallible *magisterium* of the Church rests also on the authority of Holy Scripture, the first thing to be done is to vindicate the trustworthiness of the sacred records, at least as human documents, from which can be clearly proved, as from primitive and authentic testimony, the divinity and mission of Christ our Lord, the institution of a hierarchical Church, and the primacy of Peter and his successors. It is most desirable, therefore, that there

should be numerous members of the clergy well prepared to enter upon a contest of this nature, and to repulse hostile assaults, chiefly trusting in that armor of God recommended by the Apostle (*Eph.* 6:13-17), but also not unaccustomed to modern methods of attack.

This is beautifully alluded to by St. John Chrysostom, when describing the duties of priests: 327

> We must use every endeavor that the "Word of God may dwell in us abundantly" (*Col.* 3:16); not merely for one kind of fight must we be prepared—for the contest is many-sided and the enemy is of every sort; and they do not all use the same weapons nor make their onset in the same way. Wherefore it is needful that the man who has to contend against all should be acquainted with the engines and the arts of all—that he should be at once archer and slinger, commandant and officer, general and private soldier, foot-soldier and horseman, skilled in sea-fight and in siege; for, unless he knows every trick and turn of war, the devil is well able, if only a single door be left open, to get in his fierce bands and carry off the sheep.[39]

The sophism of the enemy and his manifold arts of attack we have already touched upon. Let Us now say a word of advice on the means of defense.   328

The first means is the study of the Oriental languages and of the art of criticism. These two acquirements are in these days held in high estimation, and, therefore, the clergy, by making themselves more or less fully acquainted with them as time and place may demand, will the better be able to discharge their office with becoming credit; for they must make themselves "all things to all men" (*I Cor.* 9:22), always "ready with an answer to everyone who asks a reason for the hope that is in you" (*I Peter* 3:15). Hence it is most proper that professors of sacred Scripture and theologians should master those tongues in which the sacred books were originally written: and it would be well that ecclesiastical students also should cultivate them, more especially those who aspire to academic degrees. And endeavors should be made to estab-   329 lish in all academic institutions—as has already been laudably done in many—chairs of the other ancient languages, especially the Semitic, and of subjects connected therewith, for the benefit, principally, of those who are intended to profess sacred literature. These latter, with a similar object in view, should make themselves well and thoroughly acquainted with the art of true criticism.

330   There has arisen, to the great detriment of religion, an inept method, dignified by the name of the "higher criticism," which pretends to judge of the origin, integrity, and authority of each book from internal indications alone. It is clear, on the other hand, that in historical questions, such as the origin and the handing down of writings, the witness of history is of primary importance, and that historical investigation should be made with the utmost care; and that in this matter internal evidence is seldom of great value, except as confirmation. To look upon it in any other light will be to open the door to many evil consequences. It will make the enemies of religion much more bold and confident in attacking and mangling the sacred books; and this vaunted "higher criticism" will resolve itself into the reflection of the bias and the prejudice of the critics. It will not throw on the Scripture the light which is sought, or prove of any advantage to doctrine; it will only give rise to disagreement and dissension, those sure notes of error, which the critics in question so plentifully exhibit in their own persons; and seeing that most of them are tainted with false philosophy and rationalism, it must lead to the elimination from the sacred writings of all prophecy and miracles, and of everything else that is outside the natural order.

331   In the second place, we have to contend against those who, making an evil use of physical science, minutely scrutinize the sacred book in order to detect the writers in a mistake, and to take occasion to vilify its contents. Attacks of this kind, bearing as they do on matters of sensible experience, are peculiarly dangerous to the masses, and also to the young who are beginning their literary studies; for the young, if they lose their reverence for the Holy Scripture on one or more points, are easily led to give up believing in it altogether.

It need not be pointed out how the nature of science, just   332
as it is so admirably adapted to show forth the glory of the
Great Creator, provided it be taught as it should be, so, if it
be perversely imparted to the youthful intelligence, it may
prove most fatal in destroying the principles of true philosophy and in the corruption of morality. Hence, to the professor
of sacred Scripture a knowledge of natural science will be of
very great assistance in detecting such attacks on the sacred
books, and in refuting them. There can never, indeed, be any
real discrepancy between the theologian and the physicist, as
long as each confines himself within his own lines, and both
are careful, as St. Augustine warns us, "not to make rash
assertions, or to assert what is not known as known."[40] If
dissension should arise between them, here is the rule also
laid down by St. Augustine for the theologian:

> Whatever they can really demonstrate to be true of physical
> nature we must show to be capable of reconciliation with
> our Scriptures; and whatever they assert in their treatises,
> which is contrary to these Scriptures of ours, that is to
> Catholic faith, we must either prove it as well as we can to
> be entirely false, or at all events we must, without the
> smallest hesitation, believe it to be so.[41]

To understand how just is the rule here formulated we   333
must remember, first, that the sacred writers, or to speak
more accurately, the Holy Spirit "who spoke by them, did not
intend to teach men these things (that is to say, the essential
nature of the things of the visible universe), things in no way
profitable unto salvation."[42] Hence they did not seek to
penetrate the secrets of nature, but rather described and dealt
with things in more or less figurative language, or in terms
which were commonly used at the time, and which in many
instances are daily used at this day, even by the most eminent
men of science. Ordinary speech primarily and properly
describes what comes under the senses; and somewhat in the
same way the sacred writers—as the Angelic Doctor also re-
minds us—"went by what sensibly appeared,"[43] or put down

what God, speaking to men, signified, in the way men could understand and were accustomed to.

334   The unshrinking defense of the Holy Scripture, however, does not require that we should equally uphold all the opinions which each of the Fathers or the more recent interpreters have put forth in explaining it; for it may be that, in commenting on passages where physical matters occur, they have sometimes expressed the ideas of their own times, and thus made statements which in these days have been abandoned as incorrect. Hence, in their interpretations, we must carefully note what they lay down as belonging to faith, or as intimately connected with faith—what they are unanimous in. For "in those things which do not come under the obligation of faith, the saints were at liberty to hold divergent opinions, just as we ourselves are,"[44] according to the saying of St. Thomas. And in another place he says most admirably:

> When philosophers are agreed upon a point, and it is not contrary to our faith, it is safer in my opinion, neither to lay down such a point as a dogma of faith, even though it is perhaps so presented by the philosophers, nor to reject it as against faith, lest we thus give to the wise of this world an occasion of despising our faith.[45]

335   The Catholic interpreter, although he should show that these facts of natural science which investigators affirm to be now quite certain are not contrary to the Scripture rightly explained, must, nevertheless, always bear in mind, that much which has been held and proved as certain has afterwards been called in question and rejected. And if writers on physics travel outside the boundaries of their own branch, and carry their erroneous teaching into the domain of philosophy, let them be handed over to philosophers for refutation.

336   The principles here laid down will apply to cognate sciences, and especially to history. It is a lamentable fact that there are many who with great labor carry out and publish investigations on the monuments of antiquity, the manners and institutions of nations, and other illustrative subjects, and whose chief purpose in all this is too often to find mis-

takes in the sacred writings and so to shake and weaken their authority. Some of these writers display not only extreme hostility, but the greatest unfairness; in their eyes a profane book or ancient document is accepted without hesitation, whilst the Scripture, if they only find in it a suspicion of error, is set down with the slightest possible discussion as quite untrustworthy. It is true no doubt, that copyists have made mistakes in the text of the Bible; this question, when it arises, should be carefully considered on its merits, and the fact not too easily admitted, but only in those passages where the proof is clear.

It may also happen that the sense of a passage remains   337
ambiguous, and in this case good hermeneutical methods will greatly assist in clearing up the obscurity. But it is absolutely wrong and forbidden either to narrow inspiration to certain parts only of Holy Scripture or to admit that the sacred writer has erred. As to the system of those who, in order to rid themselves of these difficulties, do not hesitate to concede that divine inspiration regards the things of faith and morals, and nothing beyond, because (as they wrongly think) in a question of the truth or falsehood of a passage we should consider not so much what God has said as the reason and purpose which He had in mind in saying it—this system cannot be tolerated.

For all the books which the Church receives as sacred and   338
canonical are written wholly and entirely, with all their parts, at the dictation of the Holy Spirit; and so far is it from being possible that any error can coexist with inspiration, that inspiration not only is essentially incompatible with error, but excludes and rejects it as absolutely and necessarily as it is impossible that God Himself, the supreme Truth, can utter that which is not true. This is the ancient and unchanging faith of the Church, solemnly defined in the Councils of Florence and of Trent, and finally confirmed and more expressly formulated by the Council of the Vatican. These are the words of the last:

The books of the Old and New Testament, whole and entire, with all their parts, as enumerated in the decree of the same Council (Trent) and in the ancient Latin Vulgate, are to be received as sacred and canonical. And the Church holds them as sacred and canonical not because, having been composed by human industry, they were afterwards approved by her authority; nor only because they contain revelation without errors, but because, having been written under the inspiration of the Holy Spirit, they have God for their Author.[46]

339   Hence, the fact that it was men whom the Holy Spirit took up as his instruments for writing does not mean that it was these inspired instruments—but not the primary author—who might have made an error. For, by supernatural power, He so moved and impelled them to write—He so assisted them when writing—that the things which He ordered, and those only, they, first, rightly understood, then willed faithfully to write down, and finally expressed in apt words and with infallible truth. Otherwise, it could not be said that He was the Author of the entire Scripture. Such has always been the persuasion of the Fathers. "Therefore," says St. Augustine, "since they wrote the things which He showed and uttered to them, it cannot be pretended that He is not the writer; for His members executed what their head dictated."[47] And St. Gregory the Great thus pronounces: "Most superfluous it is to inquire who wrote these things—we loyally believe the Holy Spirit to be the author of the book. He wrote it who dictated it for writing; He wrote it who inspired its execution."[48]

340   It follows that those who maintain that an error is possible in any genuine passage of the sacred writings either pervert the Catholic notion of insipiration or make God the author of such error. And so emphatically were all the Fathers and Doctors agreed that the divine writings, as left by the hagiographers, are free from all error, that they labored earnestly, with no less skill than reverence, to reconcile with each other those numerous passages which seem at variance—the very passages which in great measure have been taken up by the "higher criticism"; for they were unanimous in laying it down that those writings, in their entirety and in all their parts were equally from the *afflatus* of Almighty God, and

that God, speaking by the sacred writers, could not set down anything but what was true. The words of St. Augustine to St. Jerome may sum up what they taught:

> On my own part I confess to your charity that it is only to those books of Scripture which are now called canonical that I have learned to pay such honor and reverence as to believe most firmly that none of their writers has fallen into any error. And if in these books I meet anything which seems contrary to truth, I shall not hesitate to conclude either that the text is faulty, or that the translator has not expressed the meaning of the passage, or that I myself do not understand.[49]

But to undertake fully and perfectly, and with all the weap-　341
ons of the best science, the defense of the Holy Bible is far more than can be looked for from the exertions of commentators and theologians alone. It is an enterprise in which we have a right to expect the cooperation of all those Catholics who have acquired reputation in any branch of learning whatever. As in the past, so at the present time, the Church is never without the graceful support of her accomplished children; may their services to the Faith grow and increase! For there is nothing which We believe to be more needful than that truth should find defenders more powerful and more numerous than the enemies it has to face; nor is there anything which is better calculated to impress the masses with respect for truth than to see it boldly proclaimed by learned and distinguished men.

Moreover, the bitter tongues of objectors will be silenced　342
or at least they will not dare to insist so shamelessly that faith is the enemy of science, when they see that scientific men of eminence in their profession show towards faith the most marked honor and respect. Seeing, then, that those can do so much for the advantage of religion on whom the goodness of Almighty God has bestowed, together with the grace of the faith, great natural talent, let such men, in this bitter conflict of which the Holy Scripture is the object, select each of them the branch of study most suitable to his circum-

stances, and endeavor to excel therein, and thus be prepared to repulse with credit and distinction the assaults on the Word of God. And it is Our pleasing duty to give deserved praise to a work which certain Catholics have taken up—that is to say, the formulation of societies and the contribution of considerable sums of money, for the purpose of supplying studious and learned men with every kind of help and assistance in carrying out complete studies. Truly an excellent manner of investing money, and well suited to the times in which we live! The less hope of public patronage there is for Catholic study, the more ready and the more abundant should be the liberality of private persons—those to whom God has given riches thus willingly making use of their means to safeguard the treasure of His revealed doctrine.

343   In order that all these endeavors and exertions may really prove advantageous to the cause of the Bible, let scholars keep steadfastly to the principles which We have in this letter laid down. Let them loyally hold that God, the Creator and Ruler of all things, is also the Author of the Scriptures—and that, therefore, nothing can be proved either by physical science or archaeology which can really contradict the Scriptures. If then, apparent contradiction be met with, every effort should be made to remove it. Judicious theologians and commentators should be consulted as to what is the true or most probably meaning of the passage in discussion and the hostile arguments should be carefully weighed. Even if the difficulty is after all not cleared up and the discrepancy seems to remain, the contest must not be abandoned; truth cannot contradict truth, and we may be sure that some mistake has been made either in the interpretation of the sacred words or in the polemic discussion itself; and if no such mistake can be detected, we must then suspend judgment for the time being.

344   There have been objections without number perseveringly directed against the Scripture for many a long year, which have been proved to be futile and are now never heard of; and not infrequently interpretations have been placed on certain passages of Scripture (not belonging to the rule of faith or morals) which have been rectified by more careful investi-

gations. As time goes on, mistaken views die and disappear; but "truth remaineth and groweth stronger forever and ever" (*III Esdr.* 4:38). Wherefore, as no one should be so presumptuous as to think that he understands the whole of the Scripture, in which St. Augustine himself confessed that there was more that he did not know, than that he knew,[50] so, if he should come upon anything that seems incapable of solution, he must take to heart the cautious rule of the same holy Doctor: "It is better even to be oppressed by unknown but useful signs, than to interpret them uselessly and thus to throw off the yoke only to be caught in the trap of error."[51]

As to those who pursue the subsidiary studies of which We   345
have spoken, if they honestly and modestly follow the counsels We have given—if by their pen and their voice they make their studies profitable against the enemies of truth, and useful in saving the young from the loss of their faith—they may justly congratulate themselves on their worthy service to the sacred writings, and on affording to Catholicism that assistance which the Church has a right to expect from the piety and learning of her children.

Such, Venerable Brethren, are the admonitions and the in-   346
structions which, by the help of God, We have thought it well, at the present moment, to offer to you on the study of Holy Scripture. It will now be your province to see that what We have said be observed and put in practice with all due reverence and exactness; that so We may prove Our gratitude to God for the communication to man of the words of His wisdom, and that all the good results so much to be desired may be realized, especially as they affect the training of the students of the Church, which is Our own great solicitude and the Church's hope.

Exert yourselves with willing alacrity, and use your author-   347
ity and your persuasion in order that these studies may be held in just regard and may flourish in seminaries and in the educational institutions which are under your jurisdiction. Let them flourish in completeness and in happy success, under the direction of the Church, in accordance with the salutary teaching and example of the holy Fathers, and the laudable traditions of antiquity; and, as time goes on, let

them be widened and extended as the interests and glory of truth may require—the interests of that Catholic truth which comes from above, the never-failing source of man's salvation. Finally, We admonish, with paternal love, all students and ministers of the Church always to approach the sacred writings with reverence and piety; for it is impossible to attain to the profitable understanding thereof unless the arrogance of "earthly" science be laid aside, and there be excited in the heart the holy desire for that wisdom "which is from above." In this way the intelligence, which is once admitted to these sacred studies, and thereby illuminated and strengthened, will acquire a marvelous facility in detecting and avoiding the fallacies of human science, and in gathering and using for eternal salvation all that is valuable and precious; whilst, at the same time, the heart will grow warm, and will strive, with ardent longing, to advance in virtue and in divine love. "Blessed are they who examine His testimonies; they shall seek Him with their whole heart" (*Ps.* 18:2).

348   And now, filled with hope in the divine assistance, and trusting to your pastoral solicitude—as a pledge of heavenly grace, and a sign of Our special good will—to you all, and to the clergy, and the whole flock entrusted to you, We lovingly impart in Our Lord the Apostolic Benediction.

349   Given at St. Peter's, at Rome, the 18th day of November, 1893, the sixteenth year of Our Pontificate.

VIGILANTIAE
Apostolic Letter of Leo XIII
on the Institution of a Commission for Biblical Studies
October 30, 1902

Faithful to the tradition of watchfulness and zeal by which We, first of all, because of Our office, are bound to preserve the deposit of faith safe and inviolate, We gave to the world in the year 1893 the Encyclical *Providentissimus*. In it We included, after due examination, a number of questions concerning the study of Holy Scripture. The grandeur and extreme utility of the subject impelled Us, in effect, to determine, as far as in Us lay, the directive principle of those studies so necessary now that the increase of erudition confronts Us every day with the consideration of novel questions which are sometimes in danger of being treated in a manner fraught with rashness.

Wherefore, We have warned all Catholics, and especially those in Holy Orders, of the work which each one should undertake in this matter in accordance with the abilities with which he is endowed, and We applied Ourselves with the greatest care to show how and in what manner these studies should be developed in conformity with the needs of our epoch. This document has not been without result, and it is with joy that We recall the testimonies of submission which the bishops and a great number of men eminent in science hastened to give Us while proclaiming at the same time the opportuneness and the importance of what We had written; and promising to conform with the greatest diligence to Our instructions. Another remembrance no less agreeable comes to Us in the fact that excellent beginnings were immediately made by some in the direction indicated, and an enthusiasm awakened in various places in the prosecution of such studies. Nevertheless, We remark that the causes which prompted Us to publish the previous letter are still persistent and more serious. It is therefore necessary to insist more emphatically on what has already been enjoined and more than ever to express Our desire that Our Venerable Brethren of the episcopate should watch with the greatest vigilance over these studies. To ensure greater facility as well as fruitfulness, We have resolved to add new strength to Our authority in this matter. As the task now before Us of explaining these divine books and maintaining them intact is too difficult for our Catholic interpreters to acquit themselves well of, if left to their individual efforts, and because the work is nevertheless so necessary on account of the manifold development of science and the appearance of such multitudinous error, it is deemed proper that a federation of energies should be made, and that assistance should be afforded under the auspices and direction of the Apostolic See. This result, it appears to Us, can be easily attained if We make use in the present instance of the means which We have already employed for advancing other studies.

352   Wherefore it has seemed good to Us to institute a council or, as it is termed, a Commission of men of learning whose duty shall be to effect that in every possible manner the divine text will find here and from every quarter the most thorough interpretation which is demanded by our times, and be shielded not only from every breath of error, but also from every temerarious opinion. It is proper that the principal seat of this Commission should be in Rome, under the very eyes of the Sovereign Pontiff. As it is the seat of the mistress and guardian of Christian knowledge, it should also be the center from which there should flow through the whole body of the Christian commonwealth the pure and incorruptible teaching of this science which is now so indispensable. The men of whom this Commission shall be composed, in order to satisfy fully the serious obligation which is laid upon them and which confers on them such distinction, should regard as

peculiarly and especially their own the tasks which are here proposed to their zeal.

In the first place, having established exactly what is the   353 actual intellectual trend of the present day with regard to this science, they should bear in mind that none of the recent discoveries which the human mind has made are foreign to the purpose of their work. On the contrary, let them make haste in any case where our times have discovered something useful in the matter of biblical exegesis to avail themselves of it forthwith and by their writings to put it at the service of all.

Wherefore they should devote themselves with the greatest   354 care to the study of philology and kindred sciences and keep themselves abreast of the progress of the day. As it is generally on this point that the attacks on Holy Scripture are made, it is there that we should likewise gather our arms of defense; so that there may be no inequality in the struggle between truth and error. Likewise they shall take measures that the knowledge of the ancient and oriental languages, and above all the art of deciphering the ancient texts, should be assiduously cultivated. In our contest with unbelievers, both of these kinds of studies are, as a matter of fact, a precious help in biblical studies.

In what concerns the integral safeguarding of the authority   355 of the Scriptures, the members of the Commission will employ an active vigilance and unremitting assiduity. The main point to be attained is that Catholics should not admit the malignant principle of granting more than is due to the opinion of heterodox writers, and of thinking that the true understanding of the Scriptures should be sought first of all in the researches which the erudition of unbelievers has arrived at. Indeed, no Catholic can consider as subject to doubt these truths which We have elsewhere referred to at greater length, and they must know that God has not delivered the Scriptures to the private judgment of the learned, but has confided the interpretation of them to the teaching of the Church.

In the matter of faith and morals which pertain to the   356 teaching of Christian Doctrine, the sense of Holy Scripture, which must be considered as the true sense, is that which has been adopted and is adopted by our holy mother, the Church, whose office it is to judge of the real meaning and interpretation of Holy Scripture. It is therefore not permitted to anyone to interpret the Holy Scripture in any way contrary to this sense, or even in any way contrary to the universal opinion of the Fathers (Conc. Vat. sess. III, cap. ii).

357   As We were saying, the nature of the divine books is such that in order to dissipate the religious obscurity with which they are shrouded we must never count on the laws of hermeneutics, but must address ourselves to the Church, which has been given by God to mankind as a guide and teacher. In brief, the legitimate sense of the divine Scriptures ought not to be found outside the Church nor be pronounced by those who have repudiated its teaching and authority.

358   The men who are to compose this Commission should therefore watch with great care to safeguard these principles and to keep them, as time goes on, with still greater strictness. And if certain minds profess an exaggerated admiration for heterodox writers, they must be led by persuasion to follow and to obey more faithfully the direction of the Church.

359   Doubtless there may arise an occasion when the Catholic interpreter may find some assistance in authors outside of the Church, especially in matters of criticism, but here there is need of prudence and discernment. Let our doctors cultivate with care the science of criticism, for it is of great utility in order to grasp in its complete sense the opinion of hagiographers; and in that they will receive Our warmest approbation. Let them draw from this science new resources by availing themselves even of the assistance of non-Catholic scholars. In doing so they need not fear Our disapprobation. They should, however, be careful not to draw from habitual association with such writers independence of judgment, for in point of fact the system which is known in our days as higher criticism frequently leads to such results. Its dangerous rashness We have more than once already condemned.

In the third place, it is of importance that this Commis-   360
sion should consecrate its most special attention to that part
of these studies which properly concerns the explanation of
the Scriptures and which opens to the faithful a great source
of spiritual profit. In whatever touches the texts whose sense
has been fixed in an authentic manner, either by the sacred
writers or by the Church, the Commission, it is needless to
say, should be convinced that only that interpretation can be
adopted. Such is the rule of sound hermeneutics. But there
exist numerous passages upon which the Church has not yet
given any fixed or precise definition, with regard to which it
is permitted to each doctor in his individual capacity to profess and to sustain the opinion which seems to him to be
correct. They must know, however, that on these points they
should keep as the rule of interpretation the analogy of faith
and of Catholic doctrine. Moreover, we must be on our guard
in this matter against transgressing, in the excessive ardor of
debate, the limits of mutual charity. It is also of importance
not to seem to discuss revealed truths and divine traditions. If
they make light of intellectual concord, and if these principles
are not safeguarded, we cannot have any right to expect that
the divergent labors of such a great number of scholars will
accomplish any notable progress in this science.

Hence this Commission will have as its task to regulate in a   361
legitimate and suitable manner the principal questions which
are pending between Catholic doctors in order to arrive at a
conclusion. To settle them the assembly will lend sometimes
the light of its judgment, sometimes the weight of its authority. Their investigations will also have a result of the greatest
advantage, namely, that of furnishing to the Holy See an
opportune occasion to declare what ought to be inviolably
maintained by Catholics, what ought to be reserved for more
profound research, and what ought to be left to the free
judgment of each.

Having, therefore, in view to ensure the maintenance of   362
Catholic authority in its integrity, and to promote the studies
which relate to Holy Scripture in conformity with the rules
which have been herein laid down, We, by these present

Letters, establish in this illustrious city a council or a special Commission. We wish it to be composed of some Cardinals of the Holy Roman Church who shall be chosen in virtue of Our authority. It is Our intention to add to them with the functions and titles of consultors, and to take part in the same studies and the same labors, as it is customary in the sacred Roman commissions, certain eminent men who belong to different nationalities, who are recommended by their knowledge in sacred studies, and above all, in whatever appertains to biblical science.

363   The Commission will hold its fixed reunions and publish its writings, which will appear periodically or as need may require. If advice is asked of it, it will reply to those who consult it. In a word, it will labor by all means in its power to maintain and to develop the studies of which we speak. We desire that a report concerning all the questions which may be treated in common should be addressed to the Sovereign Pontiff by the Consultor to whom the Commission will have confided the office of secretary.

364   In order to furnish members of the Commission with available help, which will be of service to them in any of these studies, We herewith assign to them for this purpose a certain portion of Our Vatican Library. We shall take care that a numerous collection of manuscripts and volumes of every epoch which treat of biblical questions shall without delay be classified and placed at the disposition of the commissioners. It is very desirable that well-to-do Catholics should come to Our assistance to establish and enlarge this library in sending to Us resources to be employed for this end, or useful books, and in so doing they will render a service in a most fitting manner to Almighty God, who is the Author of the Scriptures and of the Church.

365   Moreover, We have confidence that divine Providence will amply bless this undertaking, which has for its direct object the safeguarding of Christian faith and the eternal salvation of souls, and that Catholics who are devoted to the holy books will respond with an absolute and complete submission to the declarations of the Holy See on this point. We wish and We ordain that all and every one of these prescriptions

and decisions which it has seemed good to Us to make and to formulate on this point shall be and shall remain ratified and confirmed in the manner which We have adopted and formulated, anything to the contrary notwithstanding.

Given at Rome at St. Peter's under the Ring of the Fisherman, the 30th of October, the year 1902, the twenty-fifth of Our Pontificate.

366

Fourteen Decisions
of the Pontifical Biblical Commission
1905-1915

I

On the Tacit Quotations Contained in Holy Scripture

In order to establish a guide for students of Holy Scripture the following question has been proposed to the Biblical Commission:

367   Whether it is allowable for a Catholic commentator to solve difficulties occurring in certain texts of Holy Scripture, which apparently relate historical facts, by asserting that we have in such texts tacit or implied quotations from documents written by a non-inspired author, and that the inspired author by no means intends to approve of these statements or make them his own, and that these statements cannot, in consequence, be regarded as free from error.

368   *Answer*: To this the Commission judged proper to reply: In the negative; except in the case when, subject to the mind and decision of the Church, it can be proved by solid arguments, first, that the sacred writer really does cite another's sayings or writings; and secondly, that he does not intend in so doing, to approve them or make them his own, in such a way that he be rightly considered not to speak in his own name.

February 13, 1905.

II

Concerning the Narratives in the Historical Books Which Have Only the Appearances of Being Historical

The Biblical Commission answers the following question:

Whether we may admit as a principle of sound exegesis the opinion which holds that those books of Holy Scripture which are regarded as historical, either wholly or in part, sometimes narrate what is not history properly so-called and objectively true, but only have the appearance of history and are intended to convey a meaning different from the strictly literal or historical sense of the words. 369

Answer: In the negative; excepting always the case—not to be easily or rashly admitted, and then only on the supposition that it is not opposed to the teaching of the Church and subject to her decision—that it can be proved by solid arguments that the sacred writer did not intend to give a true and strict history, but proposed rather to set forth, under the guise and form of history, a parable or an allegory or some meaning distinct from the strictly literal or historical signification of the words. 370

June 23, 1905.

III

On the Mosaic Authorship of the Pentateuch

The Biblical Commission answers the following questions:

1. *Authenticity*—Whether the arguments amassed by critics to impugn the Mosaic authenticity of the sacred books designated by the name Pentateuch are of sufficient weight, notwithstanding the very many evidences to the contrary contained in both Testaments, taken collectively, the persistent 371

agreement of the Jewish people, the constant tradition of the Church, and internal arguments derived from the text itself, to justify the statement that these books have not Moses for their author but have been compiled from sources for the most part posterior to the time of Moses.

372   *Answer:* In the negative.

373   2. *Writer*—Whether the Mosaic authenticity of the Penta-teuch necessarily postulates such a redaction of the whole work as to render it absolutely imperative to maintain that Moses wrote with his own hand or dictated to amanueses all and everything contained in it; or whether it is possible to admit the hypothesis of those who think that he entrusted the composition of the work itself, conceived by himself under the influence of divine inspiration, to some other person or persons, but in such a manner that they render faithfully his own thoughts, wrote nothing contrary to his will, and omitted nothing; and that the work thus produced, approved by Moses as the principal and inspired author, was made public under his name.

374   *Answer:* In the negative to the first part, in the affirmative to the second part.

375   3. *Sources*—Whether it may be granted, without prejudice to the Mosaic authenticity of the Pentateuch, that Moses employed sources in the production of his work, i.e., written documents or oral traditions, from which, to suit his special purpose and under the influence of divine inspiration, he selected some things and inserted them in his work, either literally or in substance, summarized or amplified.

376   *Answer:* In the affirmative.

377   4. *Changes and Textual Corruptions*—Whether, granted the substantial Mosaic authenticity and the integrity of the Pentateuch, it may be admitted that in the long course of

centuries some modifications have been introduced into the work, such as additions after the death of Moses, either appended by an inspired author or inserted into the text as glosses and explanations; certain words and forms translated from the ancient language to more recent language, and finally, faulty readings to be ascribed to the error of amanuenses, concerning which it is lawful to investigate and judge according to the laws of criticism.

Answer: In the affirmative, subject to the judgment of the Church.   378

June 27, 1906.

IV

On the Author and Historical Truth of the Fourth Gospel

The Biblical Commission answers the following questions:

1. *External Evidence for Authenticity*—Whether from the constant, universal, and solemn tradition of the Church coming down from the second century, as it is gathered chiefly: *a.* from the testimonies and allusions of the holy Fathers and ecclesiastical writers, nay even those of heretics, which since they must have been derived from the disciples or first successors of the Apostles, are joined by a necessary connection to the very origin of the book; *b.* from the fact that the name of the author of the Fourth Gospel was received always and everywhere in the canons and catalogues of the sacred books; *c.* from the most ancient manuscripts, codices and their versions in various languages of the same books; *d.* from the public liturgical use obtaining throughout the whole world from the very beginnings of the Church; leaving aside the theological argument, it is proved by such a solid historical argument that the Apostle John and no other must be acknowledged as the author of the Fourth Gospel, that the reasons to the contrary, brought forward by the critics, in no wise weaken this tradition.   379

380   *Answer:* In the affirmative.

381   2. *Internal Evidence for Authenticity*—Whether also the internal reasons, which are drawn from the text of the Fourth Gospel considered separately, and from the testimony of the writer and the manifest kinship of the Gospel itself with the First Epistle of the Apostle John, must be considered to confirm the tradition which unhesitatingly attributes the Fourth Gospel to the same Apostle. And whether the difficulties which are drawn from the comparison of the same Gospel with the other three, bearing in mind the diversity of time, of scope, and of the hearers for whom or against whom the author wrote, can be reasonably solved, as the holy Fathers and Catholic commentators have done at some times.

382   *Answer*: In the affirmative to both parts.

383   3. *Historical Character*—Whether, notwithstanding the practice which has constantly obtained in the whole Church from the first ages, of arguing from the Fourth Gospel as from a strictly historical document, and considering moreover the peculiar character of the same Gospel and the author's manifest intention of illustrating and vindicating the divinity of Christ from His own deeds and words, it can be said that the facts narrated in the Fourth Gospel are wholly or in part invented to serve as allegories or doctrinal symbols, and that discourses of our Lord are not properly and truly the discourses of our Lord Himself, but the theological compositions of the writer, albeit they are placed in the mouth of our Lord.

384   *Answer*: In the negative.

May 29, 1907.

V

On the Character of the Book of Isaias and Its Author

The Biblical Commission answers the following questions:

1. *Prophetical Character*—Whether it may be taught that   385
the prophecies which are read in the book of Isaias, and here
and there in the Scriptures, are not real prophecies, but either
narratives composed subsequent to the event, or, if it must be
acknowledged that something was foretold before the event,
that the prophet foretold the same, not from a supernatural
revelation of God who foreknows the future, but by conjec-
turing through a happy sagacity and acuteness of natural
intelligence from things that had already happened.

Answer: In the negative.   386

2. *Time of Fulfillment*—Whether the opinion which holds   387
that Isaias and the other prophets uttered prophecies concerning only those things which were to take place immediately
or after a short space of time, can be reconciled with the
prophecies, particularly the Messianic and eschatological,
which were undoubtedly uttered by the same prophets about
the remote future, as well as with the common opinion of the
Fathers who unanimously assert that the prophets foretold
also those things which should be fulfilled after many ages.

Answer: In the negative.   388

3. *Character of the Prophetic Office*—Whether it may be   389
admitted that the prophets not only as correctors of human
wickedness and heralds of the divine Word for the good of
their hearers, but also as foretellers of future events, must
always have addressed themselves to a present and contemporary and not to a future audience, so that they could be

clearly understood by them; and that therefore, the second part of the book of Isaias (chapter 40-66), in which the prophet addresses and consoles not the Jews contemporary with Isaias, but, as one living among them, those mourning in the exile of Babylon, cannot have for its author Isaias himself then long dead, but must be attributed to some unknown prophet living among the exiles.

390   *Answer*: In the negative.

391   4. *Unity of Authorship*—Whether the philological argument, one derived from the language and the style, and employed to impugn the identity of the author of the book of Isaias, is to be considered weighty enough to compel a man of judgment, versed in the principles of criticism and well acquainted with Hebrew, to acknowledge in the same book a plurality of authors.

392   *Answer*: In the negative.

393   5. *Cumulative Arguments against Unity*—Whether there are solid arguments, even when taken cumulatively, to prove that the book of Isaias is to be attributed not to Isaias alone, but to two or even more authors.

394   *Answer*: In the negative.

June 28, 1908.

VI

**On the Historical Character of the First Three Chapters
of Genesis**

The Biblical Commission answers the following questions:

395   1. *False Exegesis*—Whether the various exegetical systems, which have been elaborated and defended by the aid of a science falsely so-called, for the purpose of excluding the

literal historical sense of the first three chapters of Genesis, are based upon solid arguments.

Answer: In the negative.   396

2. *Historical Character of the Three Chapters*—Whether we   397
may, in spite of the character and historic form of the book
of Genesis, of the close connection of the first three chapters
with one another and with those which follow, of the manifold testimony of the Scriptures both of the Old and the New
Testament, of the almost unanimous opinion of the Fathers,
and of the traditional view which—transmitted also by the
Jewish people—has always been held by the Church, teach
that the three aforesaid chapters do not contain the narrative
of things which actually happened, a narrative which corresponds to objective reality and historic truth; and whether
we may teach that these chapters contain fables derived from
mythologies and cosmologies belonging to older nations, but
purified of all polytheistic error and accommodated to mono-
theistic teaching by the sacred author or that they contain
allegories and symbols destitute of any foundation in objective reality but presented under the garb of history for the
purpose of inculcating religious and philosophical truth; or,
finally, that they contain legends partly historical and partly
fictitious, freely handled for the instruction and edification
of souls.

Answer: In the negative to each part.   398

3. *Historical Character of Certain Parts*—Whether, in par-   399
ticular, we may call in question the literal and historical
meaning where there is question of facts narrated in these
chapters which touch the fundamental teachings of the
Christian religion, as for example, the creation of all things
which was accomplished by God at the beginning of time, the
special creation of man, the formation of the first woman
from man, the unity of the human race, the original happiness of our first parents in a state of justice, integrity, and

immortality, the divine command laid upon man to prove his obedience, the transgression of that divine command at the instigation of the devil under the form of a serpent, the fall of our first parents from their primitive state of innocence, and the promise of a future Redeemer.

400   *Answer*: In the negative.

401   4. *Interpretation*—Whether, in interpreting those passages of these chapters which the Fathers and Doctors have interpreted in divers ways without leaving us anything definite or certain, anyone may, subject to the decision of the Church and following the analogy of faith, follow and defend that opinion at which he has prudently arrived.

402   *Answer*: In the affirmative.

403   5. *Literal Sense*—Whether all and each of the parts, namely, the single words and phrases, in these chapters must always and of necessity be interpreted in a proper literal sense, so that it is never lawful to deviate from it, even when expressions are manifestly used figuratively, that is, metaphorically or anthropomorphically, and when reason forbids us to hold, or necessity impels us to depart from, the proper literal sense.

404   *Answer*: In the negative.

405   6. *Allegory and Prophecy*—Whether, granting always the literal and historical sense, the allegorical and prophetical interpretation of certain passages of these chapters—an interpretation justified by the example of the Fathers and the Church—may be prudently and usefully applied.

406   *Answer*: In the affirmative.

407   7. *Scientific Expression*—Whether, since it was not the intention of the sacred author, when writing the first chapter of Genesis, to teach us in a scientific manner the innermost

nature of visible things, and to present the complete order of creation but rather to furnish his people with a popular account, such as the common parlance of that age allowed, one, namely, adapted to the senses and to man's intelligence, we are strictly and always bound, when interpreting these chapters to seek for scientific exactitude of expression.

Answer: In the negative. 408

8. *Yom*—Whether the Word *Yom* (day), which is used in the first chapter of Genesis to describe and distinguish the six days, may be taken either in its strict sense as the natural day, or in a less strict sense as signifying a certain space of time; and whether free discussion of this question is permitted to interpreters. 409

Answer: In the affirmative. 410

June 30, 1909.

VII

On the Author, Time of Composition, and Character of The Psalms

The Biblical Commission answers the following questions:

1. *Authorship*—Whether the terms *Psalms of David, Hymns of David,* the *Book of the Psalms of David,* the *Davidic Psalter,* which in the old collections and even in the Councils are used to designate the Old Testament Book of 150 psalms, as also the opinion of many Fathers and Doctors who held that absolutely all the psalms of the Psalter were to be attributed to David alone, are of such force that we have to consider David as the sole author of the entire Psalter. 411

Answer: In the negative. 412

2. *Antiquity of the Titles*—Whether, from the agreement of the Hebrew text with the Alexandrian Greek text and with 413

other old versions, we can rightly conclude that the titles prefixed to the psalms in the Hebrew text are of older date than the aforesaid LXX version, and that consequently they are due, if not directly to the authors of the psalms, at least to very ancient Jewish tradition.

414   *Answer:* In the affirmative.

415   3. *Genuineness of the Titles*—Whether the aforesaid titles, witnesses to the Jewish tradition, can be prudently called in question except when there is no solid reason against their genuine character.

416   *Answer:* In the negative.

417   4. *Davidic Authorship*—Whether, considering the not infrequent testimonies in the Bible to David's natural skill, a skill further illumined by the special gift of the Holy Spirit, for the composition of religious odes; whether, considering too, the arrangement drawn up by him for the liturgical chanting of the psalms; the attributions also, both in the Old Testament and the New, of psalms to him, as also in the actual inscriptions anciently affixed to the psalms; whether, considering, moreover, the common opinion of the Jews, and of the Fathers and Doctors of the Church, it can be prudently denied that David was the principal author of the odes contained in the Psalter. Whether, on the other hand, it can be maintained that only a few of these odes are to be attributed to the Royal Psalmist.

418   *Answer:* In the negative to both questions.

419   5. *Davidic Authorship in Particular*—Whether we can in particular deny the Davidic origin of the psalms which, in both the Old and New Testaments, are expressly cited under David's name, especially such as Ps. 2, *Why have the Gentiles raged;* Ps. 15, *Preserve me, O Lord;* Ps. 17, *I will love Thee, O Lord, my strength;* Ps. 31, *Blessed are they whose iniquities*

are forgiven; Ps. 68, *Save me, O God;* Ps. 109, *The Lord said to my Lord.*

Answer: In the negative.   420

6. *Changes and Additions*—Whether we can admit the view   421
held by some, namely, that certain psalms, whether by David
or by other authors, have, for liturgical or musical reasons, or
through the carelessness of copyists, or for other unexplained
reasons, been divided or even welded together. Further,
whether we can hold that some psalms, e.g., the *Miserere*, in
order to be better adapted to historical circumstances or
Jewish festivals, have been slightly remolded or modified,
either by the removal or addition of one or two verses, without detriment to the inspiration of the whole sacred text.

Answer: In the affirmative to both questions.   422

7. *Recent Psalms*—Whether we can maintain with any real   423
probability the opinion of those recent writers who, basing
their views only upon internal grounds or upon an unsound
interpretation of the sacred text, strive to demonstrate that
not a few psalms were composed after the date of Esdras and
Nehemias, nay, even in the Machabean age.

Answer: In the negative.   424

8. *Prophetic and Messianic Psalms*—Whether, judging by   425
the repeated testimonies of the Books of the New Testament,
the unanimous consent of the Fathers, in agreement, too,
with Jewish writers, we must hold that some psalms are to be
recognized as prophetic and Messianic, i.e., as foretelling the
coming of a future Redeemer, His kingdom, His priesthood,
His passion, death, and resurrection. And whether we must in
consequence, reject the opinion of those who, perverting the
prophetic and Messianic character of the psalms, limit these
oracles, concerning Christ, to mere predictions of the future
lot of the chosen people.

426   *Answer:* In the affirmative to both questions.

May 1, 1910.

VIII

On the Author, Date of Composition, and Historical Truth of the Gospel According to St. Matthew

The Biblical Commission answers the following questions:

427   1. *Author*—Whether, bearing in mind the universal and constant tradition of the Church dating from the first centuries, which explicit testimonies of the Fathers, the inscriptions of the codices of the Gospels, the oldest version of the sacred books as well as their catalogues transmitted to us by the holy Fathers, ecclesiastical writers, Supreme Pontiffs and the Councils, and finally, the liturgical usages of the Eastern and Western Church clearly record, it may and must be affirmed with certainty that Matthew, an Apostle of Christ, is in truth the author of the Gospel published under his name.

428   *Answer:* In the affirmative.

429   2. *Order of Composition and Language*—Whether the opinion must be considered as sufficiently supported by the testimony of tradition, which holds that Matthew wrote before the other Evangelists and that he wrote the first Gospel in the native dialect then in use by the Jews of Palestine, for whom this work was intended.

430   *Answer:* in the affirmative to both parts.

431   3. *Date of Composition*—Whether the publication of this original text may be deferred beyond the time of the destruction of Jerusalem, so that the prophecies which are therein recorded concerning that event, were written after the destruction and whether the frequently quoted testimony of St. Irenaeus,[1] the interpretation of which is uncertain and controverted, must be considered of such authority as to necessi-

tate the rejection of the opinion of those who consider it more in conformity with tradition that the first Gospel was completed even before the arrival of St. Paul at Rome.

Answer: In the negative to both parts.   432

4. *Compilation*—Whether the opinion of certain moderns   433
may be held as probable according to which Matthew is said to have composed the Gospel not exactly as it has been transmitted to us, but only a collection of the sayings and discourses of Christ, which an anonymous author, whom these moderns call the compiler of the Gospel, has used as sources.

Answer: In the negative.   434

5. *Identity of Hebrew and Greek*—Whether, from the fact   435
that the Fathers, all ecclesiastical writers, and even the Church herself, from the very beginning, have used only the Greek text of the Gospel known under the name of Matthew as canonical, not even excepting those who have explicitly testified that Matthew, the Apostle, wrote in the native dialect, it can be proved with certainty that the Greek Gospel is identical in substance with the Gospel written in the vernacular by the same Apostle.

Answer: In the affirmative.   436

6. *Historical Character*—Whether, from the fact that the   437
purpose of the author is principally dogmatic and apologetic, demonstrating to the Jews that Jesus is the Messias foretold by the prophets and a descendant of the House of David, and that, moreover, the author does not always follow the chronological order in arranging the deeds and sayings which he narrates and records, it is consequently lawful to conclude that they are not to be considered as true; and whether it may also be affirmed that the narration of the deeds and words of Christ, which is contained in the Gospel, has been subjected to changes and adaptations under the influence of the prophecies of the Old Testament and the more developed status

of the Church, and that, consequently, this narration is not in conformity with historical truth.

438   *Answer*: In the negative to both parts.

439   7. *Integrity*—Whether in particular the opinion of those ought to be considered devoid of solid foundation, who call in question the historical authenticity of the first two chapters, in which the genealogy and the infancy of Christ are narrated, as also certain passages of great importance in dogma, such as those referring to the primacy of Peter (16: 17-19), the form of Baptism given to the Apostles together with the universal mission of teaching (29:19-20), the Apostles' profession of faith in the divinity of Christ (14:33), and others of this character, which are expressed in a manner peculiar to Matthew.

440   *Answer*: In the affirmative.

June 19, 1911.

IX

On the Author, Time of Composition and Historical Truth of the Gospels According to St. Mark and St. Luke

The Biblical Commission answers the following questions:

441   1. *Authenticity*—Whether the clear evidence of tradition, wonderfully harmonious from the earliest ages of the Church and supported by numerous arguments, viz., by the explicit testimonies of the Fathers and ecclesiastical writers, by the citations and allusions occurring in their writings, by the usage of the ancient heretics, by the versions of the books of the New Testament, by the most ancient and almost universal manuscript codices, and also by intrinsic arguments from the text itself of the sacred books, certainly compels us to affirm that Mark, the disciple and interpreter of Peter, and Luke, a physician, the assistant and companion of Paul, are

really the authors of the Gospels which are respectively attributed to them.

Answer: In the affirmative. 442

2. *Integrity of the Second Gospel*—Whether the reasons by 443 which some critics endeavor to prove that the last twelve verses of the Gospel of Mark (16:9-20) were not written by Mark himself but added by another hand, are of a kind to justify the statement that these verses are not to be received as inspired and canonical, or at least prove that Mark is not the author of said verses.

Answer: In the negative to both parts. 444

3. *Integrity of the Third Gospel*—Whether likewise it is 445 lawful to doubt of the inspiration and canonicity of the narrations of Luke on the infancy of Christ (chapter 1-2) or on the apparition of the Angel comforting Jesus and on the bloody sweat (22:43-44); or whether at least it can be shown by solid reasons—as ancient heretics used to think and certain more recent critics hold—that these narrations do not belong to the genuine Gospel of Luke.

Answer: In the negative to both parts. 446

4. *The Magnificat*—Whether those very rare and altogether 447 singular documents in which the Canticle *Magnificat* is attributed not to the Blessed Virgin Mary, but to Elizabeth, can and should at all prevail against the harmonious testimony of nearly all the codices both of the original Greek text and of the versions, as well as against the interpretation clearly required no less by the context than by the mind of the Virgin herself and constant tradition of the Church.

Answer: In the negative. 448

5. *Chronological Order*—Whether, with regard to the chro- 449 nological order of the Gospels, it is lawful to abandon the

opinion, supported as it is by the most ancient as well as constant testimony of tradition, which testifies that, after Matthew, who first of all wrote his Gospel in his native language, Mark wrote second and Luke third; or is this opinion to be regarded as opposed to that which asserts that the second and third Gospels were composed before the Greek version of the first Gospel.

450   *Answer*: In the negative to both parts.

451   6. *Date of Composition*—Whether it is lawful to set the date of the composition of the Gospels of Mark and Luke as late as the destruction of the city of Jerusalem; or whether, from the fact that in Luke the prophecy of our Lord concerning the overthrow of this city seems to be more definite, it can at least be held that his Gospel was written after the siege had been begun.

452   *Answer*: In the negative to both parts.

453   7. *Date of Composition of the Third Gospel*—Whether it is to be affirmed that the Gospel of Luke preceded the book of the Acts of the Apostles (Acts 1:1-2); and since this book of which the same Luke is author, was finished at the end of the Roman imprisonment of the Apostle (Acts 28:30-31), his Gospel was composed not after this date.

454   *Answer*: In the affirmative.

455   8. *Sources*—Whether, in view both of the testimony of tradition and of internal arguments, with regard to the sources which both Evangelists used in writing their Gospels, the opinion can prudently be called in question which holds that Mark wrote according to the preaching of Peter and Luke according to the preaching of Paul, and which at the same time asserts that these Evangelists had at their disposal other trustworthy sources, either oral or already written.

Answer: In the negative.   456

9. *Historical Truth*—Whether the sayings and doings which   457
are accurately and almost graphically narrated by Mark,
according to the preaching of Peter, and are most faithfully
set forth by Luke, having diligently learned all these things
from the beginning from eminently trustworthy witnesses,
viz., "who from the beginning were eyewitnesses and ministers of the word" (Luke 1:2-3), have a just claim to the full
historical credence which the Church has ever given them; or
whether, on the contrary, the sayings and doing are to be
regarded as devoid of historical truth at least in part, either
because the writers were not eyewitnesses, or because in both
Evangelists lack of order and discrepancy in the succession of
facts are not infrequently found, or because, since they came
and wrote later, they must necessarily have related conceptions foreign to the mind of Christ and the Apostles, or facts
more or less infected by popular imagination, or, finally because they indulged in preconceived dogmatic ideas, each
according to the scope he had in view.

Answer: In the affirmative to the first part; in the nega-   458
tive to the second.

June 26, 1912.

X

On the Synoptic Question or the Mutual Relations Between the First Three Gospels

The Biblical Commission answers the following questions:

1. *Synoptic Question*—Whether, observing all things that   459
are to be absolutely observed according to what has been already laid down, especially as regards the authenticity and
integrity of the three Gospels of Matthew, Mark, and Luke,
the substantial identity of the Greek Gospel of Matthew with
its primitive original, and the order of time in which they

were written, it is lawful for exegetes, in order to explain the similarities or dissimilarities between them, to dispute freely about all the varying and opposing opinions of authors and to appeal to hypotheses of oral or written tradition or even to the dependence of one on the one or both that precede.

460   *Answer*: In the affirmative.

461   2. *Two Source Theory*—Whether what has been laid down above is to be considered as observed by those who, unsupported by any testimony of tradition or by any historical argument, lightly embrace the hypothesis commonly known as that of "the two sources," which strives to explain the composition of the Greek Gospel of Matthew and the Gospel of Luke mainly by their dependence on the Gospel of Mark and on the so-called collection of "Sayings of the Lord"; and can they, therefore, freely advocate it.

462   *Answer*: In the negative to both parts.

                                              June 26, 1912.

XI

On the Author, Time of Composition, and Historical Character of Acts

The Biblical Commission answers the following questions:

463   1. *Author*—Whether, in view especially of the tradition of the universal Church going back to the earliest ecclesiastical writers, considering the internal reasons furnished by the book of the Acts considered in itself and its relation to the third Gospel, and particularly the mutual affinity and connection of the prologues of each (Luke 1:1-4; Acts 1:1-2), it is to be held as certain that the volume entitled The Acts of the Apostles has the Evangelist Luke for its author.

Answer: In the affirmative.   464

2. *Unity of Authorship*—Whether it can be proved by criti-   465
cal reasons based on the language and style, on the method of
narration, on the unity of scope and doctrine, that the book
of the Acts of the Apostles is to be attributed to one sole
author; and that, therefore, the opinion of recent writers that
Luke is not the sole author of the book, but that different
authors of it must be admitted, is destitute of all foundation.

Answer: In the affirmative to both parts.   466

3. *We-Sections*—Whether in particular, those well-known   467
passages in the Acts in which the use of the third person is
discarded and the first person plural (Wir-stuecke, we-sections)
introduced, weaken the unity of composition and the authenticity; or whether these passages considered historically and
philologically must rather be said to confirm the unity of
composition and the authenticity.

Answer: In the negative to the first part, in the affirmative   468
to the second part.

4. *Integrity and Time of Composition*—Whether from the   469
fact that the book itself, after barely mentioning the two
years of the first Roman captivity of Paul, abruptly closes, it
is lawful to infer that the author either wrote another volume
which has been lost, or intended to write one, and that the
date of composition of the book can therefore be assigned to
a time far later than this captivity; or whether rather it is
rightly and properly to be held that Luke finished the book
at the end of the first Roman captivity of the Apostle Paul.

Answer: In the negative to the first part, in the affirmative   470
to the second part.

5. *Historical Character*—Whether, if we consider at once   471
the frequent and easy relations which Luke undoubtedly had

with the first and chief founders of the Church of Palestine as well as with Paul, Apostle of the Gentiles, to whom he was an assistant in his evangelical preaching and companion in his journeys; Luke's customary industry and diligence in examining witnesses and in seeing things for himself; and finally the evident and most remarkable agreement of the Acts of the Apostles with the Epistles of Paul and with the more genuine historical records; it is to be held for certain that Luke had in his hands most trustworthy sources and that he used them accurately, honestly, and faithfully, so that complete historical authority may be claimed for him.

472   *Answer*: In the affirmative.

473   6. *Objections to Historical Character*—Whether the difficulties commonly alleged from the supernatural facts narrated by Luke; from his account of certain discourses which, being given summarily, are considered as made up and adapted to circumstances; from certain passages which are at least apparently in conflict with profane or biblical history; and, finally, from certain narrations which seem to be in opposition with the author of the Acts himself or with other sacred writers; are of a kind to render doubtful or at least in some way to diminish the historical authority of the Acts.

474   *Answer*: In the negative.

June 12, 1913.

XII

On the Authenticity, Integrity, and Time of Composition of the Pastoral Epistles

The Biblical Commission answers the following questions:

475   1. *Authenticity*—Whether, having in view the tradition of the Church universally and firmly persevering from the beginning, as ancient ecclesiastical records testify in various ways, it is to be held for certain that the Epistles known as Pastoral,

viz., the two to Timothy and the one to Titus, notwithstanding the efforts of certain heretics who have without cause eliminated them from the number of Pauline Epistles as being contrary to their own teachings, were written by the Apostle Paul himself and ever counted as genuine and canonical.

Answer: In the affirmative.   476

2. *Compilation Theory*—Whether the so-called "fragmentary hypothesis," advanced and set forth in various ways by certain recent critics who, without indeed any probable ground and actually fighting among themselves, contend that the Pastoral Epistles were made up at a later period by unknown authors from fragments of Epistles or from lost Pauline Epistles, and greatly added to, can create the slightest prejudice against the conspicuous and most firm testimony of tradition.   477

Answer: In the negative.   478

3. *Difficulties*—Whether the difficulties commonly advanced in various ways from the style and language of the author, from the errors, especially of the Gnostics, which are described as already current at the time, from the state of the ecclesiastical hierarchy which is supposed to be already in an evolved condition, and other such reasons to the contrary, in any way weaken the opinion which holds as ratified and certain the genuineness of the Pastoral Epistles.   479

Answer: In the negative.   480

4. *Time of Composition*—Whether, since not only from historical reasons and from ecclesiastical tradition in harmony with the testimony of the Eastern and Western Fathers, as well as from the very indications easily furnished both by the abrupt conclusion of the book of the Acts and by the Pauline Epistles written at Rome, especially the second to Timothy, the opinion as to the two Roman imprisonments of the Apostle Paul is to be held as certain, it can be safely af-   481

firmed that the Pastoral Epistles were written during the period between the liberation from the first imprisonment and the death of the Apostle.

482   *Answer*: In the affirmative.

June 12, 1913.

XIII

On the Author and the Manner and Circumstances of Composition of the Epistle to the Hebrews

The Biblical Commission answers the following questions:

483   1. *Canonicity and Authenticity*—Whether so much importance should be attached to the doubts concerning the inspiration and Pauline authorship of the Epistle to the Hebrews—which, owing chiefly to its misuse by the heretics, occupied the minds of some in the West in the first centuries—that when we take into account the abiding, unanimous, and constant testimony of the Eastern Fathers, with which since the fourth century the whole Western Church has been in perfect accord; considering also the decrees of the Supreme Pontiffs and of the Sacred Councils, that of Trent especially, and finally the continuous practice of the universal Church, we may hesitate in reckoning the Epistle with certainty not only among the canonical Epistles (for that has been defined to be of faith), but among the genuine Epistles of the Apostle Paul as well.

484   *Answer*: In the negative.

485   2. *Objections*—Whether the arguments generally advanced, drawn from the singular absence of St. Paul's name and the omission of the regular introduction and greeting in the Epistle to the Hebrews; from the faultlessness of its Greek, its accuracy in phraseology and polish of style; from the way in which the Old Testament is quoted and argued from in it; or from some discrepancies which are alleged to exist between

its teaching and that of the other Epistles of St. Paul, can in the least impair its Pauline authorship; or whether, on the other hand, the complete harmony of doctrine and principles; the similarity of the cautions and counsels; and the close correspondence in phrases and in the very words, proclaimed by some non-Catholics even, which are all discovered to exist between this and the other works of the Apostle of the Gentiles, do not rather go to prove beyond doubt this Pauline authorship.

Answer: In the negative to the first part, in the affirmative   486
to the second part.

3. *Writer*—Whether the Apostle Paul must be accounted so   487
to have been the author of this letter, that it must needs be asserted that he not only planned and composed it in its entirety under the inspiration of the Holy Ghost, but also that he put it in exactly the form in which it now stands.

Answer: In the negative, subject to further decision of the   488
Church.

June 24, 1914.

XIV

On the Parousia or the Second Coming of Our Lord Jesus Christ

The Biblical Commission answers the following questions:

1. *Inerrancy*—Whether to solve the difficulties which occur   489
in the Epistles of St. Paul and of other Apostles, where the Parousia, as it is called, or the second coming of our Lord Jesus Christ is spoken of, it is permitted to the Catholic exegete to assert that the Apostles, although under the inspiration of the Holy Ghost they teach no error, nevertheless express their own human views, into which error or deception can enter.

490   *Answer*: In the negative.

491   2. *Harmony of the Apostle's Teaching*—Whether, keeping before one's eyes the genuine idea of the Apostolic Office and of St. Paul's undoubted fidelity to the teaching of the Master; likewise, the Catholic dogma regarding the inspiration and inerrancy of the Scriptures, whereby all that the sacred writer asserts, enunciates, suggests, must be held to be asserted, enunciated, suggested by the Holy Ghost; also, weighing the text of the Apostle's Epistles, considered in themselves, which are before all in harmony with the speech of the Lord Himself, it is meet to affirm that the Apostle Paul in his writings certainly said nothing which is not in perfect harmony with that ignorance of the time of the Parousia which Christ Himself proclaimed to be men's portion.

492   *Answer*: In the affirmative.

493   3. *Traditional Interpretation*—Whether, attention being paid to the Greek phrase, ἡμεῖς οἱ ζῶντες περιλειπόμενοι, also the explanation of the Fathers being weighed, especially that of St. John Chrysostom, who was highly versed both in his country's language and in the Pauline Epistles, it is lawful to reject as farfetched and destitute of solid foundation, the interpretation traditional in the Catholic schools—also retained by the reformers of the sixteenth century themselves—which explains the words of St. Paul (1 Thess. 4:15-17) without in any wise implying the affirmation of a Parousia so imminent that the Apostle added himself and his readers to those of the faithful who should survive to meet Christ.

494   *Answer*: In the negative.

June 18, 1915.

QUONIAM IN RE BIBLICA
Apostolic Letter of Pius X
on the Study of Holy Scripture in Clerical Seminaries
March 27, 1906

The Biblical Question has, perhaps, never been of such importance as it is today, and it is therefore absolutely necessary that young clerics should be assiduously trained in the knowledge of the Scriptures, so that they may not only know and understand the force and character and teaching of the Bible, but that they may be skillfully and rightly trained in the ministry of the Divine Word, and able to defend the books written by the inspiration of God from the attacks of those who deny that anything has been divinely handed down to us. To this end Our illustrious Predecessor in his encyclical *Providentissimus* decreed: "Let our first care be to see that in seminaries and academical institutions the study of Holy Scripture be placed on such a footing as its own importance and the circumstances of the time demand." On this same subject, then, We now lay down the following rules which We regard as of the greatest utility:

1. The instruction in Sacred Scripture to be imparted in 496 every seminary should embrace, first, the principal ideas concerning inspiration, the canon of the Scripture, the original text and the most important versions, the laws of hermeneutics; secondly, the history of both Testaments; and, thirdly, the analysis and exegesis of the different books according to the importance of each.

2. The curriculum of Biblical studies is to be divided over 497 the entire period during which ecclesiastical students pursue

their course of sacred studies within the walls of the seminary; so that when the course is finished each student may have gone through the entire curriculum.

498

3. The chairs of Scripture shall be organized according to the condition and the means of the different seminaries, but always in such a way that no student shall be deprived of the means of learning those things of which a priest may not lawfully be ignorant.

499

4. Since, on the one hand, it is not possible to have a detailed exposition of the whole of Scripture given in school, and, on the other, it is necessary that the whole of Scripture should be in some sense known to the priest, the professor shall take care to have special treatises or introductions for each of the books to prove their authority, and, when occasion requires, to teach the analysis of them; but he will, at the same time, dwell at greater length on the more important books and parts of books.

500

5. With regard to the Old Testament, he will make use of the latest results of research in illustrating the history of the Hebrew people and their relations with other Oriental nations; he will treat of the main features of the Mosaic Law; and he will explain the principal prophecies.

501

6. He will take special pains to imbue his students with zeal to study and understand those Psalms which they recite daily in the Divine Office; he will select some of those Psalms for interpretation in order to show by way of example the method to be followed by the students in their private studies to interpret the others.

502

7. Treating of the New Testament, he will explain briefly and clearly the special characteristics of each of the four Gospels, and the proofs of their authenticity; he will also illustrate the general characters of the entire Gospel story, and the doctrine in the Epistles and the other books.

503

8. He will pay special attention in treating of those parts of both Testaments which concern Christian faith and morals.

504

9. He will always remember, especially in treating of the New Testament, to conform to the precepts he explains to those who are afterwards by their words and their example to teach the people the doctrine of salvation. He will, therefore,

in the course of his instruction explain to his students the best way of preaching the Gospel, and will stimulate them, as occasion may offer, to observe diligently the commands of the Lord Jesus Christ and the Apostles.

10. The more promising students are to be instructed in the   505
Hebrew tongue, in Biblical Greek, and whenever possible, in some other Semitic language, such as Syriac or Arabic. "It is most proper that Professors of Sacred Scripture and theologians should master those tongues in which the sacred books were originally written; and it would be well that ecclesiastical students also should cultivate them, more especially those who aspire to academic degrees. And endeavors should be made to establish in all academic institutions chairs of the other oriental languages, especially the Semitic" (*Providentissimus Deus*).

11. In seminaries which enjoy the right of conferring aca-   506
demical degrees it will be necessary to increase the number of lectures on Sacred Scripture and consequently to go more deeply into general and special questions, and to devote more time and study to Biblical exegesis, archaeology, geography, chronology, theology and history.

12. Special diligence is to be shown in preparing select   507
students for the academical degrees in Sacred Scripture according to the rules laid down by the Biblical Commission—a matter of no small importance for securing suitable professors for Scripture for the seminaries.

13. Every doctor in Sacred Scripture will be most careful   508
never to swerve in the least in his teaching from the doctrine and tradition of the Church; he will of course make use of the real additions to our knowledge which modern research supplies, but he will avoid the rash commentaries of innovators; so, too, he will confine himself to the treatment of those questions which contribute to the elucidation and defense of the Sacred Scriptures; and finally he will be guided in his plan of teaching by those rules, full of prudence, contained in the Encyclical *Providentissimus*.

14. Students should endeavor to make up by private study   509
what the schools fail to supply in this branch of sacred learning. As lack of time will render it impossible for the professor

to go over the whole of Scripture in detail, they will by themselves devote a certain portion of time every day to a careful perusal of the Old and New Testaments—and in this way they will be greatly helped by the use of some brief commentary to throw light on obscure passages and explain the more difficult ones.

510   15. Students are to undergo an examination in Scripture, as well as in other parts of theology, to show the profit they have derived from the lessons, before they are allowed to pass into another class or to be initiated in sacred orders.

511   16. In all academies every candidate for academical degrees in theology will be asked certain questions on Scripture relating to the historical and critical introduction as well as to exegesis; and will prove by examination that he is sufficiently acquainted with the Hebrew tongue and has knowledge of Biblical Greek.

512   17. The students of Sacred Scripture are to be exhorted to read not only interpretations of the Scripture, but good authors who treat of subjects connected with this study—for instance, the history of both Testaments, the life of Our Lord and the Apostles, and books of travel in Palestine—from all of which they will easily acquire knowledge of Biblical places and customs.

513   18. To further this object efforts will be made to supply each seminary, as far as circumstances will permit, with a small library in which books of this kind will be at the disposal of the students.

514   This is Our will and Our command, everthing to the contrary notwithstanding.

515   Given at Rome at St. Peter's on the 27th day of March, 1906, the third of Our Pontificate.

LAMENTABILI
Decree of Congregation of the Inquisition
July 3, 1907

With truly lamentable results, our age, intolerant of all check in its investigations of the ultimate causes of things, not unfrequently follows what is new in such a way as to reject the legacy, as it were, of the human race, and thus fall into the most grievous errors. These errors will be all the more pernicious when they affect sacred disciplines, the interpretation of the Sacred Scripture, the principal mysteries of the faith. It is to be greatly deplored that among Catholics also not a few writers are to be found who, crossing the boundaries fixed by the Fathers and by the Church herself, seek out, on the plea of higher intelligence and in the name of historical considerations, that progress of dogmas which is in reality the corruption of the same.

But lest errors of this kind, which are being daily spread among the faithful, should strike root in their minds and corrupt the purity of the faith, it has pleased His Holiness Pius X, by Divine Providence Pope, that the chief among them should be noted and condemned through the office of this Holy Roman and Universal Inquisition.

Wherefore, after a most diligent investigation, and after having taken the opinion of the Reverend Consultors, the Most Eminent and Reverend Lords Cardinals, the general inquisitors in matters of faith and morals, decided that *the following propositions are to be condemned and proscribed,*

517

518

as they are, by this general Decree, condemned and pro-scribed:

519   1. The ecclesiastical law, which prescribes that books regarding the Divine Scriptures are subject to previous censorship, does not extend to critical scholars or students of the scientific exegesis of the Old and New Testament.

520   2. The Church's interpretation of the Sacred Books is not indeed to be condemned, but it is subject to the more accurate judgment and to the correction of the exegetes.

521   3. From the ecclesiastical judgments and censures passed against free and more scientific (*cultiorem*) exegesis, it may be gathered that the faith proposed by the Church contradicts history and that the Catholic dogmas cannot be reconciled with the true origins of the Christian religion.

522   4. The magisterium of the Church cannot, even through dogmatic definitions, determine the genuine sense of the Sacred Scriptures.

523   5. Since in the deposit of the faith only revealed truths are contained, under no respect does it appertain to the Church to pass judgment concerning the assertions of human sciences.

524   6. In defining truths the Church learning (*discens*) and the Church teaching (*docens*) collaborate in such a way that it only remains for the Church *docens* to sanction the opinions of the Church *discens*.

525   7. The Church, when it proscribes errors, cannot exact from the faithful any internal assent by which the judgments issued by it are embraced.

526   8. Those who treat as of no weight the condemnations passed by the Sacred Congregation of the Index or by the other Roman Congregations are free from all blame.

527   9. Those who believe that God is really the author of the Sacred Scripture display excessive simplicity or ignorance.

528   10. The inspiration of the books of the Old Testament consists in the fact that the Israelite writers have handed down religious doctrines under a peculiar aspect, either little or not at all known to the Gentiles.

529   11. Divine inspiration is not to be so extended to the whole of Sacred Scriptures that it renders its parts, all and single, immune from all error.

12. The exegete, if he wishes to apply himself usefully to   530
Biblical studies, must first of all put aside all preconceived
opinions concerning the supernatural origin of the Sacred
Scripture, and interpret it not otherwise than other merely
human documents.

13. The evangelists themselves and the Christians of the   531
second and third generation arranged (*digesserunt*) artifici-
ally the evangelical parables, and in this way gave an explanation of the scanty fruit of the preaching of Christ among the
Jews.

14. In a great many narrations the evangelists reported not   532
so much things that are true as things which even though
false they judged to be more profitable for their readers.

15. The Gospels until the time the canon was defined and   533
constituted were increased by additions and corrections;
hence in them there remained of the doctrine of Christ only a
faint and uncertain trace.

16. The narrations of John are not properly history, but   534
the mystical contemplation of the Gospel; the discourses
contained in his Gospel are theological meditations, devoid of
historical truth concerning the mystery of salvation.

17. The Fourth Gospel exaggerated miracles not only that   535
the wonderful might stand out but also that they might become more suitable for signifying the work and the glory of
the Word Incarnate.

18. John claims for himself the quality of a witness con-   536
cerning Christ; but in reality he is only a distinguished witness
of the Christian life, or of the life of Christ in the Church, at
the close of the first century.

19. Heterodox exegetes have expressed the true sense of   537
the Scriptures more faithfully than Catholic exegetes.

20. Revelation could be nothing but the consciousness   538
acquired by man of his relation with God.

21. Revelation, constituting the object of Catholic faith,   539
was not completed with the Apostles.

22. The dogmas which the Church gives out as revealed,   540
are not truths which have fallen down from heaven, but are
an interpretation of religious facts, which the human mind
has acquired by laborious effort.

541 23. Opposition may and actually does exist between the facts which are narrated in Scripture and the dogmas of the Church which rest on them; so that the critic may reject as false facts which the Church holds as most certain.

542 24. The exegete is not to be blamed for constructing premises from which it follows that the dogmas are historically false or doubtful, provided he does not directly deny the dogmas themselves.

543 25. The assent of faith rests ultimately on a mass of probabilities.

544 26. The dogmas of faith are to be held only according to their practical sense, that is, as preceptive norms of conduct, but not as norms of believing.

545 27. The Divinity of Jesus Christ is not proved from the Gospels but is a dogma which the Christian conscience has derived from the notion of the Messias.

546 28. Jesus, while He was exercising His Ministry, did not speak with the object of teaching that He was the Messias, nor did His miracles tend to prove this.

547 29. It is lawful to believe that the Christ of history is far inferior to the Christ who is the object of faith.

548 30. In all the evangelical texts the name *Son of God* is equivalent only to Messias, and does not at all signify that Christ is the true and natural Son of God.

549 31. The doctrine concerning Christ taught by Paul, John, the Councils of Nicea, Ephesus and Chalcedon, is not that which Jesus taught, but that which the Christian conscience conceived concerning Jesus.

550 32. It is not possible to reconcile the natural sense of the Gospel texts with the sense taught by our theologians concerning the conscience and the infallible knowledge of Jesus Christ.

551 33. It is evident to everybody who is not led by preconceived opinions that either Jesus professed an error concerning the immediate Messianic coming, or that the greater part of His doctrine as contained in the Gospels is destitute of authenticity.

552 34. The critic cannot ascribe to Christ a knowledge circumscribed by no limits except on a hypothesis which cannot be

historically conceived and which is repugnant to the moral sense, viz., that Christ as man had the knowledge of God and yet was unwilling to communicate the knowledge of a great many things to His Disciples and to posterity.

35. Christ had not always the consciousness of His Messi-   553
anic dignity.

36. The Resurrection of the Saviour is not properly a fact   554
of the historical order, but a fact of merely supernatural order, neither demonstrated nor demonstrable, which the Christian conscience gradually derived from other facts.

37. Faith in the Resurrection of Christ was in the beginning   555
not so much in the fact itself of the Resurrection, as in the immortal life of Christ with God.

38. The doctrine of the expiatory death of Christ is not   556
Evangelical but Pauline.

39. The opinions concerning the origin of the sacraments   557
with which the Fathers of Trent were imbued and which certainly influenced their dogmatic canons are very different from those which now rightly obtain among historians who examine into Christianity.

40. The sacraments had their origin in the fact that the   558
Apostles and their successors, swayed and moved by circumstances and events, interpreted some idea or intention of Christ.

41. The sacraments are merely intended to bring before   559
the mind of man the ever-beneficent presence of the Creator.

42. The Christian community imposed (*iuduxit*) the neces-   560
sity of baptism, adopting it as a necessary rite, and adding to it the obligations of the Christian profession.

43. The practice of conferring baptism on infants was a   561
disciplinary evolution, which became one of the causes why the sacrament was divided into two, viz.: baptism and penance.

44. There is nothing to prove that the rite of the sacrament   562
of confirmation was employed by the Apostles: but the formal distinction of the two sacraments, baptism and confirmation, does not belong to the history of primitive Christianity.

563   45. Not everything which Paul narrates concerning the institution of the Eucharist (1 Cor. 11, 23-25) is to be taken historically.

564   46. In the primitive Church the conception of the Christian sinner reconciled by the authority of the Church did not exist, but it was only very slowly that the Church accustomed itself to this conception. Nay, even after penance was recognized as an institution of the Church, it was not called a sacrament, for it would be held as an ignominious sacrament.

565   47. The words of the Lord: *Receive ye the Holy Ghost; whose sins ye shall forgive they are forgiven them, and whose sins ye shall retain they are retained* (John 20, 22, 23) do not at all refer to the sacrament of penance, whatever the Fathers of Trent may have been pleased to say.

566   48. James in his Epistle (v. 14 and 15) did not intend to promulgate a sacrament of Christ, but to commend a pious custom, and if in this custom he happens to distinguish (*cernit*) a means of grace, it is not in that rigorous manner in which it was received by the theologians who laid down the notion and the number of the sacraments.

567   49. The Christian Supper gradually assuming the nature of a liturgical action, those who were wont to preside at the Supper acquired the sacerdotal character.

568   50. The elders who filled the office of watching over the gatherings of the faithful, were instituted by the Apostles as priests or bishops to provide for the necessary ordering (*ordinationi*) of the increasing opportunities, not properly for perpetuating the Apostolic mission and power.

569   51. It is not possible that matrimony could have become a sacrament of the new Law until later in the Church; for in order that matrimony should be held as a sacrament it was necessary that a full theological development (*explicatio*) of the doctrine of grace and the sacraments should first take place.

570   52. It was foreign to the mind of Christ to found a Church as a Society which was to last on the earth for a long course of centuries; nay, in the mind of Christ the Kingdom of Heaven together with the end of the world was about to come immediately.

53. The organic constitution of the Church is not immu-   571
table; but Christian society, like human society, is subject to
perpetual evolution.

54. Dogmas, sacraments, hierarchy, both as regards the   572
notion of them and the reality, are but interpretations and
evolutions of the Christian intelligence which by external
increments have increased and perfected the little germ latent
in the Gospel.

55. Simon Peter never even suspected that the primacy in   573
the Church was intrusted to him by Christ.

56. The Roman Church became the head of all the churches   574
not through the ordinance of Divine Providence but through
merely political conditions.

57. The Church has shown herself to be hostile to the pro-   575
gress of natural and theological sciences.

58. Truth is not any more immutable than man himself,   576
since it is evolved with him, in him, and through him.

59. Christ did not teach a determinate body of doctrine   577
applicable to all times and to all men, but rather inaugurated
a religious movement adapted or to be adapted for different
times and place.

60. Christian doctrine in its origin was Judaic, but through   578
successive evolutions became first Pauline, then Joannine,
and finally Hellenic and universal.

61. It may be said without paradox that there is no chap-   579
ter of Scripture, from the first of Genesis to the last of the
Apocalypse, which contains a doctrine absolutely identical
with that which the Church teaches on the same matter, and
that, therefore, no chapter of Scripture has the same sense
for the critic and for the theologian.

62. The chief articles of the Apostolic Symbol had not for   580
the Christians of the first ages the same sense that they have
for the Christians of our time.

63. The Church shows itself unequal to the task of effica-   581
ciously maintaining evangelical ethics, because it obstinately
adheres to immutable doctrines which cannot be reconciled
with modern progress.

64. The progress of science involves a remodeling (*ut*   582
reformentur) of the conceptions of Christian doctrine con-

cerning God, Creation, Revelation, the Person of the Incarnate
Word, Redemption.

583   65. Modern Catholicism cannot be reconciled with true
science unless it be transformed into a non-dogmatic Christianity, that is into a broad and liberal Protestantism.

*LAMENTABILI was followed on September 8, 1907 by
Pope Pius X's Encyclical Letter PASCENDI DOMINICI
GREGIS, reiterating the rejection of the Modernist proposi-
tions. The full text of PASCENDI DOMINICI GREGIS can be
found in "Christ Our Lord," in the OFFICIAL CATHOLIC
TEACHINGS series.   Ed.*

PRAESTANTIA SACRAE SCRIPTURAE
Motu Proprio of Pius X
on the Decisions of the Pontifical Biblical Commission
November 18, 1907

In his encyclical letter *Providentissimus Deus,* given on November 18, 1893, Our predecessor, Leo XIII, of immortal memory, after describing the dignity of the Sacred Scripture and commending the study of it, set forth the laws which govern the proper study of the Holy Bible; and having proclaimed the divinity of these books against the errors and calumnies of the rationalists, he at the same time defended them against the false teachings of what is known as the higher criticism, which, as the Pontiff most wisely wrote, are clearly nothing but the commentaries of rationalism derived from a misuse of philology and kindred studies.

Our predecessor, too, seeing that the danger was constantly on the increase, and desiring to provide against the conse- 585 quences of the propagation of rash and erroneous views, by his apostolical letter *Vigilantiae,* given on October 30, 1902, established a Pontifical Council, or Commission on biblical matters, composed of several Cardinals of the Holy Roman Church, distinguished for their learning and prudence, adding to these, under the title, Consultors, a considerable body of men in sacred orders, chosen from among the learned in theology and in the Holy Bible, of various nationalities and differing in their methods and views concerning exegetical studies. In this the Pontiff had in mind, as an advantage admirably adapted for the promotion of study and for the time in which we live, that in this Commission there should be the fullest freedom of proposing, examining, and judging all opinions whatsoever; and the letter also ordained that the Cardinals of the Commission were not to come to any definite decision until they had taken cognizance of and examined the arguments on both sides, omitting nothing which might serve to show in the clearest light the true and genuine state of biblical questions proposed for solution; and when all this had been done, that the decisions reached should be submitted for approval to the Supreme Pontiff and then promulgated.

586   After mature examination and the most diligent consultations, certain decisions have been happily given by the Pontifical Biblical Commission, and these of a kind very useful for the proper promotion and direction on safe lines of biblical studies. But we observe that some persons, unduly prone to opinions and methods tainted by pernicious novelties, and excessively devoted to that principle of false liberty, which is really immoderate license, and in sacred studies proves itself to be most insidious and a fruitful source of the worst evils against the purity of the faith, have not received and do not receive these decisions with a proper obedience.

587   Wherefore We find it necessary to declare and prescribe, as We do now declare and expressly prescribe, that all are bound in conscience to submit to the decisions of the Biblical Commission, which have been given in the past and which shall be given in the future, in the same way as to the Decrees which appertain to doctrine, issued by the Sacred Congregations and approved by the Sovereign Pontiff; nor can they escape the stigma both of disobedience and temerity nor be free from grave guilt as often as they impugn these decisions either in word or writing; and this, over and above the scandal which they give and the sins of which they may be the cause before God by making other statements on these matters which are very frequently both rash and false.[1]

588   All these things We will and order to be sanctioned and established by Our apostolic authority, nothing to the contrary notwithstanding.

589   Given at Rome at St. Peter's, November 18, 1907, in the fifth year of Our Pontificate.

SPIRITUS PARACLITUS
Encyclical Letter of Pope Benedict XV
on the Fifteenth Centenary of the Death of St. Jerome
September 15, 1920

S ince the Holy Spirit, the Comforter, had bestowed the Scriptures on the human race for their instruction in Divine things, He also raised up in successive ages saintly and learned men whose task it should be to develop that treasure and so provide for the faithful plenteous "consolation from the Scriptures."[1] Foremost among these teachers stands St. Jerome. Him the Catholic Church acclaims and reveres as her "Greatest Doctor," divinely given her for the understanding of the Bible. And now that the fifteenth centenary of his death is approaching we would not willingly let pass so favorable an opportunity of addressing you on the debt we owe him. For the responsibility of our Apostolic office impels us to set before you his wonderful example and so promote the study of Holy Scripture in accordance with the teaching of our predecessors, Leo XIII and Pius X, which we desire to apply more precisely still to the present needs of the Church. For St. Jerome—"strenuous Catholic, learned in the Scriptures,"[2] "teacher of Catholics,"[3] "model of virtue, world's teacher"[4]—has by his earnest and illuminative defense of Catholic doctrine on Holy Scripture left us most precious instructions. These we propose to set before you and so promote among the children of the Church, and especially among the clergy, assiduous and reverent study of the Bible.

No need to remind you, Venerable Brethren, that Jerome was born in Stridonia, in a town "on the borders of Dalmatia

591

and Pannonia";[5] that from his infancy he was brought up a Catholic;[6] that after his baptism here in Rome[7] he lived to an advanced age and devoted all his powers to studying, expounding, and defending the Bible. At Rome he had learned Latin and Greek, and hardly had he left the school of rhetoric than he ventured on a Commentary on Abdias the Prophet. This "youthful piece of work"[8] kindled in him such love of the Bible that he decided—like the man in the Gospel who found a treasure—to spurn "any emoluments the world could provide."[9] and devote himself wholly to such studies. Nothing could deter him from this stern resolve. He left home, parents, sister, and relatives; he denied himself the more delicate food he had been accustomed to, and went to the East so that he might gather from studious reading of the Bible the fuller riches of Christ and true knowledge of his Saviour.[10] Jerome himself tells us in several places how assiduously he toiled:

> An eager desire to learn obsessed me. But I was not so foolish as to try and teach myself. At Antioch I regularly attended the lectures of Apollinarius of Laodicea; but while I learned much from him about the Bible, I would never accept his doubtful teaching abouts its interpretation.[11]

592 From Antioch he betook himself to the desert of Chalcis, in Syria, to perfect himself in his knowledge of the Bible, and at the same time to curb "youthful desires" by means of hard study. Here he engaged a convert Jew to teach him Hebrew and Chaldaic.

593 What a toil it was! How difficult I found it! How often I was on the point of giving it up in despair, and yet in my eagerness to learn took it up again! Myself can bear witness of this, and so, too, can those who had lived with me at the time. Yet I thank God for the fruit I won from the bitter seed.[12]

594 Lest, however, he should grow idle in this desert where there were no heretics to vex him, Jerome betook himself to Constantinople, where for nearly three years he studied Holy

Scripture under St. Gregory the Theologian, then Bishop of
that See and in the height of his fame as a teacher. While
there he translated into Latin Origen's *Homilies on the Prophets* and Eusebius' *Chronicle*; he also wrote on Isaias' vision of
the Seraphim. He then returned to Rome on ecclesiastical
business, and Pope Damasus admitted him into his court.[13]
However, he let nothing distract him from continual occupation with the Bible,[14] and the task of copying various manuscripts,[15] as well as answering the many questions put to him
by students of both sexes.[16]

Pope Damasus had entrusted to him a most laborious task,   595
the correction of the Latin text of the Bible. So well did
Jerome carry this out that even today men versed in such
studies appreciate its value more and more. But he ever yearned
for Palestine, and when the Pope died he retired to Bethlehem
to a monastery nigh to the cave where Christ was born. Every
moment he could spare from prayer he gave to Biblical studies.

> Though my hair was now growing gray and though I looked   596
> more like professor than student, yet I went to Alexandria
> to attend Didymus' lectures. I owe him much. What I did
> not know I learned. What I knew already I did not lose
> through his different presentation of it. Men thought I
> had done with tutors; but when I got back to Jerusalem
> and Bethlehem how hard I worked and what a price I
> paid for my night-time teacher Baranius! Like another
> Nicodemus he was afraid of the Jews![17]

Nor was Jerome content merely to gather up this or that   597
teacher's words; he gathered from all quarters whatever might
prove of use to him in this task. From the outset he had accumulated the best possible copies of the Bible and the best
commentators on it, but now he worked on copies from the
synagogues and from the library formed at Caesarea by
Origen and Eusebius; he hoped by assiduous comparison of
texts to arrive at greater certainty touching the actual text
and its meaning. With this same purpose he went through
Palestine. For he was thoroughly convinced of the truth of
what he once wrote to Domnio and Rogatian:

> A man will understand the Bible better if he has seen Judaea with his own eyes and discovered its ancient cities and sites either under the old names or newer ones. In company with some learned Hebrews I went through the entire land, the names of whose sites are on every Christian's lips.[18]

598   He nourished his soul unceasingly on this most pleasant food: he explained St. Paul's Epistles; he corrected the Latin version of the Old Testament by the Greek; he translated afresh nearly all the books of the Old Testament from Hebrew into Latin; day by day he discussed Biblical questions with the brethren who came to him, and answered letters on Biblical questions which poured in upon him from all sides; besides all this, he was constantly refuting men who assailed Catholic doctrine and unity. Indeed, such was his love for Holy Scripture that he ceased not from writing or dictating till his hand stiffened in death and his voice was silent forever. So it was that, sparing himself neither labor nor watching nor expense, he continued to extreme old age meditating day and night beside the Crib on the Law of the Lord; of greater profit to the Catholic cause by his life and example in his solitude than if he had passed his life at Rome, the capital of the world.

599   After this preliminary account of St. Jerome's life and labors we may now treat of his teaching on the divine dignity and absolute truth of Scripture.

600   You will not find a page in his writings which does not show clearly that he, in common with the whole Catholic Church, firmly and consistently held that the Sacred Books—written as they were under the inspiration of the Holy Spirit—have God for their Author, and as such were delivered to the Church. Thus he asserts that the Books of the Bible were composed at the inspiration, or suggestion, or even at the dictation of the Holy Spirit; even that they were written and edited by Him. Yet he never questions but that the individual authors of these Books worked in full freedom under the Divine afflatus, each of them in accordance with his individual nature and character. Thus he is not merely content to affirm

as a general principle—what indeed pertains to all the sacred writers—that they followed the Spirit of God as they wrote, in such sort that God is the principal cause of all that Scripture means and says; but he also accurately describes what pertains to each individual writer. In each case Jerome shows us how, in composition, in language, in style and mode of expression, each of them uses his own gifts and powers; hence he is able to portray and describe for us their individual character, almost their very features; this is especially so in his treatment of the Prophets and of St. Paul. This partnership of God and man in the production of a work in common Jerome illustrates by the case of a workman who uses instruments for the production of his work; for he says that whatsoever the sacred authors say, "Is the word of God, and not their own; and what the Lord says by their mouths He says, as it were, by means of an instrument."[19]

If we ask how we are to explain this power and action of God, the principal cause, on the sacred writers we shall find that St. Jerome in no wise differs from the common teaching of the Catholic Church. For he holds that God, through His grace, illumines the writer's mind regarding the particular truth which, "in the person of God," he is to set before men; he holds, moreover, that God moves the writer's will—nay, even impels it—to write; finally, that God abides with him unceasingly, in unique fashion, until his task is accomplished. Whence the Saint infers the supreme excellence and dignity of Scripture, and declares that knowledge of it is to be likened to the "treasure"[20] and the "pearl beyond price."[21] since in them are to be found the riches of Christ[22] and "silver wherewith to adorn God's house."[23]   601

Jerome also insists on the supereminent authority of Scripture. When controversy arose he had recourse to the Bible as a storehouse of arguments, and he used its testimony as a weapon for refuting his adversaries' arguments, because he held that the Bible's witness afforded solid and irrefutable arguments. Thus when Helvidius denied the perpetual virginity of the Mother of God, Jerome was content simply to reply: 602

Just as we do not deny these things which are written, so

do we repudiate things that are not written. That God was born of a Virgin we believe, because we read it. That Mary was married after His birth we do not believe because we do not read it.[24]

603   In the same fashion he undertakes to defend against Jovinian, with precisely the same weapons, the Catholic doctrines of the virginal state, of perseverance, of abstinence, and of the merit of good works:

In refuting his statements I shall rely especially on the testimony of Scripture, lest he should grumble and complain that he has been vanquished rather by my eloquence than by the truth.[25]

604   So, too, when defending himself against the same Helvidius, he says: "He was, you might say, begged to yield to me, and be led away as a willing and unresisting captive in the bonds of truth."[26] Again, "We must not follow the errors of our parents, nor of those who have gone before us; we have the authority of the Scriptures and God's teaching to command us."[27] Once more, when showing Fabiola how to deal with critics, he says:

When you are really instructed in the Divine Scriptures, and have realized that its laws and testimonies are the bonds of truth, then you can contend with adversaries; then you will fetter them and lead them bound into captivity; then of the foes you have made captive you will make freemen of God.[28]

605   Jerome further shows that the immunity of Scripture from error or deception is necessarily bound up with its Divine inspiration and supreme authority. He says he had learned this in the most celebrated schools, whether of East or West, and that it was taught him as the doctrine of the Fathers, and generally received. Thus when, at the instance of Pope Damasus, he had begun correcting the Latin text of the New Testament, and certain "manikins" had vehemently attacked

him for "making corrections in the Gospels in face of the authority of the Fathers and of general opinion." Jerome briefly replied that he was not so utterly stupid nor so grossly uneducated as to imagine that the Lord's words needed any correction or were not divinely inspired.[29] Similarly, when explaining Ezechiel's first vision as portraying the *Four Gospels*, he remarks:

> That the entire body and the back were full of eyes will be plain to anybody who realizes that there is nought in the Gospels which does not shine and illumine the world by its splendor, so that even things that seem trifling and unimportant shine with the majesty of the Holy Spirit.[30]

What he has said here of the Gospels he applies in his Commentaries to the rest of the Lord's words; he regards it as the very rule and foundation of Catholic interpretation; indeed, for Jerome, a true prophet was to be distinguished from a false by this very note of truth:[31] "The Lord's words are true; for Him to say it, means that it is."[32] Again, "Scripture cannot lie";[33] it is wrong to say Scripture lies,[34] nay, it is impious even to admit the very notion of error where the Bible is concerned.[35] "The Apostles," he says, "are one thing; other writers"—that is, profane writers—"are another"; "the former always tell the truth; the latter—as being mere men—sometimes err,"[36] and though many things are said in the Bible which seem incredible, yet they are true;[37] in this "word of truth" you cannot find things or statements which are contradictory, "there is nothing discordant nor conflicting";[38] consequently, "when Scripture seems to be in conflict with itself both passages are true despite their diversity."[39]

Holding principles like these, Jerome was compelled, when he discovered apparent discrepancies in the Sacred Books, to use every endeavor to unravel the difficulty. If he felt that he had not satisfactorily settled the problem, he would return to it again and again, not always, indeed, with the happiest results. Yet he would never accuse the sacred writers of the slightest mistake—"that we leave to impious folk like Celsus, Porphyry, and Julian."[40] Here he is in full agreement with

606

607

Augustine, who wrote to Jerome that to the Sacred Books alone had he been wont to accord such honor and reverence as firmly to believe that none of their writers had ever fallen into any error; and that consequently, if in the said books he came across anything which seemed to run counter to the truth, he did not think that that was really the case, but either that his copy was defective or that the translator had made a mistake, or again, that he himself had failed to understand. He continues:

> Nor do I deem that you think otherwise. Indeed I absolutely decline to think that you would have people read your own books in the same way as they read those of the Prophets and Apostles; the idea that these latter could contain any errors is impious.[41]

608   St. Jerome's teaching on this point serves to confirm and illustrate what our predecessor of happy memory, Leo XIII, declared to be the ancient and traditional belief of the Church touching the absolute immunity of Scripture from error:

> So far is it from being the case that error can be compatible with inspiration, that, on the contrary, it not only of its very nature precludes the presence of error, but as necessarily excludes it and forbids it as God, the Supreme Truth, necessarily cannot be the Author of error.

609   Then, after giving the definitions of the Councils of Florence and Trent, confirmed by the Council of the Vatican, Pope Leo continues:

> Consequently it is not to the point to suggest that the Holy Spirit used men as His instruments for writing, and that therefore, while no error is referable to the primary Author, it may well be due to the inspired authors themselves. For by supernatural power the Holy Spirit so stirred them and moved them to write, so assisted them as they wrote, that their minds could rightly conceive only those and all those things which He Himself bade them conceive;

only such things could they faithfully commit to writing and aptly express with unerring truth; else God would not be the Author of the entirety of Sacred Scripture.[42]

But although these words of our predecessor leave no room for doubt or dispute, it grieves us to find that not only men outside, but even children of the Catholic Church—nay, what is a peculiar sorrow to us, even clerics and professors of sacred learning—who in their own conceit either openly repudiate or at least attack in secret the Church's teaching on this point. 610

We warmly commend, of course, those who, with the assistance of critical methods, seek to discover new ways of explaining the difficulties in Holy Scripture, whether for their own guidance or to help others. But we remind them that they will only come to miserable grief if they neglect our predecessor's injunctions and overstep the limits set by the Fathers. 611

Yet no one can pretend that certain recent writers really adhere to these limitations. For while conceding that inspiration extends to every phrase—and, indeed, to every single word of Scripture—yet, by endeavoring to distinguish between what they style the primary or religious and the secondary or profane element in the Bible, they claim that the effect of inspiration—namely, absolute truth and immunity from error—are to be restricted to that primary or religious element. Their notion is that only what concerns religion is intended and taught by God in Scripture, and that all the rest—things concerning "profane knowledge," the garments in which Divine truth is presented—God merely permits, and even leaves to the individual author's greater or less knowledge. Small wonder, then, that in their view a considerable number of things occur in the Bible touching physical science, history and the like, which cannot be reconciled with modern progress in science! 612

Some even maintain that these views do not conflict with what our predecessor laid down, since—so they claim—he said the sacred writers spoke in accordance with the external—and thus deceptive—appearance of things in nature. But the Pontiff's own words show that this is a rash and false deduction. 613

For sound philosophy teaches that the senses can never be deceived as regards their own proper and immediate object. Therefore, from the merely external appearance of things—of which, of course, we have always to take account, as Leo XIII, following in the footsteps of St. Augustine and St. Thomas, most wisely remarks—we can never conclude that there is any error in Sacred Scripture.

614   Moreover, our predecessor, sweeping aside all such distinctions between what these critics are pleased to call primary and secondary elements, says in no ambiguous fashion that "those who fancy that when it is a question of the truth of certain expressions we have not got to consider so much what God said as why He said it," are very far indeed from the truth. He also teaches that Divine inspiration extends to every part of the Bible without the slightest exception, and that no error can occur in the inspired text: "It would be wholly impious to limit inspiration to certain portions only of Scripture or to concede that the sacred authors themselves could have erred."[43]

615   Those, too, who hold that the historical portions of Scripture do not rest on the absolute truth of the facts but merely upon what they are pleased to term their relative truth, namely, what people then commonly thought, are—no less than are the aforementioned critics—out of harmony with the Church's teaching, which is endorsed by the testimony of Jerome and other Fathers. Yet they are not afraid to deduce such views from the words of Leo XIII on the ground that he allowed that the principles he had laid down touching the things of nature could be applied to historical things as well. Hence they maintain that precisely as the sacred writers spoke of physical things according to appearance, so, too, while ignorant of the facts, they narrated them in accordance with general opinion or even on baseless evidence; neither do they tell us the sources whence they derived their knowledge, nor do they make other peoples' narrative their own. Such views are clearly false, and constitute a calumny on our predecessor. After all, what analogy is there between physics and history? For whereas physics is concerned with "sensible appearances" and must consequently square with phenomena, history, on

the contrary, must square with facts, since history is the written account of events as they actually occurred. If we were to accept such views, how could we maintain the truth insisted on throughout Leo XIII's Encyclical—viz., that the sacred narrative is absolutely free from error?

And if Leo XIII does say that we can apply to history and cognate subjects the same principles which hold good for science, he yet does not lay this down as a universal law, but simply says that we can apply a like line of argument when refuting the fallacies of adversaries and defending the historical truth of Scripture from their assaults.   616

Nor do modern innovators stop here: they even try to claim St. Jerome as a patron of their views on the ground that he maintained that historic truth and sequence were not observed in the Bible, "precisely as things actually took place, but in accordance with what men thought at that time," and that he even held that this was the true norm for history.[44] A strange distortion of St. Jerome's words! He does not say that when giving us an account of events the writer was ignorant of the truth and simply adopted the false views then current; he merely says that in giving names to persons or things he followed general custom. Thus the Evangelist calls St. Joseph the father of Jesus, but what he meant by the title "father" here is abundantly clear from the whole context. For St. Jerome "the true norm of history" is this: when it is question of such appellatives (as "father" etc.), and when there is no danger of error, then a writer must adopt the ordinary forms of speech simply because such forms of speech are in ordinary use. More than this: Jerome maintains that belief in the Biblical narrative is as necessary to salvation as is belief in the doctrines of the faith; thus in his Commentary on the Epistle to Philemon he says: 617

What I mean is this: Does any man believe in God the Creator? He cannot do so unless he first believe that the things written of God's Saints are true." He then gives examples from the Old Testament and adds: "Now unless a man believes all these and other things too which are written of the Saints he cannot believe in the God of the Saints."[45]

618   Thus St. Jerome is in complete agreement with St. Augustine, who sums up the general belief of Christian antiquity
when he says:

> Holy Scripture is invested with supreme authority by reason
> of its sure and momentous teachings regarding the faith.
> Whatever, then, it tells us of Enoch, Elias and Moses—that
> we believe. We do not, for instance, believe that God's Son
> was born of the Virgin Mary simply because He could not
> otherwise have appeared in the flesh and "walked amongst
> men"—as Faustus would have it—but we believe it simply
> because it is written in Scripture; and unless we believe in
> Scripture we can neither be Christians nor be saved.[46]

619   Then there are other assailants of Holy Scripture who misuse principles—which are only sound if kept within due bounds
—in order to overturn the fundamental truth of the Bible and
thus destroy Catholic teaching handed down by the Fathers.
If Jerome were living now, he would sharpen his keenest con-
troversial weapons against people who set aside what is the
mind and judgment of the Church, and take too ready a
refuge in such notions as "implicit quotations" or "pseudo-
historical narratiaves," or in "kinds of literature" in the Bible
such as cannot be reconciled with the entire and perfect
truth of God's word, or who suggest such origins of the Bible
as must inevitably weaken—if not destroy—its authority.

620   What can we say of men who in expounding the very
Gospels so whittle away the human trust we should repose in
them as to overturn Divine faith in them? They refuse to allow
the things which Christ said or did have come down to us
unchanged and entire through witnesses who carefully committed to writing what they themselves had seen or heard.
They maintain—and particularly in their treatment of the
Fourth Gospel—that much is due of course to the Evangelists
—who, however, added much from their own imaginations;
but much, too, is due to narratives compiled by the faithful
at other periods, the result, of course, being that the twin
streams now flowing in the same channel cannot be distinguished from one another. Not thus did Jerome and Augustine

and the other Doctors of the Church understand the historical trustworthiness of the Gospels; yet of it one wrote: "He who saw it has borne witness, and his witness is true; and he knows that he tells the truth, that you also may believe" (*Jn.* 19:35). So, too, St. Jerome: after rebuking the heretical framers of the apocryphal Gospels for "attempting rather to fill up the story than to tell it truly,"[47] he says of the Canonical Scriptures: "None can doubt but that what is written took place."[48] Here again he is in fullest harmony with Augustine, who so beautifully says: "These things are true; they are faithfully and truthfully written of Christ; so that whosoever believes His Gospel may be thereby instructed in the truth and misled by no lie."[49]

All this shows us how earnestly we must strive to avoid, as children of the Church, this insane freedom in ventilating opinions which the Fathers were careful to shun. This we shall more readily achieve if you, Venerable Brethren, will make both clergy and laity committed to your care by the Holy Spirit realize that neither Jerome nor the other Fathers of the Church learned their doctrine touching Holy Scripture save in the school of the Divine Master Himself. We know what He felt about Holy Scripture: when He said, "It is written," and "the Scripture must needs be fulfilled," we have therein an argument which admits of no exception and which should put an end to all controversy.   621

Yet it is worth while dwelling on this point a little: when Christ preached to the people, whether on the Mount, by the lakeside, or in the synagogue at Nazareth, or in His own city of Capharnaum, He took His points and His arguments from the Bible. From the same source came His weapons when disputing with the Scribes and Pharisees. Whether teaching or disputing, He quotes from all parts of Scripture and takes His example from it; he quotes it as an argument which must be accepted. He refers without any discrimination of sources to the stories of Jonas and the Ninivites, of the Queen of Sheba and Solomon, of Elias and Eliseus, of David and of Noe, of Lot and the Sodomites, and even of Lot's wife (cf. *Matt.* 12: 3, 39-42; *Lk.* 17:26-29, 32). How solemn His witness to the truth of the sacred books: "One jot or one tittle shall not pass   622 of the Law till all be fulfilled" (*Matt.* 5:18); and again: "The Scripture cannot be broken" (*Jn.* 10:35); and consequently: "He therefore that shall break one of these least commandments, and shall so teach men shall be called the least in the kingdom of heaven" (*Matt.* 5:19). Before His Ascension, too, when He would steep His Apostles in the same doctrine: "He opened their understanding that they might understand the Scriptures. And He said to them: thus it is written, and thus it behooved Christ to suffer, and to rise again from the dead the third day" (*Lk.* 24:45).

623   In a word, then: Jerome's teaching on the superexcellence and truth of Scripture is Christ's teaching. Wherefore we exhort all the Church's children, and especially those whose duty it is to teach in seminaries, to follow closely in St. Jerome's footsteps. If they will but do so, they will learn to prize as he prized the treasure of the Scriptures, and will derive from them most abundant and blessed fruit.

624   Now, if we make use of the "Greatest of Doctors" as our guide and teacher we shall derive from so doing not only the gains signalized above, but others too, which cannot be regarded as trifling or few. What these gains are, Venerable Brethren, we will set out briefly. At the outset, then, we are deeply impressed by the intense love of the Bible which St. Jerome exhibits in his whole life and teaching: both are steeped in the Spirit of God. This intense love of the Bible he was ever striving to kindle in the hearts of the faithful, and his words on this subject to the maiden Demetrias are really addressed to us all: "Love the Bible and wisdom will love you; love it and it will preserve you; honor it and it will embrace you; these are the jewels which you should wear on your breast and in your ears."[50]

625   His unceasing reading of the Bible and his painstaking study of each book—nay, of every phrase and word—gave him a knowledge of the text such as no other ecclesiastical writer of old possessed. It is due to this familiarity with the text and to his own acute judgment that the Vulgate version Jerome made is, in the judgment of all capable men, preferable to any other ancient version, since it appears to give us the sense of the original more accurately and with greater elegance than they.

The said Vulgate, "approved by so many centuries of use in the Church" was pronounced by the Council of Trent "authentic," and the same Council insisted that it was to be used in teaching and in the liturgy.[51] If God in His mercy grants us life, we sincerely hope to see an amended and faithfully restored edition. We have no doubt that, when this arduous task—entrusted by our predecessor, Pius X, to the Benedictine Order—has been completed, it will prove of great assistance in the study of the Bible.

But to return to St. Jerome's love of the Bible: this is so   626 conspicuous in his letters that they almost seem woven out of Scripture texts; and, as St. Bernard found no taste in things which did not echo the most sweet Name of Jesus, so no literature made any appeal to Jerome unless it derived its light from Holy Scripture. Thus he wrote to Paulinus, formerly senator and even consul and only recently converted to the faith:

> If only you had this foundation (knowledge of Scripture); nay, more—if you would let Scripture give the finishing touches to your work—I should find nothing more beautiful, more learned, even nothing more Latin than your volumes. . . . If you could but add to your wisdom and eloquence study of and real acquaintance with Holy Scripture, we should speedily have to acknowledge you a leader amongst us.[52]

How we are to seek for this great treasure, given as it is by   627 our Father in heaven for our solace during this earthly pilgrimage, St. Jerome's example shows us. First, we must be well prepared and must possess a good will. Thus Jerome himself, immediately on his baptism, determined to remove whatever might prove a hindrance to his ambitions in this respect. Like the man who found a treasure and "for joy thereof went and sold all that he had and bought that field" (*Matt.* 13:44), so did Jerome say farewell to the idle pleasures of this passing world; he went into the desert, and since he realized what risks he had run in the past through the allurements of vice, he adopted a most severe style of life. With all obstacles thus removed he prepared his soul for the knowledge of Jesus Christ and for putting on Him Who was "meek and humble of heart" (*Matt.* 11:29). But he went through what Augustine also experienced when he took up the study of Scripture. For the latter has told us that to him, steeped as a youth in Cicero and profane authors, the Bible seemed unfit to be compared with Cicero.

628   My swelling pride shrank from its modest garb, while my gaze could not pierce to what the latter hid. Of a truth Scripture was meant to grow up with the childlike; but then I could not be childlike; turgid eloquence appealed mightily to me.[53]

629   So, too, St. Jerome; even though withdrawn into the desert he still found such delight in profane literature that at first he failed to discern the lowly Christ in His lowly Scriptures:

Wretch that I was! I read Cicero even before I broke my fast! And after the long night-watches, when memory of my past sins wrung tears from my soul, even then I took up my Platus! Then perhaps I would come to my senses and would start reading the Prophets. But their uncouth language made me shiver, and, since blind eyes do not see the light, I blamed the sun and not my own eyes.[54]

630   But in a brief space Jerome became so enamored of the "folly of the Cross" that he himself serves as a proof of the extent to which a humble and devout frame of mind is conducive to the understanding of Holy Scripture. He realized that "in expounding Scripture we need God's Holy Spirit";[55] he saw that one cannot read or understand it otherwise "than the Holy Spirit by Whom it was written demands."[56] Consequently, he was ever humbly praying for God's assistance and for the light of the Holy Spirit, and asking his friends to do the same for him. We find him commending to the Divine assistance and to his brethren's prayers his Commentaries on various books as he began them, and then rendering God due thanks when they were completed.

As he trusted to God's grace, so too did he rely upon the   **631**
authority of his predecessors: "What I have learned I did not
teach myself—a wretchedly presumptuous teacher!—but I
learned it from illustrious men in the Church."[57] Again: "In
studying Scripture I never trusted to myself."[58] To Theophilus, Bishop of Alexandria, he imparted the rule he had laid
down for his own student life: "It has always been my custom
to fight the prerogatives of a Christian, not to overpass the
limits set by the Fathers, always to bear in mind that Roman
faith praised by the Apostles."[59]

He ever paid submissive homage to the Church, our supreme   **632**
teacher through the Roman Pontiffs. Thus, with a view to
putting an end to the controversy raging in the East concerning the mystery of the Holy Trinity, he submitted the question
to the Roman See for settlement, and wrote from the Syrian
desert to Pope Damasus as follows:

> I decided, therefore, to consult the Chair of Peter and that
> Roman faith which the Apostle praised; I ask for my soul's
> food from that city wherein I first put on the garment of
> Christ. . . . I, who follow no other leader save Christ, asso-
> ciate myself with Your Blessedness, in communion, that is,
> with the Chair of Peter. For I know the Church was built
> upon that Rock. . . . I beg you to settle this dispute. If
> you desire it I shall not be afraid to say there are Three
> Hypostases. If it is your wish let them draw up a Symbol
> of faith subsequent to that of Nicaea, and let us orthodox
> praise God in the same form of words as the Arians em-
> ploy.[60]

And in his next letter: "Meanwhile I keep crying out, 'Any   **633**
man who is joined to Peter's Chair, he is my man.' "[61] Since
he had learned this "rule of faith" from his study of the Bible,
he was able to refute a false interpretation of a biblical text
with the simple remark: "Yes, but the Church of God does
not admit that."[62] When, again, Vigilantius quoted an
Apocryphal book, Jerome was content to reply: "A book I
have never so much as read! For what is the good of soiling
one's hands with a book the Church does not receive?"[63]
With his strong insistence on adhering to the integrity of the

faith, it is not to be wondered at that he attacked vehemently those who left the Church; he promptly regarded them as his own personal enemies. "To put it briefly," he says, "I have never spared heretics, and have always striven to regard the Church's enemies as my own."[64] To Rufinus he writes: "There is one point in which I cannot agree with you: you ask me to spare heretics—or, in other words—not to prove myself a Catholic."[65] Yet at the same time Jerome deplored the lamentable state of heretics and adjured them to return to their sorrowing Mother, the one source of salvation;[66] he prayed, too, with all earnestness for the conversion of those "who had quitted the Church and put away the Holy Spirit's teaching to follow their own notions."[67]

634   Was there ever a time, Venerable Brethren, when there was greater call than now for us all, lay and cleric alike, to imbibe the spirit of this "Greatest of Doctors"? For there are many contumacious folk now who sneer at the authority and government of God, Who has revealed Himself, and of the Church which teaches. You know—for Leo XIII warned us—"how insistently men fight against us; You know the arms and arts they rely upon."[68] It is our duty, then, to train as many really fit defenders of this holiest of causes as you can. They must be ready to combat not only those who deny the existence of the Supernatural Order altogether, and are thus led to deny the existence of any divine revelation or inspiration, but those, too, who—through an itching desire for novelty— venture to interpret the sacred books as though they were of purely human origin; those, too, who scoff at opinions held of old in the Church, or who, through contempt of its teaching office, either reck little of, or silently disregard, or at least obstinately endeavor to adapt to their own views, the Constitutions of the Apostolic See or the decisions of the Pontifical Biblical Commission.

635   Would that all Catholics would cling to St. Jerome's golden rule and obediently listen to their Mother's words, so as modestly to keep within the bounds marked out by the Fathers and ratified by the Church.

636   To return, however, to the question of the formation of Biblical students. We must lay the foundations in piety and

humility of mind; only when we have done that does St.
Jerome invite us to study the Bible. In the first place, he
insists, in season and out, on daily reading of the text. "Provided," he says, "our bodies are not the slaves of sin, wisdom
will come to us; but exercise your mind, feed it daily with
Holy Scripture."[69] And again: "We have got, then, to read
Holy Scripture assiduously; we have got to meditate on the
Law of God day and night so that, as expert money-changers,
we may be able to detect false coin from true."[70]

For matrons and maidens alike he lays down the same rule.   637
Thus, writing to the Roman matron Laeta about her daughter's
training, he says:

> Every day she should give you a definite account of her
> Bible reading. . . . For her the Bible must take the place
> of silks and jewels. . . . Let her learn the Psalter first, and
> find her recreation in its songs; let her learn from Solomon's
> Proverbs the way of life, from Ecclesiastes how to trample
> on the world. In Job she will find an example of patient
> virtue. Thence let her pass to the Gospels; they should
> always be in her hands. She should steep herself in the Acts
> and the Epistles. And when she has enriched her soul with
> these treasures she should commit to memory the Prophets,
> the Heptateuch, Kings and Chronicles, Esdras and Esther;
> then she can learn the Canticle of Canticles without any
> fear."[71]

He says the same to Eustochium: "Read assiduously and   638
learn as much as you can. Let sleep find you holding your
Bible, and when your head nods let it be resting on the sacred
page."[72]

When he sent Eustochium the epitaph he had composed   639
for her mother Paula, he especially praised that holy woman
for having so wholeheartedly devoted herself and her daughter
to Bible study that she knew the Bible through and through,
and had committed it to memory. He continues:

> I will tell you another thing about her, though evil-disposed
> people may cavil at it: she determined to learn Hebrew, a

language which I myself, with immense labor and toil from my youth upwards, have only partly learned, and which I even now dare not cease studying lest it should quit me. But Paula learned it, and so well that she could chant the Psalms in Hebrew, and could speak it, too, without any trace of a Latin accent. We can see the same thing even now in her daughter Eustochium.[73]

640   He tells us much the same of Marcella, who also knew the Bible exceedingly well.[74] And none can fail to see what profit and sweet tranquility must result in well-disposed souls from such devout reading of the Bible. Whosoever comes to it in piety, faith and humility, and with a determination to make progress in it, will assuredly find therein and will eat the "Bread that cometh down from heaven" (*Jn.* 6:33); he will, in his own person, experience the truth of David's words: "The hidden and uncertain things of Thy Wisdom Thou hast made manifest to me!" (*Ps.* 50:8), for this table of the "Divine Word" does really "contain holy teaching, teach the true faith, and lead us unfalteringly beyond the veil into the Holy of Holies."[76]

641   Hence, as far as in us lies, we, Venerable Brethren, shall, with St. Jerome as our guide, never desist from urging the faithful to read daily the Gospels, the Acts and the Epistles, so as to gather thence food for their souls.

642   Our thoughts naturally turn just now to the Society of St. Jerome, which we ourselves were instrumental in founding; its success has gladdened us, and we trust that the future will see a great impulse given to it.

643   The object of this Society is to put into the hands of as many people as possible the Gospels and Acts, so that every Christian family may have them and become accustomed to reading them. This we have much at heart, for we have seen how useful it is. We earnestly hope, then, that similar Societies will be founded in your dioceses and affiliated to the parent Society here.

644   Commendation, too, is due to Catholics in other countries who have published the entire New Testament, as well as selected portions of the Old, in neat and simple form so as to

popularize their use. Much again must accrue to the Church of God when numbers of people thus approach this table of heavenly instruction which the Lord provided through the ministry of His prophets, Apostles and Doctors for the entire Christian world.

If, then, St. Jerome begs for assiduous reading of the Bible by the faithful in general, he insists on it for those who are called to "bear the yoke of Christ" and preach His word. His words to Rusticus the monk apply to all clerics: 645

> So long as you are in your own country regard your cell as your orchard; there you can gather Scripture's various fruits and enjoy the pleasures it affords you. Always have a book in your hands—and read it; learn the Psalter by heart; pray unceasingly; watch over your senses lest idle thoughts creep in.[76]

Similarly to Nepotian: 646

> Constantly read the Bible; in fact, have it always in your hands. Learn what you have got to teach. Get firm hold of that "faithful word that is according to doctine, that you may be able to exhort in sound doctrine and convince the gainsayers."[77]

When reminding Paulinus of the lessons St. Paul gave to Timothy and Titus, and which he himself had derived from the Bible, Jerome says: 647

> A mere holy rusticity only avails the man himself; but however much a life so meritorious may serve to build up the Church of God, it does as much harm to the Church if it fails to "resist the gainsayer." Malachias the Prophet says, or rather the Lord says it by Malachias: "Ask for the Law from the priests." For it is the priest's duty to give an answer when asked about the Law. In Deuteronomy we read: "Ask thy father and he will tell thee; ask the priests and they will tell thee. . . ." Daniel, too, at the close of his glorious vision, declares that "the just shall shine like stars

and they that are learned as the brightness of the firmament." What a vast difference, then, between a righteous
rusticity and a learned righteousness! The former likened
to the stars; the latter to the heavens themselves![78]

648   He writes ironically to Marcella about the "self-righteous
lack of education" noticeable in some clerics, who "think
that to be without culture and to be holy are the same thing,
and who dub themselves 'disciples of the fisherman'; as though
they were holy simply because ignorant!"[79]

649   Nor is it only the "uncultured" whom Jerome condemns.
Learned clerics sin through ignorance of the Bible; therefore
he demands of them an assiduous reading of the text.

650   Strive then, Venerable Brethren, to bring home to your
clerics and priests these teachings of the Sainted Commentator.
You have to remind them constantly of the demands made by
their divine vocation if they would be worthy of it: "The lips
of the priest shall keep knowledge, and men shall ask the Law
at his mouth, for he is the Angel of the Lord of hosts" (*Mal.*
2:7). They must realize, then, that they cannot neglect study
of the Bible, and that this can only be undertaken along the
lines laid down by Leo XIII in his Encyclical *Providentissimus
Deus.*[80] They cannot do this better than by frequenting the
Biblical Institute established by our predecessor, Pius X, in
accordance with the wishes of Leo XIII. As the experience of
the past ten years has shown, it has proved a great gain to the
Church. Not all, however, can avail themselves of this. It will
be well, then, Venerable Brethren, that picked men, both of
the secular and regular clergy, should come to Rome for
Biblical study. All will not come with the same object. Some,
in accordance with the real purpose of the Institute, will so
devote themselves to Biblical study that "afterwards, both in
private and in public, whether by writing or by teaching,
whether as professors in Catholic schools or by writing in
defense of Catholic truth, they may be able worthily to uphold the cause of Biblical study."[81] Others, however, already
priests, will obtain here a wider knowledge of the Bible than
they were able to acquire during their theological course;
they will gain, too, an acquaintance with the great com-

mentators and with Biblical history and geography. Such knowledge will avail them much in their ministry; they will be "instructed to every good work" (II *Tim.* 3:17).

We learn, then, from St. Jerome's example and teaching   651
the qualities required in one who would devote himself to Biblical study. But what, in his view, is the goal of such study? First, that from the Bible's pages we learn spiritual perfection. Meditating as he did day and night on the Law of the Lord and on His Scriptures, Jerome himself found there the "Bread that cometh down from heaven," the manna containing all delights.[82] And we certainly cannot do without that bread. How can a cleric teach others the way of salvation if through neglect of meditation on God's word he fails to teach himself? What confidence can he have that, when ministering to others, he is really "a leader of the blind, a light to them that are in darkness, and instructor of the foolish, having the form of knowledge and of truth in the law" (*Rom.* 2:19), if he is unwilling to study the said Law and thus shuts the door on any divine illumination on it?

Alas! many of God's ministers, through never looking at   652
their Bible, perish themselves and allow many others to perish also. "The children have asked for bread, and there was none to break it unto them" (*Lam.* 4:4); and "With desolation is all the land made desolate, for there is none that meditateth in the heart" (*Jer.* 12:11).

Secondly, it is from the Bible that we gather confirmations   653
and illustrations of any particular doctrine we wish to defend. In this Jerome was marvellously expert. When disputing with the heretics of his day he refuted them by singularly apt and weighty arguments drawn from the Bible. If men of the present age would but imitate him in this we should see realized what our predecessor, Leo XIII, in his Encyclical, *Providentissimus Deus*, said was so eminently desirable: "The Bible influencing our theological teaching and indeed becoming its very soul."[83]

Lastly, the real value of the Bible is for our preaching—if   654
the latter is to be fruitful. On this point it is a pleasure to illustrate from Jerome what we ourselves said in our Encyclical on "preaching the Word of God," entitled *Humani generis*.

How insistently Jerome urges on priests assiduous reading of the Bible if they would worthily teach and preach! Their words will have neither value nor weight nor any power to touch men's souls save in proportion as they are "informed" by Holy Scripture: "Let a priest's speech be seasoned with the Bible,"[84] for "the Scriptures are a trumpet that stirs us with a mighty voice and penetrates to the soul of them that believe,"[85] and "nothing so strikes home as an example taken from the Bible."[86]

655   These mainly concern the exegetes, yet preachers, too, must always bear them in mind. Jerome's first rule is careful study of the actual words so that we may be perfectly certain what the writer really does say. He was most careful to consult the original text, to compare various versions, and, if he discovered any mistake in them, to explain it and thus make the text perfectly clear. The precise meaning, too, that attaches to particular words has to be worked out, for "when discussing Holy Scripture it is not words we want so much as the meaning of words."[87] We do not for a moment deny that Jerome, in imitation of Latin and Greek doctors before him, leaned too much, especially at the outset, towards allegorical interpretations. But his love of the Bible, his unceasing toil in reading and re-reading it and weighing its meaning, compelled him to an ever-growing appreciation of its literal sense and to the formulation of sound principles regarding it. These we set down here, for they provide a safe path for us all to follow in getting from the Sacred Books their full meaning.

656   In the first place, then, we must study the literal or historical meaning:

> I earnestly warn the prudent reader not to pay attention to superstitious interpretations such as are given cut and dried according to some interpreter's fancy. He should study the beginning, middle, and end, and so form a connected idea of the whole of what he finds written.[88]

657   Jerome then goes on to say that all interpretation rests on the literal sense,[89] and that we are not to think that there is no literal sense merely because a thing is said metaphorically,

for "the history itself is often presented in metaphorical dress and described figuratively."[90] Indeed, he himself affords the best refutation of those who maintain that he says that certain passages have no historical meaning: "We are not rejecting the history, we are merely giving a spiritual interpretation of it."[91] Once, however, he has firmly established the literal or historical meaning, Jerome goes on to seek out deeper and hidden meanings, so as to nourish his mind with more delicate food. Thus he says of the Book of Proverbs—and he makes the same remark about other parts of the Bible—that we must not stop at the simple literal sense: "Just as we have to seek gold in the earth, for the kernel in the shell, for the chestnut's hidden fruit beneath its hairy coverings, so in Holy Scripture we have to dig deep for its divine meaning."[92]

When teaching Paulinus "how to make true progress in the Bible," he says: "Everything we read in the Sacred Books shines and glitters even in its outer shell; but the marrow of it is sweeter. If you want the kernel you must break the shell."[93]

.658

At the same time, he insists that in searching for this deeper meaning we must proceed in due order, "lest in our search for spiritual riches we seem to despise the history as poverty-stricken."[94] Consequently he repudiates many mystical interpretations alleged by ancient writers; for he feels that they are not sufficiently based on the literal meaning:

659

When all these promises of which the Prophets sang are regarded not merely as empty sounds or idle tropological expressions, but as established on earth and having solid historical foundations, then can we put on them the coping-stone of spiritual interpretation.[95]

On this point he makes the wise remark that we ought not to desert the path mapped out by Christ and His Apostles, who, while regarding the Old Testament as preparing for and foreshadowing the New Covenant, and whilst consequently explaining various passages in the former as figurative, yet do not give a figurative interpretation of all alike. In confirmation of this he often refers us to St. Paul, who, when

660

"explaining the mystery of Adam and Eve, did not deny that they were formed, but on that historical basis erected a spiritual interpretation, and said: "Therefore shall a man leave,' etc."[96]

661   If only Biblical students and preachers would but follow this example of Christ and His Apostles; if they would but obey the directions of Leo XIII, and not neglect "those allegorical or similar explanations which the Fathers have given, especially when these are based on the literal sense, and are supported by weighty authority";[97] if they would pass from the literal to the more profound meaning in temperate fashion, and thus lift themselves to a higher plane, they would, with St. Jerome, realize how true are St. Paul's words: "All Scripture is inspired by God and useful for teaching, for reproving, for correcting, for instructing in justice" (II *Tim.* 3:16).

662   They would, too, derive abundant help from the infinite treasury of facts and ideas in the Bible, and would thence be able to mould firmly but gently the lives and characters of the faithful.

663   As for methods of expounding Holy Scripture—"for amongst the dispensers of the mysteries of God it is required that a man be found faithful" (I *Cor.* 4:2)—St. Jerome lays down that we have got to keep to the "true interpretation, and that the real function of a commentator is to set forth not what he himself would like his author to mean, but what he really does mean."[98]

664   And he continues: It is dangerous to speak in the Church, lest through some faulty interpretation we make Christ's Gospel into man's Gospel."[99] And again: "In explaining the Bible we need no florid oratorical composition, but that learned simplicity which is truth."[100]

665   This ideal he ever kept before him; he acknowledges that in his Commentaries he "seeks no praise, but so to set out what another has well said that it may be understood in the sense in which it was said."[101] He further demands of an

expositor of Scripture a style which, while leaving no impression of haziness . . . yet explains things, sets out the meaning, clears up obscurities, and is not mere verbiage."[102]

And here we may set down some passages from his writings   666
which well serve to show to what an extent he shrank from
that declamatory kind of eloquence which simply aims at
winning empty applause by an equally empty and noisy flow
of words. He says to Nepotian:

I do not want you to be a declaimer or a garrulous brawler;
rather be skilled in the Mysteries, learned in the Sacraments
of God. To make the populace gape by spinning words and
speaking like a whirlwind is only worthy of empty-headed
men.[103]

And once more: 667

Students ordained at this time seem not to think how they
may get at the real marrow of Holy Scripture, but how best
they may make peoples' ears tingle by their flowery dec-
lamations![104]

Again: 668

I prefer to say nothing of men, who like myself, have
passed from profane literature to Biblical study, but who,
if they happen once to have caught men's ears by their
ornate sermons, straightway begin to fancy that whatsoever
they say is God's law. Apparently they do not think it
worth while to discover what the Prophets and Apostles
really meant; they are content to string together texts
made to fit the meaning they want. One would almost fancy
that instead of being a degraded species of oratory, it must
be a fine thing to pervert the meaning of the text and
compel the reluctant Scripture to yield the meaning one
wants![105]

669   "As a matter of fact, mere loquacity would not win any credit unless backed by Scriptural authority, that is, when men see that the speaker is trying to give his false doctrine Biblical support."[106] Moreover, this garrulous eloquence and wordy rusticity "lacks biting power, has nothing vivid or life-giving in it; it is flaccid, languid and enervated; it is like boiled herbs and grass, which speedily dry up and wither away."

670   On the contrary the Gospel teaching is straightforward, it is like that "least of all seeds"—the mustard seed—"no mere vegetable, but something that 'grows into a tree so that the birds of the air come and dwell in its branches.' "[107] The consequence is that everybody hears gladly this simple and holy fashion of speech, for it is clear and has real beauty without artificiality:

> There are certain eloquent folk who puff out their cheeks and produce a foaming torrent of words; may they win all the eulogiums they crave for! For myself, I prefer so to speak that I may be intelligible; when I discuss the Bible I prefer the Bible's simplicity. . . .[108] A cleric's exposition of the Bible should, of course, have a certain becoming eloquence; but he must keep this in the background, for he must ever have in view the human race and not the leisurely philosophical schools with their choice coterie of disciples.[109]

671   If the younger clergy would but strive to reduce principles like these to practice, and if their elders would keep such principles before their eyes, we are well assured that they would prove of very real assistance to those to whom they minister.

672   It only remains for us, Venerable Brethren, to refer to those "sweet fruits" which Jerome gathered from "the bitter seed" of literature. For we confidently hope that his example will fire both clergy and laity with enthusiasm for the study of the Bible. It will be better, however, for you to gather from the lips of the saintly hermit rather than from our words what real spiritual delight he found in the Bible and its study. Notice, then, in what strain he writes to Paulinus, "my com-

panion, friend, and fellow-mystic": "I beseech you to live amidst these things. To meditate on them, to know nought else, to have no other interests, this is really a foretaste of the joys of heaven."[110]

He says much the same to his pupil Paula: 673

Tell me whether you know of anything more sacred than this sacred mystery, anything more delightful than the pleasure found herein? What food, what honey could be sweeter than to learn of God's Providence, to enter into His shrine and look into the mind of the Creator, to listen to the Lord's words at which the wise of this world laugh, but which really are full of spiritual teaching? Others may have their wealth, may drink out of jewelled cups, be clad in silks, enjoy popular applause, find it impossible to exhaust their wealth by dissipating it in pleasures of all kinds; but our delight is to meditate on the Law of the Lord day and night, to knock at His door when shut, to receive our food from the Trinity of Persons, and, under the guidance of the Lord, trample underfoot the swelling tumults of this world.[112]

And in his Commentary on the Epistle to the Ephesians,   674
which he dedicated to Paula and her daughter Eustochium, he says: "If aught could sustain and support a wise man in this life or help him to preserve his equanimity amid the conflicts of the world, it is, I reckon, meditation on and knowledge of the Bible."[112]

And so it was with Jerome himself: afflicted with many   675
mental anxieties and bodily pains, he yet ever enjoyed an interior peace. Nor was this due simply to some idle pleasure he found in such studies: it sprang from love of God and it worked itself out in an earnest love of God's Church—the divinely appointed guardian of God's Word. For in the Books of both Testaments Jerome saw the Church of God foretold. Did not practically every one of the illustrious and sainted women who hold a place of honor in the Old Testament prefigure the Church, God's Spouse? Did not the priesthood, the

sacrifices, the solemnities, nay, nearly everything described in the Old Testament shadow forth that same Church? How many Psalms and Prophecies he saw fulfilled in that Church? To him it was clear that the Church's greatest privileges were set forth by Christ and His Apostles. Small wonder, then, that growing familiarity with the Bible meant for Jerome growing love of the Spouse of Christ. We have seen with what reverent yet enthusiastic love he attached himself to the Roman Church and to the See of Peter, how eagerly he attacked those who assailed her. So when applauding Augustine, his junior yet his fellow-soldier, and rejoicing in the fact that they were one in their hatred of heresy, he hails him with the words:

> Well done! You are famous throughout the world. Catholics revere you and point you out as the establisher of the old-time faith; and—an even greater glory—all heretics hate you. And they hate me too; unable to slay us with the sword, they would that wishes could kill.[113]

676   Sulpicius Severus quotes Postumianus to the same effect:

> His unceasing conflict with wicked men brings on him their hatred. Heretics hate him, for he never ceases attacking them; clerics hate him, for he assails their criminal lives. But all good men admire him and love him.[114]

677   And Jerome had to endure much from heretics and abandoned men, especially when the Pelagians laid waste the monastery at Bethlehem. Yet all this he bore with equanimity, like a man who would not hesitate to die for the faith:

> I rejoice when I hear that my children are fighting for Christ. May He in whom we believe confirm our zeal so that we may gladly shed our blood for His faith. Our very home is—as far as worldly belongings go—completely ruined by the heretics; yet through Christ's mercy it is filled with spiritual riches. It is better to have to be content with dry bread than to lose one's faith.[115]

And while he never suffered errors to creep in unnoticed,   678
he likewise never failed to lash with biting tongue any looseness in morals, for he was always anxious "to present" unto
Christ "the Church in all her glory, not having spot or wrinkle
or any such things, but that she might be holy and without
blemish" (*Eph.* 5:27). How terribly he upbraids men who
have degraded the dignity of the priesthood! With what vigor
he inveighs against the pagan morals then infecting Rome!
But he rightly felt that nothing could better avail to stem this
flood of vice than the spectacle afforded by the real beauty
of the Christian life; and that a love of what is really good is
the best antidote to evil. Hence he urged that young people
must be piously brought up, the married taught a holy integrity of life, pure souls have the beauty of virginity put before
them, that the sweet austerity of an interior life should be
extolled, and since the primal law of Christian religion was
the combination of toil with charity, that if this could only
be preserved human society would recover from its disturbed
state. Of this charity he says very beautifully: "The believing
soul is Christ's true temple. Adorn it, deck it out, offer your
gifts to it, in it receive Christ. Of what profit to have your
walls glittering with jewels while Christ dies of hunger in
poverty?"[116]

As for toil, his whole life and not merely his writings afford   679
the best example. Postumianus, who spent six months with
him at Bethlehem, says: "He is wholly occupied in reading
and with books; he rests neither day nor night; he is always
either reading or writing something."[117] Jerome's love of the
Church, too, shines out even in his Commentaries wherein he
lets slip no opportunity for praising the Spouse of Christ:

The choicest things of all the nations have come and the
Lord's House is filled with glory: that is, "the Church of
the Living God, the pillar and the ground of truth.". . .
With jewels like these is the Church richer than ever was
the synagogue; with these living stones is the House of God
built up and eternal peace bestowed upon her.[118]

> Come, let us go up to the Mount of the Lord: for we must needs go up if we would come to Christ and to the House of the God of Jacob, to the Church which is "the pillar and ground of truth."[119]

> By the Lord's voice is the Church established upon the rock, and her hath the King brought into His chamber, to her by secret condescension hath He put forth His hand through the lattices.[120]

680   Again and again, as in the passages just given, does Jerome celebrate the intimate union between Christ and His Church. For since the Head can never be separated from the mystical body, so, too, love of Christ is ever associated with zeal for His Church; and this love of Christ must ever be the chiefest and most agreeable result of a knowledge of Holy Scripture. So convinced indeed was Jerome that familiarity with the Bible was the royal road to the knowledge and love of Christ that he did not hesitate to say: "Ignorance of the Bible means ignorance of Christ."[121] And "what other life can there be without knowledge of the Bible, wherein Christ, the life of them that believe, is set before us?"[122] Every single page of either Testament seems to center around Christ; hence Jerome, commenting on the words of the Apocalypse about the River and the Tree of Life, says:

> One stream flows out from the throne of God, and that is the grace of the Holy Spirit, and that grace of the Holy Spirit is in the Holy Scriptures, that is, in the stream of the Scriptures. Yet has that stream twin banks, the Old Testament and the New, and the Tree planted on either side is Christ.[123]

681   Small wonder, then, if in his devout meditations he applied everything he read in the Bible to Christ:

> When I read the Gospel and find there testimonies from the Law and from the Prophets, I see only Christ; I so see Moses and the Prophets that I understand them of Christ.

Then when I come to the splendor of Christ Himself, and when I gaze at that glorious sunlight, I care not to look at the lamplight. For what light can a lamp give when lit in the daytime? If the sun shines out, the lamplight does not show. Not that I would detract from the Law and the Prophets; rather do I praise them in that they show forth Christ. But I so read the Law and the Prophets as not to abide in them but from them to pass to Christ.[124]

Hence was Jerome wondrously uplifted to love for and knowledge of Christ through his study of the Bible, in which he discovered the precious pearl of the Gospel: "There is one most priceless pearl: the knowledge of the Savior, the mystery of His Passion, the secret of His Resurrection."[125] Burning as he did with the love of Christ we cannot but marvel that he, poor and lowly with Christ, with soul freed from earthly cares, sought Christ alone, by His spirit was he led, with Him he lived in closest intimacy, by imitating Him he would bear about the image of His sufferings in himself. For him nought more glorious than to suffer with and for Christ. Hence it was that when on Damasus' death he, wounded and weary from evil men's assaults, left Rome and wrote just before he embarked:

682

> Though some fancy me a scoundrel and guilty of every crime—and, indeed, this is a small matter when I think of my sins—yet you do well when from your soul you reckon evil men good. Thank God I am deemed worthy to be hated by the world. . . . What real sorrows have I to bear— I who fight for the Cross? Men heap false accusations on me; yet I know that through ill report and good report we win the kingdom of heaven.[126]

In like fashion does he exhort the maiden Eustochium to courageous and lifelong toil for Christ's sake:

683

> To become what the Martyrs, the Apostles, what even Christ Himself was, means immense labor—but what a reward!. . . . What I have been saying to you will sound hard

to one who does not love Christ. But those who consider worldly pomp a mere offscouring and all under the sun mere nothingness if only they may win Christ, those who are dead with Christ, have risen with Him and have crucified the flesh with its vices and concupiscences—they will echo the words: "Who shall separate us from the charity of Christ?"[127]

684   Immense, then, was the profit Jerome derived from reading Scripture; hence came those interior illuminations whereby he was ever more and more drawn to knowledge and love of Christ; hence, too, that love of prayer of which he has written so well; hence his wonderful familiarity with Chirst, Whose sweetness drew him so that he ran unfalteringly along the arduous way of the Cross to the palm of victory. Hence, too, his ardent love for the Holy Eucharist: "Who is wealthier than he who carries the Lord's Body in his wicker basket, the Lord's Blood in his crystal vessel?"[128] Hence, too, his love for Christ's Mother, whose perpetual virginity he had so keenly defended, whose title as God's Mother and as the greatest example of all the virtues he constantly set before Christ's spouses for their imitation.[129] No one, then, can wonder that Jerome should have been so powerfully drawn to those spots in Palestine which had been consecrated by the presence of our Redeemer and His Mother. It is easy to recognize the hand of Jerome in the words written from Bethlehem to Marcella by his disciples, Paula and Eustochium:

> What words can serve to describe to you the Savior's cave? As for the manger in which He lay—well, our silence does it more honor than any poor words of ours. . . . Will the day ever dawn when we can enter His cave to weep at His tomb with the sister (of Lazarus) and mourn with His Mother; when we can kiss the wood of His Cross and, with the ascending Lord on Olivet, be uplifted in mind and spirit?[130]

685   Filled with memories such as these, Jerome could, while far away from Rome and leading a life hard for the body but

inexpressibly sweet to the soul, cry out: "Would that Rome had what tiny Bethlehem possesses!"[131]

But we rejoice—and Rome with us—that the Saint's desire has been fulfilled, though far otherwise than he hoped for. For whereas David's royal city once gloried in the possession of the relics of "the Greatest Doctor" reposing in the cave where he dwelt so long, Rome now possesses them, for they lie in St. Mary Major's beside the Lord's Crib. His voice is now still, though at one time the whole Catholic world listened to it when it echoed from the desert; yet Jerome still speaks in his writings, which "shine like lamps throughout the world,"[132] Jerome still calls to us. His voice rings out, telling us of the superexcellence of Holy Scripture, of its integral character and historical trustworthiness, telling us, too, of the pleasant fruits resulting from reading and meditating upon it. His voice summons all the Church's children to return to a truly Christian standard of life, to shake themselves free from a pagan type of morality which seems to have sprung to life again in these days. His voice calls upon us, and especially on Italian piety and zeal, to restore to the See of Peter divinely established here that honor and liberty which its Apostolic dignity and duty demand. The voice of Jerome summons those Christian nations which have unhappily fallen away from Mother Church to turn once more to her in whom lies all hope of eternal salvation. Would, too, that the Eastern Churches, so long in opposition to the See of Peter, would listen to Jerome's voice. When he lived in the East and sat at the feet of Gregory and Didymus, he said only what the Christians of the East thought in his time when he declared that "If anyone is outside the Ark of Noe he will perish in the overwhelming flood."[133] Today this flood seems on the verge of sweeping away all human institutions—unless God steps in to prevent it. And surely this calamity must come if men persist in sweeping on one side God the Creator and Conserver of all things! Surely whatever cuts itself off from Christ must perish! Yet He Who at His disciples' prayer calmed the raging sea can restore peace to the tottering fabric of society. May Jerome, who so loved God's Church and so strenuously defended it against its enemies, win for us the removal of every element of discord, in accor-

686

dance with Christ's prayer, so that there may be "one fold and one shepherd."

687   Delay not, Venerable Brethren, to impart to your people and clergy what on the fifteenth centenary of the death of "the Greatest Doctor" we have here set before you. Urge upon all not merely to embrace under Jerome's guidance Catholic doctrine touching the inspiration of Scripture, but to hold fast to the principles laid down in the Encyclical *Providentissimus Deus*, and in this present Encyclical. Our one desire for all the Church's children is that, being saturated with the Bible, they may arrive at the all-surpassing knowledge of Jesus Christ. In testimony of which desire and of our fatherly feeling for you we impart to you and all your flocks the Apostolic blessing.

688   *The "Joannine Comma" is the name given to a longer reading of I John 5:7-8 which is found in some Old Latin versions and made its way into the Sixto-Clementine Vulgate. Between the words "testify" and "Spirit" it inserts: "in heaven: the Father, the Word, and the Holy Spirit, and these three are one. And there are three who testify on earth." On January 13, 1897, the Congregation of the Inquisition, having been asked "whether the authenticity [of the Joannine Comma] can safely be denied or at least called into doubt", issued a decree replying "in the negative". A dispute followed as to whether this was meant to close debate and prevent further study of the issue. Finally, on June 2, 1927, the same Congregation (by then renamed the Holy Office) made public a clarification that had been circulating privately. It stated that "the decree was issued to restrain the audacity" of those deciding the question completely on their own. "But it was by no means intended to hinder Catholic writers from investigating the case more fully and, after weighing accurately all the arguments, inclining to the opinion against genuineness with that moderation and temperance which the gravity of the matter requires, provided they profess themselves ready to submit to the judgment of the Church. . ." Today no serious scholar defends the Comma as part of the original text of I John. It is widely viewed as an allegorical gloss, probably of fourth century Spanish or African origin, that slipped from the margin into the text of some Latin versions as of the fifth century.   Ed.*

Decisions of the Pontifical Biblical Commission on the False Interpretation of Two Texts
July 1, 1933

The Biblical Commission answers the following questions:

1. *Ps.* 15:10-11—Whether, especially considering the authentic interpretations of Sts. Peter and Paul, Princes of the Apostles (Acts 2:24-33; 13:35-37), a Catholic may interpret the words of Psalm 15:10-11, "Thou wilt not leave my soul in hell; nor wilt thou give thy holy one to see corruption. Thou hast made known to me the ways of life," as if the sacred author had not spoken of the resurrection of our Lord Jesus Christ.

689

Answer: In the negative.

690

2. *Matt.* 16:26; *Lk.* 9:25—Whether one may assert that the words of Jesus Christ—Matt. 16:26, "What doth it profit a man if he gain the whole world and suffer the loss of his own soul? Or what exchange shall a man give for his soul;" and Lk. 9:25, "What is a man advantaged, if he gain the whole world, and lose himself?"—do not refer, in their literal sense, to the eternal salvation of the soul, but only to the temporal life of man, notwithstanding the meaning of the words themselves and their context, as also the unanimous interpretation of Catholics.

691

Answer: In the negative.

692

Pontifical Biblical Commission
Letter to the Archbishops and Bishops of Italy
August 20, 1941

According to the Pontifical Biblical Commission there was sent to the Most Eminent Members of the Sacred College, to the Most Excellent Ordinaries of Italy, and to certain Superiors General of Religious Orders an anonymous brochure entitled: *A Most grave danger for the church and for souls. The critical-scientific system of studying and interpreting Holy Scripture, its evil misconceptions and aberrations* (48 pages in 8°).

694 On the first page of this pamphlet is the line: "Manuscript! Very secret matter of conscience!" But, with absurd contradiction, it was sent throughout the whole of Italy in open envelopes.

695 Moreover at the bottom of the last page one finds the following sentence: "This is a copy conformable to one presented to the Holy Father Pius XII." Since this is most true, one need only mention the discourtesy—as your Most Reverend Excellency will have immediately noticed—of sending a document, which was written with the intention of presenting it to the examination of the Holy Father, simultaneously to His Holiness and to many other ecclesiastical persons.

696 The above two facts suffice to prove how much the author of the brochure, whoever he is, lacks judgment and prudence and reverence. One could dismiss the matter without further ado. However, fearful lest certain of the accusations and insinuations made might trouble one or the other shepherd of

souls and perhaps turn him from the duty of procuring for
his future priests that sane and just study of Holy Scripture
which is so close to the heart of the Holy Father, the Most
Eminent Fathers comprising the Pontifical Biblical Commission, gathered together in solemn conference for the examination of this matter, have decided to propose the following
considerations to your Most Reverend Excellency.

The pamphlet pretends to be a defense of a certain type of   **697**
exegesis called *meditative*; but it is before everything else a
virulent attack against the scientific study of the Holy Scriptures: the philological, historical, archaeological, etc., study of
the Bible is nothing but rationalism, naturalism, modernism,
scepticism, atheism, etc.; to really comprehend the Bible one
must give free reign to the spirit, as though each individual
were in personal communion with the Divine Wisdom, and received from the Holy Spirit special individual lights, as the
first Protestants supposed. Indeed the anonymous author
attacks with extreme violence persons and pontifical scientific institutions; he inveighs against the whole idea of scientific biblical studies, "accursed spirit of pride, presumption,
and superficiality, disguised under minute investigations and
hypocritical literal exactness" (p. 40); he looks with disdain
on erudition, the study of the oriental languages, and other
auxiliary studies, and finally ends up in grave errors about the
fundamental principles of Catholic hermeneutics which flow
from the theological definition of biblical inspiration; misunderstanding the doctrine of the various senses of Holy Writ,
he utterly disregards the literal meaning and its exact investigation; finally, ignoring the history of the original texts and
of the ancient versions, as well as the nature and importance
of textual criticism, he proposes a false theory concerning the
authenticity of the Vulgate.

Since it would be out of place here, and even disrespectful   **698**
to the pastors and teachers of the Church, to dwell on the
real meaning of inspiration and biblical hermeneutics, it will
suffice now to counterbalance the pretensions of this anonymous writer with a few of the more recent pronouncements
of the Holy See about the scientific study of Holy Scripture
from Pope Leo XIII onward.

699   1. The Literal Sense. The anonymous author of the pamphlet, although he affirms "pro forma" that the literal sense is
the "basis of biblical interpretation" (p. 6), recognizes exclusively an exegesis that is purely subjective and allegorical,
flowing from personal inspiration, or rather, from the more
or less vivacious and fertile imagination of each individual.
Although it is a dogma of faith and a fundamental principle
of interpretation, as the practice of our Lord and the Apostles
proves, that there is in Holy Scripture, over and above the
literal sense, a meaning that is spiritual or typical, nevertheless not every sentence or narrative has a typical meaning.
This was the grave exaggeration of the Alexandrian School,
that they wished to find a symbolical meaning everywhere,
even to the detriment of the literal and historical meaning of
the text. The spiritual or typical sense, besides being based
on the literal sense, must conform to the practice of our
Lord, of the Apostles and of inspired writers, as well as to the
traditional usage of the Holy Fathers of the Church, especially as they express themselves in the voice of the Sacred
Liturgy, for "As prayer, so faith." A freer application of the
sacred text is permissible in sermons and ascetical works for
the expression of an edifying idea; but the resulting thought,
no matter how beautiful it may be, if it has not been established as above explained, cannot be proposed truly and
strictly as the sense of the Bible, nor as inspired by God in
the sacred text.

700   Contrary to all this, this anonymous author, making none
of these elementary distinctions between the various senses
of Holy Scripture, wishes to impose the outpourings of his
own imagination as the sense of the Bible, as "the true spiritual communications of the wisdom of God" (p. 45), and, not
understanding the supreme importance of the literal sense, he
calumniates Catholic exegetes by saying that they take into
consideration *"only* the literal sense" and that they study
even that "in a human way, understanding it *only* in the
material signification and sound of the words" (p. 11), and
finally that they are "obsessed by the literal meaning of
Scripture" (p. 46). Thus he rejects the golden rule of the doctors of the Church, clearly expressed by Aquinas: "All the

senses are founded on one—the literal—from which *alone* can any argument be drawn" (1a, q. 1, art. 10, ad 1); that rule which the Supreme Pontiffs have sanctioned and consecrated by prescribing that, before everything else, one must seek out the literal sense. For example, Pope Leo XIII writes in his Encyclical *Providentissimus Deus*: "Whilst weighing the meanings of words, the connection of ideas, the parallelism of passages, and the like, we should by all means make use of such illustrations as can be drawn from apposite erudition of an external sort" (*supra*, p. 13); and also: "provided [the exegete] carefully observes the rule so wisely laid down by St. Augustine—not to depart from the literal and obvious sense, except only where reason makes it untenable or necessity requires" (*supra*, p. 16). Pope Benedict XV likewise in his Encyclical *Spiritus Paraclitus* writes: "Jerome's first rule is careful study of the actual words so that we may be perfectly certain what the writer really does say" (*supra*, p. 67). In this encyclical he cites the example and exegetical principles of "that greatest of all the doctors in explaining Holy Scripture," St. Jerome. "Once, however, he has firmly established the literal or historical meaning, Jerome goes on to seek out deeper and hidden meanings, so as to nourish his mind with more delicate food" (*supra*, pp. 67-68). Finally, both Leo XIII and Benedict XV quote the exact words of St. Jerome insisting on the true obligation of an exegete: "The office of a commentator is to set forth not what he himself would prefer, but what his author says" (*supra*, 13 and 69).

2. **The Use of the Vulgate.** The error of the anonymous author concerning the meaning and extent of the Tridentine decree about the use of the Latin Vulgate is even more tangible. The Council of Trent, wishing to counteract the confusion arising from the new translations into the Latin and into the vernacular, at that time first appearing, wished to sanction for public use in the Western Church that common Latin version which had already been used by the Church herself for centuries. By so doing the Council did not wish in any way to minimize the authority of any of those ancient versions which had been produced in the Eastern Church, most

especially of the Septuagint used by the Apostles themselves, nor still less the authority of the original texts. For this reason it opposed the desire of one group of the Fathers who wished to make the Vulgate the sole authoritative text to the exclusion of all the others.

702   The anonymous writer delcares that by the decree of Trent the Latin version has been declared a text superior to every other. For this reason he would reprove the exegetes for wishing to interpret the Vulgate with the aid of the original text and of other ancient versions. For him the decree gives "certitude to the Sacred Text," so that there is no longer any need for the Church "to search further for the authentic word of God" (p. 7); this holds not only *in matters of faith and morals* but in every other matter as well, as, for example, in matters literary, geographical, or chronological. With this decree the Church has given us "the authentic and official text, from which it is illicit to deviate" (p. 6). To make any textual criticism is "to mutilate the Sacred Scripture" (p. 8). To do so is "to presumptuously impugn the authority (of the Church) which alone can declare a text authentic, and which in fact has done so in this Decree of the Council of Trent" (p. 28). Every critical study of the Vulgate text is "a free, irrational, and personal examination supplanting the authority of the Church" (p. 9).

703   Such a position is not only opposed to common sense, which can never accept a version as being superior to the original text, but it is also contrary to the mind of the Fathers of the Council as is clear from the *Acta*. The Council was fully aware of the necessity for a revision and correction of the Vulgate text and remitted to the Supreme Pontiffs the responsibility for the accomplishment of the work. A corrected edition of the Septuagint was made (under Sixtus V), according to the mind of the most authoritative collaborators of the Council itself; the same was ordered for the Hebrew of the Old Testament and for the Greek of the New Testament, and committees appointed accordingly. Moreover, to say that the Vulgate is the only text to be considered is wholly contrary to the Encyclical *Providentissimus Deus*: "At the same time, the other versions, which Christian antiquity has ap-

proved, should not be neglected, more especially the more
ancient MSS" (*supra*, p. 13).

In a word, the Council of Trent declared the Vulgate the   704
"authentic" text in the juridical meaning of that word, that
is, that it has "probatory force in matters of faith and morals,"
but by no means excluded the possibility of divergences from
the original text and from the ancient versions. Every good
book on Biblical Introduction makes this clear. It is implied
in the Acts of the Council itself.

3. **Textual Criticism.** With the idea, as above expounded,   705
of the almost unique value of the Vulgate and the correspond-
ingly small, almost insignificant, worth of the original texts,
and of the other ancient versions, one is not surprised that
the anonymous author denies both the necessity and the
utility of any textual criticism; and this he does despite the
fact that recent discoveries of some most precious texts have
proved the contrary. Since "it is the Church that presents and
guarantees the Sacred Text" (p. 10), any attempt at textual
criticism "is to treat the Divine Book as though it were produced by man alone" (p. 23). The one and only usefulness of
an original text, or of the other ancient versions, is for *consultation* "in order to clarify some difficulty" (p. 6); the
Greek text cannot "stand" against another text nor "against
the official text of the Church" (p. 8); "it is never permitted
to expunge from the text, not only from the official text of
the Church (the Vulgate, but even from the original, an ex-
tire narrative or an entire verse" (p. 7), even when these sec-
tions are absent from the more ancient texts and are found
only in more recent ones; to try to determine the Sacred
Text by means of textual criticism is "to massacre" the Bible
(p. 9). The few remaining pages of the pamphlet are filled
with invectives against "scientific criticism," "naturalism,"
and "modernism."

Catholic biblical science, from the time of Origen and St.   706
Jerome down to the "Commission for the revision and correction of the Vulgate," instituted by the Pope of the Encyclical
Pascendi, has always labored to establish the purest possible
form both of the original text and of the versions, primarily
of the Vulgate. Pope Leo XIII strongly recommended that

"Catholic exegetes, with our full approval, should cultivate the art of textual criticism as being very useful for a thorough understanding of the meaning of the sacred writers; and let them perfect their ability in this art even by the use of the works of heterodox authors, provided we have not forbidden it in certain cases" (Apost. Letter *Vigilantiae, supra,* p. 33). The Pontifical Biblical Commission also has declared that in the Pentateuch (and one can apply the same rule to the other books of the Bible; cf. the decision on the Psalms, *supra,* pp. 122-124), "it may be admitted that in the long course of centuries some modifications have been introduced into the work, such as additions after the death of Moses, either appended by an inspired author or inserted into the text as glosses and explanations; certain words and forms translated from the ancient language to more recent language, and finally, faulty readings to be ascribed to the error of amanuenses, concerning which it is lawful to investigate and judge according to the laws of criticism" (*supra,* p. 117).

707   The Holy Office, likewise, permitted, and still does permit, Catholic exegetes to study the question of the *Comma Joanneum* and, "after having well considered the arguments for both sides, with the moderation and circumspection which the gravity of the matter requires, even to favor the opinion which stands against the genuineness of the text" (Decree of the Holy Office, June 2, 1927, *Ench. Bibl.,* n. 121). The author of the pamphlet in question forgets or conceals all these facts in order to discredit the work of Catholic commentators, who, faithful to Catholic traditions and to the norms taught by the supreme authority of the Church, prove by the very fact of their exacting and difficult labors in textual criticism in what great veneration they hold the Sacred Text.

708   4. **The Study of Oriental Languages and of Auxiliary Sciences:** The levity and incredible arrogance of the anonymous author when speaking of these subjects move one both to pity and to indignation. "The Hebrew, the Syriac, the Aramaic" serve nowadays only as an occasion of pride and a "vain show of learning" (p. 14) for "men of science" (p. 4).

"Orientalism has become downright fetishism"; and "Modern Oriental science is often questionable" (p. 46).

Such assertions, which tend to turn one away from these   709 difficult studies and to cause levity and cynicism in the treatment of the divine books, lead inevitably to a lessening, not only of that supreme reverence and respect which we owe to the Holy Scriptures, but also of that salutary fear lest we use them in an unbecoming way. Such assertions are in open conflict with the tradition of the Church which, from the times of St. Jerome to our own, has always encouraged the study of the Oriental languages, realizing that "it is most proper that professors of Sacred Scripture . . . should master those tongues in which the sacred books were originally written" (Leo XIII, Ency. *Providentissimus Deus, supra,* p. 20), and recommending that "endeavors should be made to establish in all academic institutions . . . chairs of the other ancient languages, especially the Semitic, and of subjects connected therewith . . ." (*ibid*.). The Church demands also that "the knowledge of the ancient Oriental languages should not be less esteemed by Catholics than by non-Catholics" (Leo XIII, Apost. Letter *Vigilantiae, supra,* p. 32). The anonymous author forgets that the study of biblical languages, of Greek and Hebrew, recommended by Pope Leo XIII for theological institutions, was made obligatory by Pope Pius X (*supra,* p. 39, n. 16), and that this law has been restated in the Constitution *Deus scientiarum Dominus* (art. 33-34; *Ordinationes,* art. 27, I).

Naturally the study of Oriental languages and of auxiliary   710 sciences is not for the exegete an end in itself but it is directed towards a clear and precise understanding and insight into the divine words so that they might build up the spiritual life as much as possible. In this sense, and not because of any narrow pedantry or an ill-concealed distrust of the spiritual meaning, does the Church recommend and urge us to search out the literal meaning with the aid of philology and of textual criticism. In the same way she disapproves the excessive or exclusive use of these means, and much more their abuse, as though the book were not divine. But at the same time one cannot permit, because of abuse, that one should throw discredit on or endeavor to take away entirely the use of the true principles of exegesis: "Misuse does not destroy the use."

711   The anonymous author has added four pages to his booklet with the title: "Confirmation drawn from the Encyclical *Pascendi*," as if to place his ill-advised work under the patronage of the saintly Pope Pius X. This attempt is unsuccessful for, even if the study of Sacred Scripture was given its *Magna Charta* by Pope Leo XIII in his Encyclical *Providentissimus Deus* which centered the attention of the entire Church on this most important subject, nevertheless it was Pope Pius X who, by his own personal initiative, gave the definitive character and direction to this study, especially in Rome and Italy, since he had observed at first hand, in his experience as Bishop, the lack of biblical instruction and the disastrous effects flowing therefrom.

712   Indeed Pope Pius X began, only a few months after his election, February 23, 1904, by instituting the academic degrees of the licentiate and the doctorate in Sacred Scripture, well knowing that the granting of special titles would be an efficacious means of insuring that students devote themselves in a special way to such studies. Being unable for the moment, due to lack of means, to realize his proposed Institute devoted to higher biblical studies he actively encouraged in 1906 the teaching of Holy Scripture in the Pontifical Roman Seminary. In 1908 and 1909 he approved the erection of a higher course of studies in Sacred Scripture in the Gregorianum and in the Angelicum. Finally, in that same year of 1909 he established the Pontifical Biblical Institute which has not ceased to develop under the eyes of the Roman Pontiffs with a steady growth so evident that one need only mention it. What the Biblical Institute has done to promote true progress in the study of Sacred Scripture, especially in Italy, is demonstrated by the number of students and auditors who are Italian, as well as by the number of those who attend the Biblical Weeks which are held every year with good attendance and with ever-increasing fruit. It was also Pope Pius X who determined the important place biblical studies should have in the Seminaries when he published the Apostolic Letter *Quoniam in re*

biblica of March 27, 1906 (*supra*, pp. 36-39), and provided for its immediate application in the Seminaries of Italy by the special program issued by the Sacred Congregation of Bishops and Regulars on May 10, 1907.

It is unnecessary to insist further. Whoever may be the au-   713
thor of the brochure in question and whatever may be his opinions, the study of Sacred Scripture must continue, also in the Italian Seminaries, according to the directions given by the recent Supreme Pontiffs, for today, no less than yesterday, it is important that priests and ministers of the Word of God should be well prepared and able to give satisfactory answers, not only to questions of dogma and Catholic morals, but also to the difficulties alleged against the historical truth and against the religious doctrine of the Bible, especially of the Old Testament. In this connection it is good to end this letter with the very words which Pope Benedict XV of holy memory used in the Encyclical *Spiritus Paraclitus*: "Strive, then, Venerable Brethren, to bring home to your clerics and priests these teachings of the Sainted Commentator, St. Jerome. You have to remind them constantly of the demands made by their divine vocation if they would be worthy of it: 'The lips of the priest shall keep knowledge, and men shall seek the Law at his mouth, for he is the Angel of the Lord of hosts' (*Mal.* 2:7). They must realize, then, that they cannot neglect the study of the Bible, and that this can only be undertaken along the lines laid down by Leo XIII in his Encyclical *Providentissimus Deus*" (*supra*, pp. 64-65).

The Holy Father, to whom the entire question was pro-   714
posed in the audience of August 16, 1941, granted to the Most Reverend Secretary of the Pontifical Biblical Commission, has seen fit to approve the decisions of the Most Eminent Cardinals of the Commission and to command the publication of this present letter.

Decisions of the Pontifical Biblical Commission
on the Use of Versions of Sacred Scripture in the Vernacular
August 22, 1943

The Pontifical Biblical Commission deems it opportune to establish and commend the following norms as a solution to the question proposed to it concerning the use and the authority of biblical versions in the vernacular, especially those translated from the ancient texts. These norms likewise explain more fully the Commission's decree: *De usu versionum Sacrae Scripturae in ecclesiis*, of April, 1934.

716   Since it was recommended by the Supreme Pontiff Leo XIII of happy memory in Encyclical Letter *Providentissimus Deus* (*Acta Leonis XIII*, vol. 13, p. 342; *Enchiridion Biblicum*, n. 106), that the ancient texts of the Bible be used in order to gain a deeper knowledge and a richer expression of the divine word; and since by that recommendation, evidently not meant only for the help of exegetes and the theologians, it was seen and is seen to be almost necessary that the texts themselves be translated according to the approved rules for sacred as well as profane science into the commonly used or vernacular languages, always of course under the vigilant care of the competent ecclesiastical authority, and especially since for the most part the biblical pericopes which must be used in the liturgical books for the most holy Sacrifice of the Mass and for the public recitation of the Divine Office are taken from the Vulgate edition, which the Sacred ecumenical Council of Trent declared the one and only authentic version of all

the Latin versions then in use (*Conc. Trid.*, sess. IV, *decr. De editione et usu Ss. Librorum; Ench. Bibl.*, n. 61); all things considered:

1. Versions of Sacred Scripture translated into the vernacular either from the Vulgate or from the ancient texts may certainly be used and read by the faithful for their own private devotion, provided they have been edited with the permission of the competent ecclesiastical authority; moreover, if any version, after its text and notes have been seriously examined by men who excel in biblical and theological knowledge, is found more faithful or better expressed, the Bishops, either singly or jointly in provincial or plenary councils, may commend it to the faithful entrusted to their special care, if they see fit.

2. Any vernacular version of the biblical pericopes, which perhaps priests while celebrating Mass, according to custom or as opportunity presents itself, will read to the people after they have read the liturgical text must conform to the Latin, the liturgical text, according to the response of the Pontifical Biblical Commission (*Acta Ap. Sedis*, 1934, p. 315), although they are permitted to explain properly this version, if need be, by using the original text or another more clear version.

The Holy Father, Pope Pius XII, in the audience of August   717
22, 1943, granted to the Most Reverend Secretary, approved this *Responsum* and commanded it to be published.

DIVINO AFFLANTE SPIRITU
Encyclical Letter of Pope Pius XII
on The Most Opportune Way
to Promote Biblical Studies
September 30, 1943

Inspired by the Divine Spirit, the Sacred Writers composed those books, which God, in His paternal charity towards the human race, deigned to bestow on them in order "to teach, to reprove, to correct, to instruct in justice: that the man of God may be perfect, furnished to every good work.[1] This heaven-sent treasure Holy Church considers as the most precious source of doctrine on faith and morals. No wonder, therefore, that as she received it intact from the hands of the Apostles, so she kept it with all care, defended it from every false and perverse interpretation and used it diligently as an instrument for securing the eternal salvation of souls, as almost countless documents in every age strikingly bear witness. In more recent times, however, since the divine and the correct interpretation of the Sacred Writings have been very specially called in question, the Church has with even greater zeal and care undertaken their defense and protection. The sacred Council of Trent ordained by solemn decree that "the entire books with all their parts, as they have been wont to be read in the Catholic Church and are contained in the old vulgate Latin edition, are to be held sacred and canonical."[2] In our own time the Vatican Council, with the object of condemning false doctrines regarding inspiration, declared that these same books were to be regarded by the Church as sacred and canonical "not because, having been composed by human industry, they were afterwards approved by her authority, nor merely because they contain revelation without error, but because, having been written under the inspiration of the Holy Spirit, they have God for their author, and as such were handed down to the Church herself."[3] When, subsequently, some Catholic writers, in spite of this solemn definition of Catholic doctrine, by which such divine authority is claimed for the "entire books with all their parts" as to secure freedom from any error whatsoever, ventured to restrict the truth of Sacred Scripture solely to matters of faith and morals, and to regard other matters, whether in the domain of physical science or history, as "obiter dicta" and—as they contended—in no wise connected with faith, Our Predecessor of immortal memory, Leo XIII, in the Encyclical Letter *Providentissimus Deus,* published on November 18th in the year 1893, justly and rightly condemned these errors and safeguarded the studies of the Divine Books by most wise precepts and rules.

2. Since then it is fitting that We should commemorate the fiftieth anniversary of the publication of this Encyclical Letter, which is considered the supreme guide in biblical studies, We, moved by that solicitude for sacred studies, which We manifested from the very beginning of Our Pontificate,[4] have considered that this may most opportunely be done by ratifying and inculcating all that was wisely laid down by Our Predecessor and ordained by His Successors for the consolidating and perfecting of the work, and by pointing out what seems necessary in the present day, in order to incite ever more earnestly all those sons of the Church who devote themselves to these studies, to so necessary and so praiseworthy an enterprise. 719

3. The first and greatest care of Leo XIII was to set forth the teaching on the truth of the Sacred Books and to defend it from attack. Hence with grave words did he proclaim that there is no error whatsoever if the sacred writer, speaking of things of the physical order "went by what sensibly appeared" as the Angelic Doctor says,[5] speaking either "in figurative language, or in terms which were commonly used at the time, and which in many instances are in daily use at this day, even among the most eminent men of science." For "the sacred 720

writers, or to speak more accurately—the words are St. Augustine's[6]—the Holy Spirit, Who spoke by them, did not intend to teach men these things—that is the essential nature of the things of the universe—things in no way profitable to salvation";[7] which principle "will apply to cognate sciences, and especially to history," that is, by refuting, "in a somewhat similar way the fallacies of the adversaries and defending the historical truth of Sacred Scripture from their attacks."[8] Nor is the sacred writer to be taxed with error, if "copyists have made mistakes in the text of the Bible," or, "if the real meaning of a passage remains ambiguous." Finally it is absolutely wrong and forbidden "either to narrow inspiration to certain passages of Holy Scripture, or to admit that the sacred writer has erred," since divine inspiration "not only is essentially incompatible with error but excludes and rejects it as absolutely and necessarily as it is impossible that God Himself, the supreme Truth, can utter that which is not true. This is the ancient and constant faith of the Church."[9]

721   4. This teaching, which Our Predecessor Leo XIII set forth with such solemnity, We also proclaim with Our authority and We urge all to adhere to it religiously. No less earnestly do We inculcate obedience at the present day to the counsels and exhortations which he, in his day, so wisely enjoined. For whereas there arose new and serious difficulties and questions, from the widespread prejudices of rationalism and more especially from the discovery and investigation of the antiquities of the East, this same Predecessor of Ours, moved by zeal of the apostolic office, not only that such an excellent source of Catholic revelation might be more securely and abundantly available to the advantage of the Christian flock, but also that he might not suffer it to be in any way tainted, wished and most earnestly desired "to see an increase in the number of the approved and persevering laborers in the cause of Holy Scripture; and more especially that those whom Divine Grace has called to Holy Orders, should day-by-day, as their state demands, display greater diligence and industry in reading, meditating and explaining it."[10]

722   5. Wherefore the same Pontiff, as he had already praised and approved the school for biblical studies, founded at St.

Stephen's, Jerusalem, by the Master General of the Sacred Order of Preachers—from which, to use his own words, "biblical science itself had received no small advantage, while giving promise of more"[11]—so in the last year of his life he provided yet another way, by which these same studies, so warmly commended in the Encyclical Letter *Providentissimus Deus*, might daily make greater progress and be pursued with the greatest possible security. By the Apostolic Letter *Vigilantiae*, published on October 30 in the year 1902, he founded a Council or Commission, as it is called, of eminent men, "whose duty it would be to procure by every means that the sacred texts may receive everywhere among us that more thorough exposition which the times demand, and be kept safe not only from every breath of error, but also from all inconsiderate opinions."[12] Following the example of Our Predecessors, We also have effectively confirmed and amplified this Council using its good offices, as often before, to remind commentators of the Sacred Books of those safe rules of Catholic exegesis, which have been handed down by the Holy Fathers and Doctors of the Church, as well as by the Sovereign Pontiffs themselves.[13]

6. It may not be out of place here to recall gratefully the   **723** principal and more useful contributions made successively by Our Predecessors toward this same end, which contributions may be considered as the complement or fruit of the movement so happily initiated by Leo XIII. And first of all Pius X, wishing "to provide a sure way for the preparation of a copious supply of teachers, who, commended by the seriousness and the integrity of their doctrine, might explain the Sacred Books in Catholic schools . . ." instituted "the academic degrees of licentiate and doctorate in Sacred Scripture. . . ; to be conferred by the Biblical Commission";[14] he later enacted a law "concerning the method of Scripture studies to be followed in Clerical Seminaries" with this end in view, viz.: that students of the sacred sciences "not only should themselves fully understand the power, purpose and teaching of the Bible, but should also be equipped to engage in the ministry of the Divine Word with elegance and ability and repel attacks against the divinely inspired books";[15] finally

"in order that a center of higher biblical studies might be established in Rome, which in the best way possible might promote the study of the Bible and all cognate sciences in accordance with the mind of the Catholic Church" he founded the Pontifical Biblical Institute, entrusted to the care of the illustrious Society of Jesus, which he wished endowed "with a superior professorial staff and every facility for biblical research"; he prescribed its laws and rules, professing to follow in this the "salutary and fruitful project" of Leo XIII.[16]

724   7. All this in fine Our immediate Predecessor of happy memory, Pius XI, brought to perfection, laying down among other things "that no one should be appointed professor of Sacred Scripture in any Seminary, unless, having completed a special course of biblical studies, he had in due form obtained the academic degrees before the Biblical Commission or the Biblical Institute." He wished that these degrees should have the same rights and the same effects as the degrees duly conferred in Sacred Theology or Canon Law; likewise he decreed that no one should receive "a benefice having attached the canonical obligation of expounding the Sacred Scripture to the people, unless, among other things, he had obtained the licentiate or doctorate in biblical science." And having at the same time urged the Superiors General of the Regular Orders and of the religious Congregations, as well as the Bishops of the Catholic world, to send the more suitable of their students to frequent the schools of the Biblical Institute and obtain there the academical degrees, he confirmed these exhortations by his own example, appointing out of his bounty an annual sum for this very purpose.[17]

725   8. Seeing that, in the year 1907, with the benign approval of Pius X, of happy memory, "to the Benedictine monks had been committed the task of preparing the investigations and studies on which might be based a new edition of the Latin version of the Scriptures, commonly called the Vulgate,"[18] the same Pontiff, Pius XI, wishing to consolidate more firmly and securely this "laborious and arduous enterprise," which demands considerable time and great expense, founded in Rome and lavishly endowed with a library and other means

of research, the monastery of St. Jerome, to be devoted
exclusively to this work.[19]

9. Nor should We fail to mention here how earnestly these   726
same Predecessors of Ours, when the opportunity occurred,
recommended the study or preaching or in fine the pious
reading and meditation of the Sacred Scriptures. Pius X most
heartily commended the Society of St. Jerome, which strives
to promote among the faithful—and to facilitate with all its
power—the truly praiseworthy custom of reading and meditating on the holy Gospels; he exhorted them to persevere in the
enterprise they had begun, proclaiming it "a most useful
undertaking, as well as most suited to the times," seeing that
it helps in no small way "to dissipate the idea that the Church
is opposed to or in any way impedes the reading of the Scriptures in the vernacular."[20] And Benedict XV, on the occasion of the fifteenth centenary of the death of St. Jerome,
the greatest Doctor of the Sacred Scriptures, after having
most solemnly inculcated the precepts and examples of the
same Doctor, as well as the principles and rules laid down by
Leo XIII and by himself, and having recommended other
things highly opportune and never to be forgotten in this
connection, exhorted "all the children of the Church, especially clerics, to reverence the Holy Scripture, to read it
piously and meditate on it constantly"; he reminded them
"that in these pages is to be sought that food, by which the
spiritual life is nourished unto perfection," and "that the
chief use of Scripture pertains to the holy and fruitful exercise of the ministry of preaching"; he likewise once again
expressed his warm approval of the work of the society called
after St. Jerome himself, by means of which the Gospels and
Acts of the Apostles are being so widely diffused, "that there
is no Christian family any more without them and that all are
accustomed to read and meditate on them daily."[21]

10. But it is right and pleasing to confess openly that it is   727
not only by reason of these initiatives, precepts and exhortations of Our Predecessors that the knowledge and use of the
Sacred Scriptures have made great progress among Catholics;
for this is also due to the works and labors of all those who

diligently cooperated with them, both by meditating, investigating and writing, as well as by teaching and preaching and by translating and propagating the Sacred Books. For from the schools in which are fostered higher studies in theological and biblical science, and especially from Our Pontifical Biblical Institute, there have already come forth, and daily continue to come forth, many students of Holy Scripture who, inspired with an intense love for the Sacred Books, imbue the younger clergy with this same ardent zeal and assiduously impart to them the doctrine they themselves have acquired. Many of them also, by the written word, have promoted and do still promote, far and wide, the study of the Bible; as when they edit the sacred text corrected in accordance with the rules of textual criticism or expound, explain, and translate it into the vernacular; or when they propose it to the faithful for their pious reading and meditation; or finally when they cultivate and seek the aid of profane sciences which are useful for the interpretation of the Scriptures. From these therefore and from other initiatives which daily become more widespread and vigorous, as, for example, biblical societies, congresses, libraries, associations for meditation on the Gospels, We firmly hope that in the future reverence for, as well as the use and knowledge of, the Sacred Scriptures will everywhere more and more increase for the good of souls, provided the method of biblical studies laid down by Leo XIII, explained more clearly and perfectly by his Successors, and by Us confirmed and amplified—which indeed is the only safe way and proved by experience—be more firmly, eagerly and faithfully accepted by all, regardless of the difficulties which, as in all human affairs, so in this most excellent work will never be wanting.

728   11. There is no one who cannot easily perceive that the conditions of biblical studies and their subsidiary sciences have greatly changed within the last fifty years. For, apart from anything else, when Our Predecessor published the Encyclical Letter *Providentissimus Deus*, hardly a single place in Palestine had begun to be explored by means of relevant excavations. Now, however, this kind of investigation is much more frequent and, since more precise methods and technical

skill have been developed in the course of actual experience, it gives us information at once more abundant and more accurate. How much light has been derived from these explorations for the more correct and fuller understanding of the Sacred Books all experts know, as well as all those who devote themselves to these studies. The value of these excavations is enhanced by the discovery from time to time of written documents, which help much towards the knowledge of the languages, letters, events, customs, and forms of worship of most ancient times. And of no less importance are papyri which have contributed so much to the knowledge of the discovery and investigation, so frequent in our times, of letters and institutions, both public and private, especially of the time of Our Savior.

12. Moreover ancient codices of the Sacred Books have been found and edited with discerning thoroughness; the exegesis of the Fathers of the Church has been more widely and thoroughly examined; in fine the manner of speaking, relating and writing in use among the ancients is made clear by innumerable examples. All these advantages which, not without a special design of Divine Providence, our age has acquired, are as it were an invitation and inducement to interpreters of the Sacred Literature to make diligent use of this light, so abundantly given, to penetrate more deeply, explain more clearly and expound more lucidly the Divine Oracles. If, with the greatest satisfaction of mind, We perceive that these same interpreters have resolutely answered and still continue to answer this call, this is certainly not the last or least of the fruits of the Encyclical Letter *Providentissimus Deus*, by which Our Predecessor Leo XIII, foreseeing as it were this new development of biblical studies, summoned Catholic exegetes to labor and wisely defined the direction and the method to be followed in that labor.   729

13. We also, by this Encyclical Letter, desire to insure that the work may not only proceed without interruption, but may also daily become more perfect and fruitful; and to that end We are specially intent on pointing out to all what yet remains to be done, with what spirit the Catholic exegete should undertake, at the present day, so great and noble a   730

work, and to give new incentive and fresh courage to the laborers who toil so strenuously in the vineyard of the Lord.

731   14. The Fathers of the Church in their time, especially Augustine, warmly recommended to the Catholic scholar, who undertook the investigation and explanation of the Sacred Scriptures, the study of the ancient languages and recourse to the original texts.[22] However, such was the state of letters in those times, that not many—and these few but imperfectly—knew the Hebrew language. In the middle ages, when Scholastic Theology was at the height of its vigor, the knowledge of even the Greek language had long since become so rare in the West, that even the greatest Doctors of that time, in their exposition of the Sacred Text, had recourse only to the Latin version, known as the Vulgate.

732   15. On the contrary in this our time, not only the Greek language, which since the humanistic renaissance has been, as it were, restored to new life, is familiar to almost all students of antiquity and letters, but the knowledge of Hebrew also and of other Oriental languages has spread far and wide among literary men. Moreover there are now such abundant aids to the study of these languages that the biblical scholar, who by neglecting them would deprive himself of access to the original texts, could in no wise escape the stigma of levity and sloth. For it is the duty of the exegete to lay hold, so to speak, with the greatest care and reverence of the very least expressions which, under the inspiration of the Divine Spirit, have flowed from the pen of the sacred writer, so as to arrive at a deeper and fuller knowledge of his meaning.

733   16. Wherefore let him diligently apply himself so as to acquire daily a greater facility in biblical as well as in other Oriental languages and to support his interpretation by the aids which all branches of philology supply. This indeed St. Jerome strove earnestly to achieve, as far as the science of his time permitted; to this also aspired with untiring zeal and no small fruit not a few of the great exegetes of the sixteenth and seventeenth centuries, although the knowledge of languages then was much less than at the present day. In like manner therefore ought we to explain the original text which, having been written by the inspired author himself, has more

authority and greater weight than any, even the very best, translation, whether ancient or modern; this can be done all the more easily and fruitfully, if to the knowledge of languages be joined a real skill in literary criticism of the same text.

17. The great importance which should be attached to   734 this kind of criticism was aptly pointed out by Augustine, when, among the precepts to be recommended to the student of the Sacred Books, he put in the first place the care to possess a corrected text. "The correction of the codices"—so says this most distinguished Doctor of the Church—"should first of all engage the attention of those who wish to know the Divine Scripture so that the uncorrected may give place to the corrected."[23] In the present day indeed this art, which is called textual criticism and which is used with great and praiseworthy results in the editions of profane writings, is also quite rightly employed in the case of the Sacred Books, because of that very reverence which is due to the Divine Oracles. For its very purpose is to insure that the sacred text be restored, as perfectly as possible, be purified from the corruptions due to the carelessness of the copyists and be freed, as far as may be done, from glosses and omissions, from the interchange and repetition of words and from all other kinds of mistakes, which are wont to make their way gradually into writings handed down through many centuries.

18. It is scarcely necessary to observe that this criticism,   735 which some fifty years ago not a few made use of quite arbitrarily and often in such wise that one would say they did so to introduce into the sacred text their own preconceived ideas, today has rules so firmly established and secure, that it has become a most valuable aid to the purer and more accurate editing of the sacred text and that any abuse can easily be discovered. Nor is it necessary here to call to mind—since it is doubtless familiar and evident to all students of Sacred Scripture—to what extent namely the Church has held in honor these studies in textual criticism from the earliest centuries down even to the present day.

19. Today therefore, since this branch of science has at-   736 tained to such high perfection, it is the honorable, though

not always easy, task of students of the Bible to procure by every means that as soon as possible may be duly published by Catholics editions of the Sacred Books and of ancient versions, brought out in accordance with these standards, which, that is to say, unite the greatest reverence for the sacred text with an exact observance of all the rules of criticism. And let all know that this prolonged labor is not only necessary for the right understanding of the divinely-given writings, but also is urgently demanded by that piety by which it behooves us to be grateful to the God of all providence, Who from the throne of His majesty has sent these books as so many paternal letters to his own children.

737   20. Nor should anyone think that this use of the original texts, in accordance with the methods of criticism, in any way derogates from those decrees so wisely enacted by the Council of Trent concerning the Latin Vulgate.[24] It is historically certain that the Presidents of the Council received a commission, which they duly carried out, to beg, that is, the Sovereign Pontiff in the name of the Council that he should have corrected, as far as possible, first a Latin, and then a Greek, and Hebrew edition, which eventually would be published for the benefit of the Holy Church of God.[25] If this desire could not then be fully realized owing to the difficulties of the times and other obstacles, at present it can, We earnestly hope, be more perfectly and entirely fulfilled by the united efforts of Catholic scholars.

738   21. And if the Tridentine Synod wished "that all should use as authentic" the Vulgate Latin version, this, as all know, applies only to the Latin Church and to the public use of the same Scriptures; nor does it, doubtless, in any way diminish the authority and value of the original texts. For there was no question then of these texts, but of the Latin versions, which were in circulation at that time, and of these the same Council rightly declared to be preferable that which "had been approved by its long-continued use for so many centuries in the Church." Hence this special authority or as they say, authenticity of the Vulgate was not affirmed by the Council particularly for critical reasons, but rather because of its legitimate use in the Churches throughout so many

centuries; by which use indeed the same is shown, in the sense in which the Church has understood and understands it, to be free from any error whatsoever in matters of faith and morals; so that, as the Church herself testifies and affirms, it may be quoted safely and without fear of error in disputations, in lectures and in preaching; and so its authenticity is not specified primarily as critical, but rather as juridical.

22. Wherefore this authority of the Vulgate in matters of   739 doctrine by no means prevents—nay rather today it almost demands—either the corroboration and confirmation of this same doctrine by the original texts or the having recourse on any and every occasion to the aid of these same texts, by which the correct meaning of the Sacred Letters is everywhere daily made more clear and evident. Nor is it forbidden by the decree of the Council of Trent to make translations into the vulgar tongue, even directly from the original texts themselves, for the use and benefit of the faithful and for the better understanding of the divine word, as We know to have been already done in a laudable manner in many countries with the approval of the Ecclesiastical authority.

23. Being thoroughly prepared by the knowledge of the   740 ancient languages and by the aids afforded by the art of criticism, let the Catholic exegete undertake the task, of all those imposed on him the greatest, that, namely of discovering and expounding the genuine meaning of the Sacred Books. In the performance of this task let the interpreters bear in mind that their foremost and greatest endeavor should be to discern and define clearly that sense of the biblical words which is called literal. Aided by the context and by comparison with similar passages, let them therefore by means of their knowledge of languages search out with all diligence the literal meaning of the words; all these helps indeed are wont to be pressed into service in the explanation also of profane writers, so that the mind of the author may be made abundantly clear.

24. The commentators of the Sacred Letters, mindful of   741 the fact that here there is question of a divinely inspired text, the care and interpretation of which have been confided to the Church by God Himself, should no less diligently take

into account the explanations and declarations of the teaching authority of the Church, as likewise the interpretation
given by the Holy Fathers, and even "the analogy of faith" as
Leo XIII most wisely observed in the Encyclical Letter
Providentissimus Deus.[26] With special zeal should they apply
themselves, not only to expounding exclusively these matters
which belong to the historical, archaeological, philological and
other auxiliary sciences—as, to Our regret, is done in certain
commentaries—but, having duly referred to these, insofar as
they may aid the exegesis, they should set forth in particular
the theological doctrine in faith and morals of the individual
books or texts so that their exposition may not only aid the
professors of theology in their explanations and proofs of the
dogmas of faith, but may also be of assistance to priests in
their presentation of Christian doctrine to the people, and in
fine, may help all the faithful to lead a life that is holy and
worthy of a Christian.

742   25. By making such an exposition, which is above all, as
We have said, theological, they will efficaciously reduce to
silence those who, affirming that they scarcely ever find anything in biblical commentaries to raise their hearts to God, to
nourish their souls or promote their interior life, repeatedly
urge that we should have recourse to a certain spiritual and,
as they say, mystical interpretation. With what little reason
they thus speak is shown by the experience of many, who,
assiduously considering and meditating the word of God, advanced in perfection and were moved to an intense love for
God; and this same truth is clearly proved by the constant
tradition of the Church and the precepts of the greatest
Doctors. Doubtless all spiritual sense is not excluded from
the Sacred Scripture.

743   26. For what was said and done in the Old Testament was
·   ordained and disposed by God with such consummate wisdom, that things past prefigured in a spiritual way those that
were to come under the new dispensation of grace. Wherefore
the exegete, just as he must search out and expound the literal
meaning of the words, intended and expressed by the sacred
writer, so also must he do likewise for the spiritual sense, provided it is clearly intended by God. For God alone could have

known this spiritual meaning and have revealed it to us. Now Our Divine Savior Himself points out to us and teaches us this same sense in the Holy Gospel; the Apostles also, following the example of the Master, profess it in their spoken and written words; the unchanging tradition of the Church approves it; and finally the most ancient usage of the liturgy proclaims it, wherever may be rightly applied the well-known principle: "The rule of prayer is the rule of faith."

27. Let Catholic exegetes then disclose and expound this   744
spiritual significance, intended and ordained by God, with that care which the dignity of the divine word demands; but let them scrupulously refrain from proposing as the genuine meaning of Sacred Scripture other figurative senses. It may indeed be useful, especially in preaching, to illustrate, and present the matters of faith and morals by a broader use of the Sacred Text in the figurative sense, provided this be done with moderation and restraint; it should, however, never be forgotten that this use of the Sacred Scripture is, as it were, extrinsic to it and accidental, and that, especially in these days, it is not free from danger, since the faithful, in particular those who are well-informed in the sacred and profane sciences, wish to know what God has told us in the Sacred Letters rather than what an ingenious orator or writer may suggest by a clever use of the words of Scripture. Nor does "the word of God, living and effectual and more piercing than any two-edged sword and reaching unto the division of the soul and the spirit, of the joints also and the marrow, and a discerner of the thoughts and intents of the heart"[27] need artificial devices and human adaptation to move and impress souls; for the Sacred Pages, written under the inspiration of the Spirit of God, are of themselves rich in original meaning; endowed with a divine power, they have their own value; adorned with heavenly beauty, they radiate of themselves light and splendor, provided they are so fully and accurately explained by the interpreter, that all the treasures of wisdom and prudence, therein contained are brought to light.

28. In the accomplishment of this task the Catholic exe-   745
gete will find invaluable help in an assiduous study of those works, in which the Holy Fathers, the Doctors of the Church

and the renowned interpreters of past ages have explained the Sacred Books. For, although sometimes less instructed in profane learning and in the knowledge of languages than the scripture scholars of our time, nevertheless by reason of the office assigned to them by God in the Church, they are distinguished by a certain subtle insight into heavenly things and by a marvellous keenness of intellect, which enables them to penetrate to the very innermost meaning of the divine word and bring to light all that can help to elucidate the teaching of Christ and promote holiness of life.

746   29. It is indeed regrettable that such precious treasures of Christian antiquity are almost unknown to many writers of the present day, and that students of the history of exegesis have not yet accomplished all that seems necessary for the due investigation and appreciation of so momentous a subject. Would that many, by seeking out the authors of the Catholic interpretation of Scripture and diligently studying their works and drawing thence the almost inexhaustible riches therein stored up, might contribute largely to this end, so that it might be daily more apparent to what extent those authors understood and made known the divine teaching of the Sacred Books, and that the interpreters of today might thence take example and seek suitable arguments.

747   30. For thus at long last will be brought about the happy and fruitful union between the doctrine and spiritual sweetness of expression of the ancient authors and the greater erudition and maturer knowledge of the modern, having as its result new progress in the never fully explored and inexhaustible field of the Divine Letters.

748   31. Moreover we may rightly and deservedly hope that our time also can contribute something towards the deeper and more accurate interpretation of Sacred Scripture. For not a few things, especially in matters pertaining to history, were scarcely at all or not fully explained by the commentators of past ages, since they lacked almost all the information which was needed for their clearer exposition. How difficult for the Fathers themselves, and indeed well nigh unintelligible, were certain passages, is shown, among other things, by the oft-repeated efforts of many of them to explain the first chapters

of Genesis; likewise by the reiterated attempts of St. Jerome so to translate the Psalms that the literal sense, that, namely, which is expressed by the words themselves, might be clearly revealed.

32. There are, in fine, other books or texts, which contain   **749** difficulties brought to light only in quite recent times, since a more profound knowledge of antiquity has given rise to new questions, on the basis of which the point at issue may be more appropriately examined. Quite wrongly therefore do some pretend, not rightly understanding the conditions of biblical study, that nothing remains to be added by the Catholic exegete of our time to what Christian antiquity has produced; since, on the contrary, these our times have brought to light so many things, which call for a fresh investigation, and which stimulate not a little the practical zest of the present-day interpreter.

33. As in our age, indeed new questions and new difficul-   **750** ties are multiplied, so, by God's favor, new means and aids to exegesis are also provided. Among these it is worthy of special mention that Catholic theologians, following the teaching of the Holy Fathers and especially of the Angelic and Common Doctor, have examined and explained the nature and effects of biblical inspiration more exactly and more fully than was wont to be done in previous ages. For having begun by expounding minutely the principle that the inspired writer, in composing the sacred book, is the living and reasonable instrument of the Holy Spirit, they rightly observe that, impelled by the divine motion, he so uses his faculties and powers, that from the book composed by him all may easily infer "the special character of each one and, as it were, his personal traits."[2][8] Let the interpreter then, with all care and without neglecting any light derived from recent research, endeavor to determine the peculiar character and circumstances of the sacred writer, the age in which he lived, the sources written or oral to which he had recourse and the forms of expression he employed.

34. Thus can be the better understanding who was the in-   **751** spired author, and what he wishes to express by his writings. There is no one indeed but knows that the supreme rule of

interpretation is to discover and define what the writer intended to express, as St. Athanasius excellently observes: "Here, as indeed is expedient in all other passages of Sacred Scripture, it should be noted, on what occasion the Apostle spoke; we should carefully and faithfully observe to whom and why he wrote, lest, being ignorant of these points, or confounding one with another, we miss the real meaning of the author."[29]

752   35. What is the literal sense of a passage is not always as obvious in the speeches and writings of the ancient authors of the East, as it is in the works of our own time. For what they wished to express is not to be determined by the rules of grammar and philology alone, nor solely by the context; the interpreter must, as it were, go back wholly in spirit to those remote centuries of the East and with the aid of history, archaeology, ethnology, and other sciences, accurately determine what modes of writing, so to speak, the authors of that ancient period would be likely to use, and in fact did use.

753   36. For the ancient peoples of the East, in order to express their ideas, did not always employ those forms or kinds of speech which we use today; but rather those used by the men of their time and countries. What those exactly were the commentator cannot determine as it were in advance, but only after a careful examination of the ancient literature of the East. The investigation, carried out, on this point, during the past forty or fifty years with greater care and diligence than ever before, has more clearly shown what forms of expression were used in those far-off times, whether in poetic description or in the formulation of laws and rules of life or in recording the facts and events of history. The same inquiry has also clearly shown the special preeminence of the people of Israel among all the other ancient nations of the East in their mode of compiling history, both by reason if its antiquity and by reason of the faithful record of the events; qualities which may well be attributed to the gift of divine inspiration and to the peculiar religious purpose of biblical history.

754   37. Nevertheless no one, who has a correct idea of biblical inspiration, will be surprised to find, even in the Sacred

Writers, as in other ancient authors, certain fixed ways of expounding and narrating, certain definite idioms, especially of a kind peculiar to the Semitic tongues, so-called approximations, and certain hyperbolical modes of expression, nay, at times, even paradoxical, which even help to impress the ideas more deeply on the mind. For the modes of expression which, among ancient peoples, and especially those of the East, human language used to express its thought, none is excluded from the Sacred Books, provided the way of speaking adopted in no wise contradicts the holiness and truth of God, as, with his customary wisdom, the Angelic Doctor already observed in these words: "In Scripture divine things are presented to us in the manner which is in common use amongst men."[30] For as the substantial Word of God became like to men in all things, "except sin,"[31] so the words of God, expressed in human language, are made like to human speech in every respect, except error. In this consists that "condescension" of the God of providence, which St. John Chrysostom extolled with the highest praise and repeatedly declared to be found in the Sacred Books.[32]

38. Hence the Catholic commentator, in order to comply   755
with the present needs of biblical studies, in explaining the Sacred Scripture and in demonstrating and proving its immunity from all error, should also make a prudent use of this means, determine, that is, to what extent the manner of expression or the literary mode adopted by the sacred writer may lead to a correct and genuine interpretation; and let him be convinced that this part of his office cannot be neglected without serious detriment to Catholic exegesis. Not infrequently—to mention only one instance—when some persons reproachfully charge the Sacred Writers with some historical error or inaccuracy in the recording of facts, on closer examination it turns out to be nothing else than those customary modes of expression and narration peculiar to the ancients, which used to be employed in the mutual dealings of social life and which in fact were sanctioned by common usage.

39. When then such modes of expression are met with in   756
the sacred text, which, being meant for men, is couched in human language, justice demands that they be no more taxed

with error than when they occur in the ordinary intercourse of daily life. By this knowledge and exact appreciation of the modes of speaking and writing in use among the ancients can be solved many difficulties, which are raised against the veracity and historical value of the Divine Scriptures, and no less efficaciously does this study contribute to a fuller and more luminous understanding of the mind of the Sacred Writer.

757   40. Let those who cultivate biblical studies turn their attention with all due diligence towards this point and let them neglect none of those discoveries, whether in the domain of archaeology or in ancient history or literature, which serve to make better known the mentality of the ancient writers, as well as their manner and art of reasoning, narrating and writing. In this connection Catholic laymen should consider that they will not only further profane science, but moreover will render a conspicuous service to the Christian cause if they devote themselves with all due diligence and application to the exploration and investigation of the monuments of antiquity and contribute, according to their abilities, to the solution of questions hitherto obscure.

758   41. For all human knowledge, even the non-sacred, has indeed its own proper dignity and excellence, being a finite participation of the infinite knowledge of God, but it acquires a new and higher dignity and, as it were, a consecration, when it is employed to cast a brighter light upon the things of God.

759   42. The progressive exploration of the antiquities of the East, mentioned above, the more accurate examination of the original text itself, the more extensive and exact knowledge of languages both biblical and oriental, have with the help of God, happily provided the solution of not a few of those questions, which in the time of Our Predecessor Leo XIII of immortal memory, were raised by critics outside or hostile to the Church against the authenticity, antiquity, integrity and historical value of the Sacred Books. For Catholic exegetes, by a right use of those same scientific arms, not infrequently abused by the adversaries, proposed such interpretations, which are in harmony with Catholic doctrine and

the genuine current of tradition, and at the same time are seen to have proved equal to the difficulties, either raised by new explorations and discoveries, or bequeathed by antiquity for solution in our time.

43. Thus has it come about that confidence in the author-   760
ity and historical value of the Bible, somewhat shaken in the case of some by so many attacks, today among Catholics is completely restored; moreover there are not wanting even non-Catholic writers, who by serious and calm inquiry have been led to abandon modern opinion and to return, at least in some points, to the more ancient ideas. This change is due in great part to the untiring labor by which Catholic commentators of the Sacred Letters, in no way deterred by difficulties and obstacles of all kinds, strove with all their strength to make suitable use of what learned men of the present day, by their investigations in the domain of archae- ology or history or philology, have made available for the solution of new questions.

44. Nevertheless no one will be surprised, if all difficulties   761
are not yet solved and overcome, but that even today serious problems greatly exercise the minds of Catholic exegetes. We should not lose courage on this account; nor should we forget that in the human sciences the same happens as in the natural world; that is to say, new beginnings grow little by little and fruits are gathered only after many labors. Thus it has hap- pened that certain disputed points, which in the past remained unsolved and in suspense, in our days, with the progress of studies, have found a satisfactory solution. Hence there are grounds for hope that those also will by constant effort be at last made clear, which now seem most complicated and difficult.

45. And if the wished-for solution be slow in coming or   762
does not satisfy us, since perhaps a successful conclusion may be reserved to posterity, let us not wax impatient thereat, seeing that in us also is rightly verified what the Fathers, and especially Augustine,[33] observed in their time, viz. God wished difficulties to be scattered through the Sacred Books inspired by Him, in order that we might be urged to read and scrutinize them more intently, and, experiencing in a salutary

manner our own limitations, we might be exercised in due submission of mind. No wonder if to one or the other question no solution wholly satisfactory will ever be found, since sometimes we have to do with matters obscure in themselves and too remote from our times and our experience; and since exegesis also, like all other most important sciences, has its secrets, which, impenetrable to our minds, by no efforts whatsoever can be unravelled.

763   46. But this state of things is no reason why the Catholic commentator, inspired by an active and ardent love of his subject and sincerely devoted to Holy Mother Church, should in any way be deterred from grappling again and again with these difficult problems, hitherto unsolved, not only that he may refute the objections of the adversaries, but also may attempt to find a satisfactory solution, which will be in full accord with the doctrine of the Church, in particular with the traditional teaching regarding the inerrancy of Sacred Scripture, and which will at the same time satisfy the indubitable conclusion of profane sciences.

764   47. Let all the other sons of the Church bear in mind that the efforts of these resolute laborers in the vineyard of the Lord should be judged not only with equity and justice, but also with the greatest charity; all moreover should abhor that intemperate zeal which imagines that whatever is new should for that very reason be opposed or suspected. Let them bear in mind above all that in the rules and laws promulgated by the Church there is immense matter contained in the Sacred Books—legislative, historical, sapiential and prophetical— there are but few texts whose sense has been defined by the authority of the Church, nor are those more numerous about which the teaching of the Holy Fathers is unanimous. There remain therefore many things, and of the greatest importance, in the discussion and exposition of which the skill and genius of Catholic commentators may and ought to be freely exercised, so that each may contribute his part to the advantage of all, to the continued progress of the sacred doctrine and to the defense and honor of the Church.

765   48. This true liberty of the children of God, which adheres faithfully to the teaching of the Church and accepts and uses

gratefully the contributions of profane science, this liberty, upheld and sustained in every way by the confidence of all, is the condition and source of all lasting fruit and of all solid progress in Catholic doctrine, as Our Predecessor of happy memory Leo XIII rightly observes, when he says: "Unless harmony of mind be maintained and principles safeguarded, no progress can be expected in this matter from the varied studies of many."[34]

49. Whosoever considers the immense labors undertaken by Catholic exegetes during well nigh two thousand years, so that the word of God, imparted to men through the Sacred Letters, might daily be more deeply and fully understood and more intensely loved, will easily be convinced that it is the serious duty of the faithful, and especially of priests, to make free and holy use of this treasure, accumulated throughout so many centuries by the greatest intellects. For the Sacred Books were not given by God to men to satisfy their curiosity or to provide them with material for study and research, but, as the Apostle observes, in order that these Divine Oracles might "instruct us to salvation, by the faith which is in Christ Jesus" and "that the man of God may be perfect, furnished to every good work."[35]   766

50. Let priests therefore, who are bound by their office to procure the eternal salvation of the faithful, after they have themselves by diligent study perused the sacred pages and made them their own by prayer and meditations, assiduously distribute the heavenly treasures of the divine word by sermons, homilies and exhortations; let them confirm the Christian doctrine by sentences from the Sacred Books and illustrate it by outstanding examples from sacred history and in particular from the Gospel of Christ Our Lord; and—avoiding with the greatest care those purely arbitrary and far-fetched adaptations, which are not a use, but rather an abuse of the divine word—let them set forth all this with such eloquence, lucidity and clearness that the faithful may not only be moved and inflamed to reform their lives, but may also conceive in their hearts the greatest veneration for the Sacred Scripture.   767

768   51. The same veneration the Bishops should endeavor daily to increase and perfect among the faithful committed to their care, encouraging all those initiatives by which men, filled with apostolic zeal, laudably strive to excite and foster among Catholics a greater knowledge of love for the Sacred Books. Let them favor therefore and lend help to those pious associations whose aim it is to spread copies of the Sacred Letters, especially of the Gospels, among the faithful, and to procure by every means that in Christian families the same be read daily with piety and devotion; let them efficaciously recommend by word and example, whenever the liturgical laws permit, the Sacred Scriptures translated, with the approval of the Ecclesiastical authority, into modern languages; let them themselves give public conferences or dissertations on biblical subjects, or see that they are given by other public orators well-versed in the matter.

    52. Let the ministers of the Sanctuary support in every way possible and diffuse in fitting manner among all classes of the faithful the periodicals which so laudably and with such heartening results are published from time to time

769   in various parts of the world, whether to treat and expose in a scientific manner biblical questions, or to adapt the fruits of these investigations to the sacred ministry, or to benefit the faithful. Let the ministers of the Sanctuary be convinced that all this, and whatsoever else in apostolic zeal and a sincere love of the divine word may find suitable to this high purpose, will be an efficacious help to the cure of souls.

770   53. But it is plain to everyone that priests cannot duly fulfill all this, unless in their Seminary days they have imbibed a practical and enduring love for the Sacred Scriptures. Wherefore let the Bishops, on whom devolves the paternal care of their Seminaries, with all diligence see to it that nothing be omitted in this matter which may help towards the desired end. Let the professors of Sacred Scripture in the Seminaries give the whole course of biblical studies in such a way, that they may instruct the young aspirants to the Priesthood and to the ministry of the divine word with that knowledge of

the Sacred Letters and imbue them with that love for the same, without which it is vain to hope for copious fruits of the apostolate.

54. Hence their exegetical explanation should aim especially at the theological doctrine, avoiding useless disputations and omitting all that is calculated rather to gratify curiosity than to promote true learning and solid piety. The literal sense and especially the theological let them propose with such definiteness, explain with such skill and inculcate with such ardor that in their students may be in a sense verified what happened to the disciples on the way to Emmaus, when, having heard the words of the Master, they exclaimed: "Was not our heart burning within us, whilst he opened to us the Scriptures?"[36]   771

55. Thus the Divine Letters will become for the future priests of the Church a pure and never-failing source for their own spiritual life, as well as food and strength for the sacred office of preaching which they are about to undertake. If the professors of this most important matter in the Seminaries accomplish all this, then let them rest joyfully assured that they have most efficaciously contributed to the salvation of souls, to the progress of the Catholic faith, to the honor and glory of God, and that they have performed a work most closely connected with the apostolic office.   772

56. If these things which We have said, Venerable Brethren and beloved sons, are necessary in every age, much more urgently are they needed in our sorrowful times, when almost all peoples and nations are plunged in a sea of calamities, when a cruel war heaps ruins upon ruins and slaughter upon slaughter, when, owing to the most bitter hatred stirred up among the nations, We perceive with greatest sorrow that in not a few has been extinguished the sense not only of Christian moderation and charity, but also of humanity itself. Who can heal these mortal wounds of the human family if not He, to Whom the Prince of the Apostles, full of confidence and love, addresses these words: "Lord, to whom shall we go? Thou hast the words of eternal life."[37]   773

57. To this Our most merciful Redeemer we must therefore bring all back by every means in our power; for He is the divine consoler of the afflicted: He it is Who teaches all,   774

whether they be invested with public authority or are bound in duty to obey and submit, true honesty, absolute justice and generous charity; it is He in fine, and He alone, Who can be the firm foundation and support of peace and tranquility: "For other foundations no man can lay, but that which is laid: which is Christ Jesus."[38] This the author of salvation, Christ, will men more fully know, more ardently love and more faithfully imitate in proportion as they are more assiduously urged to know and meditate the Sacred Letters, especially the New Testament, for, as St. Jerome the Doctor of Stridon says: "To ignore the Scripture is to ignore Christ";[39] and again: "If there is anything in this life which sustains a wise man and induces him to maintain his serenity amidst the tribulations and adversities of the world, it is in the first place, I consider, the meditation and knowledge of the Scriptures."[40]

775 58. There those who are wearied and oppressed by adversities and afflictions will find true consolation and divine strength to suffer and bear with patience; there—that is in the Holy Gospels—Christ, the highest and greatest example of justice, charity and mercy, is present to all; and to the lacerated and trembling human race are laid open the fountains of that divine grace without which both peoples and their rulers can never arrive at, never establish, peace in the state and unity of heart; there in fine will all learn Christ, "Who is the head of all principality and power"[41] and "Who of God is made unto us wisdom and justice and sanctification and redemption."[42]

776 59. Having expounded and recommended those things which are required for the adaptation of Scripture studies to the necessities of the day, it remains, Venerable Brethren and beloved sons, that to biblical scholars who are devoted sons of the Church and follow faithfully her teaching and direction, We address with paternal affection, not only Our congratulations that they have been chosen and called to so sublime an office, but also Our encouragement to continue with ever renewed vigor and with all zeal and care, the work so happily begun. Sublime office, We say; for what is more sublime than to scrutinize, explain, propose to the faithful

and defend from unbelievers the very word of God, communicated to men under the inspiration of the Holy Spirit?

60. With this spiritual food the mind of the interpreter is   777
fed and nourished "to the commemoration of faith, the consolation of hope, the exhortation of charity."[43] "To live
amidst these things, to meditate these things, to know nothing else, to seek nothing else, does it not seem to you already here below a foretaste of the heavenly kingdom?"[44]
Let also the minds of the faithful be nourished with this
same food, that they may draw from thence the knowledge
and love of God and the progress in perfection and the happiness of their own individual souls. Let, then, the interpreters
of the Divine Oracles devote themselves to this holy practice
with all their heart. "Let them pray, that they may understand";[45] let them labor to penetrate ever more deeply into
the secrets of the Sacred Pages; let them teach and preach, in
order to open to others also the treasures of the word of God.

61. Let the present-day commentators of the Sacred Scrip-   778
ture emulate, according to their capacity, what those illustrious interpreters of past ages accomplished with such great
fruit; so that, as in the past, so also in these days, the Church
may have at her disposal learned doctors for the expounding
of the Divine Letters; and, through their assiduous labors, the
faithful may comprehend all the splendor, stimulating language, and joy contained in the Holy Scriptures. And in this
very arduous and important office let them have "for their
comfort the Holy Books"[46] and be mindful of the promised
reward: since "they that are learned shall shine as the brightness of the firmament, and they that instruct many unto
justice, as stars for all eternity."[47]

62. And now, while ardently desiring for all sons of the   779
Church, and especially for the professors in biblical science,
for the young clergy and for preachers, that, continually
meditating on the divine word, they may taste how good
and sweet is the spirit of the Lord;[48] as a presage of heavenly
gifts and a token of Our paternal good will, We impart to you
one and all, Venerable Brethren and beloved sons, most
lovingly in the Lord, the Apostolic Benediction.

780 63. Given at Rome, at St. Peter's, on the 30th of September, the feast of St. Jerome, the greatest Doctor in the exposition of the Sacred Scriptures, in the year 1943, the fifth of Our Pontificate.

IN COTIDIANIS PRECIBUS
Apostolic Letter of Pope Pius XII
on the new Latin Psalter and its use in the Divine Office
March 24, 1945

Following the Example of her divine Redeemer and His apostles the Church has from her earliest beginnings made constant use of those illustrious songs which the holy prophet David and other sacred writers composed under the inspiration of the Divine Spirit. They occupy a place apart in the official prayer that priests recite each day in praise of God's goodness and majesty, for their own needs, and for those of the universal Church and of the entire world.

It should be remembered, however, that the Latin Church   782
possesses these psalms as a heritage from a Church whose language was Greek. Originally translated almost word for word from Greek into Latin, they were in course of time given a number of careful corrections and revisions, most notably by the "Greatest Doctor" in the Sacred Scriptures, St. Jerome. But these corrections did not remove many of the obvious inaccuracies occurring already in the Greek version, inaccuracies which leave the force and meaning of the original (Hebrew) text quite obscure. As a result the generality of Latin readers still could not grasp with ease the sense of the sacred psalms.

And it is a well-known fact that St. Jerome himself was   783
not satisfied with having offered the Roman world that ancient Latin translation, even in his own "most diligently corrected" edition. With even greater diligence therefore he set to work translating the psalms directly from "the Hebrew

truth." However this latter translation of St. Jerome never came into general use in the Church. Instead his revised edition of the old Latin version, now known as the Gallican Psalter, gained such widespread popularity that finally Our sainted predecessor, Pius V, decided to include it in the Roman Breviary, thereby prescribing it for practically universal use.

784 Now in preparing this edition of the psalms, St. Jerome had made no effort to eliminate its obscurities and inaccuracies, his sole purpose was to correct the Latin text in accordance with the better Greek manuscripts. In our day, however, these obscurities and inaccuracies are becoming ever more glaring. For recent times have witnessed remarkable progress in the mastery of oriental languages, particularly Hebrew, and in the art of translation. Scholarly research into the laws of meter and rhythm governing oriental poetry has advanced apace. The rules for what is called textual criticism are now seen in clearer light. In various countries, moreover, many excellent vernacular translations of the psalter were published with the Church's approval, translations based on the original texts. These publications have made increasingly apparent the exquisite clarity, the poetic beauty, the wealth of doctrine those hymns possess in their original tongue.

785 It is not at all surprising, then, that a good many priests began to hope for a new Latin version of the psalms for their daily use. The hope was a very praiseworthy one, springing as it did from their endeavor to recite the canonical Hours not only with sincere devotion but with fuller understanding as well. What they desired was a Latin psalter that would bring out more clearly the meaning the Holy Spirit has inspired, that would give truer expression to the devout sentiments of the Psalmist's soul, that would reflect his style and his very words more exactly. This eager wish was voiced repeatedly both in books written by learned men of high repute and in various periodicals. The matter was furthermore referred to Us by not a few Ecclesiastics and Bishops and likewise by members of the Sacred College of Cardinals.

786 Now as We explained not so very long ago in the Encyclical Letter *Divino Afflante Spiritu*, We are, in keeping with the

profound reverence We cherish for the words of divine Writ,
determined on this: no pains, no energy is to be spared in
making it possible for the faithful to perceive ever more
plainly the meaning of the Scriptures as intended by the Holy
Spirit who inspired it and as expressed by the sacred writer.
We fully appreciated, of course, what a difficult undertaking
this would be. We realized, too, how intimately bound up the
Latin Vulgate is with the writings and interpretations of the
Holy Fathers and Doctors, how by its long centuries of use it
has obtained in the Church the very highest authority.

Nevertheless We decided to comply with these devout   787
wishes and gave orders that a new Latin translation of the
psalms be provided. It was to follow the original texts, follow
them exactly, faithfully. At the same time it was, as far as
possible, to take into account the venerable Vulgate along
with other ancient versions, and to apply sound critical norms
where their readings differed. Not even the Hebrew text, as
We are well aware, has reached us altogether free from error
and obscurity. It needs to be compared with other texts that
have come down to us from ancient times with a view to discovering which of them renders the sense more truly and
exactly. In fact there are times when, even after every help
that text criticism and a knowledge of languages can offer has
been exhausted, the meaning of the words is still not perfectly
clear and their more definite clarification will have to be left
to future study.

Still we are confident that today, thanks to the painstaking   788
use made of all the latest findings, it has been possible to
provide a translation of the psalms such as was desired. It
presents their meaning and content clearly enough to enable
priests reciting the Divine Office to grasp readily what the
Holy Spirit intended to convey by the lips of the Psalmist;
clearly enough, too, for them to be stirred up by the divine
words and urged on to true and genuine piety.

Now that the professors of Our Pontifical Biblical Institute   789
have completed the longed-for new translation with the
diligence befitting such a task, We offer it with fatherly
affection to all who have the obligation to recite the canonical
Hours daily. After due consideration of all the issues involved,

We hereby of Our own free choice (*motu proprio*) and upon mature deliberation permit them to use it, should they wish to do so, in either private or public recitation as soon as it has been adapted to the psalter of the Roman Breviary and published by the Vatican Printing Office.

790   We hope that this pastoral solicitude and fatherly affection of ours for the men and women who have dedicated their life to God will prove helpful to them. May it assist them all to draw ever more light and grace and comfort from their Divine Office. May those benefits open their eyes in these days of bitter trial through which the Church is passing, and inspire them to conform their lives more and more to the examples of holiness that shine forth so radiantly in the psalms. Let them nourish and cultivate in their hearts those sentiments of divine love, vigorous courage and sincere repentance to which the Holy Spirit moves us as we read the sacred songs.

791   What We have decided and decreed by this *motu priprio* letter shall have the force of law, anything to the contrary notwithstanding, whatever it may be, even though worthy of very special mention.

792   Given in Rome at St. Peter's on the 24th day of March in the year 1945, the 7th of Our Pontificate.

MEDIATOR DEI
Encyclical Letter of Pope Pius XII
On the Psalms (Excerpt)
November 20, 1947

The Psalms, as all know, form the chief part of the Divine Office. They encompass the full round of the day and sanctify it. Cassiodorus speaks beautifully about the Psalms as distributed in his day throughout the Divine Office: "with the celebration of matins they bring a blessing on the coming day, they set aside for us the first hour and consecrate the third hour of the day, they gladden the sixth hour with the breaking of bread, at the ninth they terminate our fast, they bring the evening to a close and at nightfall they shield our minds from darkness."

The Psalms recall to mind the truths revealed by God to 794 the chosen people, which were at one time frightening and at another filled with wonderful tenderness: they keep repeating and fostering the hope of the promised Liberator which in ancient times was kept alive with song, either around the hearth or in the stately Temple; they show forth in splendid light the prophesied glory of Jesus Christ: first, His supreme and eternal power, then His lowly coming to this terrestrial exile, His kingly dignity and priestly power and finally His beneficent labors, and the shedding of His Blood for our redemption. In a similar way they express the joy, the bitterness, the hope and fear of our hearts and our desire of loving God and hoping in Him alone, and our mystic ascent to divine tabernacles.

795   "The psalm is . . . a blessing for the people, it is the praise of God, the tribute of the nation, the common language and acclamation of all, it is the voice of the Church, the harmonious confession of faith, signifying deep attachment to authority: it is the joy of freedom, the expression of happiness, an echo of bliss."

Letter of Pontifical Biblical Commission
to Cardinal Suhard
Concerning the Time of Documents of the Pentateuch
and Concerning the Literary Form of the Eleven Chapters
of Genesis
January 16, 1948

Your Eminence,

The holy Father has been pleased to entrust to the exam- 796
ination of the Pontifical Commission for Biblical Studies two
questions, which have been recently submitted to His Holiness
concerning the sources of the Pentateuch and the historicity
of the first eleven chapters of Genesis. These two questions
with their considerations and propositions have been the
object of the most careful study on the part of the Right
Reverend Consultors and the Most Eminent Cardinals,
Members of the above mentioned Commission. As the result
of their deliberations, His Holiness has deigned to approve
the following reply in the audience granted to the undersigned on the 16th of January, 1948.

The Pontifical Biblical Commission is pleased to pay hom- 797
age to the sense of filial confidence that has inspired this step,
and wishes to correspond by a sincere effort to promote biblical studies, while safeguarding for them the greatest freedom
within the limits of the traditional teaching of the Church.
This freedom has been explicitly affirmed by the encyclical
of the Sovereign Pontiff gloriously reigning, *Divino Afflante
Spiritu,* in the following terms: "The Catholic commentator,
inspired by an active and ardent love of his subject and sincerely devoted to Holy Mother Church, should in no way be
deterred from grappling again and again with these difficult
problems, hitherto unsolved, not only that he may refute the

objections of the adversaries, but also may attempt to find a satisfactory solution, which will be in full accord with the doctrine of the Church, in particular with the traditional teaching regarding the inerrancy of Sacred Scripture, and which will at the same time satisfy the indubitable conclusions of profane sciences. Let all the other sons of the Church bear in mind that the efforts of these resolute laborers in the vineyard of the Lord should be judged not only with equity and justice, but also with the greatest charity; all, moreover, should abhor that intemperate zeal which imagines that whatever is new should for that reason be opposed or suspected" (*A.A.S.*, 1943), page 319; English Edition (Vatican Press), page 22.

798   If one would rightly understand and interpret in the light of this recommendation of the Sovereign Pontiff the three official answers previously given by the Biblical Commission regarding the above-named questions, namely, that of 23rd June, 1905, on the narratives in the historical books of Holy Scripture which have only the appearance of being historical (*Ench. Bibl.*, 154), that of 27th June, 1906, on the Mosaic authenticity of the Pentateuch (*Ench. Bibl.*, 174-177), and that of 30th June, 1909, on the historical character of the first three chapters of Genesis (*Ench. Bibl.*, 332-339), one will readily grant that these answers are in no way opposed to further and truly scientific examination of these problems in accordance with the results obtained during these last forty years. Consequently, the Biblical Commission believes that there is no need, at least for the moment, to promulgate any new decrees regarding these questions.

799   1. In what concerns the composition of the Pentateuch, in the above-named decree of 27th June, 1906, the Biblical Commission already recognized that it may be affirmed that Moses "in order to compose his work, made use of written documents or oral traditions," and also that modifications and additions have been made after the time of Moses (*Ench. Bibl.*, 176-177). There is no one today who doubts the existence of these sources or refuses to admit a progressive development of the Mosaic Laws due to social and religious condi-

tions of later times, a development which is also manifest in the historical narratives. Even, however, within the field of non-Catholic commentators very divergent opinions are professed today concerning the nature and number of these documents, their denomination and date. There are, indeed, not a few authors in different countries who, for purely critical and historical reasons and with no apologetic intention, resolutely set aside the theories most in vogue until now, and who look for the elucidation of certain redactional peculiarities of the Pentateuch, not so much in the diversity of the supposed documents as in the special psychology, the peculiar processes of thought and expression, better known today, of the early Oriental peoples, or again in the different literary style demanded by the diversity of subject-matter. Therefore, we invite Catholic scholars to study these problems, without prepossession, in the light of sound criticism and of the findings of other sciences connected with the subject-matter. Such study will doubtless establish the great part and deep influence exercised by Moses both as author and lawgiver.

2. The question of the literary forms of the first eleven 800 Chapters of Genesis is far more obscure and complex. These literary forms correspond to none of our classical categories and cannot be judged in the light of Greco-Latin or modern literary styles. One can, therefore, neither deny nor affirm their historicity, taken as a whole, without unduly attributing to them the canons of a literary style within which it is impossible to classify them. If one agrees not to recognize in these chapters history in the classical and modern sense, one must, however, admit that the actual scientific data do not allow of giving all the problems they set a *positive* solution. The first duty here incumbent upon scientific exegesis consists before all in the attentive study of all the literary, scientific, historical, cultural and religious problems connected with these chapters; one should then examine closely the literary processes of the early Oriental peoples, their psychology, their way of expressing themselves and their very notion of historical truth; in a word, one should collate without

prejudice all the subject-matter of the palaeontological and historical, epigraphic and literary sciences. Only thus can we hope to look more clearly into the true nature of certain narratives in the first Chapters of Genesis. To declare *a priori* that their narratives contain no history in the modern sense of the term would easily convey the idea that they contain no history whatever, whereas they relate in simple and figurative language, adapted to the understanding of a less developed people, the fundamental truths presupposed for the economy of salvation, as well as the popular description of the origin of the human race and of the Chosen People. Meanwhile we must practice that patience which is living prudence and wisdom. This is what the Holy Father likewise inculcates in the Encyclical already quoted: "No one," he says, "will be surprised, if all difficulties are not yet solved and overcome. . . . We should not lose courage on this account; nor should we forget that in the human sciences the same happens as in the natural world; that is to say, new beginnings grow little by little and fruits are gathered only after many labors. . . . Hence there are grounds for hope that those (difficulties) also will by constant effort be at last made clear, which now seem most complicated and difficult" (*ibid.*, p. 318; English Edition, pp. 21-22).

801   Kissing the Sacred Purple with sentiments of the deepest veneration,

> I acknowledge myself to be
> Your Most Reverend Emminence's
> Most humble servant,
> James M. Vosté, O. P.
> Secretary of the Pontifical Biblical Commission.

An Instruction of the Pontifical Biblical Commission
to the Most Excellent Local Ordinaries, Superiors General
of Religious Institutes and the Very Reverend Rectors
of Seminaries and Professors of Sacred Scripture: on the
Proper Way to Teach Sacred Scripture in the Seminaries
of Clerics and the Colleges of Religious
May 13, 1950

To commemorate in a worthy manner the fiftieth year elapsing after the publication of the Encyclical *Providentissimus Deus*, our most holy lord, Pope Pius XII, the Supreme Pontiff happily reigning, likewise issued an Encyclical, *Divino Afflante Spiritu*, September 30, 1943. After a luminous exposition of what his predecessors had zealously achieved in promoting biblical studies during the past ten lustra, the Supreme Pontiff gravely reminded all, both superiors and the faithful, of the high value enjoyed by these studies in the Church and of the procedure to be followed that these very studies may progress favorably and conduce effectively towards spreading the kingdom of God among men. In the same way he wisely determined and enjoined the way and the method by which they are ever more to be cultivated and perfected.

In order that the measures recommended and sanctioned   803
by the will of the Supreme Pontiff be executed with the
utmost care and fidelity, the Pontifical Biblical Commission
deemed it opportune to apply them, in appropriate fashion,
to the teaching of biblical subjects in the seminaries of clerics
and the colleges of religious, in which they cannot be taught
as extensively as they are proposed in theolgocial faculties
and special institutes. For in the latter, professors are formed
whose function it will be to train future priests in sacred
sciences as well as to investigate these subjects more pro-

foundly. This formation is restricted to only a few. But in the seminaries of clerics and in the colleges of religious, men are prepared to be future priests and shepherds of the Lord's flock; it will be their task to impart the truths of faith to the Catholic people and to defend divine revelation against the attacks of unbelievers.

804   Within recent decades the Supreme Pontiffs have not infrequently inculcated in explicit terms the great care with which the Local Ordinaries and Superiors General of religious institutes are obligated to provide, by exhortation no less than by the exercise of authority, that the study of Sacred Scripture in the seminaries of clerics and the colleges of religious "be maintained in due honor and flourish," as Leo XIII[1] wrote, and that the Divine Literature be taught there "as the gravity of the subject and the requirement of the times suggest."[2]

805   Recently, however, our most holy lord, Pope Pius XII, happily reigning, in summing up the admonitions of his predecessors and confirming by his own authority, gravely warned that the Sacred Books can in no wise be correctly and fruitfully expounded and elucidated by priests deputed to the care of souls "unless they have previously imbibed an active and abiding love of Sacred Scripture during their sojourn in the seminary. Hence religious superiors, upon whom a fatherly care for their seminaries is incumbent, should be vigilant that in this regard also nothing be omitted which may aid the attainment of this purpose."[3]

806   But at that time, when so many nations were oppressed by the weight of calamities and ruins, the Local Ordinaries also and the Rectors of seminaries, distracted as they were by the worries of daily subsistence and security, may perhaps have been less able to bestow the effective attention upon this obligation which the gravity and importance of the matter demanded. But now when the clash of arms is hushed, it seems that the admonitions and injunctions of the Supreme Pontiffs should be recalled to memory and inculcated anew, in order that the education of future priests in the Sacred books be fervently restored and promoted through the judicious care of superiors and the diligent effort of professors,

with the purpose of leading the faithful back to the most salutary sources of Christian life and of again imbuing and permeating the world, so terribly afflicted, with the teaching of Christ, who alone is the fount of liberty, love, and peace.

For the proper restoration and furtherance of biblical studies in the seminaries of clerics and the colleges of religious we need primarily professors fitted in all respects for teaching this subject, which surpasses all others in sanctity and sublimity.   807

It is hardly necessary to note that the professor of Sacred Scripture should be distinguished among the others for a priestly life and virtue; in fact, he should even surpass the others, since he daily enjoys an intimate familiarity with the Word of God.   808

Moreover, he should be equipped with a due knowledge of biblical subjects, which he has acquired by serious study and which he conserves and augments by unremitting toil.   809

To be able to ascertain with greater surety the amount and the character of the learning considered rightly acquired, the wise provision of Pius XI, of holy memory, is to be deemed ratified and valid also for the present time: No one is to be a professor of the Sacred Literature in a seminary "unless he has legitimately received academic decrees from the Biblical Commission or from the Biblical Institute after having completed a special course of studies in this subject."[5]   810

A general conspectus of this subject may indeed be obtained in a few years together with the method of study and teaching and the knowledge of some of the more important problems. But the range of this subject is so wide that the remainder must be left to the ulterior *study and industry of the professor.* Hence additional assiduous effort on the part of each individual is necessary that the knowledge previously acquired may be increased, perfected, and solidified, that problems newly arising may be competently examined and discussed, that the various branches of the subject which must be given to seminarians may be investigated on a higher level and with greater profundity. To attain these ends he must read attentively the newly published books and period-   811 icals on biblical subjects; he must consult libraries; he must participate in meetings instituted to further biblical science; he should, also, if conditions permit, make a journey at a favorable time to the Holy Land to inspect with his own eyes and to traverse the cities and regions connected with sacred history. So vast is the scope of biblical knowledge, so many and so great are the advances made in the explanation of the Sacred Books, so numerous are the sciences whose aid must be invoked that the professor, unless he devotes himself daily to diligent study, soon becomes unequal to his arduous office and is incapable of rendering the service which priests engaged in the ministry of souls and even the faithful rightly demand of him.

812   From this it is evident without difficulty how necessary it is that the professor of Sacred Scripture *should be able to dedicate himself entirely* to his office "in order that he may continue the work, happily begun, with every endeavor and every care."[6] Wherefore, he is not to be compelled to teach any other important branches in the seminary at the same time, in addition to the subjects pertaining to Sacred Scripture. For the Code of Canon Law determines in explicit language that care is to be taken "that there should be distinct professors at least of *Sacred Scripture*, Dogmatic Theology, Moral Theology, and Ecclesiastical History, equal to these subjects in number."[7] Furthermore, he should not be burdened with other onerous offices and ministries even outside the seminary, be they ever so holy and praiseworthy, lest he be hampered by the latter in the performance of the former for which he needs time no less than mental vigor and peace of soul.

813   Now, with regard to the method of teaching Sacred Scripture in the seminaries of clerics and the colleges of religious, the following points seem to be worthy of commemoration.

814   1. It is the task of the biblical professor to excite and foster in the students "an active and abiding love of the Sacred Books"[8] together with a proper knowledge of them. This mode of instruction is to nourish and daily increase in the future priests such a veneration for the Divine Word that all their lives they may find it to be the chief object cultivated

by the mind and the occupation of the soul, the solace and delight of the heart.

(a) To achieve this goal in the right way, _the daily reading_   815
of Sacred Scripture is even today most advantageous. In former ages it was the daily practice of priests, secular as well as religious; it was not less sacred than the daily meditation; in fact, this pious reading was their meditation.[9] Let, therefore, the professor urge his students to esteem the daily reading of the Sacred Books highly and to practice it with a humble faith and religious piety.[10] Let him recommend that they continue this exercise, which is so useful, unremittingly through the whole time of their studies, in such a way that they _repeatedly peruse the entire Scriptures in cursory fashion._ They may use either the Vulgate or some other more recent vernacular version from the original text properly approved by ecclesiastical superiors, unless they are helped more by the primitive text. This reading of Sacred Scripture will be done with greater fruitfulness if the students are intelligently instructed and directed in reading the Sacred Books from the very beginning of their course of studies. A brief conspectus or analysis of the individual books may even be proposed as is usually done in "Special Introduction."[11] If this daily reading is continuous and accomplished in an orderly and planned fashion, the candidates for the priesthood will be excellently prepared to understand rightly and celebrate worthily the sacred liturgy no less than to pursue fruitfully the theological studies themselves. Now this daily reading of Sacred Scripture should not be omitted even in the time of vacation, whether it be performed by all in common or by individuals in their homes. Nay, it should even be practiced with greater intensity during these days of greater leisure. This fidelity in striving to know and relish Sacred Scripture ever more intimately will indicate clearly how sincere their love is for the Word of God and how much they endeavor to satisfy the obligations imposed upon them by their sacerdotal vocation.

2. _When teaching his classes,_ the professor of Sacred Scrip-   816
ture will take care to give his students all that they will need

in their sacerdotal work for leading a holy life as well as for winning souls to God. Wherefore:

(a) Sacred Scripture in the seminaries of clerics and the colleges of religious should be taught so scientifically, solidly, and completely that they may know it in its entirety and in all its parts, that they may be thoroughly conversant with the more important questions which are agitated these days with regard to individual books, with the objections and difficulties proposed against sacred doctrine and history, and, finally, that they may base their explanations of biblical passages on valid scientific foundations.

(b) The time allotted to the teaching of Sacred Scripture is generally too short to be able to cover completely the immense quantity of biblical subjects. Hence the teacher should take care to make a prudent choice of the more important questions in preference to others. In doing so, he ought not to seek the objects of his own personal studies or mental propensities; he ought rather to bear in mind conscientiously the utility required by the students who are to be preachers of the Divine Word. This utility will be satisfied only then when the the professor has clearly and perspicuously expounded the teachings proposed by the Holy Spirit in both the Old and New Testaments, the progress in revelation discernible from the beginnings down to Christ and the Apostles, the relationship and union subsisting between the Old and New Testaments. Let him also, not neglect to point out aptly the great spiritual importance of the Old Testament even for our times. Accordingly, he should endeavor skillfully to make this clear wherever he has an opportunity in General or Special Introduction or in Exegesis. It will be useful, also, to illustrate, by apposite examples from sacred and profane history, the magnitude of the exertions made by God to save all and to bring them to the knowledge of the truth[12] and the manner in which His fatherly providence has disposed and directed all things "that they might work together for good to those who are called to be saints."[13]

817   If these supernatural and religious features are explained and proven as they should be, a kind of deeper love and greater esteem of the Sacred Books will undoubtedly spring

up in the minds of the students, rendering the more arid studies, such as Hebrew and Greek, more easy and pleasant. These studies cannot be altogether eliminated in seminaries and colleges, without the danger that clerics be kept away from the original inspired texts through ignorance of the languages and that they be unable to understand rightly and appraise competently the modern versions.[14] Although these studies of the languages and criticism must be reduced to summary proportions in seminaries and colleges, they will when illumined by this supernatural light, become more fecund and agreeable and will, day by day, produce greater fruit in perceiving the meaning of the Sacred Books.

When teaching *General Introduction*, without omitting the other questions altogether, the time should be devoted especially to the doctrine of inspiration, the truth of Sacred Scripture, and the laws of interpretation (hermeneutics). In *Special Introduction* to the Old and especially to the New Testament, let him treat the Sacred Books with care; let him set forth lucidly the theme of each book, its purpose, authorship, and date.[15] In this matter vain erudition on the opinions of critics, which rather disturbs than instructs the minds of the students, should be avoided. Let him rather propose and forcefully bring out the topics which are of greater spiritual utility to men of our age and which afford them suitable help in solving problems and difficulties. To enable him to deal adequately with all the Sacred Books the professor should use the time granted him sedulously, without delaying over useless or inconsequential matters.   818

In *exegetical exposition* the professor ought never to be oblivious of the fact that Sacred Scripture has been consigned to the *Church* not only to be guarded but to be interpreted and that it is not to be explained except in the name and according to the mind of the Church, since she is "pillar and basis of truth."[16] Wherefore, "he will consider it sacred never to depart in the least from the common teaching and tradition of the Church; he will, of course, turn to his use whatever modern ingenuity has brought forth, but he will neglect the rash theories of innovators."[17]   819

820   In choosing the parts to be explained more accurately, mere erudition should not be his consideration, but he should expound those points by which the *doctrine* of both Testaments is declared and defined, lest, in the words of St. Gregory, he gnaw the bark, without reaching the core.[18] Hence let him explain *chiefly* the doctrine of the Old Testament on the origin of the human race, the messianic prophecies, and the Psalms. In the New Testament let him give an orderly conspectus of the whole life of Christ the Lord; let him explain at least those portions of the Gospels and the Epistles which are read publicly in church on Sundays and feastdays. Moreover, he ought to give a history of the Passion and the Resurrection of our Lord and he ought to expound completely at least one of the principle Epistles of St. Paul, without omitting the passages of the other Epistles which refer to doctrine.

821   The professor is to discharge his office of interpreter in such a way as to explain, first of all, the so-called *literal sense*, having recourse, also, when the occasion demands, to the primal text itself. In determining the literal sense of texts let him not follow the way pursued nowadays, unfortunately, by not a few exegetes by merely considering the words and their proximate context. Let him rather sedulously have before his eyes those ancient norms inculcated anew by the Supreme Pontiff, Pius XII, gloriously reigning, in his encyclical *Divino Afflante Spiritu*. Specifically, he ought to search out accurately what Sacred Scripture teaches in other similar passages, what the explanation of the text is in the Holy Fathers and in Catholic tradition, and finally, if the case warrants it, what the teaching authority of the Church has decided about the text in question.[19] To be able to carry all this into effect, he should be eminently versed in Sacred Theology; he should be imbued with a great and genuine love of sacred doctrine. Let him never, relying upon critical and literary principles exclusively, sever his exegetical task from the universal theological teaching.

822   He should, also, take care to explain the *spiritual sense* properly provided that the fact of its being intended by God is sufficiently evident, according to the very wise norms laid down by the Supreme Pontiffs.[20] The professor will under-

stand this spiritual sense—set forth by the Holy Fathers and the great interpreters with so high a degree of zeal and love— the more readily and propound it the more religiously to the students, the greater the purity of heart, the excellence of mind, the humility of spirit, the reverence and love for the revealing God are with which he is adorned.

The professor should not attenuate nor conceal the *difficul-* **823** *ties* and *obscurities* not infrequently encountered by the interpreter of the Books of the Old Testament. He should rather attempt to unravel the problem, as far as his powers permit, with the aid of various sciences, after a fair and honest exposition of the question. Nevertheless, let him not forget "that God, who inspired the Sacred Books deliberately scattered difficulties over them in order that we may be incited to a more intense perusal and scrutiny of them and that we may practice a becoming humility of mind after having had a wholesome experience of our mental limitations."[21]

As far as possible, the professor should expound all this by **824** the so-called method of *synthesis*, treating the more important matters with greater exactness and the others to the extent and in the place proper to them. Let him cultivate this art of exposition intelligently from the very outset and let him strive to perfect himself in it ever more and more, cherishing the conviction that the fruit and efficacy of teaching is to a large extent dependent upon it.

3. *The purpose and character* of the lectures on Sacred **825** Scripture by which the students in seminaries and colleges are instructed are defined by the fact that they are not directed to the formation of so-called specialists but to the preparation of future priests and apostles. But though the formation of priests depends upon all the conditions of life and order existing in a seminary and college, it is undoubtedly, aided in a distinct way by biblical study and knowledge. For the primary purpose to be attained by these lectures is that the future priests may understand and convince themselves that the Sacred Books contribute very much towards the fruitful discharge of their sacerdotal duties. Wherefore the professor should not be at all satisfied with merely giving out points of information and useful and necessary knowledge about bibli-

cal matters. He ought, also zealously point out to his pupils, when he has the opportunity, how they may sustain, strengthen, and promote[22] the holiness of their own sacerdotal life and how they may fructify the apostolic ministry, especially that of sacred preaching and catechetical instruction, by a solid knowledge and assiduous reading of Sacred Scripture and by pious meditation upon it.[23]

826   Consequently, since biblical studies are of such great value for sacerdotal piety and for the fruitfulness of the apostolic ministry, no one can fail to see that they are to be pursued and promoted with the greatest diligence. Therefore, it is very deplorable that they are not always held in due honor and that they are not rarely accorded an unworthy position, inferior to the study of other branches; nay, at times, they are mistakenly neglected. Accordingly, this Pontifical Biblical Commission, perturbed by information and petitions received from various parts of the world, has decided that the following recommendations should be earnestly made to the Most Excellent Local Ordinaries and the Superiors General of religious institutes as well as to the Very Reverend Rectors of seminaries and the professors of biblical subjects.

827   1. The *biblical library*[24] of seminaries and colleges ought to contain, besides the Holy Fathers and the commentaries of the more distinguished Catholic interpreters, the better works on biblical theology, archeology, and sacred history as well as encyclopedias or biblical dictionaries and biblical periodicals. These works, for various reasons, cannot be easily acquired by individual professors, certainly to their own immense loss and to that of the students.

828   2. With no less care and diligence, superiors of seminaries and colleges should see to it that *clerics* may also have at their disposal in their library, besides the volume of the Holy Bible and the Manual of instruction used by all, those works which can aid them better and more effectively in reviewing and aptly complementing the lectures heard in class.

829   3. To discharge his office in a praiseworthy manner, the professor of biblical subjects is to be *devoted entirely to his task*. No other duties of great moment are to be entrusted to him. He is to be encouraged so much by his superiors—even

by financial grants and other suitable means of assistance—
that he will persevere with a willing heart in the office of
teaching even for his whole life.

For the first condition for advancing biblical study in semi-   830
naries and colleges consists in this that the professor of biblical subjects be supplied with all those aids in books and money
which will enable him to make progress himself in science as
well as to make the progress of science his own, to participate
in meetings instituted for the purpose of study, to visit the
Holy Land at a favorable opportunity, and to publish the
results of his labors in printed form.

But it is advisable that two lecturers on biblical subjects   831
be appointed, one for the Old, the other for the New Testament, in places where there is a larger number of students
(nay, even elsewhere, to provide in good time for future
needs).

4. We urgently recommend to the professor of biblical   832
subjects who is solicitous about the progress of the pupils
that he give a special free course in the biblical languages and
in others necessary or useful for the study of the Sacred
Scripture[25] or in biblical theology, history, archeology, or
any other auxiliary discipline *to select students of greater
talents.* In this course he will also be able to treat special
questions concerning individual books which at the present
time are more debated and which he may have investigated
more thoroughly by personal research or by reading books.

5. We likewise counsel the professor of biblical subjects to   833
prepare students of greater promise who display an unusual
love of Holy Writ, for special studies.[26] This should be done
in obedience to the advice of superiors, with prudence and
moderation, without, however, neglecting the other branches
in any way. He should also afford them an opportunity to
learn the modern languages more necessary for these studies
and he should teach them to know and read works "on the
life of Christ, on the life of the Apostles, on journeys, and
pilgrimages to Palestine."[27] Let him conscientiously bear in
mind the serious injury suffered by these students when they
are sent to make special studies without the requisite preparation, especially in literature. Let him persuade himself that it

is one of his chief duties to train, on the basis of his own experience, excellent teachers for his seminary, men through whose endeavors biblical subjects will be cultivated and flourish ever more and more.

834   6. All the requirements for the theological and ascetical education of clerics, for teaching the proper use of the Sacred Books in the liturgy and preaching can scarcely be duly satisfied in the meager time generally assigned to the classes of Sacred Scripture. Hence it is very praiseworthy and earnestly recommended to give *a form of compendious introduction* at the very beginning of the course of higher studies—a laudable practice, as we know, in the colleges of some orders—by which the cursory reading of the whole Scriptures to be done by the students during the time of studies is opportunely stimulated and directed. If this has been done properly, the professor will be able to devote more time to the exposition of biblical doctrine during the four years of the theological curriculum.

835   7. Once or twice a year the clerics in theology should be obliged to compose a *homily* on some biblical passage. This work is to be directed and conscientiously criticized by the professor himself. In this way, through appropriate study and pious meditation, the students learn, from the very inception of their theological education, to prepare and accurately write homilies to be delivered on Sundays and feastdays and to propose and explain from the pulpit to the people the true and genuine sense of the Word of God rightly, appositely, and reverently.

836   8. Finally, to cultivate and perfect, also, the study of Sacred Scripture in due fashion after the completion of the theological course and to continue it faithfully thereafter through life, some more important questions to be prepared from General and Special Introduction and from Exegesis should be inserted each year in the *examinations* on the various sacred sciences which Canon Law prescribes for secular priests at least for three years and for religious at least for five years after the completion of the course of studies.[28] Moreover, in the *convocations* or *conferences* to be held by the clergy, secular as well as regular, at stated periods, in con-

formity with the same Canon Law,[29] some biblical passage,
either of the Old or the New Testament, should be proposed,
as is done in a highly praiseworthy manner in some regions.
This should be chosen aptly by the professor of biblical subjects in the seminary. After it has been explained in accordance with the method of biblical science, it should be published by him in the diocesan periodicals, if this is possible, or
elsewhere.

We urgently request the Most Excellent Ordinaries and the   837
Most Reverend Generals of religious institutes, animated as
they are by a conscientious care for the common good, to
accept and execute the points of the preceding exposition in
such a way that the education of our future priests be daily
ever more perfected and that they may be imbued with that
solid sacred science which they must already use during the
time of their theological studies and later, throughout their
whole life, not frivolously and rashly, nor according to their
own caprice and sense, but in harmony with the standards of
sacred science, in harmony with the laws and precepts of the
Church, in harmony with the rules of genuine Catholic tradition. Thus the Sacred Books will be, as it were, their daily
bread, their light and strength in nourishing and developing
their own spiritual life; but in the apostolic ministry it will be
an effective aid assisting them to lead as many as possible to
the truth, to the fear and love of God, to virtue and holiness.
We are, of course, not ignorant of the many difficulties
standing in the way of a speedy and perfect fulfillment of our
recommendations. But we rest assured that the Superiors of
Churches and the Generals of religious institutes will, with
absolutely unfailing courage, not neglect a single detail by
which the study and the love of the Divine Literature on the
part of all clerics and priests may flourish with new vigor and
produce in their souls and in the discharge of their task most
abundant fruit of life and grace.

Our most holy lord, Pope Pius XII, in an audience granted   838
to the undersigned Very Reverend Consultor–Secretary,
May 13, 1950, approved this instruction and ordered it to be
made public.

Athanasius Miller, O.S.B.,
Consultor-Secretary

HUMANI GENERIS
Encyclical Letter of Pope Pius XII
on the Inspiration of the Scriptures (Excerpt)
August 12, 1950

For some go so far as to pervert the sense of the Vatican Council's definition that God is the author of Holy Scripture, and they put forward again the opinion, already often condemned, which asserts that immunity from error extends only to those parts of the Bible that treat of God or of moral and religious matters. They even wrongly speak of the human sense of the Scriptures, beneath which a divine sense, which they say is the only infallible meaning, lies hidden. In interpreting Scripture, they will take no account of the analogy of faith and the Tradition of the Church. Thus they judge the doctrine of the Fathers and of the Teaching Church by the norm of Holy Scripture interpreted by the purely human reason of exegetes, instead of explaining Holy Scripture according to the mind of the Church which Christ Our Lord has appointed guardian and interpreter of the whole deposit of divinely revealed truth.

840   Further, according to their fictitious opinions, the literal sense of Holy Scripture and its explanation, carefully worked out under the Church's vigilance by so many great exegetes, should yield now to a new exegesis which they are pleased to call symbolic or spiritual. By means of this new exegesis the Old Testament, which today in the Church is a sealed book, would finally be thrown open to all the faithful. By this method, they say, all difficulties vanish, difficulties which

hinder only those who adhere to the literal meaning of the Scriptures.

Everyone sees how foreign all this is to the principles and   841
norms of interpretation rightly fixed by Our Predecessors of
happy memory, Leo XIII in his Encyclical *Providentissimus*,
and Benedict XV in the Encyclical *Spiritus Paraclitus*, as also
by Ourselves in the Encyclical *Divino Afflante Spiritu*.

It remains for Us now to speak about those questions   842
which, although they pertain to the positive sciences, are
nevertheless more or less connected with the truths of the
Christian faith. In fact, not a few insistently demand that the
Catholic religion take these sciences into account as much as
possible. This certainly would be praiseworthy in the case of
clearly proved facts; but caution must be used when there is
rather question of hypotheses, having some sort of scientific
foundation, in which the doctrine contained in Sacred Scripture or in Tradition is involved. If such conjectural opinions
are directly or indirectly opposed to the doctrine revealed by
God, then the demand that they be recognized can in no way
be admitted.

For these reasons the Teaching Authority of the Church   843
does not forbid that, in conformity with the present state of
human sciences and sacred theology, research and discussions,
on the part of men experienced in both fields, take place
with regard to the doctrine of evolution, in as far as it inquires
into the origin of the human body as coming from pre-exis-
tent and living matter—for the Catholic faith obliges us to
hold that souls are immediately created by God. However
this must be done in such a way that the reasons for both
opinions, that is, those favorable and those unfavorable to
evolution, be weighed and judged with the necessary seriousness, moderation and measure, and provided that all are prepared to submit to the judgment of the Church, to whom
Christ has given the missions of interpreting authentically the
Sacred Scriptures and of defending the dogmas of faith.
Some however rashly transgress this liberty of discussion,
when they act as if the origin of the human body from pre-
existing and living matter were already completely certain

and proved by the facts which have been discovered up to now and by reasoning on those facts, and as if there were nothing in the sources of divine revalation which demands the greatest moderation and caution in this question.

844   When, however, there is question of another conjectural opinion, namely polygenism, the children of the Church by no means enjoy such liberty. For the faithful cannot embrace that opinion which maintains either that after Adam there existed on this earth true men who did not take their origin through natural generation from him as from the first parent of all, or that Adam represents a certain number of first parents. Now it is in no way apparent how such an opinion can be reconciled with that which the sources of revealed truth and the documents of the Teaching Authority of the Church propose with regard to original sin, which proceeds from a sin actually committed by an individual Adam and which through generation is passed on to all and is in everyone as his own.[1]

845   Just as in the biological and anthropological sciences, so also in the historical sciences there are those who boldly transgress the limits and safeguards established by the Church. In a particular way must be deplored a certain too free interpretation of the historical books of the Old Testament. Those who favor this system, in order to defend their cause, wrongly refer to the Letter which was sent not long ago to the Archbishop of Paris by the Pontifical Commission on Biblical Studies.[2] This Letter, in fact, clearly points out that the first eleven chapters of Genesis, although properly speaking not conforming to the historical method used by the best Greek and Latin writers or by competent authors of our time, do nevertheless pertain to history in a true sense, which however must be further studied and determined by exegetes; the same chapters, (the Letter points out), in simple and metaphorical language adapted to the mentality of a people but little cultured, both state the principal truths which are fundamental for our salvation, and also give a popular description of the origin of the human race and chosen people. If, however, the ancient sacred writers have taken anything from popular narrations (and this may be conceded), it must never

be forgotten that they did so with the help of divine inspiration, through which they were rendered immune from any error in selecting and evaluating those documents.

Therefore, whatever of the popular narrations have been inserted into the Sacred Scriptures must in no way be considered on a par with myths or other such things, which are more the product of an extravagant imagination than of that striving for truth and simplicity which in the Sacred Books, also of the Old Testament, is so apparent that our ancient sacred writers must be admitted to be clearly superior to the ancient profane writers.

846

Letter of Pope Pius XII
to Edwin O'Hara, Bishop of Kansas City
July 30, 1952

To Our Venerable Brother,

847   It has seemed fitting that the laudable initiative sponsored
by the Archconfraternity of Christian Doctrine in the United
States, to formally commemorate the 500th Anniversary of
the printing of the Gutenberg Bible by a Catholic Bible Week
from September 28th to October 5th of this year, should
receive from Us a word of paternal encouragement.

848   This noteworthy centennial is an event whose celebration
calls forth quite properly the fullest participation of Catholics
throughout the world. The very fact of the production of the
Bible as the first great work of the newly discovered art of
printing, in that period when Europe was religiously one and
undivided in its Catholic faith, is but another clear attestation
to the maternal care of the one true Church of Jesus Christ in
safeguarding, honoring and diffusing ever more widely, down
through the centuries from apostolic times, the Sacred Word
of God.

849   It is indeed a source of consolation to learn of the marked
progress being made by the Confraternity, with the cooperation of learned Scriptural scholars, in the publication of the
new English language edition of the Holy Bible; and also of
the stimulation being given to a more widespread reading of
the Holy Scriptures through Catholic Bible Week. Against the
dangers of disillusionment and despair at the failure of worldly

remedies in the present crisis affecting all of mankind, there
ever remains a shining beacon, a sure source of hope and
solace in the unchanging inspiration of the Word of God.
That the faithful of the United States, not only during Catholic Bible Week but subsequently as well, will give themselves
in increasing numbers to a more frequent reading of the Bible
and draw from meditation upon its eternal truths spiritual
light and strength for the salvation of their souls in Jesus
Christ Our Lord, is Our fervent and confident trust, in pledge
of which We impart to all who generously cooperate in this
high purpose, Our paternal Apostolic Blessing.

(In 1955 the secretary of the PBC, Athanasius Miller, OSB,   850
made some pertinent observations on interpreting the earlier
decrees of the PBC. His remarks appeared in an article on the
new edition of the *Enchiridion Biblicum*. One passage in particular caught wide attention and has often been quoted as
indicative of the changing atmosphere. The relevant section
reads as follows:

"As long as these decrees (of the PBC) propose views
which are neither immediately nor mediately connected with
truths of faith and morals, it goes without saying that the
scholar may pursue his research with full liberty, provided
always that he defers to the supreme teaching authority of
the Church. Today we can hardly picture to ourselves the
position of Catholic scholars at the turn of the century, or
the dangers that threatened Catholic teaching on Scripture
and its inspiration on the part of liberal and rationalistic
criticism, which like a torrent tried to sweep away the sacred
barriers of tradition. At present the battle is considerably less
fierce; not a few controversies have been settled and many
problems emerge in an entirely new light, so that it is easy
enough for us to smile at the narrowness and constraint that
prevailed fifty years ago."

An English translation of the full article can be found in
the *Catholic Biblical Quarterly*, 18 (1956) 23-29.)

Instruction of the Pontifical Biblical Commission
on Biblical Associations, and on
Biblical Conventions and Meetings
December 15, 1955

His Holiness, Pope Pius XII, happily reigning, in his encyclical letter *Divino Afflante Spiritu* of September 30, 1943, urged, among several other things aimed at the right promotion of biblical studies, that prelates seek to increase and perfect constantly among the faithful committed to their care a veneration for Holy Scripture, and that they try effectively to enkindle and fan a knowledge of it and a love for it. It is for this reason that they should earnestly help those pious associations founded to spread copies of the Sacred Books; that they should by word and deed commend the daily reading and meditation of Holy Scripture, especially of the Gospels; that they should either themselves give public lectures or conferences on biblical matters or have them given by other duly skilled lecturers; that they should, according to their means, lend support to published commentaries which consider and expound biblical matters in scientific fashion, and should spread them among the various groups of people making up their flocks.[1]

852   This Pontifical Biblical Commission, to which the duty of directing and encouraging biblical studies is specially entrusted, has with great joy learned from various sources with what speed their Excellencies have obeyed the exhortations of the Sovereign Pontiff, and what good results the faithful in not a few regions have gained from this renewed study of the Sacred Books. In many places the ordinaries have, in their

concern for things biblical, wisely helped those biblical associations, formed in quite recent times, which work to promote a knowledge of the Sacred Books and a love for them through published books and commentaries and through public meetings and lectures. With excellent results, too, are "scripture days" held, especially for the faithful at large, or meetings lasting for several days, "scripture weeks," arranged, in which subjects having to do with Holy Scripture are discussed more fully and deeply, for the benefit of definite classes of people.

There is no doubt that through all these things—provided that they be well done—the knowledge and love of Holy Scripture is effectively promoted and grows richer day by day. Yet, that this goal be reached as it ought, everything should be planned and directed with great care and prudence.   853

To begin with, those subjects to be handled in meetings should be selected which are appropriate; especially should they be selected on the basis of their ability to make the theology of the Sacred Books more deeply known and to arouse an ever greater reverence and veneration for Holy Writ among the faithful. But matters historical, critical, or literary which are of greater moment or are more keenly controverted in a given area should not be overlooked, either. Then, the speakers in such meetings should be well versed in the matters of which they treat, should sincerely obey the norms laid down by the Holy See, should be prudent and sensible in saying what they have to say, and should take thorough account of the intellectual and spiritual level of their hearers. What a harvest is reaped from these meetings when all these points are observed is plain to see from the numerous reports which have been brought to the attention of this Pontifical Commission.   854

But it is to be regretted that these activities are not carried out in every area in full accord with the norms just laid down, and that there is the danger at times that such meetings, whether they be arranged by biblical associations or by other people, not only fail to be of sufficient value for all those who take part, but even reach the point of being for some people more in the line of "destruction" than of "edification" (cf. *II Cor.* 10:8). The speakers, we are told, are not always   855 those men who are well versed in the matters of which they treat; some of them are entirely too ready to follow less reliable authors, or rashly and boldly to accept and spread doubtful or false opinions, to recommend books or periodicals of doubtful value or reading matter either lacking ecclesiastical approval or laboring under positive disapproval—and all this at times in the hearing of people not at all prepared to weigh such things and pass judgment on them. We have even heard it to have happened that speakers paid little heed to those norms on which the Sovereign Pontiff now happily reigning again gravely insisted in his encyclical letter *Humani generis*, that they boldly set forth theories condemned by the magisterium of the Church, or even went so far as to propose in place of the literal sense duly brought out under the Church's watchful eye, some new sense which they called "symbolic" and "spiritual," by which difficulties inherent in the literal sense were supposed to vanish. There is no one who cannot realize how incalculably dangerous all these things are when proposed to hearers not thoroughly skilled in biblical matters.[2]

856   Having weighed well all these considerations, this Pontifical Biblical Commission, in conformity with the duties entrusted to it, has decided it opportune to remind the faithful that these biblical associations and all biblical conventions and meetings, as well as books and all articles on Scripture to be published in magazines and newspapers, are subject to the authority and jurisdiction of the ordinaries, since they have to do with religious matters and with the religious instruction of the faithful. And that this may in the future be more effectively observed, the Commission has seen fit to enact and prescribe the following:

857   1. All biblical associations, with their activities and undertakings, are subject to the authority and jurisdiction of the competent ordinary. The competent ordinary in the case of any diocesan association or meeting is the local ordinary. In the case of interdiocesan associations and meetings the competent ordinary is the ordinary in whose diocese the head of the association resides, or in which the convention or meeting is to be held.

2. No new biblical association or biblical meeting whatever   858
may be organized or arranged without the approval of the
competent ordinary, whose duty it is, also to examine and
approve the statutes of such groups.

3. The president of an association, or the moderator of any   859
meeting, shall each year send a report on its situation, its
members, its activities, to the competent ordinary.

4. No meeting planned to deal with biblical matters for the   860
benefit of an audience made up of people not given *ex pro-
fesso* to the study of Holy Scripture, whether it is to last a
week or a day, may be held without the consent and approval
of the competent ordinary. To this same ordinary word should
be sent in plenty of time telling what topics are to be considered and what speakers are to consider them. When the
meeting is over, the moderator should send the ordinary a
brief report on the matters considered, the discussions held,
and conclusions drawn. He should send the same report to
the Secretary of the Pontifical Biblical Commission, adding
thereto a program of the meeting and a list of the speakers.

5. Those congresses and meetings held for scientific con-   861
sideration and discussion among professors of Holy Scripture
and other people who specialize in biblical matters are not included in the norms given in No. 4. But even in those meetings care should be taken to see that everything is done in
line with sensible and proven principles of Catholic doctrine
and the norms laid down by the Holy See. Moreover, admission to such meetings should not be open to outsiders who
cannot be reckoned among the ranks of the professors and
the specialists.

6. Those in charge of making preparations for meetings   862
such as those mentioned in No. 4 and of directing them should
carefully arrange to have topics treated that, rather than cater
to curiosity and love of novelty, give promise of promoting
the audience's solid instruction in faith and morality and
asceticism and to enkindle in them a sincere love for the
Sacred Books and to fan that love. Those in charge should
choose as speakers men who are most likely to achieve these
goals, who know and understand the state of the audience's
learning and piety. They should see to it that in the topics to

be considered stress is placed more on a positive presentation of matter that is clear and well investigated than on difficulties and doubtful questions. Yet, if in the presence of this audience it seems a good thing to consider even difficulties and objections, then the problem should be fairly and honestly proposed, and a good answer, backed by scientific reasoning be given.

863   Their excellencies the ordinaries ought out of their love for Christ's flock to give serious attention to this matter, and if they cannot do so themselves they should officially appoint some priest of their own diocese, a man endowed with competency in things biblical, with a knowledge of solid theology, and with suitable prudence, who will take charge of these associations and meetings and report to the ordinary at definite times, to be determined by the same ordinary. This priest shall also examine diligently writings on biblical topics which have been published, or are to be published, in books and periodicals, and if he judges something worthy of notice he shall report it to the ordinary.

864   If all these things are assiduously and accurately done, we can hope that these praiseworthy biblical associations, meetings, and conventions will contribute much toward an ever increasing knowledge of the Word of God and love for it, toward a more effective promotion of biblical studies, and toward a more abundant harvest of souls.

865   His Holiness Pope Pius XII has graciously deigned to approve this instruction and has ordered it to be made public.

Address of Pope John XXIII
on the Fiftieth Anniversary
of the Pontifical Biblical Institute
February 17, 1960

Venerable brethren and beloved sons! Some time ago We approved your timely and praiseworthy plan to celebrate the first fifty years of existence of the Pontifical Biblical Institute, a plan which is being realized today. It is apparent to Us that your joy on this occasion is intense; it could hardly be otherwise, for these years in the institute's history—as was aptly pointed out by Our beloved son, Cardinal Augustine Bea—have been fruitful and satisfying years, favored with heavenly blessings. That the institute has had the privilege of fulfilling a conception of St. Pius X's is in itself enough to make your memories forever joyous. We are therefore happy to offer a hymn of thanks to the Lord for all the favors which He has lavished upon you during these first fifty years of your activity.

Our heart is filled with glowing satisfaction as We express to you Our fatherly joy and good wishes. When that great and holy pope, who preceded Us both on the Chair of St. Mark and on the Throne of St. Peter, decided to found this providential institute (just one of the many wise acts of his reign) he "showed the whole extent of his foresight as universal teacher and pastor."[1] Nor do We wish to conceal from you the satisfaction We derive from seeing the symbolical Lion of St. Mark, which adorns your coat-of-arms just as it does Ours. All these things, and the close ties between that saintly pope and your institute, combine to deepen Our

867

regard for it. We solemnly express that regard today on this happy occasion.

868   The thought of fifty years of zealous and self-effacing work should give us pause, whether we consider the long way you have come, or look ahead at the horizons of future activity which are opening up before your eyes.

869   A backward glance at the outstanding events of the first half-century in the life of the Biblical Institute demands, first of all, an act of profound gratitude to the Lord for the uninterrupted sequence of extraordinary favors with which He has blessed the institute. (You, beloved Cardinal, great contributor to the development of this pontifical foundation, have stated this vividly and dramatically.) A multitude of reasons for gratitude can be found by reviewing, even hastily, these eventful and meaningful years: the founding of the institute, which encountered great difficulties and even opposition; the institute's fortunate economic arrangements; the extraordinary growth of its activities, evidenced by the multiplication of the number of its students and the increase in its teaching facilities and scholarly publications, which are continually contributing to its fame.

870   Our immediate predecessor, Pius XII of blessed memory, with providential initiative enlarged the headquarters of the institute and enhanced the value of its activity. His enlightened zeal shines in the history of the institute alongside the fatherly solicitude of its saintly founder.

871   All these events have been excellently described by you in beautiful language, beloved Cardinal, thus making it unnecessary for Us to repeat already known facts. You must allow Us, however, to say that the fountainhead of all these blessings is the Sacred Heart of Jesus, and that the institute is an impressive monument to His generosity and providence. When all the preparations for its inauguration had been completed, St. Pius X received the superiors of the institute, and entrusted to them a most precious treasure, and the pledge of all its future blessings, by saying: "I leave with you the Sacred Heart."[2] He gave to the words engraved on the institute's coat-of-arms, *"Verbum Domini manet in aeternum,"*[3] the additional meaning of lasting, certain protection

by the heart of Jesus. This bright hope was to come true, and
the years that have elapsed since that time are the confirmation of this hope.

The blessings already received are a pledge of new favors to   872
come in the future; that is why We invite you to take heart
from the consideration of past achievements and continue in
the trail you have blazed, with joy, serenity, and assurance.
Of course, as happens with all human undertakings, much
remains to be done and all difficulties are far from being
solved; new ones may occur, but you must place your trust in
Him who protects you: "I am with you,"⁴ said the Lord,
with you who are studying and deepening your knowledge of
His word. Therefore, beloved sons, onward *"in nomine
Domini"*!

Your trust in God must give you the strength to look with-   873
out fear at the horizons which are opening up before your
eyes and at the goals which your patient toil is destined to
attain.

The task entrusted to the institute is indeed a noble and   874
difficult one. In his apostolic letter *"Vinea Electa,"* which is,
as it were, the Magna Charta of your institute, St. Pius X
states with crystal clarity: "The goal of the Pontifical Biblical
Institute must be to create in Rome a center of higher
biblical studies which will promote biblical research and all
related studies, using all legitimate methods at its disposal, in
accordance with the mind of the Catholic Church."⁵ This is,
then, the wide and noble horizon which opens up before you:
sacred Scripture with all its hidden treasure; the teaching,
doctrina, contained in it. This is a magnificent challenge to
your intellect, and a personal satisfaction to the pope who is
speaking to you and whose main interests have always lain in
that direction.

In the homily which We delivered on November 23, 1958,   875
"infra Missarum sollemnia" in Our cathedral, the Lateran
Archbasilica, We stated that: " . . . the thing We feel most of
all is an obligation to keep on stirring up an enthusiasm
everywhere for every expression of the Divine Book, which
God meant to cast light on the whole path of life from infancy to the most advanced years. . . . Unfortunately, in all

ages, there are always a few dark clouds, arising from certain notions that have little to do with true science, cluttering up the horizon whenever men attempt to see the Gospel in all its clear and radiant splendor. This is the task that is called to mind by the Book laid open upon the altar: to teach true doctrine, proper discipline of life, and the ways in which man can rise toward God."[6]

876 The knowledge that this sacred obligation is the banner and the mission of your institute, is deeply gratifying to Us. The institute's dedication to the study of the Divine Book is the highest form of service to that *truth* which We have made the first objective of Our pontifical rule.[7] The Biblical Institute is, then, pledged to seek, enlighten, and divulge the truth contained in the sacred Scriptures, thereby sharing in the sublime mission of Jesus, the Redeemer: "I came into the world to bear witness to the truth."[8] This labor in the cause of truth requires many qualifications: earnestness, a solid foundation, scientific integrity in studying and teaching, and, at the same time, the strictest adherence to the sacred deposit of Faith and the infallible Magisterium of the Church.

877 *Scholarly seriousness* is your first and highest claim to the general esteem and respect your institute has earned during the years of achievement which you are today celebrating. It consists, as you know, in the use of new tools of learning, as they are gradually developed in the course of scientific progress; the courage to tackle the problems created by modern research and recent discoveries; and the reappraisal, as Pius XII said, of "hitherto unsolved difficulties in order to arrive at a satisfactory explanation."[9]

878 It is true that this type of work, which is carried out in a field that is not yet sufficiently tilled, requires great prudence and intellectual balance, in order to avoid presenting results as conclusive which are based merely on working hypotheses. This prudent reserve, however, does not forbid the consideration of the questions which trouble the minds of many Christians and present dangers and difficulties for their faith. Your patient scientific toil, while utilizing the most advanced tools of the exact sciences, is, and must be, animated by a

pastoral purpose, an effort to communicate to souls the truth
that is discovered and mastered.

You must not neglect these disciplines, for scholarly
seriousness requires their study and deep understanding;
however, you would betray your obligations if you devoted
too much of your time—in teaching and in research—to the
problems of, let us say, the present moment, and neglected a
great part of that divine treasure, which is the Word of God
and the age-old body of interpretation by the Holy Fathers
and eminent teachers of the Church.

879

As you see, Our heart is especially set on promoting the
study of all matters pertaining to sacred doctrine: "*doctrinam
biblicam . . . promoveat*," states the letter of St. Pius X,
quoted above. Herein lies the purpose of your institute,
which consists not only of training specialists in biblical and
secular disciplines, but also in forming a body of scholars,
fired with priestly enthusiasm and gifted with the souls of
prophets and apostles.

880

In the previously quoted encyclical, "*Divino afflante
spiritu*," Pius XII summed up the scope of your studies as
follows: "They must bring to light, first and foremost, the
theological teachings of the individual books and texts on
points of faith and morals, so that their commentaries . . .
may also be of assistance to priests in their expounding of
Christian doctrine to the people, and help all the faithful to
lead a holy life, worthy of a Christian."[10]

881

The Sacred Scriptures are unlike any other subject of
study, however exalted: they are God's Revelation, which
was foreshadowed in the soft dawn light of the Old Testament, and highlighted in the dazzling noonday light of the
New Testament by Jesus Christ, Savior of the World. According to the profound teaching of St. Augustine,[11] "When we
hear a psalm, a prophecy, the law . . . all our efforts must be
directed at seeing and recognizing Jesus Christ therein."
From the inspired pages, He is still speaking to us and teaching us, and giving our souls substantial spiritual nourishment.

882

These profound words by the great Doctor and Bishop of
Hippo are admirably echoed by those of another Doctor and

883

Bishop, the Protopatriarch of Venice, St. Lawrence Justinian, whose teachings on the pastoral and sanctifying value of Sacred Scripture have become familiar to Us, as We stated almost four years ago in a pastoral letter to the clergy and faithful of Venice.[12]

884   Listen to the inspired words with which he speaks of the Holy Book in his work *"De contemptu mundi"*: "To avoid the entanglements of human science, we have the oracles of the prophets, the writings of the apostles, and the enormous learning of the saints, who do not speak for themselves, but rather because Christ is in them. . . . How great is the authority of the Divine Scriptures! What treasures of truth are hidden under the veil of their words! A truth all holy, adorned with sublime sayings. The Holy Book contains nothing sordid, nothing devious, nothing empty, and nothing which is not worthy of veneration. Its truth is magnificent in itself: it offers a noble object to man's appreciation; it molds the souls of the faithful, nourishes those who love, leads those who are pilgrims on the earth, and cheers those who hope, because every time we read the Sacred Scriptures we listen to Christ speaking to us, consoling us, and giving us patience . . . "[13]

885   Yours is, therefore, a priestly work par excellence, and must be fired with a zeal which is concerned only with the welfare of souls, their needs, and the dangers which threaten them. It must be a zeal which also embraces the needs and wishes of your world-wide alumni, and continues to give them the guidance, the directives, and the constant refreshment of their learning that will enable them to form properly the modern generation of young priests.

886   In this light, you can easily understand the need, already mentioned above, which exists for absolute *adherence to the sacred deposit of Faith and to the Magisterium of the Church.* The charter of the Biblical Institute entrusts to you the delicate task of promoting sound biblical scholarship "according to the mind of the Catholic Church," that is, "in conformity with norms already established or to be established by this Apostolic See."[14] If this absolute adherence to the teachings of the Church, "the pillar and mainstay of the truth,"[15] is required from all her faithful children, it is all the more im-

perative that those teachings be the guiding light of all who, like you—by the express will of the Apostolic See, and by their own noble vocation—have made the object of their studies the lofty and inscrutable secrets of God contained in the Holy Book. Since you are dealing with sublime realities, it is necessary that those who love truth and do not wish to change it "one jot or one tittle"[16] submit to the leadership of the Church with complete loyalty.

To combine rigorous scholarship with complete submis-   **887** sion to the deposit of Faith and the teachings of the Magisterium of the Church, requires a great deal of acumen and prudence; in fact, it is necessary to establish clearly on the one hand the true significance and the degree of certainty of a scientific conclusion and, on the other hand, the sense and the weight of theological doctrine or of a decision by the Magisterium of the Church. Only serious scholarship and perfect docility toward the "mind of the Church" can help find the right answers to the various questions, and preserve scholars from lamentable errors.

Allow Us, in this connection, to recall the words which We   **888** spoke on the occasion of the recent Roman Synod in Our second address to the clergy: "The grace of God assures personal satisfaction to the well-disposed who are nourished and strengthened by good culture drawn, not from meager rivulets, but from the copious springs of scholarly works, which are produced even in our age, in a spirit of humble and courageous emulation of the great writings of the past by the Fathers, writers, and Doctors of the Church, the teachers of truth for all eternity.

"In his second Epistle, St. Peter sounds a note of caution   **889** about the special care that is necessary in biblical studies: ' . . . to which you do well to attend, as to a lamp shining in a dark place, until the day dawns, and the morning star rises in our hearts. This, then, you must understand first of all, that no prophecy of Scripture is made by private interpretation.' (*2 Peter* 1, 19-20)"[17]

Venerable brethren and beloved sons! Your task is surely   **890** not an easy one, and study alone is not enough. You must pray for the comforting illumination of the Holy Spirit, which "searches all things, even the deep things of God,"[18] and ask for the assistance of His gifts of wisdom, counsel, knowledge, and piety. Let prayer be the nourishment and inspiration of your life of study, according to the warning of St. Augustine: "Let them pray that they may understand. Indeed, in those writings of which they are students they read that 'The Lord grants knowledge, and learning and intelligence come from him.' "[19]

891   We remind you, therefore, of the precious heritage which was left by Pius X: "I leave you the Sacred Heart"; in this meek and humble Heart you will find a safeguard against intellectual arrogance and conceit; in this Heart are contained "all the treasures of wisdom and knowledge."

892   Only thus will you cause the noble mission of the institute to bear abundant fruit. If the institute perseveres in the path of work, humility, filial submission to the Church, and fervent prayer, it will continue to enjoy divine protection in the future.

893   These are the heavenly favors which We wish for you, and entreat from God for you, with Our most ardent supplication. As a pledge of divine favors, and in confirmation of Our benevolence, We are happy to impart to all members of the Biblical Institute—superiors, professors, students, and alumni, — Our Apostolic Blessing, wishing you that "grace be to you, and peace from God our Father and the Lord Jesus Christ."[20]

Monitum of the Holy Office
June 20, 1961

Through praiseworthy enthusiasm for Biblical studies, assertions and opinions are being spread in many quarters, bringing into doubt the genuine historical and objective truth of the Sacred Scriptures, not only of the Old Testament (as Pope Pius XII had already deplored in his encyclical letter *Humani Generis*, cf. *Acta Apostolicae Sedis* XLII, 576), but even of the New, even to the sayings and deeds of Christ Jesus.

Since assertions and opinions of this kind are causing 895
anxiety among both pastors and faithful, the eminent cardinals who are charged with preservation of the doctrine of faith and morals recommended that all of those who deal with the Sacred Scriptures, either in writing or orally, should be warned always to treat such subject-matter with due discretion and reverence and always to have before their eyes the doctrine of the Fathers of the Church and the mind and teaching authority of the Church, lest the consciences of the faithful be disturbed or the truths of the Faith be injured.

N.B. This admonition is published with the approval of 896
the eminent cardinals of the Pontifical Biblical Commission.

Given at Rome by the Sacred Congregation of the Holy 897
Office, June 20, 1961.

Msgr. Sebastiano Masala, *Notary*

Address of Pope John XXIII
to Participants in the Seventeenth Annual Study Week
of the Italian Biblical Association
September 24, 1962

eloved Sons. The seventeenth Biblical Study Week that is opening this morning with the invocation of the Holy Spirit carries before it the lovable name of St. John: apostle, evangelist, prophet; first among the adopted sons of the Mother of God; youngest in age of the Apostles; and the one believed to have lived longer than all the others.

899   We are very happy with the selection you have made: the Gospel, the Epistles, and the Apocalypse of St. John. You know the tenderness and devotion the Pope feels toward this St. John as well as toward the other St. John, the *Praecursor Domini* who was called to prepare a *"plebem perfectam."* Both are august protectors and custodians of the Archbasilica of the Lateran, *omnium ecclesiarum caput et mater*, and inspirations for the name We have chosen for Our service as Pope.

900   This first consideration suffices to indicate the interest We have in your labors and to assure you that We will follow them closely with Our prayers.

901   During these days, the majestic figure of St. John will rise before your eyes. His special merit and claim to honor, as the words of the Sacred Liturgy point out so effectively, is that of being the Apostle of Charity—charity which he drew from the divine font of the Lord, resting his head upon Him in a gesture of trusting abandon: *fluenta Evangelii de ipso sacro dominici pectoris fonte potavit.* This intimate familiarity

with Christ and love for Him is the point of departure for his simple yet heavenly pages, the delight of all souls: *fluenta Evangelii*. This is the distinguishing mark of the Apostle and his greatest claim to glory; and the meek and persuasive tones of his epistles help us to understand how it had sunk in and permeated the ardent nature of this *Son of thunder*,[1] transforming the very innermost fibers of his being.

The multiform riches of this apostle and prophet who set his divining eye on the secrets of God stir up affectionate respect.   902

His own personal testimony of a life devoted completely to the glory of the Word, the divine inspiration for which he was a docile instrument, the majestic Books which he left to the Church as a sacred heritage—these exact an attitude of great humility from not only the professor of scriptural studies and the sensitive, alert scholar, but the fervent Christian as well, when treating and speaking of him.   903

Let us lay stress immediately on the character of scriptural studies and on the aims that should inspire and guide all those who are dedicated to them with love and special competence.   904

Beloved sons, the scripture scholar is not and should not be merely a learned admirer, nor even an eager explorer, of immeasurable treasures. He might reduce himself to this, but by so doing he would greatly limit the field of his endeavors and would not be doing honor to his vocation.   905

You know this already, and you are wary of the dangers of this kind of limitation. You prove this by your dedication in resolutely striving toward your ideal and your noble, energetic adherence to it.   906

The scholar, the student of the Bible, is first of all an ardent and fearless listener to the Divine Message. He knows that it is not a dead letter locked away in archival documents, but rather a living and still intact message that comes from God and is to be welcomed in its entirety with the open, and we might say the impassioned, mind with which it was listened to by the prophets, the apostles, and the countless legions of men who feared God in the Old and the New Testament. In this way the scholar becomes a patient coworker with the Church in the safeguarding, the study and   907

the exact transmission of the genuine revealed thought contained in the sacred pages.

908   So it is easy to understand the Church's anxious attitude
toward scripture studies. While she has serene confidence and
trust in the seriousness of her sons' investigations, she cannot
rest content with simply gathering up the fruits these bear.
Instead, she must guide their steps, just as it is her province
to ratify their conclusions. While encouraging them to advance
along the promising path of present-day developments, she
must nevertheless urge them to prudence and to docile and
unshakeable loyalty to the norms of the supreme Magisterium.

909   Let us return to St. John, beloved son; let us turn back to
him who offers Us these topics for fatherly encouragement
and for confident exhortation.

910   The theme you have chosen—and We repeat it: the Gospel,
the Epistles, the Apocalypse of St. John—is one to which the
concluding words of the Fourth Gospel might well be applied:
*"Sunt autem et alia multa quae fecit Jesus; quae, si scribantur
per singula, nec ipsum arbitror mundum capere posse eos, qui
scribendi sunt, libros."*[2]

911   Hence the learned conferences to be held and the lucid
reports to be made during these days will form only a minute
portion of all that is offered to the mind and heart by John's
writings, as they stimulate prayer and a greater depth of
penetration.

912   We will not pause, then, to draw out specific information
and precepts for you and your pupils from the individual
chapters of this hymn that you intend to raise up to the glory
of the apostle of love. Your pupils will be, in great measure,
the shepherds of tomorrow's souls—and We say this with a
deep sense of responsibility which We would like to pass on
to you.

913   We will rest content with formulating a twofold wish:
1) Above all, may love for the Sacred Texts be spread ever
more widely and may it lead to meditation upon their message. This should be the aim of your studies. Even erudite
research and the new insights into the Sacred Book gained
from the auxiliary sciences find their ultimate justification in

this mission of spreading love for the revealed Word and in leading minds to an understanding of its spiritual and preceptive meanings.

From this point of view, you will find ever new and indispensable help in the works of the Fathers of the Church and the statements of the popes and of the episcopacy throughout the centuries, even though they must be read with an eye toward the new data furnished by textual criticism.   914

Prior to, and above and beyond, any display of erudition must come a hunger and thirst for the Divine Message, because it is life for souls, light unto minds, a life-giving breath. Jesus proclaimed it, and John reported to us the exact text: "*Verba, quae ego locutus sum vobis, spiritus et vita sunt.*"[3]   915

2) The second wish is a hope that the Divine Message will penetrate into the lives of nations, of families, of communities. Is not the *Gospel* perhaps the good news that they are awaiting? Is not it the *epistula Dei ad homines* that ought to free them from too many accretions that are sentimental, or coldly and merely scientific and technical? Is not it the revelation of the "new heavens and new earth"[4] that will attract human hearts as a foretaste of heavenly happiness?   916

The man of today, just as much as the man who read the *Biblia paumerum* on the walls of the churches of old, has a keen desire for the word of God. Man awaits it and listens to it with the same devotion with which the Hebrew people welcomed Esdras' reading of the Sacred Book after the harrowing events accompanying their return from captivity. What tones of anxious emotion are found in the account in the eighth chapter of the Book of Nehemias: 917

"*And Ezra the priest brought the law before the congregation both of men and women, and all that could hear with understanding, upon the first day of the seventh month. And he read therein before the street that was before the water gate from the morning until midday, before the men and the women, and those that could understand; and the ears of all the people were attentive unto the book . . . And Ezra opened the book in the sight of all the people; (for he was above all the people;) and when he opened it, all the people stood up: And Ezra blessed the Lord, the great God. And all the people answered, Amen, Amen, with lifting up their hands: and they bowed their heads, and worshipped the Lord with their faces to the ground. . . . So they read in the book in the law of God distinctly, and gave the sense, and caused them to understand the reading."*[5]

918   What words, beloved sons! You have there everything concerned with the teaching of and devotion to the Divine Book: your priestly mission, which is the most fruitful apostolate of sacred ministry; the duty of being clear and of showing pastoral interest and care: *distincte et aperte ad intelligendum*; the courage and zeal to propose the heavenly doctrine to all, *in conspectu virorum et mulierum et sapientium*; and the generous response of souls to your effort, *aures erectae ad librum.*

919   In this way, the renaissance of Scripture studies announces the glad tidings, and offers souls the constant nourishment of holy teaching.

920   You want to cooperate in this by offering at the same time to the Council, which is almost upon us, an example of shining faith and of high scientific ability and accomplishment that will serve as a prelude for the great ecumenical sessions. These will have for their symbol and inspiration the Sacred Books and the chalice of benediction: the Books and the chalice that We placed on the altar of the Lateran on November 23, 1958, when taking possession of that majestic Seat, as a sign of those pastoral interests and concerns that want to radiate out from the temple to the whole world.

921   Beloved sons. In view of this, We hope that your labors will bear all the fruit that you anticipate. And so that you yourselves may be more intimately transformed into apostles of light and of love, We call down upon you, upon your studies and upon your teaching, the constant assistance of the Divine Paraclete, with the desire that this propitiatory Apostolic Blessing of Ours be a reflection and a pledge of His life-giving splendor.

Instruction of Pontifical Biblical Commission Concerning the Historical Truth of the Gospels
April 21, 1964

Holy Mother the Church, "the pillar and bulwark of truth,"[1] has always used Sacred Scripture in her task of imparting heavenly salvation to men. She has always defended it, too, from every sort of false interpretations. Since there will never be an end to (biblical) problems, the Catholic exegete should never lose heart in explaining the divine word and in solving the difficulties proposed to him. Rather, let him strive earnestly to open up still more the real meaning of the Scriptures. Let him rely firmly not only on his own resources, but above all on the help of God and the light of the Church.

It is a source of great joy that there are found today, to meet the needs of our times, faithful sons of the Church in great numbers who are experts in biblical matters. They are following the exhortations of the Supreme Pontiffs and are dedicating themselves wholeheartedly and untiringly to this serious and arduous task. "Let all the other sons of the Church bear in mind that the efforts of these resolute laborers in the vineyard of the Lord are to be judged not only with equity and justice, but also with the greatest charity,"[2] since even illustrious interpreters, such as Jerome himself, tried at times to explain the more difficult questions with no great success.[3] Care should be had "that the keen strife of debate should never exceed the bounds of mutual charity. Nor should the impression be given in an argument that truths of revelation

923

and divine traditions are being called in question. For unless agreement among minds be safeguarded and principles be carefully respected, great progress in this discipline will never be expected from the diverse pursuits of so many persons."[4]

924   Today more than ever the work of exegetes is needed, because many writings are being spread abroad in which the truth of the deeds and words which are contained in the Gospels is questioned. For this reason the Pontifical Biblical Commission, in pursuit of the task given to it by the Supreme Pontiffs, has considered it proper to set forth and insist upon the following points.

925   1. Let the Catholic exegete, following the guidance of the Church, derive profit from all that earlier interpreters, especially the holy Fathers and Doctors of the Church, have contributed to the understanding of the sacred text. And let him carry on their labors still further. In order to put the abiding truth and authority of the Gospels in their full light, he will accurately adhere to the norms of rational and Catholic hermeneutics. He will diligently employ the new exegetical aids, above all those which the historical method, taken in its widest sense, offers to him—a method which carefully investigates sources and defines their nature and value, and makes use of such helps as textual criticism, literary criticism, and the study of languages. The interpreter will heed the advice of Pius XII of happy memory, who enjoined him "prudently . . . to examine what contribution the manner of expression or the literary genre used by the sacred writer makes to a true and genuine interpretation. And let him be convinced that this part of his task cannot be neglected without serious detriment to Catholic exegesis."[5] By this piece of advice Pius XII of happy memory enunciated a general rule of hermeneutics by which the books of the Old Testament as well as the New must be explained. For in composing them the sacred writers employed the way of thinking and writing which was in vogue among their contemporaries. Finally, the exegete will use all the means available to probe more deeply into the nature of Gospel testimony, into the religious life of the early churches, and into the sense and the value of apostolic tradition.

As occasion warrants, the interpreter may examine what   926
reasonable elements are contained in the "Form-Critical
method" that can be used for a fuller understanding of the
Gospels. But let him be wary, because quite inadmissable
philosophical and theological principles have often come to
be mixed with this method, which not uncommonly have
vitiated the method itself as well as the conclusions in the
literary area. For some proponents of this method have been
led astray by the prejudiced views of rationalism. They refuse
to admit the existence of a supernatural order and the intervention of a personal God in the world through strict revelation, and the possibility and existence of miracles and prophecies. Others begin with a false idea of faith, as if it had nothing to do with historical truth—or rather were incompatible
with it. Others deny the historical value and nature of the
documents of revelation almost a priori. Finally, others make
light of the authority of the apostles as witnesses to Christ,
and of their task and influence in the primitive community,
extolling rather the creative power of that community. All
such views are not only opposed to Catholic doctrine, but are
also devoid of scientific basis and alien to the correct principles of historical method.

2. To judge properly concerning the reliability of what is   927
transmitted in the Gospels, the interpreter should pay diligent
attention to the three stages of tradition by which the doctrine and the life of Jesus have come down to us.

Christ our Lord joined to Himself chosen disciples,[6] who   928
followed him from the beginning,[7] saw His deeds, heard His
words, and in this way were equipped to be witnesses of His
life and doctrine.[8] When the Lord was orally explaining His
doctrine, He followed the modes of reasoning and of exposition which were in vogue at the time. He accommodated
Himself to the mentality of His listeners and saw to it that
what He taught was firmly impressed on the mind and easily
remembered by the disciples. These men understood the
miracles and other events of the life of Jesus correctly, as
deeds performed or designed that men might believe in Christ
through them, and embrace with faith the doctrine of salvation.

929   *The apostles* proclaimed above all the death and resurrection of the Lord, as they bore witness to Jesus.[9] They faithfully explained His life and words,[10] while taking into account in their method of preaching the circumstances in which their listeners found themselves.[11] After Jesus rose from the dead and His divinity was clearly perceived,[12] faith, far from destroying the memory of what had transpired, rather confirmed it, because their faith rested on the things which Jesus did and taught.[13] Nor was He changed into a "mythical" person and His teaching deformed in consequence of the worship which the disciples from that time on paid Jesus as the Lord and the Son of God. On the other hand, there is no reason to deny that the apostles passed on to their listeners what was really said and done by the Lord with that fuller understanding which they enjoyed,[14] having been instructed by the glorious events of the Christ and taught by the light of the Spirit of Truth.[15] So, just as Jesus Himself after His resurrection "interpreted to them"[16] the words of the Old Testament as well as His own,[17] they too interpreted His words and deeds according to the needs of their listeners. "Devoting themselves to the ministry of the word,"[19] they preached and made use of various modes of speaking which were suited to their own purpose and the mentality of their listeners. For they were debtors[19] "to Greeks and barbarians, to the wise and the foolish."[20] But these modes of speaking with which the preachers proclaimed Christ must be distinguished and (properly) assessed: catecheses, stories, testimonia, hymns, doxologies, prayers—and other literary forms of this sort which were in Sacred Scripture and were accustomed to be used by men of that time.

930   This primitive instruction, which was at first passed on by word of mouth and then in writing—for it soon happened that many tried "to compile a narrative of the things"[21] which concerned the Lord Jesus—was committed to writing by the *sacred authors* in four Gospels for the benefit of the churches, with a method suited to the peculiar purpose which each (author) set for himself. From the many things handed down they selected some things, reduced others to a synthesis, (still) others they explicated as they kept in mind the sit-

uation of the churches. With every (possible) means they
sought that their readers might become aware of the reliability[22] of those words by which they had been instructed.
Indeed, from what they had received the sacred writers above
all selected the things which were suited to the various situa-
tions of the faithful and to the purpose which they had in
mind, and adapted their narration of them to the same situa-
tions and purpose. Since the meaning of a statement also
depends on the sequence, the Evangelists, in passing on the
words and deeds of our Saviour, explained these now in one
context, now in another, depending on (their) usefulness to
the readers. Consequently, let the exegete seek out the meaning intended by the Evangelist in narrating a saying or a deed
in a certain way or in placing it in a certain context. For the
truth of the story is not at all affected by the fact that the
Evangelists relate the words and deeds of the Lord in a different order,[23] and express His sayings not literally but
differently, while preserving (their) sense.[24] For, as St.
Augustine says, "It is quite probable that each Evangelist
believed it to have been his duty to recount what he had to in
that order in which it pleased God to suggest it to his memory—in those things at least in which the order, whether it be
this or that, detracts in nothing from the truth and authority
of the Gospel. But why the Holy Spirit, who apportions
individually to each one as He wills,[25] and who therefore undoubtedly also governed and ruled the minds of the holy
(writers) in recalling what they were to write because of the
pre-eminent authority which the books were to enjoy, permitted one to compile his narrative in this way, and another
in that, anyone with pious diligence may seek the reason and
with divine aid will be able to find it."[26]

Unless the exegete pays attention to all these things which
pertain to the origin and composition of the Gospels and
makes proper use of all the laudable achievements of recent
research, he will not fulfil his task of probing into what the
sacred writers intended and what they really said. From the
results of the new investigations it is apparent that the doctrine and the life of Jesus were not simply reported for the
sole purpose of being remembered, but were "preached" so

931

as to offer the Church a basis of faith and of morals. The interpreter (then), by tirelessly scrutinizing the testimony of the Evangelists, will be able to illustrate more profoundly the perennial theological value of the Gospels and bring out clearly how necessary and important the Church's interpretation is.

932   There are still many things, and of the greatest importance, in the discussion and explanation of which the Catholic exegete can and must freely exercise his skill and genius so that each may contribute his part to the advantage of all, to the continued progress of sacred doctrine, to the preparation and further support of the judgment to be exercised by the ecclesiastical magisterium, and to the defense and honor of the Church.[27] But let him always be disposed to obey the magisterium of the Church, and not forget that the apostles, filled with the Holy Spirit, preached the good news, and that the Gospels were written under the inspiration of the Holy Spirit, who preserved their authors from all error. "Now we have not learned of the plan of our salvation from any others than those through whom the Gospel has come to us. Indeed, what they once preached they later passed on to us in the Scriptures by the will of God, as the ground and pillar of our faith. It is not right to say that they preached before they had acquired perfect knowledge, as some would venture to say who boast of being correctors of the apostles. In fact, after our Lord rose from the dead and they were invested with power from on high, as the Holy Spirit came down upon them, they were filled with all (His gifts) and had perfect knowledge. They went forth to the ends of the earth, one and all with God's Gospel, announcing the news of God's bounty to us and proclaiming heavenly peace to men."[28]

933   3. Those whose *task it is to teach in seminaries and similar institutions* should have it as their "prime concern that . . . Holy Scripture be so taught as both the dignity of the discipline and the needs of the times require."[29] Let the teachers above all explain its theological teaching, so that the Sacred Scriptures "may become for the future priests of the Church both a pure and never-failing source for their own spiritual life, as well as food and strength for the sacred task of preach-

ing which they are about to undertake."[30] When they practice
the art of criticism, especially so-called literary criticism, let
them not pursue it as an end in itself, but that through it
they might more plainly perceive the sense intended by God
through the sacred writer. Let them not stop, therefore, half-
way, content only with their literary discoveries, but show in
addition how these things really contribute to a clearer
understanding of revealed doctrine, or if it be the case, to the
refutation of errors. Instructors who follow these norms will
enable their students to find in Sacred Scripture that which
can "raise the minds to God, nourish the soul, and further
the interior life."[31]

4. Those *who instruct the Christian people in sacred ser-*   934
mons have need of great prudence. Let them above all pass
on doctrine, mindful of St. Paul's warning: "Look to yourself
and your teaching; hold on to that. For by so doing you will
save both yourself and those who listen to you."[32] They are
to refrain entirely from proposing vain or insufficiently
established novelties. As for new opinions already solidly
established, they may explain them, if need be, but with
caution and due care for their listeners. When they narrate
biblical events, let them not add imaginative details which are
not consonant with the truth.

This virtue of prudence should be cherished especially *by*   935
those who publish for the faithful. Let them carefully bring
forth the heavenly riches of the divine word "that the faithful . . . may be moved and inflamed rightly to conform their
lives (to them)."[33] They should consider it a sacred duty
never to depart in the slightest degree from the common
doctrine and tradition of the Church. They should indeed
exploit all the real advances of biblical science which the
diligence of recent (students) has produced. But they are to
avoid entirely the rash remarks of innovators.[34] They are
strictly forbidden to disseminate, led on by some pernicious
itch for newness, any trial solutions for difficulties without a
prudent selection and serious discrimination, for thus they
perturb the faith of many.

This Pontifical Biblical Commission has already considered   936
it proper to recall that books and articles in magazines and

newspapers on biblical subjects are subject to the authority and jurisdiction of ordinaries, since they treat of religious matters and pertain to the religious instruction of the faithful.[35] Ordinaries are therefore requested to keep watch with great care over popular writings of this sort.

937   5. Those who are in charge of biblical associations are to comply faithfully with the norms laid down by the Pontifical Biblical Commission.[36]

938   If all these things are observed, the study of the Sacred Scriptures will contribute to the benefit of the faithful. Even in our time everyone realizes the wisdom of what St. Paul wrote: The Sacred Writings "can instruct (us) for salvation through faith in Christ Jesus. All Scripture is divinely inspired and profitable for teaching, for reproof, for correction, and for training in uprightness, so that the man of God may be perfect, equipped for every good work."[37]

939   The Holy Father, Pope Paul VI, at the audience graciously granted to the undersigned secretary on April 21, 1964, approved this Instruction and ordered the publication of it.

Benjamin N. Wambacq, O. Praem.
Secretary of the Commission

Address of Pope Paul VI
to Participants in the Eighteenth
Italian Biblical Week
September 26, 1964

We are happy to receive those taking part in the Eighteenth Italian Biblical Week: professors of Sacred Scripture, devotees of biblical studies, those furthering knowledge of the Sacred Book and devotion to it.

We are happy about the common aim that unites you in striving for a deeper understanding of the Bible. We are happy about the methods that guide your activity on the scientific and more popular levels. We are equally happy about the number of members in your association and the number of those connected with it, since this is clear proof to Us of the organizational efforts you are making to carry out the aims of your society and to have it spread systematically over a wide area; and We are glad to congratulate you on the way in which this Week has developed, for it has been filled with study, with discussions, and with signs of the filial devotion that you wanted to show Us through your visit and through the tribute of your abundant and valuable publications. But above all We are happy about the spirit with which you are devoting yourselves to an activity that is so praiseworthy and so difficult, desirous as you are to perfect the science of the Sacred Books, not in order to destroy their authority but rather to seek out the truth of the word of God in them; and not just with the resources of human erudition, but also with the help of the magisterium of the Church, the guardian and interpreter of divine revelation.

942   In this way, your activity is clearly linked with the spiritual movement that is stirring in the Catholic Church, reviving not a reverence for Sacred Scripture, since this has never faded, but rather an interest in exploring all the aspects of the Bible and in bringing it into a closer practical relationship with the acts of religious life. Thus we would draw upon it not just as a source and norm of faith but also as something nurturing the inner strength that springs up from a correct hearing of the divine messages of the holy Book. Study and piety are, at one and the same time, the motive and the goal of this devotion to Sacred Scripture. We are glad to praise it and encourage it, since We know very well that it is enlightened and guided by those superior and loving criteria that the Church professes with regard to the understanding, the explanation and the assimilation of the texts of Scripture.

943   Since you are teachers and scholars, you know these criteria very well; and there is no need for Us to remind you of them in this fleeting moment. Let it suffice for Us to remind you that papal teachings—contained especially in two great documents, the encyclicals *Providentissimus Deus* of Leo XIII and *Divino afflante Spiritu* of Pius XII—are still valid and still deserve to be studied and observed by every devotee of the scriptural sciences. We would also cite two other recent statements from the papal magisterium dealing with this vast and sacred field. In the first of these, the Constitution *De Sacra Liturgia* of the Second Ecumenical Council of the Vatican, the reading, the explanation and, We might say, the celebration of the Word of God contained in Sacred Scripture, are inculcated once again and practically exalted. The second, last May's Instruction of the Pontifical Biblical Commission,[1] while paying honor to the efforts of modern exegesis in behalf of an ever better understanding and appreciation of the sacred texts, also points out the dangers and the limits involved, and defends the historical truth of the holy Gospels in particular, with a calm and vigorous clarity.

944   No other obligation remains to Us on this occasion but that of lending support to the efforts and aims that you exemplify for us in such a noble and comforting way. We have in mind a triple recommendation.

First of all, keep up your devotion to the study and the   945
use of Sacred Scripture, taking great care to travel along the
good road which is the one marked out by holy Church. We
all know what new and immense difficulties beset this
journey, and how they are all the more serious and dangerous
the more intimately they are bound up with the development
of the biblical studies which are tempted from time to time
to take the immense and mysterious field of biblical truth
and confine it within the perimeter of human and personal
theory, to the point of depriving it of its sacred character and
of its transcendent values. Unhappily, this results in nullify-
ing the reality and the power of that Sacred Scripture which,
the studies claimed, alone and by itself constitutes the substance of religion. And thus testimony is unintentionally
given to the need of a living magisterium to safeguard and
clarify the genuine meaning of the divine Book.

The doctrinal orthodoxy that the Church recommends and   946
exhibits amid the dangerous and attractive explorations of
modern exegesis does not prevent study, nor does it obscure
one's view in the most arduous and complex biblical researches, but it does permit the faithful exegete to know
everything and lose nothing—to know whatever the old and
the new sciences can reasonably offer us in the field of
scripture, and lose nothing that the wisdom of faith sees as
contained therein.

Here, now, is Our second recommendation—one that We   947
see already being put into practice in your intelligent labors:
may your labor be sustained by a profound religious sense.
May your awareness of the divine Presence in the pages you
are studying never desert you. May a secret internal dialogue
accompany your study and reading of scripture.

The Bible is the Word of God in many different ways. An   948
attitude of joyful piety and of respectful veneration should
never be lacking in anyone who prepares to listen to it, to
explore it, to explain it. This attitude poses no obstacle for
human currents of thought and of language; it even makes
them more free and confident, and, when they grow weary,
helps them with a new impulse of a living nature, such as
prayer can give. Remember St. Augustine's advice to the

students of the *"venerabilium Literarum"*[1] : *"Orent ut intelligant. In eis quippe litteris, quarum studiosi sunt, legunt quoniam Dominus dat sapientiam, et a facie Ejus scientia et intellectus* (Prov. 2, 9); *a quo et ipsum studium, si pietate praeditum est, acceperunt."*[2]

949   And, finally, work to spread the love, the study, the meditation, the observance of the divine Word as Sacred Scripture preserves it for us and offers it to us. We all know the cautions that have to be used when preaching the Bible, especially among the people, who rarely are provided beforehand with the many complementary notions needed for an exact and beneficial understanding of the sacred text. It will be good for these cautions to find new and timely practical expressions that are all the more careful the wider the diffusion of the Bible and the closer We want to bring the reading of it to the inner and personal piety of the faithful. But this ought not stand in the way of the kind of diffusion that the higher level of general education makes more desirable and more possible, and that spiritual renewal, which the Church wants to promote at the present time by bringing souls back to the fonts of religious life, shows to be just as urgent as it is beneficial.

950   May these Our words of advice and encouragement tell you just how much We appreciate your activity and how glad We are to wish it all growth and success. And may Our Apostolic Blessing be a sign of this.

Vatican II
DEI VERBUM
Dogmatic Constitution on Divine Revelation
November 18, 1965

Prologue

Hearing the Word of God with reverence, and proclaiming it with faith, the sacred Synod assents to the words of St. John, who says: "We proclaim to you the eternal life which was with the Father and was made manifest to us—that which we have seen and heard we proclaim also to you, so that you may have fellowship with us; and our fellowship is with the Father and with his Son Jesus Christ." (1 *Jn.* 1:2-3). Following, then, in the steps of the Councils of Trent and Vatican I, this Synod wishes to set forth the true doctrine on divine Revelation and its transmission. For it wants the whole world to hear the summons to salvation, so that through hearing it may believe, through belief it may hope, through hope it may come to love.[1]

Chapter I

Divine Revelation Itself

2. It pleased God, in his goodness and wisdom, to reveal himself and to make known the mystery of his will (cf. *Eph.* 1:9). His will was that men should have access to the Father, through Christ, the Word made flesh, in the Holy Spirit, and thus become sharers in the divine nature (cf. *Eph.* 2:18; 2

Pet. 1:4). By this revelation, then, the invisible God (cf. *Col.* 1:15; 1 *Tim.* 1:17), from the fullness of his love, addresses men as his friends (cf. *Ex.* 33:11; *Jn.* 15; 14-15), and moves among them (cf. *Bar.* 3:38), in order to invite and receive them into his own company. This economy of Revelation is realized by deeds and words, which are intrinsically bound up with each other. As a result, the works performed by God in the history of salvation show forth and bear out the doctrine and realities signified by the words; the words, for their part, proclaim the works, and bring to light the mystery they contain. The most intimate truth which this revelation gives us about God and the salavation of man shines forth in Christ, who is himself both the mediator and the sum total of Revelation.[2]

953   3. God, who creates and conserves all things by his Word, (cf. *Jn.* 1:3), provides men with constant evidence of himself in created realities (cf. *Rom.* 1:19-20). And furthermore, wishing to open up the way to heavenly salvation, he manifested himself to our first parents from the very beginning. After the fall, he buoyed them up with the hope of salvation, by promising redemption (cf. *Gen.* 3:15); and he has never ceased to take care of the human race. For he wishes to give eternal life to all those who seek salvation by patience in well-doing (cf. *Rom.* 2:6-7). In his own time God called Abraham, and made him into a great nation (cf. *Gen.* 12:2). After the era of the patriarchs, he taught this nation, by Moses and the prophets, to recognize him as the only living and true God, as a provident Father and just judge. He taught them, too, to look for the promised Saviour. And so, throughout the ages, he prepared the way for the Gospel.

954   4. After God had spoken many times and in various ways through the prophets, "in these last days he has spoken to us by a Son" (*Heb.* 1:1-2). For he sent his Son, the eternal Word who enlightens all men, to dwell among men and to tell them about the inner life of God. Hence, Jesus Christ, sent as "a man among men,"[3] "speaks the words of God" (*Jn.* 3:34), and accomplishes the saving work which the Father gave him to do (cf. *Jn.* 5:36; 17:4). As a result, he himself—to see whom is to see the Father (cf. *Jn.* 14:9)—completed and

perfected Revelation and confirmed it with divine guarantees. He did this by the total fact of his presence and self-manifestation—by words and works, signs and miracles, but above all by his death and glorious resurrection from the dead, and finally by sending the Spirit of truth. He revealed that God was with us, to deliver us from the darkness of sin and death, and to raise us up to eternal life.

The Christian economy, therefore, since it is the new and definite covenant, will never pass away; and no new public revelation is to be expected before the glorious manifestation of our Lord, Jesus Christ (cf. 1 *Tim.* 6:14 and *Tit.* 2:13). **955**

5. "The obedience of faith" (*Rom.* 16:26; cf. *Rom.* 1:5; 2 *Cor.* 10:5-6) must be given to God as he reveals himself. By faith man freely commits his entire self to God, making "the full submission of his intellect and will to God who reveals,"[4] and willingly assenting to the Revelation given by him. Before this faith can be exercised, man must have the grace of God to move and assist him; he must have the interior helps of the Holy Spirit, who moves the heart and converts it to God, who opens the eyes of the mind and "makes it easy for all to accept and believe the truth."[5] The same Holy Spirit constantly perfects faith by his gifts, so that Revelation may be more and more profoundly understood. **956**

6. By divine Revelation God wished to manifest and communicate both himself and the eternal decrees of his will concerning the salvation of mankind. He wished, in other words. "to share with us divine benefits which entirely surpass the powers of the human mind to understand."[6] **957**

The sacred Synod professes that "God, the first principle and last end of all things, can be known with certainty from the created world, by the natural light of human reason' (cf. *Rom.* 1:20). It teaches that it is to his Revelation that we must attribute the fact "that those things, which in themselves are not beyond the grasp of human reason, can, in the present condition of the human race, be known by all men with ease, with firm certainty, and without the contamination of error."[7] **958**

Chapter II

The Transmission of Divine Revelation

959   7. God graciously arranged that the things he had once revealed for the salvation of all peoples should remain in their entirety, throughout the ages, and be transmitted to all generations. Therefore, Christ the Lord, in whom the entire Revelation of the most high God is summed up (cf. *Cor.* 1:20; 3:16-4, 6) commanded the apostles to preach the Gospel, which had been promised beforehand by the prophets, and which he fulfilled in his own person and promulgated with his own lips. In preaching the Gospel they were to communicate the gifts of God to all men. This Gospel was to be the source of all saving truth and moral discipline.[8] This was faithfully done: it was done by the apostles who handed on, by the spoken word of their preaching, by the example they gave, by the institutions they established, what they themselves had received—whether from the lips of Christ, from his way of life and his works, or whether they had learned it at the prompting of the Holy Spirit; it was done by those apostles who, under the inspiration of the same Holy Spirit, committed the message of salvation to writing.[9]

960   In order that the full and living Gospel might always be preserved in the Church the apostles left bishops as their successors. They gave them "their own position of teaching authority."[10] This sacred Tradition, then, and the sacred Scripture of both Testaments, are like a mirror, in which the Church, during its pilgrim journey here on earth, contemplates God, from whom she receives everything, until such time as she is brought to see him face to face as he really is (cf. *Jn.* 3:2).

961   8. Thus, the apostolic preaching, which is expressed in a special way in the inspired books, was to be preserved in a continuous line of succession until the end of time. Hence the apostles, in handing on what they themselves had received, warn the faithful to maintain the traditions which they

had learned either by word of mouth or by letter (cf. 2 *Th.* 2:15); and they warn them to fight hard for the faith that had been handed on to them once and for all (cf. *Jude* 3).[11] What was handed on by the apostles comprises everything that serves to make the People of God live their lives in holiness and increase their faith. In this way the Church, in her doctrine, life and worship, perpetuates and transmits to every generation all that she herself is, all that she believes.

The Tradition that comes from the apostles makes progress in the Church, with the help of the Holy Spirit.[12] There is a growth in insight into the realities and words that are being passed on. This comes about in various ways. It comes through the contemplation and study of believers who ponder these things in their hearts (cf. *Lk.* 2:19 and 51). It comes from the intimate sense of spiritual realities which they experience. And it comes from the preaching of those who have received, along with their right of succession in the episcopate, the sure charism of truth. Thus, as the centuries go by, the Church is always advancing towards the plenitude of divine truth, until eventually the words of God are fulfilled in her. 962

The sayings of the Holy Fathers are a witness to the life-giving presence of this Tradition, showing how its riches are poured out in the practice and life of the Church, in her belief and her prayer. By means of the same Tradition the full canon of the sacred books is known to the Church and the holy Scriptures themselves are more thoroughly understood and constantly actualized in the Church. Thus God, who spoke in the past, continues to converse with the spouse of his beloved Son. And the Holy Spirit, through whom the living voice of the Gospel rings out in the Church—and through her in the world—leads believers to the full truth, and makes the Word of Christ dwell in them in all its richness (cf. *Col.* 3:16). 963

9. Sacred Tradition and sacred Scripture, then, are bound closely together, and communicate one with the other. For both of them, flowing out from the same divine well-spring, come together in some fashion to form one thing, and move towards the same goal. Sacred scripture is the speech of God as it is put down in writing under the breath of the Holy Spirit. 964

And Tradition transmits in its entirety the Word of God which has been entrusted to the apostles by Christ the Lord and the Holy Spirit. It transmits it to the successors of the apostles so that, enlightened by the Spirit of truth, they may faithfully preserve, expound and spread it abroad by their preaching. Thus it comes about that the Church does not draw her certainty about all revealed truths from the holy Scriptures alone. Hence, both Scripture and Tradition must be accepted and honored with equal feelings of devotion and reverence.[13]

965   10. Sacred Tradition and sacred Scripture make up a single sacred deposit of the Word of God, which is entrusted to the Church. By adhering to it the entire holy people, united to its pastors, remains always faithful to the teaching of the apostles, to the brotherhood, to the breaking of bread and the prayers (cf. *Acts* 2:42 Greek). So, in maintaining, practicing and professing the faith that has been handed on there should be a remarkable harmony between the bishops and the faithful.[14]

966   But the task of giving an authentic interpretation of the Word of God, whether in its written form or in the form of Tradition,[15] has been entrusted to the living teaching office of the Church alone.[16] Its authority in this matter is exercised in the name of Jesus Christ. Yet this Magisterium is not superior to the Word of God, but is its servant. It teaches only what has been handed on to it. At the divine command and with the help of the Holy Spirit, it listens to this devotedly, guards it with dedication and expounds it faithfully. All that it proposes for belief as being divinely revealed is drawn from this single deposit of faith.

967   It is clear, therefore, that, in the supremely wise arrangement of God, sacred Tradition, sacred Scripture and the Magisterium of the Church are so connected and associated that one of them cannot stand without the others. Working together, each in its own way under the action of the one Holy Spirit, they all contribute effectively to the salvation of souls.

Chapter II

Sacred Scripture: Its Divine Inspiration and Its Interpretation

11. The divinely revealed realities, which are contained and presented in the text of sacred Scripture, have been written down under the inspiration of the Holy Spirit. For Holy Mother Church relying on the faith of the apostolic age, accepts as sacred and canonical the books of the Old and the New Testaments, whole and entire, with all their parts, on the grounds that, written under the inspiration of the Holy Spirit (cf. *Jn.* 20:31; 2 *Tim.* 3:16; 2 *Pet.* 1:19-21; 3:15-16), they have God as their author, and have been handed on as such to the Church herself.[17] To compose the sacred books, God chose certain men who, all the while he employed them in this task, made full use of their powers and faculties[18] so that, though he acted in them and by them,[19] it was as true authors that they consigned to writing whatever he wanted written, and no more.[20]   968

Since, therefore, all that the inspired authors, or sacred writers, affirm should be regarded as affirmed by the Holy Spirit, we must acknowledge that the books of Scripture, firmly, faithfully and without error, teach that truth which God, for the sake of our salvation, wished to see confided to the sacred Scriptures.[21] Thus "all Scripture is inspired by God, and profitable for teaching, for reproof, for correction and for training in righteousness, so that the man of God may be complete, equipped for every good work" (2 *Tim.* 3:16-17, Gk. text).   969

12. Seeing that, in sacred Scripture, God speaks through men in human fashion,[22] it follows that the interpreter of sacred Scriptures, if he is to ascertain what God has wished to communicate to us, should carefully search out the meaning which the sacred writers really had in mind, that meaning which God had thought well to manifest through the medium of their words.   970

971   In determining the intention of the sacred writers, attention must be paid, *inter alia*, to "literary forms for the fact is that truth is differently presented and expressed in the various types of historical writing, in prophetical and poetical texts," and in other forms of literary expression. Hence the exegete must look for that meaning which the sacred writer, in a determined situation and given the circumstances of his time and culture, intended to express and did in fact express, through the medium of a contemporary literary form.[23]

Rightly to understand what the sacred author wanted to affirm in his work, due attention must be paid both to the customary and characteristic patterns of perception, speech and narrative which prevailed at the age of the sacred writer, and to the conventions which the people of his time followed in their dealings with one another.[24]

972   But since sacred Scripture must be read and interpreted with its divine authorship in mind,[25] no less attention must be devoted to the content and unity of the whole of Scripture, taking into account the Tradition of the entire Church and the analogy of faith, if we are to derive their true meaning from the sacred texts. It is the task of exegetes to work, according to these rules, towards a better understanding and explanation of the meaning of sacred Scripture in order that their research may help the Church to form a firmer judgment. For, of course, all that has been said about the manner of interpreting Scripture is ultimately subject to the judgment of the Church which exercises the divinely conferred commission and ministry of watching over and interpreting the Word of God.[26]

973   13. Hence, in sacred Scripture, without prejudice to God's truth and holiness, the marvellous "condescension" of eternal wisdom is plain to be seen "that we may come to know the ineffable loving-kindness of God and see for ourselves how far he has gone in adapting his language with thoughtful concern for our nature."[27] Indeed the words of God, expressed in the words of men, are in every way like human language, just as the Word of the eternal Father, when he took on himself the flesh of human weakness, became like men.

Chapter IV

The Old Testament

14. God, with loving concern contemplating, and making 974
preparation for, the salvation of the whole human race, in a
singular undertaking chose for himself a people to whom he
would entrust his promises. By his covenant with Abraham
(cf. *Gen.* 15:18) and through Moses, with the race of Israel
(cf. *Ex.* 24:8), he did acquire a people for himself, and to
them he revealed himself in words and deeds as the one, true,
living God, so that Israel might experience the ways of God
with men. Moreover, by listening to the voice of God speaking
to them through the prophets, they had daily to understand
his ways more fully and more clearly, and make them more
widely known among the nations (cf. *Ps.* 21:28-29; 95:1-3;
Is. 2:1-4; *Jer.* 3:17). Now the economy of salvation, foretold,
recounted and explained by the sacred authors, appears as
the true Word of God in the books of the Old Testament,
that is why these books, divinely inspired, preserve a lasting
value: "For whatever was written in former days was written
for our instruction, that by steadfastness and the encouragement of the Scriptures we might have hope" (*Rom.* 15:4).

15. The economy of the Old Testament was deliberately 975
so orientated that it should prepare for and declare in prophecy the coming of Christ, redeemer of all men, and of the
messianic kingdom (cf. *Lk.* 24:44; *Jn.* 5:39; 1 *Pet.* 1:10), and
should indicate it by means of different types (cf. 1 *Cor.* 10:
11). For in the context of the human situation before the era
of salvation established by Christ, the books of the Old Testament provide an understanding of God and man and make
clear to all men how a just and merciful God deals with mankind. These books, even though they contain matters imperfect and provisional, nevertheless show us authentic divine
teaching.[28] Christians should accept with veneration these
writings which give expression to a lively sense of God, which

are a storehouse of sublime teaching on God and of sound wisdom on human life, as well as a wonderful treasury of prayers; in them, too, the mystery of our salvation is present in a hidden way.

976   16. God, the inspirer and author of the books of both Testaments, in his wisdom has so brought it about that the New should be hidden in the Old and that the Old should be made manifest in the New.[29] For, although Christ founded the New Covenant in his blood (cf. *Lk.* 22:20; 1 *Cor.* 11:25), still the books of the Old Testament, all of them caught up into the Gospel message,[30] attain and show forth their full meaning in the New Testament (cf. *Mt.* 5:17; *Lk.* 24:27; *Rom.* 16:25-26; 2 *Cor.* 3:14-16) and, in their turn, shed light on it and explain it.

Chapter V

The New Testament

977   17. The Word of God, which is the power of God for salvation to everyone who has faith (cf. *Rom.* 1:16), is set forth and displays its power in a most wonderful way in the writings of the New Testament. For when the time had fully come (cf. *Gal.* 4:4), the Word became flesh and dwelt among us full of grace and truth (cf. *Jn.* 1:14). Christ established on earth the kingdom of God, revealed his Father and himself by deeds and words; and by his death, resurrection and glorious ascension, as well as by sending the Holy Spirit, completed his work. Lifted up from the earth he draws all men to himself (cf. *Jn.* 10:32, Gk. text), for he alone has the words of eternal life (cf. *Jn.* 6:68). This mystery was not made known to other generations as it has now been revealed to his holy apostles and prophets by the Holy Spirit (cf. *Eph.* 3:4-6, Gk. text), that they might preach the Gospel, stir up faith in Jesus Christ and the Lord, and bring together the Church. The writings of the New Testament stand as a perpetual and divine witness to these realities.

978   18. It is common knowledge that among all the inspired writings, even among those of the New Testament, the Gos-

pels have a special place, and rightly so, because they are our principal source for the life and teaching of the Incarnate Word, our Saviour.

The Church has always and everywhere maintained, and   979
continues to maintain, the apostolic origin of the four Gospels. The apostles preached, as Christ had charged them to do, and then, under the inspiration of the Holy Spirit, they and others of the apostolic age handed on to us in writing the same message they had preached, the foundation of our faith; the fourfold Gospel, according to Matthew, Mark, Luke and John.[31]

19. Holy Mother Church has firmly and with absolute   980
constancy maintained and continues to maintain, that the four Gospels just named, whose historicity she unhesitatingly affirms, faithfully hand on what Jesus, the Son of God, while he lived among men, really did and taught for their eternal salvation, until the day when he was taken up (cf. *Acts* 1:1-2). For, after the ascension of the Lord, the apostles handed on to their hearers what he had said and done, but with that fuller understanding which they, instructed by the glorious events of Christ and enlightened by the Spirit of truth,[32] now enjoyed.[33] The sacred authors, in writing the four Gospels, selected certain of the many elements which had been handed on, either orally or already in written form, others they synthesized or explained with an eye to the situation of the churches, the while sustaining the form of preaching, but always in such a fashion that they have told us the honest truth about Jesus.[34] Whether they relied on their own memory and recollections or on the testimony of those who "from the beginning were eyewitnesses and ministers of the Word," their purpose in writing was that we might know the "truth" concerning the things of which we have been informed (cf. *Lk.* 1:2-4).

20. Besides the four Gospels, the New Testament also con-   981
tains the Epistles of St. Paul and other apostolic writings composed under the inspiration of the Holy Spirit. In accordance with the wise design of God these writings firmly establish those matters which concern Christ the Lord, formulate more and more precisely his authentic teaching, preach

the saving power of Christ's divine work and foretell its glorious consummation.

982   For the Lord Jesus was with his apostles as he had promised (cf. *Mt.* 28:20) and he had sent to them the Spirit, the Counsellor, who would guide them into all the truth (cf. *Jn.* 16:13).

Chapter VI

Sacred Scripture in the Life of the Church

983   21. The Church has always venerated the divine Scriptures as she venerated the Body of the Lord, in so far as she never ceases, particularly in the sacred liturgy, to partake of the bread of life and to offer it to the faithful from the one table of the Word of God and the Body of Christ. She has always regarded, and continues to regard the Scriptures, taken together with sacred Tradition, as the supreme rule of her faith. For, since they are inspired by God and committed to writing once and for all time, they present God's own Word in an unalterable form, and they make the voice of the Holy Spirit sound again and again in the words of the prophets and apostles. It follows that all the preaching of the Church, as indeed the entire Christian religion, should be nourished and ruled by sacred Scripture. In the sacred books the Father who is in heaven comes lovingly to meet his children, and talks with them. And such is the force and power of the Word of God that it can serve the Church as her support and vigor, and the children of the Church as strength for their faith, food for the soul, and a pure and lasting fount of spiritual life. Scripture verifies in the most perfect way the words: "The Word of God is living and active" (*Heb.* 4:12), and "is able to build you up and to give you the inheritance among all those who are sanctified"(*Acts* 20:32; cf. 1 *Th.* 2:13).

984   22. Access to sacred Scripture ought to be open wide to the Christian faithful. For this reason the Church, from the very beginning, made her own the ancient translation of the Old Testament called the Septuagint; she honors also the other Eastern translations, and the Latin translation, espe-

cially that which is called the Vulgate. But since the Word of God must be readily available at all times, the Church, with motherly concern, sees to it that suitable and correct translations are made into various languages, especially from the original texts of the sacred books. If it should happen that, when the opportunity presents itself and the authorities of the Church agree, these translations are made in a joint effort with the separated brethren, they may be used by all Christians.

23. The spouse of the incarnate Word, which is the Church,   985 is taught by the Holy Spirit. She strives to reach day by day a more profound understanding of the sacred Scriptures, in order to provide her children with food from the divine words. For this reason also she duly fosters the study of the Fathers, both Eastern and Western, and of the sacred liturgies. Catholic exegetes and other workers in the field of sacred theology should zealously combine their efforts. Under the watchful eye of the sacred Magisterium, and using appropriate techniques they should together set about examining and explaining the sacred texts in such a way that as many as possible of those who are ministers of the divine Word may be able to distribute fruitfully the nourishment of the Scriptures of the People of God. This nourishment enlightens the mind, strengthens the will and fires the hearts of men with the love of God.[35] The sacred Synod encourages those sons of the Church who are engaged in biblical studies constantly to renew their efforts, in order to carry on the work they have so happily begun, with complete dedication and in accordance with the mind of the Church.[36]

24. Sacred theology relies on the written Word of God,   986 taken together with sacred Tradition, as on a permanent foundation. By this Word it is most firmly strengthened and constantly rejuvenated, as it searches out, under the light of faith, the full truth stored up in the mystery of Christ. Therefore, the "study of the sacred page" should be the very soul of sacred theology.[37] The ministry of the Word, too—pastoral preaching, catechetics and all forms of Christian instruction, among which the liturgical homily should hold pride of place—

is healthily nourished and thrives in holiness through the Word of Scripture.

987   25. Therefore, all clerics, particularly priests of Christ and others who, as deacons or catechists, are officially engaged in the ministry of the Word, should immerse themselves in the Scriptures by constant sacred reading and diligent study. For it must not happen that anyone becomes "an empty preacher of the Word of God to others, not being a hearer of the Word in his own heart,"[38] when he ought to be sharing the boundless riches of the divine Word with the faithful committed to his care, especially in the sacred liturgy. Likewise, the sacred Synod forcefully and specifically exhorts all the Christian faithful, especially those who live the religious life, to learn "the suprassing knowledge of Jesus Christ" (*Phil.* 3:8) by frequent reading of the divine Scriptures. "Ignorance of the Scriptures is ignorance of Christ."[39] Therefore, let them go gladly to the sacred text itself, whether in the sacred liturgy, which is full of the dvine words, or in devout reading, or in such suitable exercises and various other helps which, with the approval and guidance of the pastors of the Church, are happily spreading everywhere in our day. Let them remember, however, that prayer should accompany the reading of sacred . Scripture, so that a dialogue takes place between God and man. For, "we speak to him when we pray; we listen to him when we read the divine oracles."[40]

988   It is for the bishops, "with whom the apostolic doctrine resides"[41] suitably to instruct the faithful entrusted to them in the correct use of the divine books, especially of the New Testament, and in particular of the Gospels. They do this by giving them translations of the sacred texts which are equipped with necessary and really adequate explanations. Thus the children of the Church can familiarize themselves safely and profitably with the sacred Scriptures, and become steeped in their spirit.

989   Moreover, editions of sacred Scripture, provided with suitable notes, should be prepared for the use of even non-Christians, and adapted to their circumstances. These should be prudently circulated, either by pastors of souls, or by Christians of any rank.

26. So may it come that, by the reading and study of the   990
sacred books "the Word of God may speed on and triumph"
(2 *Th.* 3:1) and the treasure of Revelation entrusted to the
Church may more and more fill the hearts of men. Just as
from constant attendance at the eucharistic mystery the life
of the Church draws increase, so a new impulse of spiritual
life may be expected from increased veneration of the Word
of God, which "stands forever" (*Is.* 40:8; cf. 1 *Pet.* 1:23-25).

Address of Pope Paul VI
to Old Testament Experts
April 19, 1968

We thank your eloquent spokesman, the very worthy Father R.A.F. MacKenzie, rector of Our Biblical Institute, and We greet with joy, sirs, an assembly of specialists so distinguished and competent in biblical studies as you are. After having held its congress in different countries of Western Europe, the International Organization for the Study of the Old Testament this time chose the city of Rome, whose immense religious, historical and artistic heritage cannot fail to lend a notable increase of interest to your learned communications. We bid you welcome. Allow Us to receive you here in the words which Our far-distant predecessor St. Damasus addressed to the great specialist of biblical studies of his time, St. Jerome: "I do not think," he wrote to him, "that there can be a more worthy topic for conversation between us than the Holy Scriptures."[1]

992   The Scriptures which are the direct object of your study are those of the Old Testament. The great interest of your congress, it seems to Us, is precisely the choice of a sphere of investigation wherein Christian theologians, both Catholic and Protestant, as well as scholars of the Jewish religion, can meet and work together. The Old Testament is our common treasure. All three families—Jewish, Protestant and Catholic—hold it in equal esteem. They can study and venerate these holy books together. We can go even further: they can pray from the same texts. What prayer is more religious, more

universal by its object, and more moving in its accents than the Psalms? Your initiative in embarking upon this study of the Scriptures in common is truly a happy one. Your previous congresses have shown how timely this has been. Here we have a really genuine and fruitful form of ecumenical endeavor.

The progress of Old Testament studies has been remarkable   993 in these past years. As far as the Catholic Church is concerned, Our predecessor Pius XII, as you know, had opened more widely the way for research by his encyclical letter *Divino Afflante Spiritu* of September 30, 1943, in which he encouraged the use of well-founded and critical methods which are suitable for explaining the sacred texts. It is your honor that you dedicate yourselves in a professional and scientific way to employ all the means given you by modern technology, in the literary, historical and archeological fields, and to use them in order to increase our knowledge of the Old Testament. We cannot but rejoice to learn that a number of scholars all over the world are engaged in this study.

Our world, as has been noted many times, is troubled   994 by a very strong tendency toward "desacralizaion," toward "secularism." The problem of the presence and action of God in this world presents itself to some, nowadays, in new and unexpected ways which are often paradoxical and disconcerting.

In this confusion of ideas and interpretations, thanks to   995 your specialization, you are to some extent the witnesses and heralds of traditional values and of that most precious of all values, which is the keystone of the whole religious structure of mankind, divine transcendency. Allow Us to say, gentlemen, that your research, your scientific investigation, dedicated to the history and literature of Israel, are in Our eyes of the greatest importance in calling attention in our modern society to the values that are highest.

Moreover, it is enough to cast a glance at the program of   996 your conferences to appreciate their worth and perceive how much they represent for the progress of the interpretation of the Old Testament.

997   The Catholic Church is well aware that it is neither the last nor the least active in this domain. Contrary to certain assertions often repeated in the course of the last centuries, the Church has always paid the most lively attention to the Holy Scriptures. We hope your learned work will leave you enough time for a brief visit to the Vatican Library. There you will observe by the abundance of Codices and editions of the Bible, the care which the Church has shown throughout the centuries for this incomparable book, which she has always considered as the privileged source of Divine Revelation.

998   Here, in fact, in the view of the Church we have not merely a literary work; rather we are dealing with a religious work put together with a religious motive, chosen and constituted according to religious criteria. It is a work jealously guarded and transmitted because it is the bearer of a divine message which at first was destined for the chosen people, but also for those who consider themselves the spiritual descendants of the Old Testament. Consequently, it differs from all human books; it is an inspired book containing and transmitting a revelation. The Church sees the harmonious prolongation and fulfillment of this revelation in the New Testament.

999   How then can such a book fail to be the object of devoted attention and study? The Church studies the Bible in all its aspects. First of all, she devotes to it in ever-increasing number, scientific works such as those in which you are engaged. On the Church's part there are also theological studies of the Bible: Is there one "theology" of the Old Testament? Or several? Or rather a single biblical theology dealing with both the Old and New Testaments, and several orders or several paths in presenting and organizing what has been revealed? These are questions which are disputed by theologians.[2] Finally, the Church is no less concerned with the spiritual aspect; and one of her religious could devote, some time ago, a book of almost a thousand pages to *L'Ancien Testament source de vie spirituelle*.[3]

1000   The wealth of revelation contained in the pages of the Old Testament, is such that it seems it will never be exhausted. It is God as Creator and as good who is revealed to us in the Old Testament, the God who is one and true, the living God and the God of all holiness; the God who is offended but who pardons, because there is a plan of salvation for men and He pursues it untiringly right through a "holy history," whose every fragment the Church gathers with immense veneration and unbounded love.

In the face of the audacious and disquieting changes of the modern world, what else can the Church desire but to see the truth, the grandeur and the beauty of this fundamental theology of the Old Testament imposing itself on every soul of good will and constituting a powerful spiritual bond for all those who are sincerely desirous of light and peace?   **1001**

Such are, gentlemen, some of the reflections which your presence here today inspires in Us. We are glad to receive you in this week of Easter, that feast whose very name evokes one of the summits of the Old Testament. Continue with your work. Keep on giving us a deeper knowledge of the holy text. Nothing could be more in keeping with the spirit of the Second Vatican Council, which as you know, devotes a special chapter of its Dogmatic Constitution on Revelation to the Old Testament. Be assured of Our lively sympathy and of all Our esteem for the important task which you are fulfilling, and on which We heartily implore the blessings of Him who is and remains forever the God of the Bible, the "God of our Fathers," the "God of Abraham, Isaac and Jacob."   **1002**

General Instruction on Roman Missal
Congregation for Divine Worship
March 26, 1970

The most important part of the Liturgy of the Word consists of the readings from sacred scripture and the songs occurring between them. The homily, the Profession of Faith (Creed) and the Prayer of the Faithful develop and conclude it. In the readings, which are interpreted by the homily, God speaks to his people, reveals to them the mysteries of redemption and salvation, and provides them with spiritual nourishment; and Christ himself, in the form of his word, is present in the midst of the faithful. The people appropriate this divine word to themselves by their singing, and testify their fidelity to God's word by their profession of faith. Strengthened by the word of God they intercede, in the Prayer of the Faithful, for the needs of the entire Church and for the salvation of the whole world.

1004   34. In the readings, the table of God's word is laid before the people and the treasures of the Bible are opened to them. By tradition the reading of the extracts from scripture is not a presidential function, but that of an assistant. Hence the deacon—or, if no deacon is present, some other priest—should read the Gospel. A lector reads the other extracts. But if neither deacon nor any other priest is available, the Gospel is to be read by the celebrant.

Apostolic Letter Issued 'Motu Proprio'
by Pope Paul VI
June 27, 1971

The diligent concern with which the Church has always endeavored to achieve an ever greater understanding of Sacred Scripture so that she may unceasingly nourish her children with the divine word[1] is especially evident in our times. For the Second Vatican Ecumenical Council prescribed that the rich treasures of the word of God be made more amply and plentifully accessible to the faithful, the better to foster the Christian life.

The excelling greatness and importance of this task, to which the spouse of Christ is applying herself today with renewed diligence, demands that she make every effort to encourage the study of Sacred Scripture. For this reason the same Ecumenical Council gave this timely advice: "Catholic exegetes and other students of sacred theology, working diligently together and using appropriate means, should devote their energies to an exploration and exposition of the divine writings, under the watchful care of the sacred teaching office of the Church. This should be done in such a way that as many ministers of the divine word as possible will be able effectively to provide the nourishment of the Scriptures for the People of God."[2]

1006

But since the progress of modern scholarship daily presents new questions in these disciplines which are not easy to solve, it follows that the work entrusted to Scripture scholars becomes very difficult. Even though these scholars must pursue

1007

their studies in accordance with recent scientific method, they know nevertheless that God has entrusted the Scriptures not to the private judgment of learned people, but to His Church. The Scriptures, therefore, must always necessarily be interpreted according to the norms of Christian tradition and hermeneutics, under the guardianship and protection of the Church's magisterium.[3]

1008 Our intention is, through a greater effectiveness of method, to assist the advance of true teaching in biblical studies; to preserve the interpretation of Scripture from all rashness of opinion; and also to give greater coordination to the work of theologians in their collaboration with the Holy See and with one another.[4] With that intention We have deemed it opportune to give careful consideration particularly to the Pontifical Biblical Commission, established by Our predecessor Leo XIII through the apostolic letter *Vigilantiae Studiique* of October 30, 1902, in order to promote in due manner the study of Scripture.

1009 The benefits for the safeguarding and growth of biblical studies so far derived from the commission's work from its very beginning confirm Our conviction regarding its usefulness and importance. In order that the Church may draw ever greater fruit from it, nothing seems to Us more apt and valid than to regulate the pontifical commission with new and more appropriate laws. Their purpose will be to ensure that with regard to its program, to the proposal and treatment of questions, to the assignment of various offices and, finally, to the number and selection of members, the commission may proceed to perform its task more expeditiously and in accordance with the increased needs of Christian society.

1010 Therefore, having duly considered all matters, We establish and decree, on Our own initiative and by Our apostolic authority, the following new laws for the regulation of the Pontifical Biblical Commission.

1011 1. The Biblical Commission, which continues in its function of suitably promoting biblical studies and of offering assistance to the Church's magisterium in interpreting Scripture, is reorganized according to new norms and is linked with the Sacred Congregation for the Doctrine of the Faith.

2. The cardinal prefect of the Sacred Congregation for the Doctrine of the Faith holds the office of president of the Biblical Commission; he may be aided by a vice-president, to be selected from the members of the commission.   1012

3. The Biblical Commission is composed of scholars of the biblical sciences from various schools and nations; they shall be outstanding for their learning, prudence and Catholic regard for the magisterium of the Church.   1013

4. Members of the Biblical Commission are appointed by the Supreme Pontiff, on the proposal of the cardinal president after consultation with the episcopal conferences. Appointment is for a term of five years, on completion of which they may be reappointed. The number of members shall not exceed 20.   1014

5. The secretary of the Biblical Commission, having been proposed by the commission president, is appointed by the Supreme Pontiff for a five-year period, and is included among the consultors of the Sacred Congregation for the Doctrine of the Faith. On the completion of his five-year term, he may be reappointed. It is useful for the cardinal president, as far as possible, to arrange a consultation among members of the commission before presenting to the Supreme Pontiff the names of candidates for this position.   1015

6. A plenary session of the Biblical Commission shall be convened at least once a year.   1016

7. If the study of particular questions should so demand, the cardinal prefect may set up special subcommissions of members with particular competence in the point at issue. Such subcommissions shall terminate with the completion of the study. The subcommission shall be able, with the assent of the commission president, to consult other experts, including non-Catholics, if the case demands it. Those invited for such consultation do not become members.   1017

8. The members of the Biblical Commission may also be consulted by letter.   1018

9. Questions and topics for study are designated by the Supreme Pontiff or by the president of the commission, on the proposal of the Sacred Congregation for the Doctrine of the Faith, or of the Synod of Bishops, or of episcopal confer-   1019

ences, or of the Biblical Commission itself on the suggestion of its members; or likewise on the proposal of Catholic universities and biblical societies, with due regard for the directive contained in article 136 of the apostolic constitution *Regimini Ecclesiae Universae.*

1020   10. The conclusions reached by the Biblical Commission in plenary session—after the work done by the subcommission, where such applies—are to be submitted to the Supreme Pontiff and transmitted for the use of the Sacred Congregation for the Doctrine of the Faith.

1021   11. It is the duty of the Biblical Commission to carry out studies, and to prepare instructions and decrees which the Sacred Congregation for the Doctrine of the Faith may publish with special mention of the Biblical Commission and with the approval of the Supreme Pontiff, unless in special cases the Supreme Pontiff shall determine otherwise.

1022   12. It shall be the concern of the Biblical Commission to foster relationships with various institutes of biblical studies, both Catholic and non-Catholic.

1023   13. The commission must be consulted before the issuance of new norms on biblical matters.

1024   14. The Biblical Commission continues to confer academic degrees in biblical studies, until further notice, according to special norms which are to be suitably revised.

1025   15. Members of the Biblical Commission shall observe strict secrecy in matters pertaining to the commission, in keeping with the nature and importance of those matters and in obedience to the current norms concering secrecy.

1026   We order that what We have decreed in this letter that We have issued on Our own initiative be regarded as established and ratified, anything to the contrary notwithstanding, even if worthy of special mention, and that it shall take effect as of July 8 of the current year.

1027   Given at Rome, at St. Peter's, June 27th, in the year 1971, the ninth of Our pontificate.

Address of Pope Paul VI
at the Vatican Library International Book Year Exhibit
March 25, 1972

It is a very remarkable circumstance, one without doubt
unique, which brings us together today in this shrine
of knowledge and culture, the Apostolic Vatican Library. It is a matter of the active and vocal witness given by
the Catholic Church to its interest in and great esteem for
what is at first sight a wholly secular initiative, the International Book Year, which the 16th session of the UNESCO
General Conference has proclaimed for 1972.

This is a secular initiative, but only in appearance. For   1029
everything that touches the human soul, the progress of
knowledge and the extension of culture necessarily has a
moral aspect which in some way concerns man's relationship
with God, and which by this very fact comes within the ambit
of religion and is the object of the Church's attentive care.

What purpose has UNESCO had in view in promoting this   1030
initiative? We have just heard the answer to this question
expressed in lofty terms by the Director General, and the
program's slogan conveys it perfectly: "Books for all." This
very worthy organization has thus wished, above all, to draw
the world's attention to the irreplaceable function of books,
considered as an eminent means of culture and education, an
incomparable factor of spiritual progress and an instrument
capable of evoking thoughts of peace, which can contribute
effectively to a better understanding among peoples. The
organization has also desired—and this is also to its praise—to

study the most appropriate means of ensuring the circulation of books, especially among young people in the developing countries.

1031   The Church notes all of this with lively satisfaction. Through a letter from Our Cardinal Secretary of State, We made the Church's voice heard at the International Book Festival held at Nice in May of last year, and expressed the conviction that the true role of books, the aim which all those concerned with their distribution must pursue, is above all to instruct and elevate mankind, and to guide it toward the achievement of its true good.

1032   In fact, anyone who reflects can see that material progress, however spectacular, is only a partial aspect of complete human progress. Man needs spiritual values in order to be fully human, in order to ensure the harmonious balance of his life and the fruitfulness of his earthly activities. And in fact, thanks to the technical aids that man has at his disposal, books are multiplying endlessly.

1033   But it is obvious that the criterion of judgment in this matter cannot be merely quantitative; it is not a question of producing an abundance of books of just any sort. It is through their quality that books can play their beneficial part. It is to the extent that books are vehicles for spiritual values that they really make mankind advance, that they help to build up and not to destroy. And it is naturally in this light that the Holy See and the Church view UNESCO's initiative as worthy of approval and encouragement.

1034   What We have said so far concerns what We might call the Church's "generic" interest in books as a means of culture. But the Church has something more specific to say on this matter. The Church too has "her" book, the book of books, if We may be permitted to call it such, a book that has been translated into every language, printed in millions of copies, distributed and read in every country of the world, a sort of permanent best-seller for mankind: the Bible. In accepting the invitation to participate in the International Book Year, the Church, as the depository and guardian of this most precious of treasures, intends above all to promote a better and wider knowledge of the Bible.

She considers that she can and must act in this way. For all believers, the Bible is something radically different from all that the human spirit has produced, something far superior; it is the Word of God. The sacred writer, whatever his talents may have been, is in this case only an instrument used by God. What is before us is an inspired book, a book which has God for its principal author. In choosing and making use of men in full possession of their faculties and abilities, God has in a sense consecrated the splendid mission of the writer.

1035

Certainly, we can find rich food for thought in the fact that God chose a book in order to communicate with men, in order to "invite and take them into fellowship with Himself," to make known to them, or to recall to them down through the centuries. His loving plan for His people and for all mankind. We can say that the Bible realizes perfectly the highest goal that any book has ever been able to set itself: to put man into contact with his Creator. It does this with a freshness that spans the centuries without ever growing old, and with a variety that charms the spirit and the heart.

1036

The Bible in fact is not just a book; it is a library in itself, a set of books of every different literary genre. Sometimes through the clarity of the narrative style, at other times with the vehemence of the prophets' chiding, at others again by means of the loftiest poetry reflecting all the nuances of divine wisdom and human psychology, God teaches successive generations, illuminates them and gladdens them with His light.

1037

By contact with the Bible, men of all times and all lands have learned the language of faith and hope, of justice and peace; millions have had horizons of light and joy revealed to them, and have drawn from the Bible or have rediscovered in it, confidence in the destiny of man and of the world.

1038

It is to the whole of these spiritual riches—and certainly without any hidden motive of self-interest—that the Holy See intends to draw the attention of men of goodwill. Its aim is to offer them, in all simplicity and cordiality, a fresh occasion for approaching this unique book, which has played so great a role in the history of culture and civilization. To believers it extends an invitation to deepen their knowledge of these

1039

familiar pages, and there to nourish their spiritual lives more intensely, as the recent Council urges.

1040   And now We are about to inaugurate, and you are going to be able to visit, the exhibition that has been prepared with great care and skill by the Prefect of Our Apostolic Library and his dovoted collaborators. As We have just been told and as you are going to see, it is a collection of especially rare or important copies of the Bible, spread over the centuries and belonging to the most varied languages and regions of the Christian world. You will be able to admire both the old and the new acquisitions of the Vatican Library. One of the most recent—although it is a very ancient text—is the Bodmer Papyrus, which has come to us from the famous Swiss collector, whose name well deserves mention here today. And among the most ancient possessions is a manuscript that is remarkable both for its content and its calligraphy, one well known to exegetes of the entire world, the *Codex B*, whose presence here has gained for it also the name of *Codex Vaticanus*.

1041   The desire to make these precious documents better known has recently given Us the idea of having a certain number of photostatic reproductions made. We intend presently to offer to you, Mr. Director General, one such copy of *Codex B*, if you will be so good as to accept it as a gift from the Holy See to UNESCO and as a symbol of the Holy See's participation in the campaign conducted by your organization.

1042   It only remains for Us to congratulate warmly all those who have so skillfully arranged this exhibition, to thank those who have done Us the honor of coming here to inaugurate it with Us this evening, and to extend Our cordial good wishes for the complete success of the International Book Year.

MYSTERIUM ECCLESIAE
The Declaration of the Sacred Congregation
for the Doctrine of the Faith
June 24, 1973

Part V

The transmission of Divine Revelation by the Church en-
counters difficulties of various kinds. These arise from
the fact that the hidden mysteries of God "by their
nature so far transcend the human intellect that even if they
are revealed to us and accepted by faith, they remain concealed by the veil of faith itself and are, as it were, wrapped
in darkness." Difficulties arise also from the historical condition that affects the expression of Revelation.

With regard to this historical condition, it must first be
observed that the meaning of the pronouncements of faith
depends partly upon the expressive power of the language
used at a given time and under given circumstances. Moreover, it sometimes happens that some dogmatic truth is first
expressed incompletely (but not falsely), and at a later date,
when considered in a broader context of faith or human
knowledge, is expressed more fully and perfectly. In addition, when the Church makes new pronouncements she intends to confirm or clarify what is in some way contained in
Sacred Scripture or in previous expressions of Tradition; but
at the same time she usually intends to solve certain questions
or remove certain errors. All these things have to be taken
into account so that these pronouncements may be properly
interpreted. Finally, even though the truths which the Church

intends to teach through her dogmatic formulas are distinct from the changeable conceptions of a given epoch and can be expressed without them, nevertheless it can sometimes happen that these truths may be enunciated by the sacred magisterium in terms that bear traces of such conceptions.

1045   In view of the above, it must be stated that the dogmatic *formulas* of the Church's magisterium have suitably communicated revealed truth from the very beginning and that, remaining the same, these formulas will continue to communicate this truth forever to those who interpret them correctly. It does not follow, however, that every one of these formulas has been or will be suitable for this purpose to the same extent. For this reason theologians seek to define exactly the intention of teaching proper to the various formulas, and in carrying out this work they are of considerable assistance to the living magisterium of the Church, to which they remain subordinate. For this reason also it often happens that ancient dogmatic formulas and others closely connected with them remain alive and fruitful in the habitual usage of the Church, but with suitable expository and explanatory additions that maintain and clarify their original meaning. In addition, it has sometimes happened that in this habitual usage certain of these formulas have given way to new expressions, proposed or at least approved by the sacred magisterium, which brought out that meaning more clearly or completely. As for the *meaning* of dogmatic formulas, this remains ever true and constant in the Church, even when it is expressed with greater clarity or fuller understanding. The faithful must therefore shun the opinion, first, that dogmatic formulas (or some category of them) cannot signify truth in a determinate way, but can only offer changeable approximations to it, which to a certain extent distort or alter it; secondly, that these formulas signify the truth only in an indeterminate way, this truth being like a goal that is constantly being sought by means of such approximations. Those who hold such opinions do not escape dogmatic relativism, and they are corrupting the concept of the Church's infallibility relative to the truth to be taught or held determinately.

Address of Pope Paul VI
to the Pontifical Biblical Commission
March 14, 1974

It is a pleasure for Us to meet with you during the first session of the Pontifical Biblical Commission as it begins a new phase of its existence. We have taken pains to nominate all its members—each and every one of you—not only as representatives of a variety of schools and nations, but also as scholars whose competence and devotion to the Church and her magisterium are well known to Us.

Here We feel obliged to acknowledge gratefully the past 1047 achievements of this Commission, particularly of its presidents and secretaries, since the time it was founded by Our predecessor Leo XIII in 1902. And We also wish to express Our confidence in your future efforts. Your work should accomplish a twofold purpose. It should effectively promote progress in the biblical studies of the Church, and it should also keep the interpretation of Sacred Scripture on the right path—faithful to the word of God to which we are subject, and responsive to the needs of human beings to whom that word is addressed.

As you know, Sacred Scripture and particularly the New 1048 Testament took shape within the community of God's people, of the Church gathered around the Apostles. Formed in the school of Jesus and transformed into witnesses to His resurrection, they transmitted His deeds and teachings, explaining the salvific import of the events which they themselves had witnessed. Thus, while it is true to say that the word of God convened and engendered the Church, it is also true to say that the Church has somehow been the matrix of Sacred Scripture. In these sacred writings the Church recognized and expressed her faith, her hope and her rule of life in the world for all generations to come.

1049   The studies of recent decades have helped greatly to highlight the close relationship and bond that inextricably link Scripture and the Church. They have pointed up the essential structure, the living environment (*Sitz im Leben*), the activity of prayer, the devoted attachment to the Lord, the cohesion of the members around the Apostles, the difficulties regarding the surrounding world, the oral and literary tradition, the missionary and catechetical effort, and the first developments in varied religious and cultural spheres. Indeed it seems that the distinctive, dominant feature of contemporary exegesis is its reflection on the deep relations existing between Scripture and the Church from the very beginning.

1050   Consider the scholarly explorations into the history of traditions, forms and redactional work (*Tradition - Form - Redaktiongeschichte*), which We encouraged—with the required methodological correctives—in the recent Instruction *Sancta Mater Ecclesia*, dealing with the historical truth of the Gospels.[1] Do not these explorations operate in terms of this perspective? And then there is the contemporary stress on the need to integrate a "diachronic" approach: the former pays attention to the historical development of the text while the latter gives due weight to the literary and existential connection of the text with the overall linguistic and cultural context in which it is situated. Once again, do they not clearly bring us into the life of the Church?

1051   Consider also the talk about a "plurality of theologies," or, to put it better, about the varied but complementary ways in which fundamental themes of the New Testament are presented and illustrated—such themes as salvation, the Church and the mystery of Christ's person. Does this not evoke for us the choral symphony of the living community, its manifold voices professing their faith in one and the same mystery? And then there is the function of hermeneutics, which has become more imperative in the last decade and which has taken its place alongside historical and literary exegesis. Does it not encourage the exegete to go beyond research into some "pure primitive text," and to remember that it is the Church, the living community, which "actualizes" the message of Scripture for contemporary man?

These various orientations of contemporary exegesis, it seems to Us, reflect the major convictions of Christian Tradition which run from the days of St. Paul, through the patristic and medieval period, to the teachings of Our great predecessor Pius XII. They find solemn reaffirmation in Vatican II: "Sacred Tradition and Sacred Scripture form one sacred deposit of the word of God, committed to the Church. Holding fast to this deposit, all the holy people united with their bishops remain always steadfast in the teaching of the Apostles, in the common life, in the breaking of the bread and in prayers. Thus there is a single common effort by the bishops and the faithful to hold on to the heritage of faith and to practice and profess it."[2]   1052

This essential connection between the Bible and the Church—or if you prefer, this reading of Sacred Scripture in the midst of the Church—bestows an important function of service to God's word on the exegetes of Sacred Scripture. And this applies especially to you who are official members of the Pontifical Biblical Commission. We, for Our part, are encouraged to be sympathetic to—indeed, to support and stimulate—the ecclesial character of contemporary exegesis.   1053

Your work is not simply to explain ancient texts, to relate the facts in a critical way, or to get back to the original, primitive form of some sacred text. The prime duty of the exegete is to present the message of Revelation to the People of God; to lay bare the meaning of the word of God in itself and in its relationship to contemporary man; and to provide people with access to God's word above and beyond the enveloping semantic signs and cultural syntheses, which are sometimes far removed from the culture and problems of our own day.   1054

What a great mission you have with regard to the Church and all humanity! What a contribution you can make to the evangelization of the contemporary world! To point up your   1055 responsibility and to protect you from some of the false byways into which exegesis is often in danger of wandering, We are going to borrow the words of a masterful exegete who displayed exceptional critical ability, faith and devotion to the Church. We refer to Father Lagrange.

1056   Writing in 1918, he drew up a negative assessment of the various schools of liberal exegesis. He then pinpointed the roots of their failure in these causes: their doctrinal opportunism, the one-sided nature of their research and the narrow rationalism of their methodology. As he put it: "Since the end of the 18th century, Christianity has been taken in tow by reason. One was supposed to bend the texts to the fashion of the day. This opportunism served as the inspiration for the commentaries of the rationalists." He then goes on to say: "All we ask of this independent exegesis is that it be purely scientific. But it can be scientific only if it breaks away from another defect that is common to all the schools we have enumerated here. All of them have been *einseitig*, one-sided."[3] Father Lagrange also challenged another feature of their critiques: their avowed intention not to accept the supernatural.

1057   His remarks retain their pertinence and urgency today. We can add another point that will further clarify them. One should not exaggerate or go beyond the possibilities of the exegetical method adopted. He should not turn it into an absolute methodology, pretending that it alone enables one to gain access to Divine Revelation. Likewise one should avoid a systematic questioning aimed at detaching any and every expression of the faith from a solid foundation of certainty.

1058   These aberrant approaches can be avoided if one adheres to the golden rule of theological hermeneutics enunciated by Vatican II. In the work of interpreting Sacred Scripture, it says: "No less serious attention must be given to the content and unity of the whole of Scripture if the meaning of the sacred texts is to be correctly worked out. The living Tradition of the whole Church must be taken into account along with the analogy of faith."[4] To quote Father Lagrange once again: "One cannot manage to recover the sense of Christianity by grouping texts together if he does not get down to the reason for existence of the whole. It is a living organism with its own unique vital principle. That principle, discovered long ago, is the Incarnation of Jesus Christ, the salvation assured to human beings by the grace of redemption. To look elsewhere is to run the risk of taking the wrong road."[5]

Expressing the message means, first and foremost, gathering all the meanings of a text and having them converge toward the oneness of the mystery. It is a unique, transcendent, inexhaustible mystery and so we can approach it under a variety of aspects. The collaboration of many people will be required in order to analyze the whole process of the insertion of the Word of God into history—what St. John Chrysostom called *synkatabasis or condescensio*[6]—in line with the variety of human languages and cultures. This will enable us to call from every page the universal, immutable sense of the message and then to propose it to the Church, so that the faith may be truly understood in the modern context and applied beneficially to the grave problems that are tormenting thoughtful minds at the present time.

1059

It is up to you exegetes to make Sacred Scripture into a reality, in line with the sense of the living Church, so that it does not remain simply a monument from the past but becomes a source of light, vitality and action. Only in this way will the fruits of exegesis be able to serve the Church's kerygmatic function and her dialogue, to offer themselves to the reflection of systematic theology and moral teaching, and to be of use to her pastoral activity in the modern world.

1060

As you realize from these words, there is evidently a real continuity between exegetical research and that of dogmatic and moral theology. There is also a real need for interdisciplinary contact between the biblical scholar, the specialist in dogmatic theology, the expert in moral theology, the jurist, and the people involved in pastoral and missionary activity. In saying this, We are merely recalling and emphasizing the directives of Vatican II. Having noted that the study of Sacrea Scripture "can be considered the soul of sacred theology,"[7] it goes on to ask that special attention be paid to the improvement of moral theology: "The scientific treatment of it should be nourished more by the teachings of Sacred Scripture."[8]

1061

For as the Pastoral Constitution on the Church in the World of Today points out: "The Church guards the heritage of God's word and draws from it moral and religious principles."[9]

1062   Without a clear biblical foundation, moral theology is in danger of turning into arid philosophical schemata. It runs the risk of becoming totally out of touch with man in his concrete, historical reality; of overlooking the fact that man is a creature of God, wounded by sin but saved in Christ. It may well forget that Christ gave us His spirit of love and liberty so that we might "live sober, upright, and godly lives in this world, awaiting our blessed hope."[10]

1063   The biblical scholar is called upon to render analogous service to the ecumenical and missionary task of the Church. It is not simply that the Bible is the privileged place of encounter with Churches and ecclesial communities that are not in complete communion with Rome. By having recourse to the message and example of Christ, all Christians should learn how to effect self-purification and reconciliation in a way that fosters and promotes the full realization of our hoped for unity.

1064   Here We want to recall what Vatican II said in its Decree on the Missionary Activity of the Church. It called for "fresh scrutiny' (*novae investigationi subiciantur*) of "the works and words revealed by God, as contained in Holy Writ," in the context of the world's cultures and religions. "Thus it will be more clearly seen along what paths faith may search for understanding, while taking into account the philosophy and wisdom of the nations, and in what way their customs, their views on the meaning of life, and their social order can be correlated with the morality taught by divine Revelation."[11]

1065   Great tasks await the exegete in the life and future of the Church. In order to meet these tasks, he will make every effort to preserve and nurture within himself each day a living relationship with the mystery of the God of love, who sent His Son to us to make us His adopted children. This mystery, along with the divine deeds that attend it, can scarcely be recognized and acknowledged by those who are primarily devoted to earthly values, however noble in themselves—such as cultural and scientific progress. Didn't Jesus Himself say that God's revelation was concealed from the wise and the clever but revealed to the lowly ones?[12]

There must be a real existential openness to the mystery of the God of love; otherwise our exegesis will remain clouded in darkness, no matter how scholarly it may be. We cannot maintain such openness without the light of divine grace, for which we should plead humbly and constantly. As St. Augustine tells us: "It is not enough to ask that those who dedicate themselves to Sacred Scripture be well versed in the particularities of language. . . . It is of prime importance and necessity that they pray in order that they may be able to understand (*orent ut intelligant*)."[13]

1066

Dear sons and brothers, We have been talking to you about the modern tasks of the exegete in the life of the Church, about the openness he should have toward other theological disciplines and about the necessity of reading the Bible in terms of the Church's Tradition. Our comments explain the decision We reached in Our recent Motu Proprio *Sedula Cura*,[14] that the Biblical Commission should henceforth be attached to the Sacred Congregation for the Doctrine of the Faith. The International Theological Commission will also be attached to the Sacred Congregation, but in a different manner.

1067

As the norms of Our Motu Proprio prove, there is no question of a levelling that would infringe upon the specialized character of your research, your own initiatives or the indispensable service you are called upon to render to the Holy See. Instead the aim is to maintain the essential task assigned to your Commission by Our predecessor Leo XIII, while fostering healthy collaboration between the organisms of the Holy See. We want to foster "interdisciplinarity" between exegetical specialists and other theological disciplines, so that they may render joint service to Our magisterium.

1068

In closing this address, We wish to tell you that We expect a great deal from your labors; and We call down upon you and your efforts the light of the Holy Spirit, giving you Our apostolic blessing.

1069

Document of the Sacred Congregation
for Catholic Education
On the Theological Formation of Future Priests (Excerpts)
February 22, 1976

The first fact about Scripture that must be taken into account in the teaching of theology is that it is the starting point, the *permanent foundation*, and the lifegiving and animating principle of all of theology.[1] The professor of the biblical sciences must therefore carry out his mission with the scientific competence and completeness that the importance of his discipline requires. If he is to execute his task as he should, he must deal with the text, with the event to which the text relates and with the tradition which communicates and interprets the text. But even while he applies textual, literary and historical analysis, he must keep alive in the souls of his students an awareness of the mystery and of God's plan. Since Scripture is passed on to us by the Church and in part even came into existence within the Church, it requires to be read and understood in the light of ecclesial tradition.[2]

1071   80. The primordial role of the Scriptures cannot but determine the nature of the relation between Scripture and theology with its various disciplines. We must bear in mind that the Scripture cannot be approached unilaterally and in function solely of the disciplines (as though it existed merely as a source of probative texts), but that, on the contrary, theology in its entirety is called upon to help to a better and increasingly profound understanding of the sacred texts, that is, of the dogmatic and moral truths they contain. Consequently, after all the introductory questions have been handled, the teaching of Sacred Scripture must culminate in a biblical theology which gives a unified vision of the Christian mystery.

81. If a biblical theology is really to yield a better understanding of the Sacred Scriptures, it must have its own proper contents which are identified according to a special methodology. It must also enjoy a certain autonomy. By this is meant that such a theology focuses exclusively on what is specific to the Scriptures and that it embraces the Scriptures in their entirety. Such an autonomy is a relative thing; it does not imply either independence from or hostility toward systematic theology, despite what we observe today in some cases.   1072

While positive and systematic theology each has its own special method, the two disciplines should always be engaged in fruitful collaboration. In fact, if we want to speak with complete accuracy, should we not say that the two disciplines are two successive stages of the total work, since the speculative approach is already present in the positive. The positive is the speculative in process of becoming, while the speculative is the positive which has achieved its goal.   1073

82. One way to secure the desired unity and harmony is for the teachers of the major disciplines involved to cooperate with one another in an effective and coordinated way. The disciplines we have in mind are exegesis, fundamental theology, dogmatic theology and moral theology. Cooperation will assure a suitable division of tasks as well as a more complete structuring and harmonizing of the subject-matter being taught.   1074

The professor of Sacred Scripture is expected to manifest a proper openness to and understanding of the problems of the other theological disciplines. Above all, he should bear constantly in mind the requirements of the integrity and internal coherence of the faith, requirements which are expressed in the principle of "the analogy of faith."[3]   1075

The importance rightly attributed to the biblical sciences today increases the Scripture scholar's responsibility to those who pursue the other disciplines but does not justify an attitude of independence or a tendency to think of him-   1076 self as the dominant partner. He must think of himself as a servant of the word of God and must be mindful of how sensitive many problems of exegesis are. Such problems must be handled in a prudent and balanced fashion, especially in the seminary, and with an awareness of the influence the treatment of such problems can have on catechetics and preaching.[4]

1077   83. The professor of Sacred Scripture will have to be conscious especially of how his teaching relates to dogmatic and moral theology, fundamental theology and the pastoral ministry and spiritual life of future priests. It will be sufficient here to recall the following points. If exegesis is to be useful for systematic theology, it must take the form of a genuine biblical theology in the proper sense of the term. In relation to fundamental theology, the biblical sciences must be up-to-date in their cognizance of the other sciences, while also taking a constructive approach when it comes to relating the assured data of the sciences to the faith. As far as the pastoral ministry is concerned, the professor must give as complete as possible a view of the Sacred Scriptures, without neglecting any of the more important problems,[5] and train the students in the wise use of the texts, these being interpreted in their proper sense. Finally, with regard to the spiritual life, the students must be taught to respect and love the Sacred Scriptures,[6] and be trained in how to use them profitably in liturgy, devotion and priestly asceticism.

1078   84. In order to give truly formative value to teaching based on the *biblical themes*, the professor of Sacred Scripture must endeavor to bring these themes together in a theological-ecclesial synthesis that draws its inspiration from *the profession of the Catholic faith*, this profession, or creed, being itself a synthesis of the Church's understanding of revelation.

References

Origen, Letter to Gregory Thaumaturgus, c. 235 A.D.

1   *John* x. 3.
2   *Matt.* vii. 7.
3   *Heb.* iii. 14.

Origen, Commentary on the Gospel According to Matthew, c. 247 A.D.

1   *Matt.* v. 9.
2   *Prov.* viii. 8, 9.
3   *Ps.* lxxii. 7.
4   *Ecc.* xii. 11
5   *I Sam.* xvi. 14.

Cyril, Bishop of Jerusalem, Catechesis IV (Excerpts), c. 348 A.D.

1   *1 Cor.* 2, 10.
2   *Matt.* 12, 32.

3   *Gal.* 2, 23.

4   *Ibid.* 24.

5   Cf. *Matt.* 5, 17.

6   The reference is to the Septuagint. In chapter 34 Cyril tells the popular legend of its origin.

7   Note the omission of the Apocalypse from Cyril's Canon.

8   This chapter gives us some idea of the pagan atmosphere in which the Christian had to live.

Augustine, Bishop of Hippo, *On Christian Instruction*, 397 A.D.

1   *Acts* 2.1ff.

2   *Wisd.* 7.13; *1 Cor.* 11.23.

3   *2 Tim.* 1.12.

4   *2 Cor.* 12.2, 4.

5   *1 Cor.* 9.1.

6   *Acts* 9.3ff.

7   *Acts* 10.1ff.

8   *1 Cor.* 3.17.

9   *Acts* 8.26ff.

10   *Exod.* 18.14ff.

11   Cf. *Matt.* 25.26, 27.

12   *John* 8.44.

13   *John* 14.6.

14   *1 Cor.* 4.7.

15   *Matt.* 13.12.

16   *2 Cor.* 9.10.

17   *Matt.* 14.17ff.; 15.34ff.

18   *2 Cor.* 9.6ff.

19   *1 Cor.* 8.2.

20   *1 Peter* 3.17.

21   *1 Tim.* 1.5.

22   *2 Cor.* 5.7.

23   *1 Cor.* 13.1ff.

24   *1 Cor.* 13.8.

25   *1 Cor.* 13.10.

26   *1 Cor.* 13.13.

27   *1 Tim.* 1.5.

Book 2

1   *John* 12.3-7; cf. Aug. *Tract. in Joan.* 50.7.

2   *Matt.* 26.29.

3   *Matt.* 9.21; cf. Aug. *De cons. Ev.* 2.20.50.

4   *Gen.* 11.1ff.

5   The reference is to Hebrew; cf. Aug. *De civ. Dei* 16.43.3.

6   *Cant.* 4.2.

7   *Matt.* 22.37, 39.

8   *1 Cor.* 13.12.

9   *2 Cor.* 5.6ff.

10   *Phil.* 3.20.

11   *Ps.* 110.10; *Eccli.* 1.16.

12   Cf. Council. Hipponense A.D. 393, Can. 38; also Concil. Carthag.
A.D. 397, Can. 47.

13   See Introduction, p. 3.

14   See Introduction p. 3f.

15   *Deut.* 25.4; *1 Cor.* 9.9; *1 Tim.* 5.18.

16   *Isa.* 58.7 (ancient version).

17   *Isa.* 58.7 (Vulgate version).

18   *Rom.* 11.14.

19   *Isa.* 7.9 (ancient version).

20   *Isa.* 7.9 (Vulgate version).

21   *2 Cor.* 5.7.

22   *Rom.* 3.15 (*Ps.* 13.3).

23   *Wisd.* 4.3.

24   *1 Cor.* 8.1.

25   Cf. *Num.* 13.20; cf. Aug. *Locut. in Heptat.* 4.35.

26   *Ps.* 131.18.

27   *1 Cor.* 1.25.

28   What ancient version St. Augustine intended as the *Italia* (Italian) is not altogether clear.

29   I.e., the Septuagint; cf. Pope, *op. cit.* I 184-192.

30   *John* 9.7; cf. Aug. *Tract. in Joan.* 44.2.

31   *Matt.* 10.16.

32   *Eph.* 4.15.

33   *Eph.* 4.22ff; *Col.* 3.9.

34   *Matt.* 7.13.

35   *Gen.* 8.11.

36   *Ps.* 50.9; cf. Aug. *Enarr. in ps.* 50.12.

37   *Exod.* 24.18; *3 Kings* 19.8; *Matt.* 4.2.

38   *Matt.* 22.37.

39   *Matt.* 17.3.

40   *John* 21.11, 6.

41   Cf. *Brev. in psalmos* (G. Morin, *Anecdota Maredsolana* III.2 312).

42   *Ps.* 32.2; *Ps.* 91.4.

43   *John* 2.20.

44   *1 Cor.* 8.1.

45   *1 Cor.* 5.7.

46   *Matt.* 11.28-30.

47   *Exod.* 12.22.

48   *Eph.* 3.17, 18.

49   *Eph.* 3.19.

50   *Ps.* 50.9, 10.

51   *3 Kings* 10.14ff.

Book 3

1   *John* 1.1, 2.

2   *Phil.* 1.23, 24.

3   *2 Cor.* 7.1, 2.

4   *1 Cor.* 7.34.

Augustine, *The Harmony of the Gospels*, Book I, 400 A.D.

1   *Luke* iii. 31.

2   *Matt.* i. 6.

3   *John* xix. 19-22.

4   *Ps.* lxxv. 1.

5   *Ps.* cx. 4.

6   I *Sam.* xxi. 6; *Matt.* xii. 3.

7   *Luke* i, 36, 5.

8   *Luke* i. 32.

9   I *Tim.* ii. 5.

10 *John* i. I, 3.

11 *John* i, 14.

12 *John* x. 30.

13 *John* xiv. 9, 10.

14 *John* xvii. 22.

15 *John* v. 19.

16 *John* xiii. 23.

17 I *Cor.* xiii. 12.

18 *Rev.* v. 5.

19 *Matt.* ii, 1-18.

20 *Luke* i. 5, 36.

21 *Luke* ii. 22-24.

22 *Acts* ix. 1-30.

23 *Gen.* xxviii. 14.

24 *Luke* iv. 41.

25 *Ps.* xcvi. 5.

26 *Jer.* xxiii, 24.

27 *Gen.* i. I.

28 *Gen.* v. 24.

29 *Gen.* vii.

30 *Gen.* xxii, 18.

31 *Gen.* xxvi. 4.

32   *Jer.* xvi. 19.

33   *Deut.* vi. 4.

34   *Exod.* xx. 4.

35   *Exod.* xxiii. 24.

36   *Isa.* vii. 14; *Matt.* i. 23.

37   *Ps.* lxxii. II.

38   *Isa.* ii. 5-21.

39   *Ps.* xix. 6.

40   *Ps.* xix. 1-6.

41   *Isa.* liv, 5.

42   *Isa.* lii. 13-liv. 5.

43   *Matt.* xxvi., xxvii.; *Mark* xiv., xv.; *Luke* xxil, xxiii.: *John* xvii, xix.

44   *Isa.* lii. 15.

45   *Rom.* xv. 15, 21.

46   *John* xii. 37, 38; *Rom.* x. 16.

47   *Rom.* v. 20.

48   *Deut.* vii. 5.

49   *Rom.* v. 5.

50   I *Tim.* ii. 5.

Pope Gregory I, Letter to Leander (Excerpt), 594 A.D.

23   Cf. John Chrysostom, *Hom. in Ioh.* 4:1 (NPNF, 1st ser., 14.16).

24   *Job* 9:13 (Vulgate; R.S.V. different).

25   The allusion is to the pagan concept of the Tital Atlas as in Hesiod, *Theog*, 517; Aeschylus, *Prom*. 347 ff.

26   *Job* 7:15.

27   *Job* 3:2.

28   *Job* 3:5.

29   *Job* 3:7.

30   *Job* 7:19.

31   *Job* 6:7.

32   *Job* 7:20.

33   *Job* 13:26.

34 *Job* 27:6.

35 *Job* 31:16-20.

36 Gregory, as well as Leander, suffered much from gout, on which see Epist. 9.121 (NPNF, 2d ser., 13.34) and 11.32 (*Ibid*. 13.58).

37 *Heb*. 12:6.

38 *Deut*. 16:32.

39 Metacism is the juxtaposition of one *m* before another or of final *m* before a word beginning with a vowel, which in the classical poets is called elision; its avoidance, hiatus.

40 Doubtless he means the *clausulae*, patterns of prose rhythm much used by certain stylists, on which see W. H. Shewring, *Oxford Classical Dictionary* (Oxford, 1949) 738-740.

41 On Aelius Donatus, fourth century grammarian, of whom Jerome had been a pupil, and who was influential in late antiquity and the Middle Ages, see H. Keil, *Grammatici latini* 4.355-402. Gregory's disdain for the rules of grammer is in sharp contrast with what his contemporary Gregory of Tours says of him (*Hist. of the Franks* 10.1), that so "accomplished was he in grammar, dialectic, rhetoric, that he was held second to none in all the city." He doubtless supposes that the pope possessed these qualities without having genuine knowledge that he did.

42 That is, Jerome's translation, now called the Vulgate, nearly two centuries old, but the *Vetus Latinum* which preceded was not yet superseded.

John Damascene, *On the Orthodox Faith*: Book Four, 745 A.D.

1 *Matt*. 5. 17.

2 *John* 5.39.

3 *Heb*. 1.1-2.

4 *2 Tim*. 3. 16.

5 *Ps*. 1.3.

6 *Luke* 11.10.

7 Cf. *Ps*. 67.14

8 *Deut*. 32.7.

9 Cf. *1 Cor*. 8.7.

10 Cf. *John* 4.14.

11   Epiphanius, *On Weights ana Measures* (*PG* 43.244A).

12   *John* 10.30; 14.9; *Phil.* 2.6.

Pope Eugene IV, Council of Florence, A Decree in Behalf of the Jacobites, from the Bull *Cantate Domino*, 1442 A.D.

1   Cf. St. Fulgentius, *De fide*, ad Petrum c. I, n. 4 [MI 65, 674].

Pius VII, Letter to Archbishop of Mohileff (Excerpt), September 3, 1816.

1   St. Augustine, *In Io.*, tr. 18, c. I [ML 35 (Aug. III b), 1536].

PROVIDENTISSIMUS DEUS, Encyclical Letter of Pope Leo XIII on the Study of Holy Scripture, November 18, 1893.

1   *Con. Vat.*, Sess. 3 cap. 2 *de revelatione.*

2   *Ibid.*

3   St. Augustine, *De civitate Dei*, 11, 3.

4   St. Clement of Rome, *Ad Cor.*, 45; St. Polycarp, *Ad. Phil.*, 7; St. Irenaeus, *Adv. haereses*, 2, 28, 2.

5   St. John Chrysostom, *In Gen.*, hom. 2, 2; St. Aug., *In Ps.* 30 sermo 2, 1; St. Gregory the Great, *Epist. ad Theod.*, 4, 31.

6   St. Aug., *De util. cred.*, 14, 32.

7   St. Jerome, *Epist. ad Paulinum*, 53, 3.

8   Id., *In Isaiam*, Prol.

9   *Ibid.*, 54:12.

10   Cf. *Jer.* 23:29.

11   St. Aug., *De doctr. christ.*, 4, c. 6-7.

12   St. Jn. Chrys., *In Gen.*, hom. 21, 2; 60, 3; St. Aug., *De discipl. christ.*, 2.

13   St. Athanasius, *Epist. fest.*, 39.

14   St. Aug., *Sermo*, 46, 24; St. Ambrose, *In Ps. 118*, sermo 14, 2.

15   St. Jerome, *Epist. ad Nepotianum*, 42, 7.

16   St. Greg. Gt., *Reg. Past.*, 2, 11; *Moral.*, 18, 26.

17   St. Aug., *Sermo*, 179, 1.

18   St. Greg. Gt., *Reg. Past.*, 3, 24.

19   St. Jerome, *In Mich.* 1:10.

20   *Conc. Trid.*, Sess. 5 cap. 1 *de ref.*

21   *Ibid.*, 1, 2.

22   *Ibid.*, Sess. 4 decr. *De edit. et usu Libr. Sacr.*

23   St. Aug., *De doctr. christ.*, 3, 4.

24   St. Jerome, *Epist. ad Pammachium*, 48, 17.

25   Id. *Epist. ad Paulinum*, 53, 6.

26   St. Iren., *Adv. haer.*, 4, 26, 5.

27   *Conc. Vat.*, Sess. 3 cap. 2 *de revel.*;   cf. *Conc. Trid.*, Sess. 4 decr. *De edit. et usu Libr. Sacr.*

28   *Conc. Vat.*, Sess. 3 cap. 3 *de fide.*

29   St. Jerome, *Epist. ad Paulinum*, 53, 6.

30   St. Aug., *De util. cred.*, 17, 35.

31   Rufinus, *Hist. eccl.*, 2, 9.

32   St. Aug., *C. Julian.*, 2, 10, 37.

33   Id., *De Gen. ad litt.*, 8, 7, 13.

34   Cf. Clement of Alexandria, *Strom.*, 7, 16; Origen, *De princ.*, 4, 8; *In Lev.*, hom. 4, 8; Tertullian, *De praescr.*, 15; St. Hilary, *In Matt.*, 13:1.

35   St. Greg. Gt., *Moral.*, 20, 2.

36   St. Thomas, *Summ. theol.*, I, q. 1, a. 5, ad 2.

37   *Ibid.*, a. 8.

38   *Con. Vat.*, Sess. 3 cap. 3 *de fide.*

39   St. Jn. Chrys., *De sacerd.*, 4, 4.

40   St. Aug., *In Gen. op. imperf.*, 9, 30.

41   Id., *De Gen. ad litt.*, 1, 21, 41.

42   *Ibid.*, 2, 9, 20.

43   St. Thom., *Summ. theol.*, I, q. 70, a. 1, ad 3.

44   Id., *In 2 Sent.* d. 2, q. 1, a. 3.

45   Id., *Opusc.*, 10.

46   *Conc. Vat.*, Sess. 3 cap. 2 *de revel.*

47   St. Aug., *De cons. Evang.*, 1, 35.

48   St. Greg. Gt., *Moral in Job*, praef. 1, 2.

49   St. Aug., *Epist.*, 82, 3 et alibi.

50   Id., *Epist. ad Ianuar.*, 55, 21.

51   Id., *De doctr. christ.*, 3, 9, 13.

PRAESTANTIA SACRAE SCRIPTURAE, Motu Proprio of Pius X on the Decisions of the Pontifical Biblical Commission, November 18, 1907.

1   We omit the portion of the Motu Proprio that refers to the censures and penalties affecting those who neglect to observe the prescriptions against the errors of the modernists.

SPIRITUS PARACLITUS, Encyclical Letter of Pope Benedict XV on the Fifteenth Centenary of the Death of St. Jerome, September 15, 1920.

1   *Rom.* 15:4.

2   Sulpicius Severus, *Dial.*, 1, 7.

3   John Cassian, *De Incarn.*, 7, 26.

4   S. Prosper, *Carmen de ingratis*, 57.

5   S. Jerome, *De viris ill.*, 135.

6   Id., *Epist. ad Theophilum*, 82, 2, 2.

7   Id., *Epist. ad Damasum*, 15, 1, 1; *Epist. ad eundum*, 16, 2, 1.

8   Id., *In Abdiam*, Prol.

9   Id., *In Matt.*, 13:44.

10   Id., *Epist. ad Eustochium*, 22, 30, 1.

11   Id., *Epist. ad Pammachium et Oceanum*, 84, 3, 1.

12   Id., *Epist. ad Rusticum*, 125, 12.

13   Id., *Epist. ad Geruchiam*, 123, 9; *Epist ad Principiam*, 127, 7, 1.

14   Id., *Epist. ad Principiam*, 127, 7, 1.

15   Id., *Epist. ad Damasum*, 36, 1; *Epist. ad Marcellum*, 32, 1.

16   Id., *Epist. ad Asellam*, 45, 2; *Epist. ad Marcellinum et Anapsychiam*, 126, 3; *Epist. ad Principiam*, 127, 7.

17   Id., *Epist ad Pammachium et Oceanum*, 84, 3, 1.

18   Id., *Ad Domnionem et Rogatianum in I Paral.*, Praef.

19   Id., *Tract. de Ps.*, 88.

20   Id., *In Matt.*, 13:44; *Tract. de Ps.*, 77.

21   Id., *In Matt.*, 13:45.

22   Id., *Quaest. in Genesim*, Praef.

23   Id., *In Agg.*, 2:1; cf. *In Gal.*, 2:10.

24   Id., *Adv. Helv.*, 19.

25   Id., *Adv. Iovin.*, 1, 4.

26   Id., *Epist. ad Pammachium*, 49, 14, 1.

27   Id., *In Jer.*, 9:12-14.

28   Id., *Epist. ad Fabiolam*, 78, 30.

29   Id., *Epist. ad Marcellam*, 27, 1, 1.

30   Id., *In Ezech.*, 1:15-18.

31   Id., *In Mich.*, 2:11; 3:5-8.

32   Id., *In Mich.*, 4:1.

33   Id., *In Jer.*, 31:35.

34   Id., *In Nah.*, 1:9.

35   Id., *Epist. ad Pammachium*, 57, 7, 4.

36   Id., *Epist. ad Theophilum*, 82, 7, 2.

37   Id., *Epist. ad Vitalem*, 72, 2, 2.

38   Id., *Epist. ad Damasum*, 18, 7, 4; cf. *Epist. Paula et Eusto Chium ad Marcellam*, 46, 6, 2.

39   Id., *Epist. ad Damasum*, 36, 11, 2.

40   Id., *Epist. ad Pammachium*, 57, 9, 1.

41   S. Augustine, *Ad S. Hieron., inter epist.* S. Hier., 116, 3.

42   Leo XIII, *Providentissimus Deus*; cf. *Supra*, p. 24.

43   Ibid., cf. *supra*, pp. 23-24.

44   S. Jerome, *In Jer.*, 23:15-17; *In Matt.*, 14:8; *Adv. Helv.*, 4.

45   Id., *In Philem.*, 4.

46   S. Aug., *Contra Faustum*, 26, 3, 6.

47   S. Jerome, *In Matt.*, Prol.; cf. *Luke*, 1:1.

48   Id., *Epist. ad Fabiolam*, 78, 1, 1; cf. *In Marc.*, 1:13-31.

49   S. Aug., *Contra Faustum*, 26, 8.

50   S. Jerome, *Epist. ad Demetriadem*, 130, 20; cf. *Prov.* 4:6, 8.

51   *Conc. Trid.*, Sess. 4 *Decr. de ed. et usu ss. librorum*; cf. *Ench. Bibl.*, n. 61.

52   S. Jerome, *Epist. ad Paulinum*, 58, 9, 2; 11, 2.

53   S. Aug., *Confessiones*, 3, 5; cf. 8, 12.

54   S. Jerome, *Epist. ad Eustochium*, 22, 30, 2.

55   Id., *In Mich.*, 1:10-15.

56   Id., *In Gal.*, 5:19-21.

57   Id., *Epist.* 108 sive *Epitaphium S. Paulae*, 26, 2.

58   Id., *Ad Domnionem et Rogatianum in I Paral.*, Praef.

59   Id., *Epist. ad Theophilum*, 63, 2.

60   Id., *Epist. ad Damasum*, 15, 1, 2, 4.

61   Id., *Epist. ad Damasum*, 16, 2, 2.

62   Id., *In Dan.*, 3:37.

63   Id., *Adv. Vigil.*, 6.

64   Id., *Dial. contra Pelagianos*, Prol. 2.

65   Id., *Contra Ruf.*, 3, 43.

66   Id., *In Mich.*, 1:10-15.

67   Id., *In Is.*, 16:1-5.

68   Leo XIII, *Providentissimus Deus*; cf. *supra*, p. 10.

69   S. Jerome, *In Tit.*, 3:9.

70   Id., *in Eph.*, 4:31.

71   Id., *Epist. ad Laetam*, 107, 9, 12.

72   Id., *Epist. ad Eustochium*, 22, 17, 2.

73   Id., *Epist.* 108 sive *Epitaphium S. Paulae*, 26.

74   Id., *Epist. ad Principiam*, 127, 7.

75   *Imitatio Christi*, 4, 11, 4.

76   S. Jerome, *Epist. ad Rusticum*, 125, 7, 3.

77   Id., *Epist. ad Nepotianum*, 52, 7, 1; cf. *Tit.* 1:9.

78   Id., *Epist. ad Paulinum*, 53, 3, 3.

79   Id., *Epist. ad Marcellam*, 27, 1, 2.

80   Leo XIII, *Providentissiumus Deus; supra*, p. 10-28.

81   Pius X, *Vinea electa*, May 7, 1909; cf. *A.A.S.*, 1 (1909) 447-451; *Ench. Bibl.*, n. 287.

82   S. Jerome, *Tract. de Ps.* 147; cf. *Ps.* 1:2; *Wis.* 16:20.

83   Leo XIII, *Providentissimus Deus*; cf. *supra*, p. 17.

84   S. Jerome, *Epist. ad Nepotianum*, 52, 8, 1.

85   Id., *In Amos*, 3:3-8.

86   Id., *In Zach.*, 9:15.

87   Id., *Epist. ad Marcellam*, 29, 1, 3.

88   Id., *In Matt.*, 25:13.

89   Cf. Id., *In Ezech.*, 38:1, 41:23, 42:13; *In Marc.*, 1:13-31; *Epist. ad Dardanum*, 129, 6, 1.

90   Id., *In Hab.*, 3:14.

91   Id., *In Marc.*, 9:1-7; cf. *In Ezech.*, 40:24-27.

92   Id., *In Eccles.*, 12:9.

93   Id., *Epist. ad Paulinum*, 58, 9, 1.

94   Id., *In Eccles.*, 2:24-26.

95   Id., *In Amos*, 9:6.

96   Id., *In Isa.*, 6:1-7.

97   Leo XIII, *Providentissimus Deus*; cf. *supra*, p. 17.

98   S. Jerome, *Epist. ad Pammachium*, 49, 17, 7.

99   Id., *In Ga.*, 1:11.

100   Id., *In Amos*, Praef.

101   Id., *In Gal.*, Praef.

102   Id., *Epist. ad Damasum*, 36, 14, 2; cf. *Epist. ad Cyprianum*, 140, 1, 2.

103   Id., *Epist. ad Nepotianum*, 52, 8, 1.

104   Id., *Dialogus contra Luciferianos*, 11.

105   Id., *Epist. ad Paulinum*, 53, 7, 2.

106   Id., *In Tit.*, 1:10.

107   Id., *In Matt.*, 13:32.

108   Id., *Epist. ad Damasum*, 36, 14, 2.

109   Id., *Epist. ad Pammachium*, 48, 4, 3.

110   Id., *Epist. ad Paulinum*, 53, 10.

111   Id., *Epist. ad Paulam*, 30, 13.

112   Id., *In Eph.*, Prol.

113   Id., *Epist. ad Augustinum*, 141, 2; cf. *Epist. ad eumdems*, 134, 1.

114   Postumianus apud Sulp. Sev., *Dial.*, 1, 9.

115   S. Jerome, *Epist. ad Apronium*, 139.

116   Id., *Epist. ad Paulinum*, 58, 7, 1.

117   Postumianus, *Dial.*, 1, 9.

118   S. Jerome, *In Agg.*, 2:1-10.

119   Id., *In Mich.*, 4:1-7.

120   Id., *In Matt.*, Prol.

121   Id., *In Isa.*, Prol.; cf. *Tract. de Ps.* 77.

122   Id., *Epist. ad Paulam*, 30, 7.

123   Id., *Tract. de Ps.* 1.

124   Id., *Tract. in Marc.*, 9:1-7.

125   Id., *In Matt.*, 13:45.

126   Id., *Epist. ad Asellam*, 45, 1, 6.

127   Id., *Epist. ad Eustochium*, 22, 38.

128   Id., *Epist. ad Rusticum*, 125, 20, 4.

129   Id., *Epist. ad Eustochium*, 22, 38, 3.

130   Id., *Epist. Paula et Eucstochium ad Marcellam*, 46, 11, 13.

131   Id., *Epist. ad Furiam*, 54, 13, 6.

132   John Cassian, *De Incarn.*, 7, 26.

133   S. Jerome, *Epist. ad Damasum*, 15, 2, 1.

DIVINO AFFLANTE SPIRITU, Encyclical Letter of Pope Pius XII on The Most Opportune Way to Promote Biblical Studies, September 30, 1943.

1   *II Tim.* 3:16-17.

2   *Conc. Trid.*, Session IV, decr. 1; *Ench. Bibl.*, n. 60.

3   *Conc. Vat.*, Session III, cap. 2; *Ench. Bibl.*, n. 77.

4   Pius XII, *Address to the Ecclesiastical Students in Rome* (June 24, 1939), *A.A.S.*, 31 (1939) 245-251.

5   St. Thomas, *Sum. Theo.*, I, art. 1 ad 3.

6   St. Augustine, *De Gen. ad litt.*, 2, 9, 20.

7   Leo XIII, *Leonis XIII Acta*, 13, 355; *supra*, p. 22.

8   Cf. Benedict XV, *Spiritus Paraclitus*, *A.A.S.*, 12 (1920) 396; *supra*, p. 53.

9 Leo XIII, *Leonis XIII Acta*, 13, 357 sq.; *supra*, pp. 23-25.

10 *Ibid.*, 328; *supra*, p. 2.

11 Id., *Hierosolymae in coenobio*, Sept. 17, 1892, *Leonis XIII Acta*, 12, 239-241; cf. p. 240.

12 Cf. *Leonis XIII Acta*, 22, 232 ss.; *supra*, p. 31.

13 *Letter of the Pontifical Biblical Commission to their Excellencies the Archbishops and Bishops of Italy*, Aug. 20, 1941, *A.A.S.*, 31 (1941) 465-472; *infra*, pp. 138-147.

14 Pius X, *Scripturae Sanctae*, Feb. 23, 1904, *Pii X Acta*, 1, 176-179; *Ench. Bibl.*, nn. 149-157; cf. nn. 150-151.

15 Id., *Quoniam in re biblica*, March 27, 1906, *Pii X Acta*, 3, 72-76; *supra*, pp. 36-39.

16 Id., *Vinea electa*, May 7, 1909, *A.A.S.*, 1 (1909) 447-449; *Ench. Bibl.*, nn. 282-298; cf. nn. 286 and 283.

17 Pius XI, *Bibliorum scientiam*, April 27, 1924, *A.A.S.*, 16 (1924) 180-182; *Ench. Bibl.*, nn. 505-512.

18 Pius X, *Letter to the Most Rev. Abbot Aidan Gasquet*, Dec. 3, 1907, *Pii X Acta*, 4, 117-119; *Ench. Bibl.*, nn. 274-275.

19 Pius XI, *Inter praecipuas*, June 15, 1933, *A.A.S.*, 26 (1934) 85-87.

20 Pius X, *Letter to Cardinal Casetta "Qui piam,"* Jan. 21, 1907, *Pii X Acta*, 4, 23-25.

21 Benedict XV, *Spiritus Paraclitus*, Sept. 15, 1920, *A.A.S.*, 12 (1920) 385-422; *Ench. Bibl.*, nn. 443-394; cf. nn. 443, 481, 483, 477; *supra*, pp. 43-78.

22 Cf., e.g., St. Jerome, *Praef. in quatuor Evang. ad Damasum*; St. Aug., *De doctr. christ.*, 2, 16.

23 St. Aug., *De doctr. christ.*, 2, 21.

24 *Decr. de editione et usu Sacrorum Librorum; Conc. Trid.*, ed. Soc. Goerres, 5, 91.

25 *Ibid.*, 10, 471; cf. 5, 29, 59, 65; 10, 446.

26 Leo XIII, *Providentissimus Deus, Leonis XIII Acta*, 13, 345-346; *supra*, pp. 15-16.

27 *Hebr.* 4:12.

28 Benedict XV, *Spiritus Paracletus*, *A.A.S.*, 12 (1920) 390; *supra*, p. 47.

29   St. Athanasius, *Contra Arianos*, 1, 54.

30   St. Thomas, *Commen. ad Hebr.*, cap. 1, lectio 4.

31   *Hebr.* 4:15.

32   Cf., e.g., St. John Chrysostom, *In Gen.*, 1:4; *In Gen.*, 2:21; *In Gen.* 3:8; *Hom. 15 in Joan.*, 1:18.

33   Cf. St. Aug., *Epist. and Paulinum*, 149, 34; *De diversis quaestionibus*, 1. 53, n. 2; *Enarr. in Ps.* 146, 12.

34   Leo XIII, *Vigilantiae, Leonis XIII Acta*, 22, 237; *supra*, p. 34.

35   Cf. *II Tim.* 3:13, 17.

36   *Luke* 24:32.

37   *John* 6:69.

38   *I Cor.* 3:11.

39   St. Jerome, *In Isaiam*, Prol.

40   Id., *In Ephesios*, Prol.

41   *Col.* 2:10.

42   *I Cor.* 1:30.

43   Cf. St. Aug., *Contra Faustum*, 13, 18.

44   St. Jerome, *Epist.*, 53, 10.

45   St. Aug., *De doctr. christ.*, 3, 56.

46   *I Mach.* 12:9.

47   *Dan.* 12:3.

48   Cf. *Wisdom* 12:1.

An Instruction of the Pontifical Biblical Commission to the Most Excellent Local Ordinaries, Superiors General of Religious Institutes and the Very Reverend Rectors of Seminaries and Professors of Sacred Scripture on the Proper Way to Teach Sacred Scripture in the Seminaries of Clerics and the Colleges of Religious, May 13, 1950.

1   The encyclical *Providentissimus; Ench. Bibl.*, n. 133. Cf. *supra*, p. 28.

2   *Ibidem*, n. 103. Cf. *supra*, pp. 11-12; cf. also n. 114; Pius X, Apostolic Letter, *Quoniam in Re Biblica*, March 27, 1906; *Ency. Bibl.*, n. 162. Cf. *supra*, p. 36.

3   Encyc. *Divino Afflante Spiritu*; *A.A.S.*, 35 (1943) 321; cf. *supra*, p. 104.

4   Cf. Leo XIII, Encyc., *Providentissimus*; cf. *supra*, pp. 5-6.

5   Motu Proprio *Bibliorum Scientiam*, April 27, 1924; *Ench. Bibl.*, n. 509.

6   Encyc. *Divino Afflante Spiritu, loc. cit.*, p. 324. Cf. *supra*, p. 106.

7   *Codex Iuris Canonici*, Can. 1366, par. 3.

8   Cf. Encyc. *Divino Afflante Spiritu, loc. cit.*, p. 321. Cf. *supra*, p. 104.

9   Cf. *Jos.* 1:18; St. Jerome, *In Titum* 3:9; *Epist.*, 52.

10   Cf. *De Imitatione Christi*, I, 5.

11   Cf. Pius X, Apost. Letter *Quoniam in Re Biblica;* *Ench. Bibl.*, n. 166. Cf. *supra*, p. 37.

12   *I Tim.* 2:4.

13   *Rom.* 8:28.

14   Cf. Pius X, Apost. Letter *Quoniam in Re Biblica; Ench. Bibl.*, n. 172. Cf. *supra*, pp. 37-38.

15   Cf. Pius X, Apost. Letter *Quoniam in Re Biblica; Ench. Bibl.*, n. 166. Cf. *supra*, p. 37.

16   *I Tim.* 3:15.

17   Cf. Pius X, Apost. Letter *Quoniam in Re Biblica; Ench. Bibl.*, n. 175. Cf. *supra*, p. 38.

18   St. Gregory, *Moralia*, 20, 9.

19   Pius XII, Encyc., *Divino Afflante Spiritu, loc, cit.*, p. 310. Cf. *supra*, p. 93.

20   Encyc. *Providentissimus; Ench. Bibl.*, n. 112; cf. *supra*, pp. 16-17; Encyc. *Spiritus Paraclitus; Ench. Bibl.*, n. 485-486; cf. *supra*, pp. 67-69; Encyc. *Divino Afflante Spiritu, loc. cit.*, p. 311; *Ench. Bibl.*, n. 552-553; cf. *supra*, pp. 93-95.

21   Pius XII, Encyc. *Divino Afflante Spiritu, loc. cit.*, p. 318. *Ench. Bibl.*, n. 563; cf. *supra*, p. 101.

22   Cf. St. Jerome, *Epist.* 130 towards the end.

23   Cf. Leo XIII, *Providentissimus; Ench. Bibl.*, n. 87; cf. *supra*, pp. 4-5; Benedict XV, Encyc. *Spiritus Paraclitus; ibid.*, n. 482-483; cf. *supra*, pp. 65-66; Pius XII, Encyc. *Divino Afflante Spiritu, loc. cit.*, p. 320; *Ench. Bibl.*, n. 566; cf. *supra*, pp. 102-104.

24   Cf. Pius X, Apost. Letter *Quoniam in Re Biblica; Ench. Bibl.*, n. 180; cf. *supra*, p. 39.

25   Thus also Pius X, Apost. Letter *Quoniam in Re Biblica; Ench. Bibl.*, n. 172; cf. *supra* ,pp. 37-38.

26   Cf. Pius X, Apost. Letter *Quoniam in Re Biblica; Ench. Bibl.*, nn. 172, 173; cf. *supra*, pp. 37-38; Pius XI, Motu Proprio *Bibliorum Scientiam; Ench. Bibl.*, n. 505-506.

27   Cf. Pius X, Apost. Letter *Quoniam in Re Biblica; Ench. Bibl.*, n. 179; cf. *supra*, p. 39.

28   *Codex Iuris Canonica*, Can. 130, 590.

29   *Ibid.*, Can. 131, 591.

HUMANI GENERIS, Encyclical Letter of Pope Pius XII (Excerpt) on the Inspiration of the Scriptures, August 12, 1950.

1   Cf. *Rom.* 5, 12-19; Conc. Trid. sess. V, can. 1-4.

2   January 16, 1948: *A.A.S.*, 40 (1948) 45-48; cf. *infra* 148-151.

Instruction of the Pontifical Biblical Commission on Biblical Associations and on Biblical Conventions and Meetings, December 15, 1955.

1   Cf. *A.A.S.*, 35 (1943) 321; *supra*, p. 103.

2   Cf. *A.A.S.*, 42 (1950) 569 f.

Address of Pope John XXIII on the Fiftieth Anniversary of the Pontifical Biblical Institute, February 17, 1960.

1   *"Esortazione al Clero Veneto," AAS* 51 (1959) 379; *TPS* (Summer 1959) v, 5, no. 3, 297.

2   Cf. *S. Pio X, Promotore degli Studi Biblici* (1955) 40.

3   "The word of the Lord remains forever."—Ed.

4   *Aggeus* 1, 13.

5   *AAS* 1, (1909) 447 ff.

6   *AAS* 50, (1958) 917; *TPS* (Summer 1959) v. 5, no. 3, 285.

7   Cf. the encyclical *"Ad Petri Cathedram," TPS* (Autumn 1959) v. 5, no. 4, 359-83.

8 *John* 18, 37.

9 The encyclical *"Divino afflante Spiritu," AAS* 35 (1943) 319.

10 *AAS* 35 (1943) 310.

11 St. Augustine, *Enarr. in Psalm. 98*, 1; ML 37, 1260.

12 See A. G. Roncalli, "La Sacra Scrittura e San Lorenzo Guistin-iani," *Revista Biblica* (1958) 289-94.

13 *Divi Laurentii Justiniani Opera Omnia* (Venice: 1721) 422.

14 Cf. *AAS* 1 (1909) 448.

15 *1 Tim.* 3, 15.

16 *Matt.* 5, 18.

17 A digest of this synodal talk appears in *TPS* (Spring 1960) v. 6, no. 2, 157-9.

18 *1 Cor.* 2, 10.

19 *De doctr. chr.* 3, 56; ML 34, 89 ff.

20 *2 Thess.* 1, 2.

Address of Pope John XXIII to Participants in the Seventeenth Annual Study Week of the Italian Biblical Association, September 24, 1962.

1 Cf. *Mark* 3, 17.

2 *John* 21, 25.

3 *John* 6, 64.

4 Cf. *Is.* 66, 22; *2 Peter* 3, 13; *Apoc.* 21, 1.

5 *2 Esd.* 8, 2-3, 5-6, 8.

Instruction of Pontifical Biblical Commission Concerning the Historical Truth of the Gospels, April 21, 1964.

1 *1 Tim.* 3:15.

2 *Divino afflante Spiritu* 46.

3 Cf. *Spiritus Paraclitus* 2, 3.

4 Apostolic Letter *Vigilantiae.*

5 *Divino afflante Spiritu* 38.

6 *Mk.* 3:14; *Lk.* 6:13.

7   *Lk.* 1:2; *Acts* 1:21-22.

8   *Lk.* 24:28; *Jn.* 15:27; *Acts* 1:8; 10:39; 13:31.

9   *Lk.* 24:44-48; *Acts* 2:32; 3:15; 5:30-32.

10   *Acts* 10:36-41.

11   Compare *Acts* 13:16-41 with *Acts* 17:22-31.

12   *Acts* 2:36; *Jn.* 20:28.

13   *Acts* 2:22; 10:37-39.

14   *Jn.* 2:22; 12:16; 11:51-52; cf. 14:26; 16:12-13; 7:39.

15   *Jn.* 14:26; 16:13.

16   *Lk.* 24:27.

17   *Lk.* 24:44-45; *Acts* 1:3.

18   *Acts* 6:4.

19   *1 Cor.* 9:19-23.

20   *Rom.* 1:14.

21   *Lk.* 1:1.

22   *Lk.* 1:4.

23   Cf. John Chrysostom, *Hom. in Math.* 1, 3.

24   Augustine, *De consensu Evangelistarum* 2, 12, 28.

25   *1 Cor.* 12:11.

26   *De consensu Evangelistarum* 2, 21, 51-52.

27   *Divino afflante Spiritu* 47.

28   Irenaeus, *Adversus haereses* 3, 1, 1̈.

29   Apostolic Letter *Quoniam in re biblica.*

30   *Divino afflante Spiritu* 55.

31   *Divino afflante Spiritu* 25.

32   *1 Tim.* 4:16.

33   *Divino afflante Spiritu* 50.

34   Apostolic Letter *Quoniam in re biblica* 13.

35   Instruction *De consociationibus biblicis.*

36   *Ibid.*

37   *2 Tim.* 3:15-17.

Address of Pope Paul VI to Participants in the Eighteenth Italian Biblical Week, September 26, 1964.

1   the venerable words.

2   *De doctrina Christiana* III, 56; *PL* 34, 89-90. "Let them pray that they may understand. For they can read in those very words that they pore over that the Lord gives wisdom, and that knowledge and understanding are from His face; and it is from Him that they have received the will to study, if it is endowed with devotion."

Vatican II, DEI VERBUM, Dogmatic Constitution on Divine Revelation, November 18, 1965.

1   St. Augustine, *De Catechizandis rudibus*, c. 4, 8: *PL* 40, 316.

2   Cf. *Mt.* 11:27; *Jn.* 1:14 and 17; 14:6; 17:1-3; 2 *Cor.* 3:16 and 4:6; *Eph.* 1:3-14.

3   *Epistle to Diognetus*, c. 7, 4: Funk, *Patres Apostolici*, I, p. 403.

4   First Vatican Council, *Dogm. Const. on Cath. Faith*, c. 3 (on Faith): *Denz.* 189 (3008).

5   Second Council of Orange, can. 7: *Denz.* 180 (377). First Vatican Council, *loc. cit.: Denz.* 1791 (3010).

6   First Vatican Council, *Dogm. Const. on Cath. Faith*, c. 2 (on Revelation): *Denz.* 1786 (3005).

7   Ibid.: *Denz.* 1785 and 1786 (3004 and 3005).

8   Cf. *Mt.* 28:19-20 and *Mk.* 16:15. Council of Trent, Session IV, Decree *On the Canonical Scriptures: Denz.* 783 (1501).

9   Cf. Council of Trent, *loc. cit.*: First Vatican Council, Session III, *Dogm. Const. on the Catholic Faith*, c. 2 (on Revelation): *Denz.* 1787 (3006).

10   St. Irenaeus, *Adv. Haer.*, III, 3, 1: *PG* 7, 848; Harvey, 2, p. 9.

11   Cf. Council of Nicea II: *Denz.* 303 (602) Council of Constantinople IV, Session X, can. 1: *Denz.* 336 (650-652).

12   Cf. First Vatican Council, *Dogm. Const. on the Catholic Faith*, c. 4 (on Faith and Reason): *Denz.* 1800 (3020).

13   Cf. Council of Trent, Session IV, *loc. cit.: Denz.* 783 (1501).

14   Cf. Pius XII, Apost. Const. *Munificentissimus Deus*, 1 Nov. 1950: *AAS* 42 (1950) 756, taken along with the words of St. Cyprian,

Epist. 66, 8; Hartel, III, B, p. 733: "The Church is the people united to its Priests, the flock adhering to its shepherd."

15 Cf. First Vatican Council, *Dogm. Const. on the Catholic Faith*, c. 3 (on Faith): *Denz.* 1972 (3011).

16 Cf. Pius XII, Encycl. *Humani Generis*, 12 Aug. 1950: *AAS* 42 (1950) 568-569: *Denz.* 2314 (3886).

17 Cf. Vatican Council I, *Const. dogm. de fide catholica*, c. 2 (de revelatione): *Denz.* 1787 (3006). *Bibl. Commission*, Decr. 18 June 1915: *Denz.* 2180 (3629); EB 420; Holy Office, *Letter*, 22 Dec. 1923; EB 499.

18 Cf. Pius XII, Encycl. *Divino Afflante Spiritu*, 30 Sept. 1943: *AAS* 35 (1943), p. 314; EB 556.

19 *In* and *by* man: cf. *Heb.* 1:1; 4:7 (*in*); 2 *Sam.* 23:2; *Mt.* 1:22 and *passim* (*by*); Vatican Council I, *Schema de doctr. cath.*, note 9; Coll. Lac., VII, 522.

20 Leo XIII, Encycl. *Providentissimus Deus*, 18 Nov. 1893: *Denz.* 1952 (3293); EB 125.

21 Cf. St.Augustine, *Gen. ad Litt.*, 2, 9, 20: *PL* 34, 270-271; *Epist.* 82, 3: *PL* 33, 277; *CSEL* 34, 2, p. 354.—St. Thomas. *De Ver.* q. 12, a. 2, C.—Council of Trent, Session IV, *de canonicis Scripturis: Denz.* 783 (1501)—Leo XIII, Encycl. *Providentissimus*; EB 121, 124, 126—127.—Pius XII, Encycl. *Divino Afflante*: EB 539.

22 St. Augustine, *De Civ. Dei*, XVII, 6, 2: *PL* 41, 537: *CSEL* XL, 2, 228.

23 St. Augustine, *De Doctr. Christ.*, III, 18, 26; *PL* 34, 75-76.

24 Pius XII, *loc. cit.: Denz.* 2294 (3829-2830); EB 557-562.

25 Cf. Benedict XV, Encycl. *Spiritus Paraclitus*, 15 Sept. 1920: EB 469. St. Jerome. *In Gal.* 5, 19-21: *PL* 26, 417 A.

26 Cf. Vatican Council I, *Const. dogm. de fide catholica*, c. 2 (de revelatione): *Denz.* 1788 (3007).

27 St. John Chrysostom, *In Gen.* 3, 8 (hom. 17, 1): *PG* 53, 134. *Attemperatio* corresponds to the Greek *synkatabasis*.

28 Pius XI, Encycl. *Mit brennender Sorge*, 14 March 1937: *AAS* 29 (1937), p. 151.

29 St. Augustine, *Quaest. in Hept.* 2, 73: *PL* 34, 623.

30 St. Irenaeus, *Adv. Haer*, III, 21, 3: *PG* 7, 950 (—25, 1; Harvey 2, p. 115). St. Cyril of Jerusalem, *Catech.* 4, 35: *PG* 33, 497. Theodore of Mopsuestia, *In Soph.* 1, 4-6: *PG* 66, 452D—453A.

31 Cf. St. Irenaeus, *Adv. Haer.* III, 11, 8: *PG* 7, 885; ed. Sagnard, p. 194.

32   Cf. *Jn.* 14:25; 16:13.

33   *Jn.* 2:22; 12-16; cf. 14:25; 16:12-13; 7:39.

34   Cf. The Instruction *Sacra Mater Ecclesia* of the Pontificial Biblical Commission: *AAS* 56 (1964), p. 715.

35   Cf. Pius XII, Encycl. *Divino Afflante*: EB 551, 553, 567. Biblical Commission, Instruction on the Teaching of S. Scripture in Seminaries of Clerics and Religious, 13 May 1950: *AAS* 42 (1950), pp. 495-505.

36   Cf. Pius XII, ibid.: EB 569.

37   Cf. Leo XIII, Encycl. *Providentissimus*: EB 114; Benedict XV, Encycl. *Spiritus Paraclitus: EB* 483.

38   St. Augustine, *Serm.* 179: *PL* 38, 966.

39   St. Jerome, *Comm. in Isaias*, Prol.: *PL* 24, 17. Cf. Benedict XV, Encycl. *Spiritus Paraclitus:* EB 475-480; Pius XII, Encycl. *Divino Afflante: EB* 544.

40   St. Ambros, *De Officiis ministrorum* I, 20, 88: *PL* 16, 50.

41   St. Irenaeus, *Adv. Haer.* IV, 32, 1: *PG* 7, 1071; (= 49, 2) Harvey, 2, p. 255.

Address of Pope Paul VI to Old Testament Experts, April 19, 1968.

1   *"Neque vero ullam puto digniorem disputationis nostrae confabulationem fore, quam si de Scripturis sermoncinemur inter nos."* Migne: *PL* 22, 451.

2   R. de Vaux, *Peut-on écrire une "théologie de l'Ancien Testament?"* in *Bible et Orient*, Paris: ed. du Cerf (1967).

3   Rev. Paul-Marie de la Croix, O.C.D., Desclée de Brouwer, 1952.

Apostolic Letter Issued 'Motu Proprio' by Pope Paul VI, June 27, 1971.

1   See *Dogmatic Constitution on Divine Revelation*, no. 23

2   Ibid.

3   See Vat. Counc I, sess. III, ch. II, *De revelatione*; Vat Coun. II, *Dogmatic Constitution on Divine Revelation*, no. 12.

4   See *Dogmatic Constitution on Divine Relevation*, nos. 12 and 23.

Address of Pope Paul VI to the Pontifical Biblical Commission, March 14, 1974.

1   *AAS* 56 (1964), 712-718.

2   *Dogmatic Constitution on Divine Revelation*, no. 10.

3   M. J. Lagrange, *Le sens du Christianisme d'après l'exegése allemande*, Paris: Gabalda (1918), pp. 323, 324, 328.

4   *Dogmatic Constitution on Divine Revelation*, no. 12

5   Lagrange, op. cit., p. 325.

6   *Hom.* 17, 1 in *Gn.* 3, 8: *PG* 53, 134.

7   *Dogmatic Constitution on Divine Revelation*, no. 24; *Decree on Training for the Priesthood*, no. 16.

8   *Decree on Training for the Priesthood*, no. 16.

9   *Pastoral Constitution on the Church in the World of Today*, no. 33.

10   *Ti.* 2, 12-13.

11   *Decree on the Missionary Activity of the Church*, no. 22.

12   See *Mt.* 11, 25; *Lk* 10, 21.

13   *De doctrina christiana*, 3, 56: *PL* 34, 89.

14   *AAS* 63 (1972), 665-669.

Document of the Sacred Congregation for Catholic Education On the Theological Formation of Future Priests (Excerpts), February 22, 1976.

1   See the *Dogmatic Constitution on Divine Revelation*, no. 24

2   See the Pontifical Biblical Commission, Instruction *Sancta Mater* on the Historicity of the Gospels (April 21, 1964): *AAS* 56 (1964) 712-718.

3   See the *Dogmatic Constitution on Divine Revelation*, no. 12

4   See the Pontifical Biblical Commission, Instruction *Sancta Mater: AAS* 56 (1964) 717-178.

5   See *Basic Program*, no. 78.

6   See the *Constitution on the Sacred Liturgy*, no. 24.